Fundamentals of Public Relations and
Marketing Communications in Canada

FUNDAMENTALS OF Public Relations IN CANADA
and Marketing Communications

PICA
PICA
PRESS

An imprint of
The University
of Alberta Press

William Wray Carney & **Leah-Ann Lymer** *Editors*

Published by

The University of Alberta Press
Ring House 2
Edmonton, Alberta, Canada T6G 2E1
www.uap.ualberta.ca

Library and Archives Canada Cataloguing in Publication

Fundamentals of public relations and marketing communications
in Canada / edited by William Wray Carney and Leah-Ann Lymer.

Includes bibliographical references and index.
ISBN 978-1-77212-044-8 (paperback).—ISBN 978-1-77212-062-2 (pdf)

1. Communication in marketing—Canada—Textbooks. 2. Public
relations—Canada—Textbooks. I. Lymer, Leah-Ann, editor
II. Carney, William Wray, 1950-, editor

HF5415.123.F85 2015   658.8'02   C2015-902111-1
                                                  C2015-902112-X

Index available in print and PDF editions.

First edition, second printing, 2016.
First printed and bound in Canada by Houghton Boston Printers, Saskatoon, Saskatchewan.
Copyediting and proofreading by Joanne Muzak.
Indexing by Judy Dunlop.

The University of Alberta Press is committed to protecting our natural environment.
As part of our efforts, this book is printed on Enviro Paper: it contains 100% post-consumer
recycled fibres and is acid- and chlorine-free.

The University of Alberta Press gratefully acknowledges the support received for its
publishing program from The Canada Council for the Arts. The University of Alberta Press
also gratefully acknowledges the financial support of the Government of Canada through
the Canada Book Fund (CBF) and the Government of Alberta through the Alberta Media
Fund (AMF) for its publishing activities.

Canada   Canada Council   Conseil des Arts   Government
           for the Arts   du Canada   of Alberta ■

This book is dedicated to the reader, whether a student beginning a career in public relations or marketing communications in Canada or a practitioner using this book as a reference.

CONTENTS

Foreword

In today's corporate environment, audiences are more interconnected than ever with social networks enabling the democratization and connection of everything in ways that put the reputations of corporations, institutions, products and individuals in the public's hands. Those publics—and there are many—have access to more information than ever before and no longer want that information filtered.

That's where communications professionals come in, as we counsel our colleagues and clients to consider the point of view of all the relevant publics at the most strategic level of decision-making. We also help them to engage the public, co-create ideas, have conversations and tell their stories.

In essence, we put the "public" back in "public relations." That's because our industry is about so much more than just media relations these days—although that remains important. Today's PR is also about the practice of direct engagement, whether through one-on-one conversations or by reaching thousands of people at the same time via the Internet. This harkens back to the origins of the PR field and the work of trailblazers such as Edward Bernays, broadly regarded as "the father of public relations." Bernays saw media and other avenues as mere amplifiers used to reach the public and share messages in a smart, strategic fashion.

The tools may have grown but the purpose has stayed the same. It's all about engaging the public.

Today, we have unparalleled access to data that we can use to better analyze the public. This allows us to craft customized, dynamic communications strategies for our clients and to execute them through a broad range of communications channels, including traditional media, social media and a wide variety of digital outlets.

In these pages, you will learn about the varied, adaptable skill set that you will be developing as you begin your journey to becoming a professional communicator. Like any career, there are many valuable lessons to be learned both in and out of the classroom. This text will provide you with a solid grounding in the former and continue to serve you as you embark on your career.

With more than three decades of experience, including my current role as President and CEO, Americas Region of Hill + Knowlton Strategies Canada, the single greatest lesson I have learned is that my education in this field will never end. Every day I come to work is another opportunity to draw on the historical roots of our industry and to take advantage of the most contemporary communications techniques. As professional communicators, this combination of old and new not only provides us with the tools we need to share the stories of our clients in a compelling, authentic fashion, it also makes communications one of the best fields in which to set one's professional stake.

Best of luck on your journey.

Mike Coates
President and CEO, Americas Region
Hill + Knowlton Strategies

HILL+KNOWLTON
STRATEGIES

Acknowledgements

The editors would like to acknowledge the significant number of people who have made this book possible.

First of all, the 19 authors from across the country who have given their time and expertise to this book have showed the highest levels of dedication to the profession and the teaching of it, and such a book would not be possible without their engagement and commitment. The editors would also like to thank the National Council on Education of the Canadian Public Relations Society for its assistance in helping recruit the authors, most of whom are CPRS members.

The funders of this book are Hill + Knowlton Strategies of Canada; without their financial support this book would not have become available to Canadian students and professionals. The editors and the University of Alberta Press deeply appreciate their support for this important project.

Special thanks to the two peer reviewers Don McCann and Jennifer Walinga who have given their time and guidance to this project.

Professor Jeremy Berry of Mount Royal University School of Communications and his students: Hailey Laycraft, Kevin Brown, Erin Jordan, and Estella Pertzold. have been particularly helpful in their review of draft chapters and their contribution of the companion website, which allows this book to continue to be relevant as the industry is in constant flux.

And a personal thank you to Sarah Carney of Montreal and Paul Tymchuk of Sudbury for their constant support.

William Wray Carney
Leah-Ann Lymer

Introduction

William Wray Carney and Leah-Ann Lymer

A long text deserves a short introduction.

This book is intended for use by students of public relations, communications, and marketing communications across Canada. It relates Canadian history, Canadian practice, and Canadian law and cites Canadian examples of public relations excellence. It is also intended as a reference for practitioners since few communicators, if any, have the range of experience the 19 authors of this text have.

The authors are experts in their fields, and as co-editors of this project we cannot thank them enough for their work in this endeavour, at their time and expense, while juggling demanding jobs, usually at a senior level, teaching, research, and personal lives. Please read their biographies at the end of the book; they have done extraordinary work for your benefit.

The work of the co-editors was divided as follows. William Wray Carney acted as the manager for this project, having the idea that the education field sorely lacked an introductory text on the topic. (Unfortunately, US texts have been used up to now, and while these texts are good, they simply do not speak to the significant differences in Canada, of law, language, and culture.) Finding the authors was the main task, working with them as they developed their chapters, and editing as necessary until such time as the book was worthy of going to external peer review. Once this vital step was completed, Leah-Ann Lymer came onboard to work with the authors to revise and prepare their chapters for publication.

Unit One of the text is required reading because the chapters in this section inform all aspects of public relations, including the role of public relations, its history in Canada, legal issues, ethics, and communications theory. Unit Two explores marketing, the role of marketing communications, research methods, and communications plans. Unit Three is essentially composed of craft chapters, focusing on writing, advertising, and the practice areas of media relations, digital communications, government relations, internal communications, and crisis communications. Instructors can choose which chapters they want to teach depending on the focus of their faculties.

Students should keep this text as a reference throughout their education and use it to start the process of determining what area within this field they wish to major in. As stated, practitioners will also find it useful as a reference text. The book can also be used by practicing communicators and marketers as a reference, along with books such as a thesaurus and dictionary and the *Canadian Press Style Guide*. Because most communicators specialize in one field, having a reference such as this volume will give them an overview of other areas of the field with which they may come into contact.

The Essentials

UNIT ONE

An Overview of Public Relations in Canada

Charles Pitts

1

LEARNING OBJECTIVES

After reading this chapter, you will be able to

- define public relations;
- describe some of the practice areas in public relations;
- explain the challenges of communicating in a bilingual and multicultural society; and
- identify the skills required to become a public relations practitioner.

INTRODUCTION

Before tackling the multi-faceted questions of what constitutes public relations (PR), it is perhaps worth determining from the practitioner's viewpoint *why* one would choose public relations as a career. The simple answer is that public relations is an exciting and seductive field, one that shows no lack of variety, challenge, or reward—personal or financial. A career in the field will appeal to the person who is inquisitive, communicative, and literate, one who appreciates the importance of social and commercial relationships and of reputation management. PR can be credited with contributing to numerous changes in social behaviours in Canada and elsewhere, including increased scholarity, public hygiene, and national vaccination levels, reduced tobacco consumption, acceptance of multiculturalism, and many other social shifts.

The PR practitioner is a strategist and a tactician. Often the PR practitioner is credited with being a master of savoir faire and savoir vivre. In reality, and contrary to general perception, the role of a PR practitioner will appeal in most instances to the people who enjoy behind-the-scenes work. The role is one of a "grey eminence" where the majority of one's time is not spent interacting personally with clients or other stakeholders, but rather counselling those who are the frontline interface with the public.

From a financial viewpoint, the profession offers a steadily growing level of opportunity. The Canadian Public Relations Society (CPRS), in its *Pathways to the Profession*, states that as of September 2009, the unemployment rate of public relations practitioners stood at 4.18 per cent, or half the national average of other fields.[1] Contributing to the positive employment levels is the fact that senior managers in industry, the non-profit sector and government have increasingly seen their businesses founder when the principles of public relations were ignored.

Since the arrival of new media, PR practitioners are now free to telecommute to the office and can work more independently on mandates of widely varying duration and degrees of complexity. For those concerned with life's other interesting occupations (such as raising a family), public relations in its many forms offers tremendous flexibility in terms of re-entering the job market later in life.

There is such a generalized need for public relations that today's practitioner in Canada can look forward to an exciting career with few barriers, except one's own lack of imagination. As to professional longevity, contrary to certain communications management functions, in public relations one does not age, one matures—one more reason that PR makes an excellent career choice for the right candidate.

WHAT IS PUBLIC RELATIONS?

The Canadian Public Relations Society (CPRS) defines public relations as "the strategic management of relationships between an organization and its diverse publics, through the use of communication, to achieve mutual understanding, realize organizational goals and serve the public interest."[2] However, in its attempts to be as comprehensive as possible, the CPRS definition may suggest too vast a range of activities for its meaning to be easily discernible. Simply stated, public relations includes everything from personal interaction with individual community members to complex management functions, communications planning, the development of strategies, tactics, budgets and financial control, people management, and information release.

Earlier definitions of public relations placed emphasis on developing, projecting, and maintaining the image of business, non-profit organizations, and public figures such as entertainers or politicians. Today, practitioners working for organizations prefer to focus on reputation rather than image. A good reputation is understood to be earned through actions conducted in the public interest—actions that are authentic and contribute to mutual understanding. By contrast, projecting an image is seen as one-way communication that contributes only to how an organization would like its publics to perceive it. A major role of the PR practitioner is to counsel business and association leaders on social, economic, and political issues and their potential impact on an organization and its stakeholders. Consequently, PR practitioners develop programs and activities to meet particular communications challenges with employees, customers, investors, legislators, and voters.

There may be as many ways of viewing public relations as there are types of activity and careers in the field. L.L.L. Golden, a senior Canadian PR specialist operating in the United States, redefined the profession or discipline as maintaining "relations with the public."[3] This sentiment could be rephrased as "relations with 'a' public," since by and large PR practitioners have abandoned the notion of public relations as concerned with a general public. It is now · widely recognized that the public is composed of distinct subgroups of communities, each with its own identities, needs, aspirations, attitudes, and opinions.

Public relations programs and activities consist of communications strategies aimed at developing mutually respectful relationships with a variety of publics and earning their understanding of (and, ideally, support for) an organization's products, services, management, or role in society. To this end, early in any public relations campaign, one must identify the public or publics to whom a message is directed and devise strategies and tactics to convey messages and achieve the desired goals. The strategy defines clear objectives based on properly targeted polling, surveys, focus groups, or other attitude research. The PR practitioner can then define the tools, tactics, and messages to be used to communicate with defined groups. (See Chapter 8 for more on research methods.) While not a panacea for all that ails an organization's relationships and reputation, public relations does convey a vast array of activities and endeavours aimed at supporting or redressing the reputations of individuals, organizations, and communities.

A Note About Terminology in This Book

As you read this book, you will notice that some chapters have a public relations focus, while others have a marketing communications focus. The following are explanations of these basic concepts. See Figure 1.1 for a quick reference.

Public Relations

The key notions in the definition of public relations by the CPRS suggest that PR aims to manage key relationships with a variety of audiences, based on mutually beneficial outcomes.[4] While there are many other ways to define the field, most modern definitions resemble this one, in essence. Underlying this definition, of course, is the notion of two-way communication and mutual benefit to the organization and to the publics and communities with which it wishes to maintain relationships.

Increasingly, marketing specialists include public relations strategies and tactics in the "marketing mix" repertoire of activities to support their objectives.[5] Nonetheless, PR and marketing remain distinct sectors.

Marketing

Marketing is often described as consisting of the four Ps: strategic *promotion* of a *product*, a service, a brand, or a social concept at an acceptable *price* (monetary or social cost) and at a time and *place* that meets the needs of a specific clientele or community. Marketing should not be confused with sales, which is just one of the elements of the marketing mix. (See Chapter 6 for an overview of marketing.)

Marketing Communications

Marketing communications is a subset of marketing. This vast sector consists of processes, including advertising, brand reinforcement, direct marketing, design, merchandising, packaging, promotion, sponsorship, sales, and sales promotion. Marketing communications underpins most commercial and economic activities. As consumers of products, services, and social messaging, we are exposed through various media (print, electronic, and social) to a variety of marketing communications elements on a daily basis. (See Chapter 7 for more about marketing communications.)

Figure 1.1 Basic Concepts

Concept	Definition
Public relations	"The strategic management of relationships between an organization and its diverse publics, through the use of communication, to achieve mutual understanding, realize organizational goals and serve the public interest."[6]
Communications	For the purposes of this book, the same definition for public relations will be used for communications. The reader will note there are some conflicting or overlapping definitions within the realms of public relations and marketing communications.
Marketing	"The process of planning the conception, pricing, promotion, and distribution of ideas, goods, and services to create exchanges that satisfy individual and organized objectives."[7]
Marketing communications	"The combination of the elements, activities, and techniques an organization employs to connect with and persuade the target market to engage in a particular action or response, such as buying a product, using a service or accepting an idea."[8]

WHAT DO PR PRACTITIONERS DO?

It is also important to define how PR practitioners spend their time and which traits, tools, and talents are most important to the trade. PR practitioners need to be able to write clearly, rapidly, and accurately for traditional media or new media. The types of documents that they create or edit include media releases, newsletters, financial reports, corporate advertising, technical or product documentation, and online messages for various social media. (See Chapter 10 for more about writing for public relations.)

Part and parcel of writing, of course, is the research needed to represent clients or employers adequately. With time, this research will lead the PR practitioner to become a well-informed spokesperson—one who is in a position to defend and represent the interests of the employer or client by offering accurate, timely, and "politically correct" information to media sources and other interested publics.

Writing and research, however, are often just the first steps in the PR process. A next step is the distribution or marketing of the writing. This step can entail media relations or pitching to media. When the information one is pitching is newsworthy, the task can be quite pleasant. When one is flogging a story of little interest, the task can be quite tedious and unsettling. On the receiving end, one also has to be available to manage inquiries from media relating to the client or employer. A thorough knowledge of the organization for which one works is of immeasurable importance.

The practice areas in which PR practitioners work include the following:

· internal communications
· social marketing advertising
· government relations
· crisis communications
· investor relations
· PR support of marketing and sales
· industry relations and association relations
· media relations
· digital communications

Many of these will practice areas be discussed in further detail later in this book.

As you expand your study of public relations, you will see discrepancies in how organizations refer to the practice areas. For example, internal communications in one organization may be called employee relations in another. There is no widely agreed upon, authoritative set of definitions in the PR field in part, perhaps, because it has never been a regulated discipline, such as law or medicine. In addition, some organizations have preferred to use terms other than *public relations* because the term has fallen into disfavour at times.

Internal Communications

Internal communications aims to provide two-way communications between management and those audiences deemed to be internal, such as employees and often their families, suppliers, shareholders, and industry associations.[9] Often, newcomers to PR find entry-level employment in internal communications, while more senior practitioners move on to more externally oriented activities. The view is that external communications requires more experience and is more difficult to manage.

Unfortunately, this situation may also reflect management's views that internal PR is less important than other functions. In fact, nothing could be further from the truth. The management of information given to employees and other internal audiences and the communications from these same people to management is crucial to the health and survival of organizations. This interdependence is particularly true during crises or periods of internal change or upheaval, such as mergers and acquisitions, downsizing, or shifts in strategic focus. Solid internal communications is also crucial in unionized environments where the viewpoints of the union bosses often contrast those of management. Staying in touch with one's employees in a positive, open, and reciprocal manner can pay tremendous dividends to an organization; not doing so may lead to disaster.

With the galloping increase in the use of social media, Internet, and intranet (e-communications within an organization), managers and PR practitioners are realizing the threats, challenges, and opportunities that these new platforms of communications represent. For the PR practitioner, the use of social media and the development of related communications policies offer employment opportunities for people who are savvy in the use of digital media. Protecting the corporation from messages that are harmful to its image will keep more and more PR practitioners busy. Facebook and Twitter, for example, are open invitations for criticism from people inside and outside the organization. Although these media are prime vehicles for open dialogue, they also provide the opportunity for abuse. (See Chapter 15 for more on internal communications.)

Social Marketing Advertising

Social marketing advertising is a practice area in which an organization purchases advertising to convey its message without interference or interpretation from news media.

Producing social marketing ads as a PR tactic can be very effective since it allows the organization to control the message without the intervention of a media editor. However, in addition to being expensive because it is paid communication, such messaging may lose some of the credibility it otherwise would have had as a PR activity. In other words, it may be seen as not being disinterested. For example, in reaction to federal changes to competition in the cellphone market in 2013, Bell Canada purchased two full pages of advertising the *Globe and Mail* and *Toronto Star*, which ran on July 23. The first page, which it called an open letter to all Canadians, criticized the opening of the Canadian market to US-based Verizon Communications. The second page was devoted to criticism of the federal policy by noted Canadian businesspersons and academics. (See Chapter 11 for more on advertising.)

Government Relations

Government relations is concerned with influencing the government to adopt your organization's point of view. The goal is to encourage the government to make changes to legislation, regulations, or policies to accommodate your organization's needs. Government relations exists at the political level and the bureaucratic level at the federal, provincial, and municipal levels.

Lobbying is a government relations strategy that involves direct contact with elected representatives. It may consist of something as simple as meeting with your city councillor to persuade her to plant flowers or trees in public spaces. At a higher level, lobbying may involve activities to persuade bureaucrats, legislators, or heads of other types of organizations to modify import duties or appoint people to certain positions. Most commonly, it involves advocating on behalf of and explaining in a detailed manner one's personal, commercial, or political cause. While the scale of lobbying in Canada does not nearly rival such activities in the United States, it remains a major function for in-house practitioners and is a lucrative business for consulting lobbyists who work outside of a corporation or NGO.

In an attempt to ensure that people lobbying various levels of government are not insiders acting as outsiders, federal and provincial legislation prohibits any person who has left a political or bureaucratic role from lobbying his or her recent associates. Usually, the prohibition lasts for two years. Notwithstanding, abuses appear to occur quite often. The federal Lobbying Act, called the Lobbyists Registration Act when it came into force in 1996, requires an individual who acts for payment on behalf of any person or organization to register publicly, whether they are a consultant or an employee. Lobbyists who must register are those who are paid to communicate with a public office holder on specified topics or to arrange meetings with that person. A public office holder is "an employee of the federal government, whether elected or appointed."[10] Similar registration legislation exits in provinces, territories, and municipalities across Canada.

Governments at all levels across Canada also use public relations, paid advertising, and social media to present messages to support their own positions regarding public policy and to change citizens' behaviours.[11] (See Chapter 14 for more on government relations.)

Crisis Communications

Crisis communications is often managed by company PR officers or external PR consultants working with senior management to help avoid an acute or smouldering crisis from having a negative impact on a corporation's image and reputation. In an age where corporations and organizations are forced to be more and more transparent, crisis management and crisis preparedness have become roles of critical importance. Issues that in the past would not have been of public concern now threaten corporations and organizations on short notice. For example, the sexual behaviour of staff and management has become an issue of public interest in business, the military, and politics.

A great deal of study has gone into understanding how to discern impending crises and avoid exacerbating issues. Preparation is key: a crisis plan must be defined in advance and be ready to be implemented when an issue grows from a problem into a critical event that might disrupt business operations and damage an image or reputation. With the arrival of the 24/7 news cycle and never-sleep social media, crises develop more quickly and more violently than at any time in the past. The PR practitioner ensures that potential issues are tracked and that the organization is vigilant and prepared to meet challenges from within and from outside the organization. (See Chapter 16 for more on crisis communications.)

Investor Relations

Investor relations (IR) activities provide support of the reputation and the perceived value (usually the share price) of companies whose common shares, bonds, or other financial instruments are listed and traded on one of the world's securities exchanges, commonly referred to as stock exchanges. The audiences for IR primarily include individual and institutional shareholders, financial analysts, and financial media.

PR practitioners are very much in demand in IR because of the popularization of stock trading, more stringent stock exchange regulations, and the constant scrutiny of trading activities in the Digital Age. IR specialists are particularly in demand with startup ventures and corporations whose stocks are or will be listed on the various security exchanges around the world. In the case of companies that are newly created or that shift from being privately held to publicly traded, PR professionals participate in initial public offerings (IPO), where company stocks are offered for sale to the public for the first time.

One of the most spectacular IPOs occurred in May 2012, when social networking company Facebook, Inc. was forced by securities law to "go public" because the number of private investors surpassed 500. In such cases, the issuing of company information to news-hungry media and investors is tightly controlled and managed by IR/PR specialists.

Regardless of which practice area a PR practitioner operates in, IR or corporate PR, he or she will need a rudimentary understanding of finance, accounting, and the ability to read a financial balance sheet.

PR Support of Marketing and Sales

Public relations is most often deemed to be used to protect an organization's reputation or persuade various publics to support certain viewpoints or issues. More and more, however, PR is being used to target consumers through unpaid public media. At times, it may be used to complement consumer advertising; at other times, PR is used alone to add credibility to the qualities of consumer products or services. In such cases, PR becomes part of the marketing mix that is meant to influence consumer habits.

This type of PR requires the practitioner to work closely with marketing and sales departments. In every launch of major consumer items (smartphones, electronic games, nutritious foods, advanced corporate jets), the hand of the PR specialist can be seen in the editorial coverage and background articles written by public media. From fashion to pharmaceuticals to aeronautics, PR strategies and tactics, including media relations, events, and social media activities, are supporting consumer and industrial marketing. As the lines between true journalism and paid coverage blur, consumer PR is taking on a greater commercial promotion role, which may appear crass to the purist.

On a cautionary note, in the longer term interest of the brand or the corporate reputation, the PR practitioner should be reminded not to be overly aggressive in his or her attempts to support marketing efforts to promote a product with news media.

Industry Relations and Association Relations

Industry relations and association relations provide information to various publics on behalf of a specific industrial sector or not-for-profit association. PR in support of a specific industrial sector can be most challenging and rewarding, affording the opportunity to conduct the most sophisticated public relations campaigns and government relations at the highest levels of influence.

Trade associations exist in support of everything from egg producers to aircraft manufacturers to hotel operators and the sex trade. Employment in such associations provides the practitioner with exposure to a variety of PR experiences and significant networking contacts, often at the national and international levels.

Media Relations

Media relations consist of communicating a corporation's or an organization's key messages to target audiences through public news media. Often the starting point of PR careers, media relations consists of establishing positive relations with news, trade, and digital media in order to influence story choices such as a company's or organization's products, services, or reputation. It involves dealing with news and story editors and journalists. The goal of media relations is to obtain unpaid, positive coverage in the media.

Since one is seeking unpaid coverage, however, results come only with diplomatic negotiations and by providing media with story ideas that truly meet audience interests. To establish credible relations, PR practitioners must be familiar with the audiences and editorial approaches of a wide variety of media outlets and follow the story coverage (or beat) of the individual journalists to whom they pitch their stories. In most North America media, PR practitioners must conform to strict codes of ethics that restrict the type of "wine-and-dine" influencing that might have prevailed in the past. (See Chapter 12 for more on media relations.)

Digital Communications

The Internet, email, social media, cellphone texting, on-demand video, e-books, blogs, citizen journalists have all been made possible because of the electronic miniaturization and the digitization of the transmission and storage of information. The use of digital media fosters symmetrical and multi-directional, interactive communications, at times to the chagrin of participants, be they corporations or individuals. Also, it has largely contributed to the phenomena of 24/7 global communications, which requires virtual around-the-clock monitoring and continual vigilance. (See Chapter 13 for more on digital communications.)

HOW TO PREPARE FOR A CAREER IN PR

PR practitioners come to the field equipped with training in sectors that range from the arts to law to engineering. Until the 1970s, however, few programs existed that provided a formal education in public relations in Canada. Today, in-class and online training exists at the certificate, diploma, BA, MA, and PhD level in Canada. In fact, there are over 100 programs available at colleges and universities across the country.

In all cases, students need to have strong communications aptitudes and skills (oral, written, and visual). They also need to acquire an understanding of news production, advertising, media relations, digital media, speechwriting, and public speaking and must develop research and analysis skills. Students would also benefit from at least a cursory understanding of the political and legislative process, how, upfront and behind the scenes, policy becomes law and laws are applied through regulations. They should also have an interest in understanding the fundamentals of how organizations function, from financial statements to organizational behaviour to management practices.

Communicating in a Bilingual and Multicultural Society

The dualities of English and French in everyday social transactions and in business contribute to Canada's charms and challenges. Until the 1970s, few PR practitioners outside Quebec were able to work in French. Almost invariably, French-speaking PR practitioners were called upon to bridge the linguistic gap. In addition, predominantly English-speaking organizations seldom released information in French; whereas predominantly French-speaking organizations most often conducted PR activities in both languages. The scene changed radically with the enactment of the Official Languages Act in 1969. Since that time, conducting PR activities in both languages has become de rigueur in national and many provincial communications programs.

Today, communications professionals in PR and advertising recognize the need to adapt texts and avoid word-for-word translation to convey the meaning of original messages accurately. Although not necessarily required to do so by law, in most cases, businesses and NGOs recognize the need to and advantages of communicating in both of Canada's official languages. For most PR practitioners, the message should be clear: being able to comprehend spoken and written French and English is desirable and can lead to greater responsibilities within most organizations and to greater financial rewards. The same applies to other languages as more Canadian corporations go global.

In addition, Canada is a vastly changed nation culturally and racially from what it was just a few decades ago. Multiculturalism is recognized as a national value in the Canadian Charter of Human Rights and Freedoms. Nothing belies the notion of a general public to which PR practitioner address their messages than multiculturalism. Not all Canadians obtain their news from English or French media. Radio, television, newspaper, and online media are produced locally in most European languages, in addition to English and French, as well as Mandarin, Punjabi, and dozens of other Asian languages. Once called *foreign languages*, the term loses it meaning in multicultural Canada. As result, the PR practitioner's messages and messaging (how messages are developed and delivered) must be modified considerably to be meaningful to the various multicultural communities.

Reflecting this new reality, the *Canadian Press Stylebook* (2010) devotes considerable space to what it entitles "Sensitive Subjects," including race names and description of race and ethnicity.[12] While one can never truly be conversant with a multitude of cultures, the Canadian PR practitioner must be conscious of the cultural milieu in which he or she operates to meet the information needs of diverse publics. Recent elections indicate that the big political winners are those parties that identify and court relevant cultural groups and work to develop policies and programs that appeal to them. Corporations are also adapting to these new opportunities and realities.

How Much Can I Earn?

In general, PR practitioners can achieve significant financial rewards. This statement is particularly true of those who have prepared well for the profession, remain current with social and technological trends, network well and track threats and opportunities.

Terms of employment are always subject to individual circumstances and negotiations. The size of the organization, its geographic location, the stability of the practice area in which it operates, and the nature of its business will influence the salaries, benefits, bonuses, and perquisites.

By and large, salaries and benefits will be higher in the corporate sector. Specialties in investor relations and crisis communications often are among the top earners, with salaries, bonuses, benefits, and stock options adding up to hefty packages. Careers in the not-for-profit sector may offer great learning experiences and a sense of contributing to one's community but they tend to offer lower financial rewards, although this is not always the case. Corporate PR employment will tend to offer more stability than PR agency employment, which is dependent on the renewal of contracts by clients in a highly competitive and unstable environment.

For some time now, the majority of PR practitioners have been women.[13] In light of this fact, one might expect that pay equity between men and women would exist in the profession. Unfortunately, recent findings indicate income discrimination between the sexes.[14]

CONCLUSION

The multi-faceted profession of public relations makes an enormous contribution to the social, political, and economic health of the nation. Knowledgeable organization leaders and PR professionals know that communicating openly, transparently, and in the public interest pays off on the bottom line and beyond. No government or organization of any significance in the twenty-first century would consider operating without robust PR support.

PR also makes a significant contribution to media itself. Particularly with cutbacks in the number of journalists and the closing of traditional media outlets, if PR practitioners were to fail to deliver story ideas and background material, print and electronic media would be left scrambling to fulfill content needs.

Within the business environment, PR has found and is continuing to find its place at the management table. Management recognizes that the maintenance of good public relations relies on guidance from in-house practitioners or outside PR counsel. Although it has always been the case, today more than ever, the actions, attitudes, and communications of every member of an organization's team, from senior manager to shopfloor worker, contribute to affirmative relations with the public, especially since the advent of the Web and social media. With colleagues and associates, clients, and other stakeholders having access to powerful information outlets, the slightest tweet or Facebook post can have significant (intentional or unintentional) impact on the image and reputation of an organization. As a result, in large organizations, policies and procedures are being put into place in an attempt to provide some control or response to these occurrences. Organizational surveillance of social media necessitates 24/7 early-warning and response systems to manage impending public relations concerns. This no doubt will require greater understanding and use of this media by PR practitioners. They will also be required to share this understanding with their colleagues and associates.

The skill set of practitioners has grown in complexity and sophistication in recent decades. Fortunately, colleges and universities are offering expanding curricula. As the world has changed to a knowledge-based economy in general, the skill set of the PR practitioner has changed to being e-knowledge-based. In many cases, electronic media have obviated the need to be acquainted with many traditional production techniques and introduced new requirements. This shift will continue to require vigilance on the part of the PR practitioner to stay current.

The society with which today's PR practitioner works is not that of his or her professional predecessors. Issues and concerns that were unheard of or unnamed are now the practitioners' stock in trade. Most generally, the PR practitioner must deal with a variety of interest groups that have sway—from disgruntled consumers to representatives of groups with diverse needs and interests, such as Aboriginals, environmentalists, persons with disabilities, persons of varied sexual orientations, and multiple ethnic groups, to name just a few. PR should no longer be practised as a one-way vehicle to "win friends and influence people." We must recognize that only two-way, symmetrical communications between organizations and communities deemed to be equals will lead to healthy relations with various publics.

KEY TERMS

Association relations: Public relations and community outreach conducted on behalf of for-proft and not-for-profit associations concerned with promoting professional, industrial, or societal issues.

Canadian Public Relations Society (CPRS): The voluntary professional association of Canadian PR practitioners, including students.

Consumer-related PR: The public relations practice area in which public relations techniques are used to support consumer marketing and sales activities.

Crisis communications: Consists of the planning and implementation of strategies and tactics allowing organizations to identify real and potential crises that may disrupt the operations and materially detract from the organization's reputation.

Digital communications: The various means by which people connect using technology. Digital communications include text, photos, audio, and video distributed through electronic devices, including computers and mobile telephones, whether to individual users (for example, through email or text message) or groups of users (for example, on social networks).

Government relations: A practice area in public relations that attempts to influence one or more governments to adopt your organization's point of view.

Industry relations: Public relations, intra-industry, or external relations used to support or promote a particular industrial sector's interests.

Internal communications: The communications practice area dealing with groups of individuals within an organization. Internal communications employs the same strategic analysis, development and evaluation tools and techniques as other communications practice areas and adapts specific tools to suit an internal environment.

Investor relations: The public relations practice area in which activities are designed to support the reputation and the perceived value of companies whose common shares, bonds, or other financial instruments are listed on securities exchanges.

Marketing: While often confused with public relations and sales, marketing is concerned with understanding target audiences through strategic research and interacting with them in a way that is beneficial to both them and your company. It is about identifying customer needs, aligning those with what you offer, and attracting and retaining the right customers to profit your organization.

Marketing communications: The various marketing and communications disciplines (e.g., direct response and advertising) organizations use to engage a particular target market and/or persuade them towards a particular action or purchase. Each discipline may be used on its own or in conjunction with others.

Media relations: The public relations practice area that focuses on interfacing with the news media, both proactively, through news releases and other tools, and reactively, providing information and facilitating interview requests.

Messaging: Statements that act as anchors for the organization's positioning on a given issue and that are delivered with consistency by designated spokespersons.

Public relations: A management function whose goal is to develop beneficial relationships between an organization and communities that are relevant to its operations.

Social advertising: Social advertising is a practice area in which an organization purchases advertising to convey its message without interference or interpretation from news media.

FOR REVIEW AND DISCUSSION

1. How would you define public relations?
2. Explain why the notion of a general public has been largely abandoned by PR practitioners.
3. Do you agree that internal communications is crucial to the health and survival of organizations? Explain your answer.
4. Describe a current example of social marketing advertising. Assess the response of news media and audiences to the advertisement. Explain the reasons for the response.
5. Why do you think the federal Lobbying Act was created?
6. Examine how digital media has affected the role of PR practitioners.

7. What impact has bilingualism and multiculturalism had on PR in Canada?
8. Examine the online investor relations section of a major Canadian corporation. What could you tell a potential share purchaser about this company?

ACTIVITIES

1. Analyze a daily newspaper and choose three articles that you think may have been influenced by a PR practitioner. Explain your rationale to a classmate.
2. Summarize what contribution you feel PR makes to society. In your opinion, is the role of PR practitioner relevant and productive today? Defend your answer to the class.
3. Which PR practice areas are you most interested in as you begin your course of study? What related skills do you already have? Which ones do you think you need to develop? Re-evaluate your answers to these questions when you have finished reading this book. How have your answers changed?

FURTHER READING

CBC News. "How Maple Leaf Foods is Handling the Listeria Outbreak." August 28, 2008. http://www.cbc.ca/news/business/story/2008/08/27/f-crisisre-sponse.html.

Gordon, Averill Elizabeth. *Public Relations*. Oxford: Oxford University Press 2011.

Gordon-Reed, Annette. "The Persuader, What Harriet Beecher Stowe Wrought." *New Yorker*, June 13 and 20, 2011, 120.

Herbert, W., and J. Jenkins, eds. *Perspectives on Public Relations in Canada*. Markham, ON: Fitzhenry and Whiteside, 1984.

"List of Social Networking Websites," s.v. *Wikipedia*. Last modified February 18, 2014. http://en.wikipedia.org/wiki/List_of_social_networking_websites.

Ross, R. *The Management of Public Relations*. New York: Wiley, 1977.

Steinberg, C. *The Creation of Consensus*. Toronto: Saunders of Toronto, 1975.

NOTES

1. Canadian Public Relations Society, *Pathways to the Profession: An Outcomes Based Approach towards Excellence in Canadian Public Relations and Communications Management* (Ottawa: CPRS National Council on Education, March 2011), http://www.cprs.ca/education/pathways.aspx.

2. Canadian Public Relations Society, "About Us," accessed March 31, 2014, http://www.cprs.ca/aboutus/mission.aspx.

3. Gerald D. Brown, "What Is Public Relations?" in *Perspectives on Public Relations in Canada*, eds. W. Herbert and J. Jenkins (Markham, ON: Fitzhenry and Whiteside, 1984), 2.

4. Canadian Public Relations Society, "About Us."

5. Keith J. Tuckwell, *Integrated Marketing Communications: Strategic Planning Perspectives* (Toronto: Pearson Prentice Hall, 2007).

6. Canadian Public Relations Society, "About Us."

7. Keith J. Tuckwell, *Canadian Marketing in Action*, 7th ed. (Toronto: Pearson Education, 2007).

8. Norman A. Govoni, *Dictionary of Marketing Communications* (Thousand Oaks, CA: Sage, 2004), 123.

9. James E. Grunig and Todd T. Hunt, *Managing Public Relations* (New York: Holt, Rinehart, and Winston, 1984).

10. Office of the Commissioner of Lobbying of Canada, "Ten Things You Need to Know About Lobbying," accessed November 19, 2012, http://www.ocl-cal.gc.ca/eic/site/012.nsf/eng/00403.html.

11. For a list of advertising campaigns by the Government of Canada, see Public Works and Government Services Canada, "2012–2013 Annual Report on Government of Canada Advertising Activities," last modified February 7, 2014, http://www.tpsgc-pwgsc.gc.ca/pub-adv/rapports-reports/2012-2013/tdm-toc-eng.html.

12. Patti Tasko, ed., *The Canadian Press Stylebook: A Guide for Writers and Editors*, 16th ed. (Toronto: Canadian Press, 2010).

13. Glen M. Broom and Bey-Ling Sha, *Cutlip and Center's Effective Public Relations*, 11th ed. (Upper Saddle River, NJ: Prentice Hall, 2012), 26.

14. David M. Dozier, Bey-Ling Sha, and Hongmei Shen, "Why Women Earn Less Than Men: The Cost of Gender Discrimination in U.S. Public Relations," *Public Relations Journal* 7, no. 1 (2012): 13, http://www.prsa.org/Intelligence/PRJournal/Documents/2013DozierShaShen.pdf.

A Brief History of Public Relations in Canada

Amy Thurlow and Anthony R. Yue

2

LEARNING OBJECTIVES

After reading this chapter, you will be able to

- describe the historical evolution of PR in Canada;
- discuss the practice and profession of public relations;
- describe and reflect upon the gradual professionalization of the profession and its current roots in
  academia; and
- identify and contextualize public relations in
  popular culture.

INTRODUCTION

The history of public relations in Canada follows an interesting path. It is different from the history of public relations in the United States or Europe. This point is important because the dominant, or most commonly known, history of PR comes from the American perspective. In this chapter, we will look specifically at the history of the practice of public relations in Canada.

Before we launch into a description of the history of public relations in Canada, it is useful to consider some basic ideas concerning history itself.

When we think of history, we usually think of "a written narrative constituting a continuous methodical record, in order of time, of important or public events, especially those connected with a particular country, people, individual."[1] History can be recounted, remembered, and recorded in a variety of ways, including images and artworks, film and video, and oral histories, all of which are valuable ways of understanding and narrating the past. This perspective on history relates to the study of historiography, which is an area of study that concerns how histories are produced. The study of how multiple accounts of the past may arise is a hallmark of contemporary research in organizational analysis and management and thus important in the study of a history of public relations in Canada.[2] This means that history may be understood as being both subjective and dynamic; not just a static thing. History influences the present in profound ways, and so we might argue that it is a living, breathing part of our ongoing experience. This understanding opens up the possibility—in fact, the likelihood—that there is more than just one accurate account of the past.

In the case of the Canadian history of public relations, we are somewhat disadvantaged by the lack of information available to tell the full and detailed story of our origins, as well as the fact that the history of our profession in the United States has been told so fully and to such a wide audience, it is difficult to make space sometimes for our own history. Although some important work has been done in this area, much remains to be done. This important work goes to the heart of our identity as a Canadian profession.

THE PRACTICE AND THE PROFESSION

When considering the history of public relations, it is necessary to consider the distinction between the practice (what PR practitioners do) and the profession (who PR practitioners are). This distinction is important for our examination of history because some of the activities and functions of the modern PR professional may have existed and been performed long before we could identify a discrete profession. This point is worth noting because public relations is often identified as a fairly new field of practice, but when we look at what professional communicators in Canada have been doing since before Confederation, we see that public relations is actually a well-established and historically situated field. The pioneering work of John Donaldson in the mid- to late 1800s and Clifford Sifton's work during the late 1800s to early 1900s are early examples of Canadian public relations practices. Yet the two professional associations that would merge to become the Canadian Public Relations Society (CPRS) in 1953 were formed as recently as 1948.

IMMIGRATION, SETTLEMENT, AND RAILROADS

The Canadian experience of public relations practice had its origins in efforts of public policy and government administration, largely aimed at immigration and settlement campaigns.

Merle Emms's 1995 master's thesis on the history of Canadian public relations traces the first full-time publicity activities to the general immigration campaign of the late 1800s.[3] After Confederation in 1867, the growth and development of Canada became a priority for the new government. In 1878, Prime Minister John A. Macdonald's National Policy provided for incentives, such as free land, in the Canadian west to encourage settlers to move there and establish farms. Although Canada was a large country geographically, the population was still quite small and large areas were unsettled. Settlement of the western Prairies was important from political, economic, and social perspectives. The government was concerned with populating the western regions as well as developing the national economy. Macdonald believed that the best way to encourage industrial development in eastern Canada and develop the national economy across all regions was to settle the Prairies with farmers who could provide a stable source of food for the growing Canadian population, and a source of grain that could be exported to Europe.[4]

As a result of this focus, the Departments of the Interior (which was responsible for immigration) and Agriculture were the largest and most important departments of the early Canadian government. By looking at the work of these two departments, we can gain some insights into what public relations activities of the time looked like.

The public relations campaign to bring settlers to the Canadian west was, for the most part, aimed at farmers from the United Kingdom during the first two decades after Confederation. In 1872 and 1873, over one million pamphlets describing the Canadian west were distributed throughout the UK. As well, 23,000 posters advertising opportunities for Canadian immigration were placed in British post offices.[5] In the years that followed, the Canadian government also organized a network of immigration agents in the UK and Europe who would give presentations to potential immigrants. These presentations often included lantern slides, an early version of a slide projector show. Photographs of the Canadian west were projected in front of a light from a lantern box to create a visual image on the wall of the presentation hall.

John Donaldson has emerged as the first "government publicist" and is linked to these Canadian immigration initiatives. Records from the federal Department of Agriculture in the late 1880s and 1890s indicate that Donaldson was an immigration agent, at that time a function housed in the Department of Agriculture. In this role, he was responsible for organizing the network of immigration agents and providing them with appropriate communications materials. During this period, one of the most sophisticated and widely distributed publications on the Canadian west was introduced. *Canada West* magazine was designed by Rand McNally and produced by the Immigration Branch of the Canadian Department of the Interior. It included black and white photographs of Canada and information on settlement and immigration. When the magazine was introduced, "the immigration agents throughout Britain and the United States found it the most useful publication in their collection for promoting the West."[6]

In 1892, responsibility for immigration was moved to the Department of the Interior. Communication strategies for immigration and settlement initiatives became more focused, and tactics such as advertising and targeted communication with specific audiences were highlighted. The specific audiences targeted by the National Policy on Immigration were farmers from the UK, the United States, and areas of Northern Europe. The communications campaign targeting these groups included speakers' tours, posters, flyers, newspaper advertising, and special promotional discounts on transportation such as trans-Atlantic crossings and railway fares to western Canada.

Although there was a great deal of interest in immigration from European farmers, there was stiff competition from the United States and Australia. Canada's persistent image among Europeans was that of a land of ice and snow with hard winters. Therefore, many immigrants chose warmer climates, and Canada was trailing in immigration numbers.

When Wilfrid Laurier was elected as prime minister of Canada in 1896, his Liberal government saw the need to enhance its communication campaign and to do a better job of "selling" the Canadian west. Laurier appointed Clifford Sifton as minister of the interior, responsible for immigration and western settlement. This department under Sifton kept well-documented records of its work in communication, advertising, and public relations. Detailed annual reports provided a clear accounting of the elements of the public relations campaigns aimed at increasing immigration. As well, a decidedly multimedia approach was applied to this campaign. Six hundred American editors (in an early version of the modern "media tour") were given free trips to Canada, as were British MPs.[7] Thousands of pamphlets and posters were distributed in the United States at state fairs and other agricultural gatherings. Over 200,000 pamphlets were distributed at the St. Louis World's Fair in 1904 alone. The campaign also included "one thousand lantern-slide lectures in England in a single year; one thousand inquiries a month at the High Commissioner's office in London; and a thirty-five thousand dollar arch at the coronation of Edward VII, trumpeting the advantages of immigration."[8] As a result of this focused public relations campaign, more than two million immigrants came to Canada between 1896 and 1911.[9]

One of the written accounts of an early public relations campaign credits Canadian political figure Clifford Sifton for the success of a communications initiative that attracted settlers to Canada from 1896 to 1911.[10] This campaign included all of the hallmarks of contemporary strategic public relations pro-grams: messages were "tested on party members, slogans were developed that created a fit between the needs of the customers (potential immigrants) and the unique appeal of the product (Canada) and diverse media were used."[11] This approach continued for decades and encouraged immigrants to settle the Canadian west. The campaign however, remains a controversial chapter in the development of the Canadian national identity. Public relations strategies were used effectively to reach a specific audience, but the focus on a mainly Anglo-Saxon public, to the exclusion of other racial and ethnic groups, sup-ported an elitist and racist immigration policy. This example of an early PR campaign in Canada, although successful in relation to the strategy employed, identifies the ongoing struggle for public relations practitioners in terms of ethical responsibilities and strategic outcomes.

There are also questions about the authenticity of the information pro-vided to potential immigrants. Many settlers complained that the images they were shown and the information they received from agents did not fully and accurately describe the hardships that they had to face during winter on the Canadian Prairies. Issues surrounding ethical practice will be further explored in Chapter 4.

Canadian Encyclopedia contributor David Norman states that Sifton's work in promotion "stands as a model in communications, targeted to specific audiences, and it probably represents the greatest and most successful public relations campaign in Canadian history."[12] Under Sifton as minister of the inte-rior in 1896, the department established a sustained public relations approach to settlement: "Important publics had been identified, PR lobbying strategies were introduced, publications were printed and distributed on a regular basis, and administrative procedures had been streamlined to incorporate a measure of accountability."[13] This accountability was documented in annual reports from the department.

By all accounts, Sifton employed a variety of public relations tactics and strategies that are still used by practitioners today, such as media tours, lectures, advertising, and special events. Sifton, however, was a government official and likely did not consider himself a public relations practitioner. The term *public relations counsellor* was not yet in common usage. It was not until Edward Bernays coined the term in 1923 in the United States that individuals practising public relations were named. Throughout the early 1900s and up until the mid-1920s in Canada, government communication and publicity campaigns were by far the most significant and most common of what would become identified as public relations practice.

As immigration expanded through the Canadian west in the late 1800s and early 1900s, the railway companies also became interested in bringing settlers to the West, particularly Manitoba, the Northwest Territories, and British Columbia. To that end, public relations practice began to emerge within the private sector. The practice was still focused on settlement initiatives, bringing farmers from European and the United States to settle in the Canadian west— but within a corporate context. John Murray Gibbon was employed with the Canadian Pacific Railway (CPR) from 1913 to 1945 as the organization's publicity agent. He is regarded as a pioneer in Canadian public relations practice for his development of strategic and sustained public relations campaigns. A former journalist, one of Gibbon's first jobs with the railway covered what we would now call media relations. He hosted European news editors and journalists on a train trip across Canada, providing information for the stories to be published abroad. During his career, he also co-ordinated special events for the railway, including the opening of several landmark CP hotels across the country.

THE EXPANSION OF PUBLIC RELATIONS

In Canada, along with the railway companies, a "handful of private institutions" had introduced full-time publicity programs by the early 1900s.[14] To the south, public relations practitioners in the United States were already firmly situated in the private sector. Journalism was in a period referred to as "yellow journalism" or muckraking. The news media were focused on scandal and sensationalism with a view to sell papers and increase circulation. To counter this approach in the press, a role emerged for public relations practitioners. This group was referred to as press agents, and these individuals (many of them former journalists themselves) were hired by wealthy business families and companies to counteract negative coverage in the press and to handle crisis management. As Cutlip, Center, and Broom point out, in this era, "for the most part, big businesses hired former reporters to counter the muckrakers with whitewashing press agentry, demonstrating little grasp of the fundamental problems in the conflict."[15] A pioneer in this era was Ivy Ledbetter Lee. An American newspaper reporter and a Princeton graduate, Lee had left his low-paying job as a reporter to take up public relations. He worked on political campaigns and for corporate clients. In 1906, he issued his "Declaration of Principles," in which he stated,

> This is not a secret press bureau. All our work is done in the open.... Our plan is, frankly and openly, on behalf of business concerns and public institutions, to supply to the press and public of the United States prompt and accurate information concerning subjects which it is of value and interest to the public to know about.[16]

This philosophy of telling the truth, and particularly of telling the truth to the public, significantly influenced the evolution of PR from publicity into public relations. In 1908, Lee was hired full-time by the Pennsylvanian Railroad to run their Publicity Department. In 1914, he was appointed as personal advisor to John D. Rockefeller Jr. Lee continued to work for the Rockefeller family until the 1930s. Then, in the early 1930s, Lee came under criticism for consulting work he did for the government of Nazi Germany. He represented the German Dye Trust, controlled by I.G. Farben, and he worked for this organization after the Nazi government had come to power and taken control. Lee refused to comment on the situation, and he died shortly after in 1934. Although still considered a founding figure of American public relations, Lee ended his career with this cloud over his reputation.

During the 1920s and 1930s, building on Lee's "Declaration of Principles," public relations began to evolve from simply publicity, to "a top management, strategic function—and a philosophy."[17] In Canada, although government remained the largest employer of public relations practitioners, the practice was expanding into the private sector, and PR consultants had begun to emerge. Consistent with this emerging consultancy role, the first formal public relations consulting agency is identified as PR consultant James Cowans's agency, established in 1930.[18]

Meanwhile, Edward L. Bernays, another pioneer in public relations, was practising in the 1920s and 1930s in the United States. In 1923, Bernays published the first book on public relations entitled *Crystallizing Public Opinion*.[19] In this book, he is credited with introducing the term *public relations counsel*— and naming the modern day profession. Bernays was the nephew of Sigmund Freud and was interested in the process of public opinion formation. In 1928, Bernays was hired by the American Tobacco Company to improve sales of its Lucky Strike cigarettes. The company had realized that it did not have access to a lucrative potential market—women—because of the opinion at the time that women could not smoke in public. Bernays developed a campaign called "Torches of Freedom" and organized a group of women in New York City to march at the front of the Easter Parade smoking Lucky Strike in a bid for complete equality with men. The campaign was successful in terms of changing social views of women smoking. By 1983, Bernays had changed his views on smoking and did some work for the American Cancer Society to communicate the serious health effects.[20]

In addition to his work in public relations practice, Bernays was also a champion of post-secondary education in PR and a strong advocate of mandatory licensing within the profession. Bernays and his wife, Doris Fleischman, ran a consulting firm for over 40 years, counselling major corporations, government agencies, and non-profit organizations.[21] Fleischman is recognized as a pioneer in public relations and one of the first women in the public relations profession. In 1939, she published a book of career advice by women who had succeeded in many different fields. In her own chapter on public relations, Fleischman showed optimism for the success of women in the field: "The profession of counsel on public relations is so new that all who are engaged in it, men as well as women, are pioneers. No traditions have grown against women's participation in it, and women will share the responsibility of developing and shaping this new profession."[22]

In Canada, women have contributed to both the practice and profession of public relations. In 1956, Ruth Hammond was one of the first women to join the Canadian Public Relations Society. Her background was originally in journalism, and she worked as a reporter and served as women's editor for the *Toronto Star* from 1946 to 1950. She later formed her own public relations firm and worked with both corporate clients and charitable organizations. In 1998, she received an honorary doctorate degree from Mount Saint Vincent University in recognition of her contributions to the field of public relations. In 2010, when CPRS presented Hammond with the title of honorary member of the board of directors on her 90th birthday, she was described as "a true trailblazer before it was even fashionable for women to be. She was driven in her quest for gender equity within the profession from a set of core values that have earned her the respect of countless colleagues."[23]

Another trailblazer, Barbara Sheffield, was the first woman elected national president of CPRS in 1990. During her tenure as president, Sheffield addressed all member societies about strategies for demonstrating professionalism in PR practice. An accredited member of CPRS herself, Sheffield encouraged all practitioners to gain accreditation in the profession by completing a work sample evaluation and a written and oral exam process with CPRS.

PROFESSIONALIZATION AND EDUCATION

The efforts of members of professional associations such as CPRS and International Association of Business Communicators (IABC) in Canada have helped to lead the way towards professionalization and formalized education within the field of public relations.

Gordon Hulme, the head of the public relations department for Shawinigan Water and Power Co. in the mid-1940s, initiated the informal discussions between PR practitioners that would lead to a call for an official Canadian public relations association.[24] On March 23, 1948, 26 Montreal-based public relations practitioners, led by Hulme, met to establish the newly formed Canadian Public Relations Society.[25] On November 22 of that same year, the Public Relations Association of Ontario was formed.

In 1953, these two organizations amalgamated at a special meeting on March 30, and "a resolution on amalgamation of the two organizations was passed unanimously."[26] This point marked the beginning of a national approach to professionalization in Canada. Other member societies joined from across the country. As of 2013, CPRS had approximately 1,700 members nationwide.[27]

By 1974, the International Association of Business Communicators had established Corporate Communicators Canada as the first district chapter of the association outside of the United States. In that same year, IABC launched its accreditation program, the ABC, the Accredited Business Communicator designation.[28]

In 1991, another professional association began as Canadian Women in Radio and Television (CWRT). This organization quickly recognized a need to support women in other communications industries, including public relations. Today, this association, now known as Women in Communications and Technology (WCT), supports members from a broad spectrum of the communications field by raising the profile of women in the industry and pro-viding professional development opportunities.[29]

During this period of growth in professional development for public relations practitioners, a number of other institutes and associations were formed in Canada to support specific sectors of public relations work. For example, in 1987, the Institute for Healthcare Communication was established as an organization that supports health care communicators in both Canada and the United States.[30]

Along with the establishment of professional associations, there has also been a transformation in public relations education in Canada from the early years of the practice to today. In 1948, Leonard Knott initiated a course in public relations at McGill University in Montreal. Knott was a founding member of CPRS (Montreal) and the author of The PR in Profit, published in 1955.[31] The University of Toronto's public relations course soon followed in 1949.[32] In 1977, the first bachelor of public relations degree program was offered in Canada at Mount Saint Vincent University in Halifax.

Charles Tisdall, one of the most prominent PR practitioners in Canada during the second half of the twentieth century, was a member of the advisory board for the Mount Saint Vincent University degree program in the late 1970s. His commitment to education in public relations was reflected in his long career as an expert in communications and reputation management. He lectured at Humber College, Ryerson University, the University of Western Ontario, and New York University, and he contributed to the establishment of practitioner accreditation programs for both the Canadian Public Relations Society and the Public Relations Society of America. In 1985, Tisdall's agency, Tisdall Clark and Partners Ltd., merged with Continental Public Relations Ltd., both based in Toronto, to create a major national public relations company.[33]

The commitment to public relations education by practitioners like Edward Bernays, Leonard Knott, and Charles Tisdall has resulted in recognition within the field of the need for formal post-secondary education in public relations. By 2011, over 44 post-secondary programs were available across Canada, ranging from certificate to diploma to undergraduate and graduate degrees. The range of focus within these programs is quite broad. Several programs focus on public relations and journalism as areas of study within a communications depart-ment. Others situate public relations within a business management context. Consequently, in addition to treating PR as a discipline in its own right, there is also a focus on PR in relation to media and culture and digital communications.

THE PORTRAYAL OF PUBLIC RELATIONS
IN POPULAR CULTURE

The notion of multiple legitimate histories was introduced at the beginning of this chapter. This explanation allows us to critically consider differing accounts of history. As Weick, Sutcliffe, and Obstfeld point out in their now classic article on sensemaking, "Our identities are importantly held in the hands of others."[34] That is to say, what others think of us matters; the image of ourselves that is projected back to us from others becomes a component of how we define ourselves.

Since the Second World War, the image of public relations practice projected through popular culture, mainstream media, cinema, and fictional writing in Canada and the United States has been decidedly negative. Prior to the 1940s, the depiction of public relations within popular culture was quite positive. Perhaps with the increased focus on propaganda highlighted in the post-war era, or the increase in the numbers of PR practitioners after this time, there was a distinct change of representation of the profession. This change spanned different types of popular media with initial negative imaging in books such as Vance Packard's The Hidden Persuaders (1957) and Walter Goodman's The Clowns of Commerce (1957).[35]

These negative images then seem to be placed in opposition to the culture and practices of reporters and journalists. Professor and expert in government public relations Mordecai Lee states, "Public Relations has had a negative image in popular culture of manipulation, artificiality and puffery. Reporters are often the conveyors and reinforcers of this negative viewpoint."[36]

Beyond the representation of PR in books and in the news media, portrayals of PR in popular culture, including Hollywood portrayals of PR practice, offer up PR as being neither professional, nor working in the interests of the public, and have become more commonplace.[37] Examples include the film The Man in the Gray Flannel Suit (1956), and the more contemporary television series Sex and the City (1998–2004) and Mad Men (2007–2015). Some authors suggest that the use of fictional depictions of situations, times, or people is especially illuminating of deeply held beliefs and so may be more revealing of underlying assumptions.[38]

The Man in the Gray Flannel Suit was a novel written by Sloan Wilson and published in 1955. This work formed the basis for a movie of the same name starring Gregory Peck, Jennifer Jones, and Fredric March. The book and film portray the life of a soldier returned from war who takes on a public relations job for a television network only to find that he seems to be required to choose between being a successful corporate man or having a more balanced life. The depiction of a choice between a balanced life and being a "company man," combined with the main character's remorse about violence and thoughts of a lover from the past, portray a conflicted and ethically distraught individual. This representation of the relentless PR company man is less than appealing.

More recently, the Samantha Jones character in the *Sex and the City* television series and films is a public relations practitioner. Her role is described in glamorous terms, as almost a socialite who plans special events. Although there may be an element of this role in some public relations jobs, it is certainly not the core of the profession or the main function of most practitioners. The character of Kelly Taylor on the television show *Beverly Hills 90210*, which aired from 1990 to 2000, also presents a picture of PR as superficial and glamorous, certainly not strategic and management-focused. PR practitioner, professor, and author Ellen Frisina contends that the portrayal of PR as glamorous has contributed to students of public relations having a sense that the field is not to be taken seriously; the power of media influence on the profession must not be trivialized.[39] This influence is especially powerful because it represents both the distant and the near past(s) such that we might see these representations as being "historical fact." Beyond simply arguing whether a representation of PR is accurate, we might more usefully ask how does one account for PR becoming more (or less) accepted. Such investigations might help us understand how misunderstandings about what PR is arise from both inside and outside of the profession. The mechanisms at work to allow for such compelling representations are especially apparent in the example of *Mad Men*.

The award-winning television series *Mad Men* is set in the 1960s and first aired in 2007. The series weaves a nostalgic sense of the 1960s, complete with themes of emerging feminism, a smoking and drinking culture, and rebelliousness on the part of the protagonist Don Draper (initially the creative director and junior partner of Sterling Cooper advertising agency). *Mad Men* portrays an advertising agency conflated with aspects of public relations in such a way as to mirror our present day understandings of integrated communication management (ICM) agency practices. This intertwining of present agency practices, along with a widespread inability of many publics to discern the differences between advertising, marketing, and PR, forms a compelling popular example of PR that is not particularly accurate.

Through portraying a fictional account, which contains enough real-life examples to be credible (for example, the firm is approached by companies such as Lucky Strike, Kodak, and Volkswagen to design campaigns), plus credible period costuming and workplace sets, the series is lauded in reviews for its authenticity and historical accuracy. The portrayal of an ethically torn male protagonist adds to the representation of the practitioner as male, ambitious, driven, busy, and at the edge of ethical acceptability, revisiting themes from *The Man in the Gray Flannel Suit*.

Mad Men is a compelling popular culture example precisely because it *appears* historically accurate enough (e.g., award-winning period costumes, references to other popular portrayals of PR) to represent an already understood and popularly held understanding of PR.[40] One might already hold a sort of nostalgic view of the 1960s that includes the idea that the women's rights movement was evident everywhere, even in advertising agencies on Madison Avenue, and that the stylized clothing seen in the television series was worn by everyone, and so the representation of the past matches deeply held biases. The question of whether such representations are historically accurate is less important than understanding that history is driven by subjective interpretations. *Mad Men* is a fine example of how staying close to commonly held assumptions makes a representation of the past seem very credible.

CONCLUSION

This chapter began with a discussion about the nature of history and how more than one account of the past may likely be true at the same time. This idea, that history is subjective, is especially important in the Canadian context because the ways in which the practice of public relations unfolded are both similar and different from what popular culture or US-based histories suggest. Because many publics gain their information and then shape their understandings of the PR profession from mass media, the role of popular culture and its focus upon the American context cannot be overemphasized. To understand a history of PR in Canada demands that one assumes a perspective towards history that is more subjective than one might normally be accustomed to.

One focus of this examination of a PR history from a Canadian perspective has been to show how the geography and settlement patterns of the day influenced both the needs and then the practices of PR. This offers a different lens through which to consider public relations in Canada and augments popular culture representations of the for-profit agency model that we observe in film, television, and written portrayals of public relations.

Through a detailed review of some of the key individuals associated with public relations in Canada and in the United States, some important considerations surface. For example, we begin to see how early pioneers of the profession were both women and men and that there were early organization and education efforts to strengthen the profession.

Our considerations of the past also point out how ethical concerns have been central to PR practitioners who try to understand what is fair, reasonable, and truthful in professional practice. When aspects of the public relations profession are brought into sharp relief through a look at the past, the present state of PR practices and professional standards and concerns are better explained. You will learn about laws affecting public relations in Chapter 3 and ethics in Chapter 4.

KEY TERMS

Canadian Public Relations Society (CPRS): Established in 1948, the Canadian Public Relations Society is an organization of men and women who practise public relations in Canada and abroad. Members work to maintain the highest standards and to share a uniquely Canadian experience in public relations.

International Association of Business Communicators (IABC): An international professional association established in 1970 for communicators, including public relations practitioners. This association is a US-based international organization with over 15,000 members in 80 countries.

Muckraking: A form of sensationalized journalism common in the early 1900s where stories were developed, largely for print newspapers, based on scandal and speculation.

National Policy: The policy of the Canadian government introduced under Prime Minister John A. Macdonald prioritizing the economic and political development of the country through policies of immigration and settlement of the West, tariffs and protectionist trade strategies, and the establishment of a national railway system.

Press agent: This individual acted as a liaison with the press to share information on behalf of an individual or organization. This role typically reflected a one-way flow of communication from the organization to the media.

Publicity: An uncontrolled (unpaid) method of placing messages in the media by creating interest among journalists for editorial content on the subject.

FOR REVIEW AND DISCUSSION

1. Compare and contrast the major differences in the evolution of the field of public relations in Canada and the United States.
2. Describe three significant events in the evolution of public relations practice in Canada.
3. Examine the importance of strategic public relations practice to the success of Prime Minster Macdonald's National Policy on immigration.
4. Choose two of the individuals introduced in this chapter who have played a role in the evolution of public relations practice. Assess their contributions to the profession.
5. Contrast the evolution of journalism from the muckraking of yellow journalism in the early 1900s to what you know of the field of journalism today.

ACTIVITIES

1. Visit the Jack Yocum Public Relations Profile Collection at http://www.cprs.ca/foundation/yocom.aspx to learn more about Canadian pioneers in public relations. Choose one of the individuals profiled in this series and write a short paper on the influence of that public relations pioneer on the evolution of Canadian PR practice.
2. To learn more about the use of lantern slides as a communication tactic in Canada's immigration campaign, see Ellen Scheinberg and Melissa K. Rombout's, "Projecting Images of the Nation: The Immigration Program and Its Use of Lantern Slides, archived at Library and Archives Canada, http://www.collectionscanada.gc.ca/publications/002/015002-2250-e.html. Compare two of the social media platforms you use today (e.g., Facebook, Twitter, YouTube, etc.) with the technology of the lantern slide. What communication objectives do these technologies share? How would the impact on audiences differ?
3. With a classmate, explore the perceptions that you have of the PR profession as you begin your course of study. Think of how your perceptions may have originated. Re-evaluate your perceptions after you have finished reading this book. How have your perceptions changed?

FURTHER READING

Bernays, Edward L. *Crystallizing Public Opinion*. New York: Boni and Liveright, 1923.

CPRS. "60 Years, 60 Milestones: The Canadian Public Relations Society: A History of Development and Achievement." Canadian Public Relations Society, 2010.

———. Jack Yocum Public Relations Profile Collection, 2013. http://www.cprs.ca/foundation/yocom.aspx.

Herbert, W.B. and J.R.G. Jenkins, eds. *Perspectives on Public Relations in Canada: Some Perspectives*. Markham, ON: Fitzhenry and Whiteside, 1984.

NOTES

1. *Oxford English Dictionary*, s.v. "History," accessed June 16, 2011, http://www.oed.com/view/Entry/87324?rskey=VGg1ug&result=1.

2. For example, see Chapter 21, "Historiography and the Past in Business Studies," in Alan Bryman, Emma Bell, Albert J. Mills, and Anthony Yue, *Business Research Methods*, Canadian edition (Don Mills, ON: Oxford University Press, 2011), 428–60. See also Gabrielle A. T. Durepos and Albert J. Mills, ANTi-History: *Theorizing the Past, History, and Historiography in Management and Organization Studies* (Charlotte, NC: Information Age Publishing, 2012).

3. Merle Emms, "The Origins of Public Relations as an Occupation in Canada" (MA thesis, Department of Communication, Concordia University, Montreal, QC, 1995).

4. Laura A. Detre, "Canada's Campaign for Immigrants and the Images in 'Canada West' Magazine," *Great Plains Quarterly* 24, no. 2 (2004): 113–29.

5. John Oldland, "How the (Canadian) West Was Won" (unpublished paper, Division of Business Administration, Bishop's University, Lennoxville, QC, 1989), 10.

6. Detre, "Canada's Campaign for Immigrants," 113.

7. *Canadian Encyclopedia Online*, s.v. "Public Relations," by David Norman, accessed March 31, 2014, http://thecanadianencyclopedia.com/en/article/public-relations/.

8. Pierre Berton, *The Promised Land: Settling the West 1896–1914* (Toronto: McClelland and Stewart, 1984), 18.

9. R.A. Jenness, "Canadian Migration and Immigration Patterns and Government Policy," *International Migration Review* 8, no. 1 (1974): 5–22.

10. *Canadian Encyclopedia Online*, s.v. "Public Relations."

11. Johnathan Rose, "Government Advertising and the Creation of National Myths: The Canadian Case," *International Journal of Nonprofit and Voluntary Sector Marketing* 8, no. 2 (2003): 153–65.

12. *Canadian Encyclopedia Online*, s.v. "Public Relations."

13. Ibid.

14. Peter Johansen, "Professionalisation, Building Respectability, and the Birth of the Canadian Public Relations Society" *Journalism Studies* 2, no. 1 (2001): 59.

15. Scott M. Cutlip, Allen H. Center, and Glen M. Broom, *Effective Public Relations*, 8th ed. (Upper Saddle River, NJ: Prentice Hall, 2009), 98.

16. Karen Miller Russell and Carl O. Bishop, "Understanding Ivy Lee's Declaration of Principles: U.S. Newspaper and Magazine Coverage of Publicity and Press Agentry, 1865–1904," *Public Relations Review* 35, no. 2 (2009): 91–101.

17. John F. Budd Jr., Joe S. Epley, and Edward L. Bernays, "Edward Bernays: Pro & Con," *Public Relations Quarterly* 28, no. 1 (1983): 3.

18. Kevin G. Putnam, *The Origins and History of the First Public Relations Consulting Agency to Operate in Toronto* (Toronto: Ryerson Polytechnic Institute, 1997).

19. Edward L. Bernays, *Crystallizing Public Opinion* (New York: Boni and Liveright, 1923).

20. Budd Jr., Epley, and Bernays, "Edward Bernays: Pro & Con," 3.

21. Cutlip, Center, and Broom, *Effective Public Relations*, 8th ed.,103.

22. Doris E. Fleischman, *Careers for Women: A Practical Guide to Opportunity for Women in American Business* (New York: Garden City Publishing, 1939), 385.

23. CPRS, "Ruth Hammond, APR, CPRS Fellow, Toronto, Ontario, Career Highlights," accessed March 14, 2014, http://cprs.ca/foundation/jack_yocom/ruth_hammond.aspx.

24. Johansen, "Professionalisation," 60.

25. CPRS, "60 Years, 60 Milestones: The Canadian Public Relations Society: A History of Development and Achievement," Canadian Public Relations Society, 2010, 2.

26. Ibid.

27. CPRS, *Annual Review 2013: Advancing Public Relations and Communications Management*, http://www.cprs.ca/uploads/Governance/Annual%20Reports/2013_Annual_Review_web.pdf. The *Annual Review* specifies 1,718 members.

28. IABC, "IABC History," accessed June 27, 2011, http://news.iabc.com/index.php?s=40&item=78.

29. CWC, "Overviews and Reports," accessed June 27, 2011, http://www.cwc-afc.com/show-content.cfm?section=who-ove. See also Women in Communications and Technology, https://www.wct-fct.com/.

30. IHC, "About IHC," accessed June 27, 2011, http://healthcarecomm.org/about-us/.

31. Leonard L. Knott, *The PR in Profit* (Toronto: McClelland and Stewart, 1955).

32. CPRS, "60 Years, 60 Milestones: The Canadian Public Relations Society: A History of Development and Achievement," Canadian Public Relations Society, 2010, 2.

33. CPRS, "Public Relations Profile Collection," accessed June 16, 2011, http://www.cprs.ca/foundation/yocom.aspx.

34. Karl E. Weick, Kathleen M. Sutcliffe, and David Obstfeld, "Organizing and the Process of Sensemaking," *Organization Science* 16, no. 4 (2005): 409–21.

35. Johansen, "Professionalisation," 63.

36. Mordecai Lee, "The Image of the Government Flack: Movie Depictions of Public Relations in Public Administration," *Public Relations Review* 27, no. 3 (2001): 298.

37. Amy Thurlow, "'I Just Say I'm in Advertising': A Public Relations Identity Crisis," *Canadian Journal of Communication* 34, no. 2 (2009): 245.

38. Anthony R. Yue, and Gabrielle Durepos, "Fiction Analysis," in *The Sage Encyclopedia of Case Studies*, eds. Albert J. Mills, Eldon Wiebe, Gabrielle Durepos (Thousand Oaks, CA: Sage Publications, 2009), 395–96.

39. Ellen Tashie Frisina, "Addressing the 'Sex and the City' Syndrome," *Public Relations Tactics* 10, no. 8 (2003): 19.

40. Anthony R. Yue, and Amy Thurlow, "Facts, Fictions, and (Re)Visionist Presentism: Public Relations and Those Mad Men" (paper presented at the 28th Standing Conference on Organizational Symbolism, Lille, FR, July 2010).

Danielle Lemon and Charmane Sing

3

LEARNING OBJECTIVES

After reading this chapter, you will have an awareness of
Canadian laws related to communications and marketing.
You will be able to

- identify the limits to the right to freedom of expression;
- explain the law of defamation;
- describe the regulations to ensure honesty in advertising;
- define intellectual property rights, including copyright
  and trademarks;
- describe the laws regarding privacy and freedom
  of information; and
- explain the purpose of industry self-regulation.

INTRODUCTION

In Canada, the right to freedom of expression, which includes freedom of the
press and other media of communication, is protected by law. The Constitution
of Canada is the supreme law in this country and outlines the system of government and civil rights. The constitution features the Canadian Charter of Rights
and Freedoms (commonly referred to as the Charter), which lists "fundamental
freedoms" belonging to everyone in Canada—citizens or non-citizens, individuals or corporations—and that must be guaranteed by the policies and actions of

all levels of government. The text of section 2(b) of the Charter states that everyone has the fundamental freedom of "thought, belief, opinion and expression, including freedom of the press and other media of communication."[1]

While the right to freedom of expression is enshrined in the Charter, there are some legal and regulatory limits to that right established by the federal and provincial governments that will have practical effects on any communications or marketing initiatives. The chapter begins with an overview of the limits to the right to freedom of expression, followed by detailed description of the various limits.

LIMITS TO THE RIGHT TO FREEDOM OF EXPRESSION

In Canada, a person's constitutional right to freedom of expression is limited by the following laws and regulations, which seek to balance that right with other individual rights and the public interest:

- the Criminal Code
- intellectual property laws
- the Competition Act
- consumer protection legislation
- the Canadian Radio-television Telecommunications Commission (CRTC)

The Criminal Code

The Criminal Code of Canada lists certain criminal offences that limit a person's ability to exercise the right to freedom of expression, in the interest of protecting public values.

Criminal Libel

Article 298 of the Criminal Code describes the offence of "defamatory libel," which is published matter that is untruthful and likely to injure the reputation of any person by exposing them to "hatred, contempt or ridicule, or that is designed to insult the person of or concerning whom it is published."[2]

Defamatory libel may be expressed directly or by "insinuation or irony," in words or otherwise.[3] A person publishes a libel when it is exhibited in public, when it is caused to be read or seen, or when it is shown or delivered by a person with the intent that it should be read or seen, by either the person whom it defames or any other person.

A person found guilty of defamatory libel could be subject to imprisonment for a term of up to two years. If a person publishes a defamatory libel and knows it to be false, he or she may face up to five years in prison. A proprietor of a newspaper can be found guilty of defamatory libel unless they can prove that the defamatory matter was inserted without their knowledge and without negligence on their part. You will learn more about the law of defamation later in this chapter.

Obscene Material

Article 163 of the Criminal Code makes it an offence for a person to make, print, publish, distribute, circulate, or possess any "obscene written matter, picture, model, phonograph record or other thing whatever," including crime comics.[4] The offence applies to a variety of offensive acts, including offering to sell, advertise, or publish an advertisement relating to methods of causing abortions or miscarriages, or methods for "restoring sexual virility" or curing venereal diseases.

An exception to this offence is provided: if a person can provide that the public good was served by the acts in question, and the acts did not extend beyond what served the public good, they are not guilty of the offence. Determining whether the act fits these exceptional criteria is determined on a case-by-case basis.

Hate Speech

Article 318 of the Criminal Code makes it an offence to advocate or promote genocide, or acts committed with the intent to destroy in whole or in part any "identifiable group." Identifiable group is defined as "any section of the public distinguished by colour, race, religion, ethnic origin, or sexual orientation."[5]

Article 319 makes it an offence to communicate statements in any public place that incite hatred against any identifiable group. "Communicating" here includes broadcasting. A person convicted of an offence under either Article 318 or 319 could face a prison sentence of two to five years.

Intellectual Property Laws

Canadian intellectual property laws established by the Government of Canada, such as the Copyright Act, the Trade-marks Act, and their associated regulations, will apply in certain situations to protect material that is copyrighted or trademarked from reproduction or publication by third parties. In these laws, the government balances the right of the creator to control the reproduction of his or her work with the right to freedom of expression. You will learn more about Canadian intellectual property laws later in this chapter.

The Competition Act

The creation of marketing materials is limited by the Competition Act. This legislation prevents a person from making false or misleading representations about the supply or use of a product when promoting the product or a business.

Promotion includes representations made on product packaging, articles accompanying a product, in-store displays, and generally made during the process of selling that product. "False or misleading" representations include those made with respect to warranties, performance guarantees, length of life of products, and testimonials as to the efficacy of products. You will see more examples of false and misleading advertising later in this chapter.

According to the Competition Act, Canada's commissioner of competition may review a person's conduct with respect to false or misleading representations. In this context, "person" includes individuals and corporations. The commissioner may also seek court orders to prevent a person from engaging in misleading or false misrepresentations; to prevent a person from publishing or making available material containing false or misleading representations; or to impose hefty financial penalties.

Consumer Protection Acts

Provincial consumer protection legislation prohibits a myriad of unfair business practices and deceptive practices, such as false representations of the standard, quality, style, or grade of a good or service. This legislation includes British Columbia's Business Practices and Consumer Protection Act, Alberta's Fair Trading Act, and Ontario's Consumer Protection Act. These acts allow a consumer to seek civil remedies, which would include monetary damages or an injunction to prevent certain kinds of conduct from a person who engages in deceptive practices.

The Canadian Radio-television Telecommunications Commission (CRTC)

The CRTC is the independent regulatory agency that governs broadcasting and telecommunications in Canada. Its policies also establish standards and practices that may affect a person's ability to exercise his or her right to freedom of expression freely.

Several of the more widespread policies that the CRTC enforces are commonly known as the "Canadian Content" rules. These rules require broadcasters to present a certain percentage of programming that is written, produced, presented, or otherwise contributed to by persons from Canada. These rules also ensure that the multicultural nature of Canadian culture is accurately represented in media, ensuring both official languages and Aboriginal peoples are given a voice in Canadian broadcasting.

The CRTC responds to the public's concerns regarding broadcasting and telecommunications, in terms of content, availability, and pricing, and holds public consultations to address these issues. Although the CRTC is an independent agency, both the federal Broadcasting Act and the federal Telecommunications Act inform the policies established by the CRTC. The CRTC reports to the minister of Canadian heritage.

Now that you have a general understanding of the limits to the right to freedom of expression, the following sections will provide further detail and examples.

A Note about Quebec

Quebec is governed by the Civil Code of Quebec. These civil laws may vary greatly from the common law of Canadian jurisdictions, discussed in this chapter. If you are working in Quebec, you should review a text that outlines the laws governing communications, marketing, and advertising practices in that province. The authors of this chapter are not licensed to practice law in the Province of Quebec and cannot comment on the Civil Code of Quebec with any authority.

THE LAW OF DEFAMATION

For centuries, society has placed immeasurable value on a person's reputation. The law of civil defamation protects an individual's reputation and places serious limits on what a person may publish or broadcast about another by giving a person a right to sue another for damage to his or her reputation caused by the publication or broadcast. Defamation has been defined as "publication, without justification or lawful excuse, which is calculated to injure the reputation of another by exposing him to hatred, contempt or ridicule."[6] To be considered defamatory, the publication or broadcast must be untrue and must tend to lower the individual profiled in the opinion of members of society generally.

For a statement to be considered defamatory, it must have been "published" —meaning it was communicated to someone other than the plaintiff. Each person who repeats a defamatory statement "publishes" that statement and is potentially liable for the defamation.

Historically, defamatory acts have been divided into two broad categories: slander (spoken defamatory statements) and libel (written words and images). Libellous statements were held to be more permanent and, therefore, more serious. To win a libel case, a plaintiff did not need proof of suffering monetary damages as a result of the defamation. In today's electronic age, however, the line between slander and libel is blurring. For example, someone may say something defamatory about another person in an online chat. It is a written statement, but is it more permanent than a broadcast on YouTube in which a person in slandered? To address the ways technology is rapidly changing our perception of defamation, several provinces have passed uniform defamation acts, which abolish the distinction between slander and libel and make all defamatory acts actionable (meaning a plaintiff may make a claim to a court) without proof of damage.

Unlike several other jurisdictions, including the United States, a Canadian victim of defamation does not need to show that the defendant was malicious to win a defamation suit. One of the most relevant Canadian court cases on defamation is Hill v. Church of Scientology of Toronto.[7]

In this case, a lawyer for the Church of Scientology, Morris Manning, held a press conference on the steps of a Toronto courthouse and commented on allegations that the Church of Scientology were intending to file in court against another lawyer, Casey Hill. The church alleged that Hill had misled a judge (a grievous allegation against any lawyer) and breached court orders. In court, these allegations were found to be untrue and unfounded. Hill then sued both Manning and the Church of Scientology for libel. At court, he won damages of $1.6 million, a judgement that was affirmed by the Court of Appeal of Ontario.

In appealing the decision to the Supreme Court of Canada, the church and Manning argued that the law of defamation had gone too far: that protecting an individual's reputation had restricted their own rights to freedom of expression to an unacceptable extent. They also argued that Hill should have to prove that defamation had actually occurred by showing that they had expressed actual malice in their statements. The Supreme Court of Canada disagreed. The court wrote that freedom of speech, like any other freedom, is subject to the law and must be balanced against the essential need of individuals to protect their reputation.

Defences to Defamation

Once a plaintiff has established that a statement was defamatory, the person who published or broadcast the defamatory statement (or defendant) must provide that the statement was defensible (meaning, there is a defence available to the defendant for their actions) in order to avoid liability. For a defamatory statement to be defensible, the defendant must prove that it was either true; fair comment; published under "privilege"; or published in the context of what may otherwise be called "responsible journalism."[8]

Truth

Truth, sometimes called the defence of "justification," is an absolute form of defence—a complete exoneration of the defendant against a defamation claim. A person can have no right to protect his or her reputation from harm if the inferences being made as a result of the defamatory statement are in fact true.

Fair Comment

For a defamatory statement to be successfully defended as "fair comment," the statement must be a matter of public interest, based on known and provable facts, an opinion that some, or any person (not just the publisher of the defamatory statement) would be capable of holding, based on those facts. In other words, the publisher of the defamatory statement does not necessarily have to believe that the inferences of the statement are true, but some person must be capable of holding such opinion, based on the facts before them.

For example, in the case of *WIC Radio Ltd. and Rafe Mair v. Kari Simpson*,[9] Kari Simpson sued Rafe Mair, a journalist in British Columbia, and his radio station for comments he made about her during an editorial radio broadcast. Simpson opposed the introduction of educational materials that deal with homosexuality into public schools. Her stance as a public opponent of homosexuality was well known in the community. Mair's editorial referred to Simpson's public opposition of positive portrayals of homosexuals as akin to "bigots" such as Hitler, George Wallace, and other individuals who had publicly displayed hostility or violence towards a minority. The courts had no problem finding that Mair's statements were defamatory. However, the courts also found that Mair could use the defence of fair comment without actually believing that Simpson was capable of or advocating violence against homosexuals. The court found it was enough that Simpson's previous public addresses had used violent imagery and metaphors. As a result, "someone" could have expressed the belief that Simpson condoned violence against homosexuals. This threshold is not particularly high; the belief does not even have to be objective or reasonable.

The key element of the defence of fair comment is the public interest. Mair's defence of fair comment would not have been accepted if the courts had not found that speaking out against intolerance towards homosexuals was in the public interest. Mair was ultimately victorious at the Supreme Court of Canada, which found that his statements had been fair comment and were not defamatory.

In the Manitoba Queen's Bench case of *Makow v. Winnipeg Sun*, Justice Monnin clearly summarized the public policy behind the defence of fair comment:

> Everyone has a right to comment on matters of public interest provided he does so fairly and honestly and such comment, however severe, is not actionable.
>
> In order to be successful, the defendants must meet the following criteria: the words objected to must be comment and not statement of fact; the comment must be fair; (and) the comment must be on a matter of public interest.[10]

The defence of fair comment is a situation where courts are willing to tip the scales back in favour of the public interest, freedom of expression, and a robust media at the expense of an individual's reputation. However, the harm must be balanced carefully against the value of the defamatory statements to the public generally.

Privilege

Some forms of reports are protected from defamation claims by provincial laws. For instance, fair and accurate reports of court proceedings are protected by privilege, as are public meetings, communications, or decisions by entities that represent governmental authority in Canada.

The most obvious forms of statements that are subject to the defence of privilege are statements made in court proceedings and in federal Parliament, to permit the fair and accurate reporting of these processes to the public.

Responsible Journalism

In two cases in 2009, *Grant v. Torstar Corporation*[11] and *Quan v. Cusson*,[12] the Supreme Court of Canada created a new defence to a libel claim, called the "responsible journalism" defence. A publisher of a libellous statement may now present a defence that the libellous statement was a "responsible communication on matters of public interest."[13] The court may consider this defence if the publisher can prove it acted according to prevailing journalistic standards and the subject matter is related to a matter of public interest, even though some of the facts may have been published incorrectly. The court, however, must also weigh the seriousness of the allegation contained in the libellous statement; the extent to which the subject matter was in the public interest; the steps taken by the publisher to verify the facts; whether the story communicated the plaintiff's point of view; and the overall tone of the story.

HONESTY IN ADVERTISING

Advertising exists in all facets of our lives. Its fundamental purpose is to influence consumers' purchasing decisions. To that end, regulations need to be in place to ensure that consumers have accurate and sufficient information to make informed purchasing decisions and to deter deceptive marketing practices.

In Canada, marketing practices are regulated primarily by the federal Competition Act (administered by the Competition Bureau); provincial consumer protection legislation (administered by a provincial consumer protection branch of a ministry or a not-for-profit corporation created by legislation, such as BC's Business Practices and Consumer Protection Act); and the Canadian Code of Advertising Standards (administered by Advertising Standards of Canada). Special rules and guidelines may apply for certain industries, such as the motor vehicle, tobacco, food, and drug and alcohol industries.

All of these regulations and guidelines share the same general principle: making false, deceptive, or misleading representations to the public for the purpose of promoting a product or service is prohibited in Canada. A "representation" could be a statement, an illustration, or a claim about a product or service.

In Canada, there are a number of cases where businesses have been found to have made false or misleading representations to the public. For example, the Competition Bureau investigated a matter where a company labelled its home improvement/hardware products as having been made in Canada when in fact the products originated from China. The bureau deemed these to be false and misleading representations, and the company had to correct its labels. Here are more examples of false, deceptive, or misleading marketing practices that contravene the various regulations and guidelines:

- Advertisements with unsubstantiated claims concerning the performance, efficacy, or length of a product. In other words, before a company can claim that its product will last longer than the competitors' products, the company must be able to prove that its product actually does so.
- Advertisements omitting material information. For example, an Ontario health club failed to disclose in some of its print and radio advertising that

consumers are required to pay mandatory "fitness assessment" fees, or that consumers are required to sign up for a one-year contract to receive the advertised "free" trial offers.

- Advertisements containing disclaimers or asterisked "fine print" information that contradicts the key representation in the advertisement, and whose disclaimers or "fine print" information are not clearly placed or described. For example, the advertisement of a magazine publisher and its marketing company was found to be misleading because the general message to the consumer—namely, the exclamatory sentences in bold uppercase letters in the advertisements—was that the consumer had already won a sweepstakes. In fact, the advertisement was simply an invitation to participate in the sweepstakes. The information clarifying that the advertisement was only an invitation to participate was in small print and phrased ambiguously.
- Advertisements where a company compares its services with the services of its competitor and in doing so makes untruthful or unsubstantiated claims about the competitor's services. For example, a telecommunications company claimed that it had the most reliable network in Canada (in comparison to its competitors). Such representations were considered to be misleading because the claim of having Canada's most reliable network was based on the company's outdated testing that was no longer accurate.

If a person (meaning an individual or corporation) is found to have engaged in any of the prohibited marketing practices, he, she, or it may be liable to criminal or civil sanctions, which include imprisonment and monetary penalties. It is important to note that in determining whether a representation is false or misleading, it does not matter whether a member of the public was in fact misled or deceived. Rather, the key considerations are the general impression conveyed by the representation and whether the representation is likely to have influenced consumers' purchasing decisions. The Supreme Court of Canada has clarified in *Richard v. Time Inc.* that the "consumer" under consideration is an average consumer who is credulous and inexperienced and takes no more than ordinary care in observing an advertisement.[14]

INTELLECTUAL PROPERTY RIGHTS

It is important to have a basic understanding of intellectual property rights to understand how they apply to your own work and the works of others that you may wish to use.

Copyright

Copyright gives certain exclusive rights to authors of original literary, dramatic, musical, and artistic works. Copyright in an original work exists automatically when it is created. To be considered "original," a work must originate with an author, cannot be copied, and must involve some intellectual effort.

Copyright protects expression of an idea, not the idea itself. It is possible to have two works that include the same idea but expressed in different ways.

The range of "works" that can be protected by copyright is broad and can include written works, paintings, photographs, musical scores, performances, and computer programs. The scope of copyright protection varies slightly depending on the type of work being protected and is subject to exceptions made by lawmakers to protect certain matters of public policy. At the most basic level, copyright protects a work from being copied, performed, displayed, distributed, or adapted without the author's permission. In Canada, copyright exists for the life of the author of a work, plus fifty years. After this point, a work becomes known as a "public domain" work and can be freely distributed and published.

Although copyright arises automatically upon creation of an original work, an author can, for added protection, register copyright with the Canadian Intellectual Property Office. This registration can be used in court as evidence of ownership.

It is important to understand that no original work should be used without the author's permission. A quotation from original works may in some circumstances be used without the author's permission, but must still be attributed to the author (their name must be included as the author of the quotation) to avoid copyright infringement. There is no "percentage rule" where usage of a small percentage of a work will ensure that you do not infringe its copyright; this is something that is often—and erroneously—believed by professionals in many creative industries. If you are going to use someone else's work, either use it with permission or do not use it at all.

Trademark

Trademarks can play an integral role in advertising and promotional activities because they can distinguish the advertised products or services from those of competitors, create or reinforce a desired brand image with consumers, and promote customer loyalty.

A trademark is a distinctive symbol that identifies the source of a product or service, and distinguishes the product or service from others. Trademarks also denote a certain quality to the products and services associated with the marks. A trademark can take various forms, such as a word, a phrase (slogan), a design (logo), or a combination of these. For example, when consumers hear the well-known phrase "RRRoll up the rim to win" on the radio, they generally associate the phrase to a promotional contest held at participating Tim Hortons restaurants.

In Canada, a company or an organization acquires rights in a trademark by using the mark in connection with a product or a service. However, trademark rights that are based solely on use are limited to the geographical area where the trademark owner can prove that there is actual use of the trademark and that the trademark has gained a reputation within that geographical area. To obtain broader rights in a trademark, including exclusive trademark rights across Canada, the trademark owner can apply to the Canadian Intellectual Property Office for a trademark registration. As long as a mark is continuously, exclusively, and properly used in Canada, a trademark owner can have perpetual rights in a trademark.

A trademark can provide tremendous value to its owner. In some cases, a company's trademark has considerably more value than the company's tangible assets. Significant emphasis and resources are often devoted to selecting a strong trademark and to protecting it from potential abuse and infringement. That said, there are a number of legal issues trademark owners and marketing professionals must consider before choosing and taking steps to protect a new trademark. For example, does the proposed trademark conflict with already existing trademarks belonging to others? Does the proposed trademark contravene the requirements set out in the Trade-marks Act? To properly address these questions and to avoid investing time and money in an unenforceable or potentially infringing trademark, it is prudent to consult with a trademark lawyer at the outset of marketing initiatives to incorporate new trademarks. Then, once a trademark has built up sufficient reputation and recognition in the marketplace, trademark owners and their marketing team must be vigilant to obtain appropriate legal advice and guidance to protect and enforce valuable trademark rights.

NEW FEDERAL LEGISLATION ON COPYRIGHT AND DIGITAL MEDIA

On June 29, 2012, Canada's Copyright Modernization Act received royal assent, and most of its provisions came into force on November 7, 2012, marking the first changes to Canada's copyright laws since 2000.[15] The new act addresses technological developments that have become a part Canadian's everyday life, including the widespread sharing of content on the Internet, which the previous Copyright Act did not address. The Copyright Modernization Act includes the following new laws:

- Copyright owners are given the exclusive right to control how their copyrighted material is published and shared on the Internet.
- Copyright owners who are affected by digital piracy now have the ability to sue digital pirates for monetary damages.
- Copyright owners who use tools to protect their digital content, such as digital locks, are protected by new rules that impose liability on individuals who circumvent technological protection measures or break digital locks, or who sell tools designed to break such digital locks.
- The distinction between commercial (infringement for profit) and non-commercial infringement (for example, for personal use) is made, with appropriately larger fines for commercial infringement of a copy righted work.

New forms of permissions for content users are also addressed. For instance, "Internet mash-ups" are now permissible, as Canadians are now permitted to use copyrighted material in the creation of new works, as long as their use of the original work is for non-commercial purposes; the work created does not have a substantial negative impact on market for the original work or the original creator's reputation; and the new "mash-up" is not a substitute for the original work.

The Copyright Modernization Act also requires the Canadian government to review the legislation every five years to ensure the law is keeping up to speed with technological developments.

PRIVACY AND FREEDOM OF INFORMATION

There are a number of laws and regulations at both the federal and provincial level that govern the collection, use, and disclosure of information by governments and businesses. These laws will affect the availability and use of certain information by journalists, advertisers, and businesses.

What the Government Must Keep Confidential

As of 1983, the Privacy Act imposed obligations on federal government agencies and institutions as to how they collect, use, and disclose the personal information of individuals. "Personal information" in this context means information about an identifiable individual, including information about race, national or ethnic origin, marital status, religion, colour, age, education, criminal or employment history, address, or fingerprints.

Personal information also includes correspondence between the government and an individual that is implicitly or explicitly private and confidential, or anything that contains an individual's views on another individual. The Privacy Act affects what you may request from the government by way of a freedom of information request.

How Businesses Collect, Use, or Disclose Personal Information

Beginning in 2001, the Personal Information Protection and Electronic Documents Act (PIPEDA) slowly phased in laws that impose restrictions on how businesses in the private sector collect, use, and disclose individuals' personal information. These restrictions are particularly relevant to how businesses can use their customers' information for communications and marketing purposes, such as electronic flyers and customer bulletins or updates.

PIPEDA requires businesses to obtain consent from customers for the purposes for which it is collecting personal information before doing so. For instance, if a business collects personal information for the purpose of recording inventory, then it cannot then use that information to create marketing contact lists.

An affected customer or the privacy commissioner appointed under PIPEDA can bring a business to the federal court for failing to comply with PIPEDA. The consequences can be audits, fines, and negative publicity for the business.

INDUSTRY SELF-REGULATION

In addition to the legal limits prescribed by regulation and common law, Canada's own communications and marketing industries self-regulate by establishing guidelines, standards, and practices that members must follow. Self-regulation relies on "buy-in" from the industry; member compliance is essential to its success. This buy-in is achieved by the persuasive argument that self-regulation is preferable to governmental regulation.

The Canadian Broadcast Standards Council (CBSC)

All of Canada's private radio and television broadcasters are members of the Canadian Association of Broadcasters (CAB). The CBSC is an independent body established by the CAB to administer standards developed by CAB members. The CBSC administers a number of codes, including a Code of Ethics,

Violence Code, Equitable Portrayal Code (to prevent stereotypical or negative portrayals of minority groups), and a Journalistic Independence Code.

Members of the public may file complaints with the CBSC if they have a complaint about a broadcaster and have not first received a satisfactory response from the broadcaster. The CBSC will then investigate further through regional and national panels of adjudicators, composed equally of volunteer members of the public and volunteer broadcasters. The CBSC will issue a ruling, which is made public and with which the broadcaster must comply.

CBC/Radio-Canada Journalistic and Advertising Standards and Practices

CBC/Radio-Canada has established its own corporate policies to which its broadcasters must adhere. Both the Journalistic Standards and Practices and Advertising Practices are wide-ranging and address diverse topics, such as

- how children and youth are interviewed;
- having respect for young audiences;
- the use of hidden cameras and microphones;
- how conflicts of interests will be handled;
- the objectives for court reporting;
- how single points of view or opinions will be presented; and
- how social media may be used.

Members of the public may complain to CBC's ombudsman if they feel a CBC or Radio-Canada broadcaster has not adhered to these standards and a satisfactory response has not been first received from the broadcaster. The ombudsman then reports directly to CBC/Radio-Canada's president and the board of directors.

Advertising Standards Canada

Advertising Standards Canada is a national not-for-profit industry member organization that administers the Canadian Code of Advertising Standards. The code, created and updated by the advertising industry, sets out the criteria for standards of truth, accuracy, and fairness, which advertising in any medium must meet. National and regional response councils are made up of members of the public and the advertising industry. The councils review and respond to public complaints about advertisements believed to violate the principles in the code.

CONCLUSION

This chapter is intended to give you a sense of the various laws affecting communications and marketing in Canada. When preparing communications material, whether in school or in the field, practitioners should keep their eyes and minds open to potential legal issues. In the event of a possible legal issue, they should contact expert legal advice from lawyers who are familiar not only with the federal legislation in the area but also the provincial legislation. Consulting a lawyer after a communications has gone out is too late. If in doubt, invest in legal advice prior to releasing communications. This tactic will prevent further legal costs if your communications do violate the law.

KEY TERMS

Canadian Charter of Rights and Freedoms: A bill of rights forming part of Canada's Constitution Act, 1982 that guarantees political rights to Canadian citizens and protects the civil rights of everyone in Canada from the actions of all levels of government.

Canadian Constitution: The supreme law of Canada, which establishes Canada's system of government, divides power between the federal government and provincial governments, and enshrines the civil rights of Canadians and those people resident in Canada.

Canadian Radio-television and Telecommunications Commission (CRTC): Canada's regulatory agency that oversees broadcasting and communications.

Consumer protection legislation: Laws enacted usually by the provinces to protect the rights of consumers when they are purchasing goods and services in the marketplace and to encourage fair competition among businesses.

Copyright: A legal concept, enshrined in Canada's Copyright Act, that gives a creator of an original work exclusive rights to the use of that work, including the right to copy that work, to be credited for that work, and to benefit financially from that work.

Criminal Code of Canada: A Canadian law that codifies criminal offences, procedures, and punishments in Canada.

Defamation: The communication of a false statement that may give an individual or business (or other organization or group) a negative or inferior image. Includes slander, libel, and criminal libel.

Defamatory libel: Also known as *criminal libel*, an umbrella term given to those forms of libel that are prohibited by law, including under the Criminal Code of Canada.

Defendant: In a lawsuit, a defendant is the party who is accused of some wrong-doing and must answer the plaintiff's complaint.

False representations: Statements that are held out to be fact but are found upon investigation to be untrue.

Intellectual property laws: Laws that grant certain exclusive rights to the creators of intangible assets such as original musical, literary or artistic works, discoveries and inventions, or words, symbols, and designs.

Plaintiff: A party who initiates a lawsuit and seeks a legal remedy from a defendant for the defendant's (alleged) wrongdoing.

Trademark: A word, design, symbol, or phrase that identifies a product or service.

FOR REVIEW AND DISCUSSION

1. Consider the general categories of limits to the right to freedom of expression (Criminal Code, intellectual property rights, competition, consumer protection, and CRTC regulation) discussed in this chapter. Do you think some limits are more valid than others? Why or why not?

2. Think of three examples of well-known trademarks that have built up significant reputation and recognition in the marketplace. What part of the trademark do you think is distinctive? What part of the trademark is most famous? What "values" would you associate with that trademark (e.g., trustworthiness, value for money, quality)? Consider how long the trademark has been in the marketplace. Has it taken a long time for the trademark to build up a reputation?

3. Imagine an advertisement that says "Natural Gas BBQ, completely assembled—$600." Consider whether the advertisement is acceptable under applicable advertising legislations if: (a) the barbecue costs $600 and (b) there is an additional charge of $50 to assemble the barbecue. If the advertisement is not acceptable in your opinion, how would you change it?

4. Do you think it is appropriate for retailers to ask for your email address when ringing up your purchase? How about your postal code? How much information is "too much?" Discuss the reasons a company might want to keep its customers' personal information on record.

5. Do you think self-regulation by an industry, such as the advertising industry's Advertising Standards Canada, is effective, or does an external regulator (such as the communications industry's CRTC) need to be in place to ensure the public is protected? What are the arguments for or against self-regulation?

ACTIVITIES

1. Find a news story anywhere in the world where an organization is suing another organization (the "defendant") relating to unauthorized use of its trademark. In groups of two, discuss why the organization commenced the lawsuit and the group's prediction as to the strengths and weaknesses of the organization's case and of the defendant's case.

2. In a group, find 5 to 10 examples of advertising; try to find print, online, and broadcast (radio or TV) examples. Consider whether each example makes a claim as to the performance or efficacy of the product. Is there "fine print"? If you were a consumer, would you be surprised if the product did not live up to the claims in the advertising? What steps would you take to address such a problem if you were the manufacturer or producer of the advertised product?

3. Find a news story anywhere in the world where a person is suing a media outlet or another person for defamation. What is the basis for the claim? What defences will the defendant present to the claim? If you were the judge, how would you rule in the matter?

4. Visit three retailers, either in person or online, and obtain their policy on collecting customer's email addresses. Compare the terms of each policy. Is there one policy you prefer? Why?

5. Visit your province's consumer protection agency or bureau online. What protections do they offer consumers? Is it easy or difficult for consumers to understand their rights? What suggestions would you offer the consumer protection bureau to improve the laws around consumer protection?

FURTHER READING[16]

Adam, Stuart G., and Robert Martin. *A Sourcebook of Canadian Media Law.* 2nd ed. Ottawa: Carleton University Press, 1994.

Advertising Standards Canada. *The Canadian Code of Advertising Standards.* 2012. http://www.adstandards.com/en/Standards/theCode.aspx.

Blake, Cassels, and Graydon LLP. *Dispute Resolution in Canada.* Accessed April 2, 2014. http://www.blakes.com/English/Resources/Pages/Litigation-and-Dispute-Resolution-in-Canada.aspx.

Canadian Intellectual Property Office website: www.cipo.ic.gc.ca

CBC Radio-Canada. *Journalistic and Advertising Standards and Practices.* 2014. http://www.cbc.radio-canada.ca/en/reporting-to-canadians/acts-and-policies/programming/journalism/.

Vaver, David. *Intellectual Property Law: Copyright, Patents, and Trade-marks*. Concord, ON: Irwin Law, 1997.

NOTES

1. Canadian Charter of Rights and Freedoms, Constitution Act, 1982, Schedule B to the Canada Act, 1982 (United Kingdom) (1982, c.11), http://laws-lois.justice.gc.ca/eng/charter/.
2. Criminal Code, 1985, c. C-46, art. 298, http://laws-lois.justice.gc.ca/eng/acts/C-46/.
3. Ibid.
4. Criminal Code, 1985, c. C-46, art. 163, http://laws-lois.justice.gc.ca/eng/acts/C-46/.
5. Criminal Code, 1985, c. C-46, art. 318, http://laws-lois.justice.gc.ca/eng/acts/C-46/.
6. Parke B stated this in *Parmiter v. Coupland* (1840) 6 M and W 105, 108, Exch., qtd. in "Defamation," s.v., *Black's Law Dictionary*, accessed April 2011, http://thelawdictionary.org.
7. Hill v. Church of Scientology of Toronto, [1995] 2 S.C.R. 1130.
8. Quan v. Cusson, 2009 SCC 62, [2009] 3 S.C.R. 712.
9. WIC Radio Ltd. and Rafe Mair v. Kari Simpson, 2007 CanLII 2769 (SCC).
10. Makow v. Winnipeg Sun, 2003 MBQB 56.
11. Grant v. Torstar Corporation, 2009 SCC 61.
12. Quan v. Cusson, 2009 SCC 62.
13. David Crerar, and Michael Skene, Borden Ladner Gervais LLP, "New Defamation Defence of Responsible Communication on Matters of Public Interest," *Lexology*, January 6, 2010, http://www.lexology.com/library/detail.aspx?g=a8c6b6e9-9e05-47c0-9a5b-43efa9292f4a.
14. Richard v. Time Inc., 2012 SCC 8.
15. Copyright Modernization Act, SC 2012, c. 20, http://laws-lois.justice.gc.ca/eng/AnnualStatutes/2012_20/page-1.html.
16. We also consulted these sources in writing this chapter.

Allison G. MacKenzie

4

Ethics: Living Your Professional Values

LEARNING OBJECTIVES

After reading this chapter you will be able to

- describe what constitutes ethical PR practice;
- differentiate between two commonly held ethical perspectives—utilitarianism and deontology—and understand key differences between them;
- identify five tenets of practice that distinguish professions from occupations;
- explain the role of professional associations in fostering an ethical PR profession;
- describe the purpose of having a code of ethics; and
- explain the advantages and disadvantages of licensing and accrediting PR practitioners.

INTRODUCTION

As a student, you face ethical issues every day. Ask yourself, is it ethical to

- work with another student on an individual assignment?
- ask one of your parents to edit an essay prior to submission?
- scan or copy a textbook rather than purchasing it?
- reuse materials developed for one assignment as part of another assignment?
- download a pirated song or movie on your computer?

How you respond to these issues shapes your character and your reputation or personal brand. Like you, practitioners face ethical issues every day. As a future practitioner, you need to think about your ethics and professional reputation now so that you are prepared to live your values when you face ethical challenges in your practice. Ask yourself, would I

- omit key facts to change the reception of a presentation in my organization's favour?
- alter a publicity photo or a photo for my organization's newsletter?
- join a chat room to conduct research for my client without revealing my identity to other participants?
- provide a journalist with a gift such as cash, a trip, or a night on the town in return for coverage of my client's issues?
- leave key facts out of a media release because those facts would cast my client in a less positive light?
- use information or knowledge I gained while working for one client to another client's advantage?

PR practitioners face these kinds of ethical issues daily. In this chapter you will explore the ethical context for professional public relations. You will learn what ethical PR is, why it is important, what it means to be a professional, and the role of professional associations in fostering ethical practice.

PR ETHICS—NOT AN OXYMORON

Ethical conduct by PR practitioners is more important today than ever before. Almost daily Canadians are inundated with high-profile scandals and frauds perpetrated by leaders within the public and private sectors. Examples include the Senate scandal, Toronto Mayor Rob Ford's 2013 cocaine use, corporate misrepresentations of Canada's contribution to global warming, and the use of performance-enhancing drugs by Olympic athletes. As a result of such ongoing revelations of corporate, organizational, and government misdoings, misrepresentations, and half-truths, Canadians' trust in their elected officials and corporate and community leaders has never been lower.

This growing lack of trust has a direct impact on the public's perception of PR. In 2007, the Vancouver PR firm Hoggan and Associates commissioned a survey of the public's perceptions of PR: 81 per cent of respondents thought the role of PR is to help clients misrepresent performance.[1] As Hoggan says, four out of five people think PR practitioners mislead people for a living.[2] The public associates PR practitioners, often the public voice of such community leaders, with wide-scale obfuscation, and this association continues to damage our collective reputation.

The public's growing lack of trust of public relations is not limited to the North America. It is global. Consider the findings of a 2003 United Kingdom report by Corporate Watch:

> There is a considerable body of evidence emerging to suggest that modern public relations practices are having a very significant deleterious impact on the democratic process...PRs have often engaged in deliberate deception on their clients' behalf and have developed a deeply unhealthy relationship with the "free press." Furthermore, by giving vested interests the opportunity to deliberately obfuscate, deceive, and derail public debate on key issues the public relations industry reduces society's capacity to respond effectively to key social, environmental and political challenges.[3]

As this passage demonstrates, there is plenty of evidence to support the theory that PR has a reputation for unethical behaviour. As you have read, the role of PR is to create mutually beneficial relationships between organizations and the stakeholders upon whom the organization's success depends. Given that effective relationships are built on mutual trust and credibility, this negative reputation seriously undermines the effectiveness of the PR function in society. For this reason, students and practitioners must foster ethical standards of practice, commit to ethical practice, and foster professionalism within the practice.

Society judges PR to be of value when it

- promotes the free, honest, and ethical exchange of ideas, opinions, and education;
- identifies the sources and goals of the participants in the discussion;
- is conducted in an ethical, open, and transparent way.[4]

Society judges PR to be unethical when it

- limits the exchange of ideas, debate, and discourse on matters of public interest;
- hides the identities of the participants and their motivations; and
- is conducted in an unethical, unfair way.[5]

INTERVIEW: THE POWER OF COMMUNICATION

Throughout this chapter, four senior communicators will share their thoughts on ethical PR practice.

Robert Campbell, Director, National Aboriginal Services, MNP LLP, Winnipeg, Manitoba (over 20 years of practice): Communication may very well be the singular most important component of any organization today. Communication has both internal and external applications, which are equally important. As our environments continue to expand and our reach continues to grow, there is a compounding effect on our need to communicate. It all boils down to this simple reality: everything we do (as people and organizations) and, more importantly, the success of our actions is predicated on our ability to communicate effectively. The better the communication, the greater the chance of a more positive outcome.

Kim Blanchette, APR, Manager, Communications, Energy Resources Conservation Board, Calgary, Alberta (over 20 years of practice): Gone are the days of simply trying to get our message to internal and external stakeholders—we now need to help them understand how to filter through the barrage of information and opinion to find the facts. American political scientist Joseph Nye says the real power in the Information Age has become the ability to determine what is truly important and that is a role that communicators must play. As we move traditional organizations away from the mindset of "knowledge is power" to "sharing knowledge is power," communicators are increasingly challenged to put information in the correct context.

Christen Downie, ABC, Manager, Communications, Methanex Corp., Vancouver, British Columbia (over 20 years of practice): Through effective communication, organizations build and grow relationships with key stakeholders, create and maintain two-way channels to foster understanding and acceptance. Factors such as increased skepticism of big business and governing bodies following the worst recession in decades, the pressure to be environmentally and socially responsible, and the global explosion of social media have made it imperative for organizations to be—and to be seen as being—transparent.

Communication has an important role in ensuring that information shared with stakeholders not only continues to be relevant and
accurate, value-added and purpose-driven, but also promotes transparency and tells the organization's story. It's also key to promoting
an organization's brand and protecting its reputation. Practitioners
are effectively the ears of their organizations, helping to monitor,
anticipate, and analyze stakeholder opinion, attitudes, and issues
that may have an impact on their organizations.

Guy Litalien, ARP, Senior Media Advisor, Hydro-Québec, Montreal, Quebec
(over 25 years of practice): Simply put, an organization without
communication within the organization and outside with its stakeholders cannot function.

WHAT ARE ETHICS?

The word *ethics* is derived from the Greek word *ethos*, which means *customs*.[6]
Ethics help you answer the questions, what is the right thing to do in this situation—how should I behave? Ethics, the rules set by individuals, professions,
and organizations that define what is fair or unfair, good, or bad to self as well
as to others, is one of five factors that regulate our social conduct and behaviour.
The other four factors are: (1) tradition—how previous generations have done
things; (2) public opinion—an aggregate of how, in general, a majority of members of a society currently think about issues. If you think about divorce you'll
see that public opinion changes over time; (3) law—the set of rules established
by a society to govern itself; and (4) morality—the rules established by religious
organizations, spiritual leaders, and social units to identify right conduct and
virtuous behaviour.[7]

Ethics provide individuals, professional associations, and organizations
with guidance regarding what is right or wrong, fair and unfair, honest or
dishonest. Many factors contribute to your ethical code, including your culture,
religion, socioeconomic and educational background, as well as your life
experiences. While the law establishes a floor for your conduct (such as stealing
is illegal), your ethics establish a ceiling for your behaviour. For example, if
a store clerk gives you too much change, depending on your personal ethical
code, you will probably return the change to him or her even though it is the
clerk's mistake.

While there are many ways of applying knowledge, understanding, and
reasoning to ethical dilemmas, utilitarianism and deontology are the two most

commonly identified ethical decision-making philosophies. Based on the work of John Stuart Mill and Jeffrey Bentham, utilitarianists make decisions based on the greater good or perceived consequences of an action. A utilitarianist asks, "Will the result of this action cause greater good or happiness for the greatest number of people than an alternative decision would?"[8] The end justifies the means. For example, a practitioner working for a local sports team may believe the quickest route to obtaining positive media coverage for the team is to deliver complimentary tickets and baseball caps to local journalists. From a utilitarian perspective, no harm is done. No one will be hurt, and this minor "gifting" will build a positive relationship with local journalists, leading to better coverage of the team.

Deontologists make decisions based on what the right thing to do is without consideration of the outcomes. Based on the work of Immanuel Kant, deontologists base their decisions on what is right or what is wrong, not on the consequences (which are not always easy to predict) or who will benefit the most. Deontologists believe a decision is ethically sound if it could be applied universally in the same circumstances.[9] In other words, the end never justifies the means; do unto others as you would have them do unto you. From a deontological perspective, gifting to gain favour is never acceptable no matter how minor the gift and even if no one is hurt by the exchange.

CASE STUDY: IS IT ETHICAL TO ALTER DIGITAL PHOTOS FOR A MEDIA RELEASE TO PROTECT NATIONAL SECURITY?

By John Larsen, MCS, ABC

It has often been said that ethics are relative (utilitarianism), meaning that ethical decision making can only be evaluated in the context of the specific situations in which they were made. The opposite of this construct is ethical absolutism (deontology), meaning that one ethical code can and should apply universally across all similar situations. On the surface both approaches make sense. However, although a utilitarian perspective often appears to fit logically, it can become a slippery slope that will eventually negate our professional ethics and diminish our reputation.

Case in point: In 1999, I was the Canadian Forces public affairs officer for NATO during the Serbian air campaign, stationed at the sprawling US airbase in Aviano, Italy. The aim of the conflict was to remove Serbian forces from Kosovo. The military effort began with a 78-day bombing campaign: each day and night fighters and bombers from NATO countries would fly combat missions into Serbia and over the occupied territory of Kosovo.

We believed that to ensure public support for the mission we needed to tell Canadians the story of our Canadian Air Force presence. However, we needed to do so without releasing specific tactical information.

The national media had been requesting photos and B-roll (unnarrated video footage) of our pilots in action. One morning, the lead military photographer came into my office with a set of crisp digital shots he'd taken of Canadian military planes taxiing and taking off, set against the stunning mountain backdrop. The photos communicated the excitement of the operation, exactly the type of highly prized shots that warrant front-page placement for Canadian daily newspapers. Unfortunately, the photos also revealed our various bomb and armament configurations, highly sensitive information that we didn't want released to the media.

Option one: digitally remove the armament, a relatively easy process using the new digital technology of the day. A utilitarian ethical perspective would have no concerns with this solution. Digital enhancement of the photos would enable us to tell this important story in a compelling way while abiding by the mandatory security restrictions. The logic behind this option was that, even though we wouldn't normally enhance media images, this was an extenuating situation and thus enhancement was understandable and warranted.

The countervailing view, option two: don't use the photos. This option recognized that faked imagery was faked imagery, pure and simple: even if we were upfront with the media, the viewers of the images wouldn't know the truth.

What would you do?

Our solution: We decided to re-shoot the entire series of photos, being extra careful not to include the armaments. Ultimately, the photos were not quite as good as the originals but they were still very good and they served the needs of a media without compromising professional integrity or reputation. Nothing was staged, nothing was photoshopped. No excuses required.

ETHICAL ADVOCACY

Professor Patricia J. Parsons of Mount Saint Vincent University in Halifax, Nova Scotia defines PR ethics as "the application of knowledge, understanding, and reasoning to questions of right and wrong behaviour in the professional practice of public relations."[10] Being an ethical practitioner is not an easy task. Practitioners must balance their responsibilities to society, employer, professional association, and self. These responsibilities often conflict.

PR practitioners are paid advocates for their clients and employers but are responsible first (and always) to act in the public's interest, a situation that often creates conflict. For this reason, it is important to be aware that as a professional your primary responsibility is to society above your professional association, employer, and self. Individual practitioners and the PR profession have a fundamental obligation to serve the welfare of the larger society as a condition of the right to serve clients[11] As paid advocates for clients, PR practitioners use persuasion to promote their clients' perspectives but ethically are obliged to do so in a way that does not hide or distort key facts or the truth.

The basic principles for ethical communication are to tell the truth, treat others as you would like to be treated, and to do no harm. Ethical PR involves having a clear understanding of how your organization's goals and objectives align or conflict with the community's interests, values, and well-being, as well as understanding what the community expects from your organization.[12] It means speaking the truth not only when it benefits you but also speaking the truth when it could potentially hurt you.[13]

INTERVIEW: ETHICAL PRACTICE REQUIRES A LIFELONG COMMITMENT

Christen: PR practitioners have a personal responsibility to tell the truth in their communication and to verify information before sharing with stakeholders. They have a role in helping their organizations consider possible outcomes of decisions and actions and the effects of communicating those decisions and actions on stakeholders. Practitioners must also counsel executives and leaders with integrity, not only on how to communicate with stakeholders but on what to disclose or not, even if it involves unpleasant facts. Ultimately, practitioners have an integral role in building trust and maintaining relationships with stakeholders based on transparency and authentic communication.

Kim: Ethics are crucial—from confidentiality to representing the public interest to ensuring senior executives fully understand the impact

of communications decisions—ethics are present in day-to-day
public relations practice regardless of the organization or industry.
Communicating with stakeholders, internal or external, is based on
trust. The ethical practice of PR helps maintain that trust, even in
times of crisis.

Guy: Ethical practice must begin as soon as students start learning and
practising PR. It should also contribute to the organizational vision
in terms of both communication and management.

Robert: To be effective you need to have high ethical standards. You must
believe in your subject matter, understand the subject, and have a
position on it. This will make you a more enthusiastic and authentic
communicator and will have a greater impact on the audience.

But how does a practitioner respond when his or her primary responsibility
to the public conflicts with an employer's interests and directions?

The first step is to approach the employer or client to explain the ethical conflict and the potential consequences of a particular course of action. Often this is
all that is required as the employer is seeking a solution and, chances are, risk-
ing reputational damage will only make the problem or issue more significant.
Look for alternative approaches and courses of action.

If your employer persists with an action you believe to be unethical, talk with
a senior practitioner or call your professional association's ethical help line
to investigate alternative perspectives and courses of action. Rarely (although
it happens), the PR practitioner will decide to resign the file or the position
because it does not align with his or her ethical code. In such a situation, the PR
practitioner should be very careful about labelling anyone or anything "unethical," which could be construed as defamatory or libellous.

WHAT DOES IT MEAN TO BE A PR PROFESSIONAL?

Instructors and practitioners often talk about the PR "profession," but have
you ever wondered what being a member of a "profession" actually means?

An occupation is a job that people do to earn money, while a profession
is work that requires specialized training and skills developed over a long
period of time and honed through practice and ongoing education. A profession operates in alignment with public purpose and has both an intellectual
tradition and a fiduciary responsibility.[14] Society gives professionals special
rights and responsibilities. We often respect professionals such as doctors,
lawyers, and engineers because of their knowledge, education, and specialized

skills. Members of these types of established professions enjoy special status in society.

For an occupation to become a profession, society must recognize it and its practitioners as having the following elements:

- specialized skills and expertise, institutionalized within a body of academic knowledge derived from research and application
- esoteric language, acquired through education and practice, unknown to those outside the profession
- a mandatory self-regulating professional body, with the power to grant and remove the privilege of practice and to discipline members
- a mandatory, enforceable code of ethics and standards of practice to which all members are held responsible
- autonomy of practice
- a service orientation based on the provision of a widely recognized service to society; recognition of a duty to society above self

While PR does not meet all of the above criteria, it is progressing towards professionalization. Many scholars argue that PR is midpoint on the professionalization continuum. Let's consider PR in light of these criteria.

Specialized Education

Until the 1970s, education and experience as a journalist was widely accepted as the career path to PR. Since the 1970s, colleges and universities across North America have offered undergraduate and post-graduate degrees in communication with a focus on PR. Because of the increased academic focus on PR research, the body of theoretical knowledge continues to expand. A growing number of scholarly journals are dedicated to reporting on academic research in PR.

Today's PR students undergo a rigorous curriculum that includes PR management, communication theory, organizational behaviour, media relations, government relations, strategic communication planning, and research methods in public relations. They draw upon the PR scholarly journals to research issues and challenges and apply their findings to practice. In the process of their studies, students acquire language and specialized knowledge that is specific to PR, and prior to graduation, students often supplement their education with international experience and/or a practicum.

INTERVIEW: CORE ATTRIBUTES FOR COMPETENT
PR PRACTITIONERS

Christen: Three attributes distinguish the best practitioners. First, the best practitioners understand the opinions, attitudes, and issues that may have an impact on their organizations so they may better counsel their executives on decisions and courses of action and develop successful communication programs to achieve strategic goals.

Second, they are committed to personal leadership, including a deep knowledge of self and personal values, and the development of leadership attributes such as professionalism and integrity— applied every day and in all aspects of their work.

Finally, they understand the value of relationships and continually build and develop their networks. They nurture relationships with mentors and colleagues in their own and other organizations, including professional business associations to collaborate, gain insight into their business, and guide their development and careers.

Guy: Competence in oral and written communication is critical; then working with an ethical philosophy and as a defender of the democracy; and finally, always looking for ways to improve the practice of PR.

Kim: Relationship/trust building is critical. PR practitioners who are able to build relationships and trust succeed within organizations. Practitioners need to be able to balance their understanding of PR practice, the awareness they have developed, and their role as advisors in order to assist senior managers in decision making. Practitioners who understand this role and use it to build trust are provided with valuable opportunities to advise and influence decision makers. At the same time, however, practitioners must not abandon the challenging function of being an advocate for those who will receive the information. Challenging decision makers to understand the consequences of their decisions and advocating for considerations of specific audiences is a key role in strategic, effective public relations.

Robert: The best PR practitioners understand the audience with whom they are communicating. Their messages have clarity and do not leave room for confusion or misunderstanding. They understand the subject matter they are communicating and, to a degree, believe in the subject matter. To be effective, you need to know the attributes of your audience.

Specialized Skills and Esoteric Language

Practitioners have special skills and expertise in communication and persuasion that most members of the public do not. PR may have far-reaching consequences for people and communities because, when practitioners advocate on behalf of a client, there is no guarantee that the other side of the discussion will be heard.[15] Effective PR involves advocacy, relationship building, and strategic, persuasive communication. To accomplish this, PR practitioners use both persuasive and accommodative techniques. Practitioners learn these skills through education, the study of communications theory and case studies, and by honing their craft in practicums, apprenticeships, and under the supervision of more senior practitioners.

Professional Associations

The Canadian Public Relations Society (CPRS) and the International Association of Business Communicators (IABC) are voluntary professional associations for Canadian PR practitioners. There are other communications associations in Canada, often associated with specific industries, such as the Canadian Health Care Public Relations Association.

Code of Ethics

Professional associations codify widely accepted standards of practice and concepts of right practice into codes of ethical conduct, which members use to guide practice excellence. PR practitioners are not obligated to adhere to a mandatory code of ethics. While both IABC and CPRS have codes of ethics, neither have powers of enforcement beyond expulsion from the association, a power rarely used, as expulsion would leave the association exposed to a potential defamation suit by the former member.

Autonomy of Practice

Professionals have knowledge and skills beyond the layperson. Clients and employers hire professionals to provide direction and solutions in response to complex issues that are beyond the understanding of a person without the same knowledge and expertise. The reality of PR practice, however, is that practitioners often report to and take direction from heads of other departments, such as human resources, and rarely have autonomy of practice.

GROWING RECOGNITION OF SOCIETAL RESPONSIBILITY

The primary purpose of the PR function is to help organizations develop and maintain effective two-way relationships with stakeholders and publics, including news media, community activists, shareholders, government officials, and employees. As this role expands, there is a growing recognition by practitioners that trust, credibility, and integrity are integral to the practice. As discussed earlier, however, the public often perceives that rather than providing a valuable service to society, PR practitioners often assist government, corporate, and community leaders in the misrepresentation of issues. In other words, there is a disconnect between the work practitioners think they are doing and the public's perception of the purpose of PR.

INTERVIEW: THE CONSTANTLY EVOLVING COMMUNICATIONS ENVIRONMENT

Kim: The biggest challenge facing communicators today is keeping up with the pace of change and understanding the impact of new technologies on both communication and PR practice.

Robert: Audiences are larger and more diverse so the information we send out goes to much larger groups or tribes. It is critical for the practitioner to understand the audience dynamic and their mediums. People are using a multitude of mediums for communication, so to be effective you need to know which are most significant to the specific audience.

Guy: Everything about Web 2.0 and social media is challenging because of the interaction between an organization and their public. Monitoring the conversations and responding to the growing demand for content is a big challenge.

Christen: The current uncertainty of today's global environment also creates challenges for practitioners. In the aftermath of the global economic crisis, public opinion has become more distrustful of organizations. Practitioners have a key role in reputation management. In a tough environment, practitioners can help their organizations rebuild trust and restore confidence with stakeholders through transparency and authentic, accurate communication.

THE MOVE TOWARDS INCREASED PROFESSIONALISM IN PR

While the professional context for PR practice has evolved, practitioners still need to make significant improvements before society recognizes PR as a profession. Prior to achieving professional status, PR will require more specialized educational programs, a more comprehensive body of knowledge, community recognition, individual accountability, and adherence to a mandatory code of ethics that protects the public interest and focuses on social responsibility.[16]

In Canada, a number of initiatives targeting increased professionalization of PR are underway. In 2010, CPRS adopted the *Pathways to the Profession* report. Among its numerous recommendations, the report advocates for the introduction of a post-graduate certification program for entry-level practitioners. Similar to the mandatory examinations faced by law, medical, and engineering graduates, candidates with a post-secondary designation in PR would undertake a series of courses, seminars, and examinations. Upon successful completion of the program, candidates would be designated as certified PR practitioners.[17]

Advocates of the proposed program say that it would ensure a standardized education for PR practitioners and a minimum level of entry-level competency. It would also provide the public with protection against unscrupulous or unqualified practitioners because all practitioners would be required to pass a series of exams prior to receiving credentials. (Currently, anyone may set up a PR practice regardless of qualifications.)

Opponents of such a program, however, believe that without government legislation that establishes a requirement for mandatory academic credentials to practice PR, participation by practitioners and educators in post-graduate certification programs would be minimal. These opponents argue that IABC and CPRS accreditation programs already certify the competency of individual practitioners across all areas of PR practice. In addition, they argue a standardized certification program would create additional layers of bureaucracy, unduly restrict individuals from moving into PR from non-traditional paths, and increase the cost of professional services to the public.

REGULATION OF PR: ACCREDITATION, LICENSING, OR VOLUNTARY ASSOCIATION?
Accreditation
Both CPRS and IABC offer accreditation designations to self-identified senior members who choose to undergo a rigorous program of peer evaluation, assessment, and evaluation. To earn accredited status, candidates undergo an extensive four-phase process of peer assessment and evaluation. Initially, the candidate submits an application detailing work experience and education. Once accepted into the process, the candidate submits a portfolio that includes two work samples and demonstrates a theoretical basis for practice. When his

or her portfolio is approved, the candidate writes a four-hour examination and undergoes a 30-minute oral examination. Successful candidates maintain their accredited designations as long as they retain their status of member in good standing. CPRS requires accredited members to engage in continued professional development; IABC does not.

Critics of accreditation argue that because less than 15 per cent of members are accredited, accreditation does not provide the public with protection against unscrupulous charlatans. Many argue that standardized licensing would establish and enforce minimum standards of competence and thus would be a more effective system of public protection. Licensing systems used by other professional associations require that candidates have a minimum educational credential, serve an apprenticeship, and successfully complete uniform examinations. Opponents of mandatory licensing argue it would create an onerous level of additional bureaucracy (including administration to track members' status, proctor and mark exams, and monitor mandatory continuing education). These additional requirements would be costly to administer and track—an additional financial cost to be borne by practitioners—that ultimately would increase the cost of PR services, to clients and the public.

Mandatory Licensing: The Brazilian Experience

Brazil is the only country that currently enforces mandatory licensing of PR practitioners. The Brazilian experience with licensing of PR practitioners provides a comprehensive example of the pros and the cons of mandatory licensing.

Since 1967, Brazil has required that PR practitioners have both a degree in PR and a state licence to practice.[18] Federal and regional councils have the power to grant licences and discipline practitioners. A 2003 study of Brazilian practitioners found most practitioners agree that although licensing protects the public from unscrupulous PR practitioners and is beneficial for both clients and organizations, licensing has not increased public recognition of public relations as a professional practice such as law or medicine.[19] Brazilian practitioners suggest there is a need for greater enforcement by the licensing body to prevent the erosion of traditional PR services to human resources, operations, and marketing. They also argue in favour of prosecution of illegal activities by unscrupulous practitioners such as event planners who call themselves "PR professionals." Brazilian practitioners also express concerns that businesses often choose to hire unlicensed versus licensed practitioners and that licensing has failed to protect against encroachment by other professions, such as journalists, marketers, event planners, and human relations practitioners.[20]

Voluntary Adherence to a Code of Ethics: The Canadian Experience

In Canada, PR is not licensed or regulated, but practitioners may choose to join one of the two voluntary professional associations.

The Canadian Public Relations Society (CPRS)

Leading Canadian PR practitioners founded CPRS in 1948 to foster professionalism, advance the professional stature of public relations, regulate the practice of PR in the public interest, and serve the public interest. CPRS delivers associative services such as professional education, events, and testing to 1,800 members affiliated with 16 member societies across Canada.[21]

According to Karen Dalton, APR, executive director of the CPRS,[22] the CPRS introduced the Code of Ethics in 1961 and has never modified it, although, in 2010, the Society approved a policy statement on social media as an addendum to the code. The code identifies nine foundational standards for ethical practice by CPRS members. The code directs that members shall practice in the public interest, be fair, honest, and open in all dealings with media, the public, and colleagues.[23]

CPRS's Judicial and Ethics Committee is responsible for enforcing the code. Sanctions, however, are limited to public sanction, suspension, and revocation of membership. While CPRS may suspend or expel a member who violates the code, it does not have the power to prohibit that practitioner from continuing to work in public relations.

As you review the code, notice how it provides specific, explicit information on what constitutes the ethical practice of PR and answers many of the questions raised earlier in this chapter. For example, principle two clearly states that a practitioner shall not provide a journalist with a gift such as cash, a trip, or a night on the town in return for favourable coverage of his or her client's issues. Principles three, four, and five direct that practitioners shall be open and honest about both their own identity and the identity of their client.

Both student and practising members are responsible for knowing the Code of Ethics and for governing their professional lives by the standards it establishes.

International Association of Business Communicators (IABC)

Founded in 1971, IABC has approximately 15,000 members practising PR in more than 80 countries, including 14 Canadian chapters. Member benefits include local and international networking, professional development events and opportunities, the annual world conference, an annual subscription to

Communication World (a monthly magazine for communications professionals), a research and library databank, and numerous communications tools and templates.

While CPRS's code is a direct, explicit code developed for Canadian practitioners, IABC's Code of Ethics for Professional Practitioners establishes a context for ethical practice in a global context. The code identifies that communications is a powerful tool that influences millions of lives worldwide and carries significant social responsibility.[24] It also recognizes that cultural context is an important factor when defining ethical practice. As a result, IABC's Code of Ethics for Professional Practitioners provides three foundational rules for practice: professional communication is legal, ethical, and in good taste. IABC provides 12 articles (many similar to CPRS's principles) in support of these rules.

Although IABC directs its code to a wider, more diverse, multicultural public, the underlying principles and direction provided to practitioners remain similar to the CPRS Code of Ethics.

Have You Joined CPRS or IABC?

PR students who are active members of either CPRS or IABC develop an enhanced professional network and knowledge by the time they graduate. Student membership in CPRS or IABC is available to students enrolled in full-time studies and provides significant advantages in networking, résumé building, and access to specialized resources. If you are not currently a member, there are a number of reasons you should consider joining. Benefits include

- PR-related volunteer opportunities;
- student pricing for professional networking and development events and conferences;
- access to online resources including job postings, reports, and library materials;
- subscription to monthly professional magazine; and
- mentorship programs.

INTERVIEW: ESTABLISH YOURSELF AS AN ETHICAL PR PRACTITIONER

Christen: Know yourself, your values, and your strengths. Know who you are and what your values are. Use this knowledge to guide your decision making and behaviour.

Know your business: To be of strategic value to your organization, learn about your business. Be good at what you do and develop a solid understanding of the business you are in.

Ask whether your prospective employers' values align with your own: research the values of prospective employers. Do their values align with your own? An interview is your opportunity to learn about the values and ethics of the organization and the people you will be working with. These are your formative career years, so consider working with an organization that is a good personal fit.

Contemplate ethical dilemmas in advance: familiarize yourself with the codes of ethics from both IABC and CPRS. These helpful guides can provide context in working through ethical dilemmas before they arise.

Robert: The average person has very good judgement skills. You know in your mind and in your heart what is right. Ultimately, you have to answer to yourself and live with yourself...I personally would prefer peace of mind versus other rewards. This may sound altruistic but as you age it becomes more important to you. In my own world, I know that my actions will reflect on my children and I want them to be proud of me as I in turn will be proud of their decisions.

Kim: Learn all you can about the values and ethics of your organization and ensure your practices exemplify that. Use that information in the building of your products, plans, messages. You have an opportunity to help your organization demonstrate its values on a regular basis and to impact on how those values and ethics are communicated to employees, stakeholders, clients, and the public.

Guy: Learn the distinction between utilitarianism and deontology. Learn to differentiate between regular situations that usually correspond with conformity of the society (laws, rules, code of ethics, etc.) and irregular situations for which the rules may not be written but in which society's beliefs and morals will play have an important role in decision making.

CONCLUSION

In our rapidly changing and evolving communications environment, it simply is impossible to identify and address all of the ethical dilemmas you will face during your career as a PR practitioner. In general, do the right thing for the right reason every time and you will not go wrong.

The following are tips for ethical PR practice:

1. Never misrepresent (by omission or error) the facts of a matter in any type of communication, including promotional materials such as websites, presentations, brochures, social media feeds, or face-to-face communication. Tell the truth regardless of whether it is favourable or unfavourable to your organization's perspective. Honesty safeguards and stewards organizational reputation, credibility, and integrity.

2. Do not mask either your or your organization's identity when acting in any professional capacity such as participating in online forums or discussions or hosting a website. Tell the truth about your identity and the identity of the organization or client you represent.

3. Do not alter publicity images in B-roll or any type of electronic media. The news media and the public believe these images to be authentic snapshots or reality. Alteration makes the message untrue.

4. Clearly identify video news releases as such. Labelling must include the names and titles of the persons interviewed as well as the name of the sponsoring organization.

5. Do not offer journalists or news media outlets any type of financial compensation or gifts for coverage or favourable press.

6. Do not blur the boundaries between paid advertising and media coverage. Increasingly, specialty magazines and special feature sections are offering organizations "news" coverage as a supplement to advertising purchases— pay for play. Insist on distinct separation between purchased coverage and news.

7. Remember, while it is important to be honest and open with journalists, as a paid advocate for a client or organization, there are circumstances when it is appropriate not to release information, particularly when restricted by law or ethics.

8. Do not use research, information, and materials gathered under contract with one client on another client file. These materials remain proprietary to the first client.

KEY TERMS
B-roll: Provided by organizations to media as part of media kits, B-roll is unnarrated video footage that is used by TV news producers to supplement news anchor narration.

Canadian Public Relations Society (CPRS): Established in 1948, the Canadian Public Relations Society is an organization of men and women who practice public relations in Canada and abroad. Members work to maintain the highest standards and to share a uniquely Canadian experience in public relations.

Code of ethics: A set of agreed upon principles for conduct within an organization or association used by members and employees to guide ethical decision making and behaviour.

Deontology: An ethical decision-making philosophy by which decisions are made based on what is right or what is wrong in a universal context, not on the consequences (which are not always easy to predict).

Ethical advocacy: As a tenet of professional practice, an ethical advocate is a public relations practitioner who communicates persuasively and truthfully on behalf of the client while recognizing his or her primary responsibility is to act in the public's interest.

Ethics: Ethics are the rules that help individuals, groups, and organizations to identify what is right or wrong, fair and unfair, honest or dishonest for themselves and for others in specific situations.

Profession: Work that requires its practitioners to have specialized education, training, and skills developed over a long period of time, honed through practice and ongoing education and operating in alignment with public service.

International Association of Business Communicators (IABC): An international professional association established in 1970 for communicators, including public relations practitioners. This association is a US-based international organization with over 15,000 members in 80 countries.

Utilitarianism (situational ethics): An ethical decision-making philosophy by which decisions are made based on the greater good or perceived consequences of an action.

FOR REVIEW AND DISCUSSION

1. What are ethics in public relations practice?
2. How important are ethics in public relations? Explain your answer.
3. Describe what it means to you to be an ethical advocate.
4. What are the advantages and disadvantages of licensing versus accreditation of PR practitioners?
5. In your opinion, is public relations a profession or an occupation? Defend your answer.

6. What advantages do students gain by joining professional associations? Predict what barriers you may face when joining a professional association. Propose how you could overcome these challenges.

7. Determine three ethical challenges PR practitioners face when using social media. Propose ways to address these challenges.

ACTIVITIES

1. Go to the websites of the CPRS and IABC and locate their codes of ethical conduct. Compare and contrast the two codes. What are the key similarities and differences? Which code is more meaningful to you as a student? Explain your answer.

2. Write your personal code of ethics for professional conduct. Include at least three guidelines for ethical behaviour and decision making.

   • Work in groups of three to compare your personal codes. Discuss your guidelines with your group and explain why you chose them and how they would clarify ethical practice.
   • Describe in which professional situations your guidelines will provide clarity.

3. Working in pairs, review three promotional activities documented on the tobacco wiki located on the Center for Media and Democracy PR Watch website (http://sourcewatch.org/index.php/Promotions). What are some of the ethical violations associated with these publicity campaigns?

   • Name three current PR campaigns targeting increased consumption of goods or services that have similar ethical violations or ambiguities. Describe the nature of these violations. What are your suggestions for remedying these ethical violations?

FURTHER READING

Business Ethics: www.businessethics.ca

Canadian Public Relations Society. *Pathways to the Profession*. March 2011. http://www.cprs.ca/uploads/education/PathwaytoProfessionEng_Final_11-07-2011.pdf.

The Ethics Network, Ryerson University: www.ryerson.ca/ethicsnetwork/
   resources/ethicaldecision/
Institute for Public Relations: www.instituteforpr.org
International Association of Business Communicators: www.iabc.com
International Public Relations Association: www.ipra.org
Journal of Business Ethics: www.springerlink.com/content/0167-4544
PR Watch, a project of the Center for Media and Democracy: www.prwatch.org
Public Relations Society of America: www.prsa.org
The W. Maurice Young Centre for Applied Ethics, University of British
   Columbia: www.ethics.ubc.ca

NOTES

1. James Hoggan, *Do the Right Thing: PR Tips for a Skeptical Public* (Sterling, VA: Capital Books, 2009), 18.
2. Ibid.
3. Corporate Watch UK, "Public Relations and Lobbying Industry: An Overview," *Corporate Watch*, April 2003, http://www.corporatewatch.org/?lid=1570.
4. S.M. Cutlip, A.H. Center, and G.M. Broom, *Effective Public Relations*, 9th ed. (Upper Saddle River, NJ: Pearson Prentice Hall, 2006), 124.
5. Ibid.
6. Erma Woods and Ian Sommerville, Chapter 10, in *The Public Relations Handbook*, by Alison Theaker (New York: Routledge, 2001), 142.
7. Allen Center, P. Jackson, S. Smith, and F.R. Stansberry, *Public Relations Practices: Managerial Case Studies and Problems*, 7th ed. (Upper Saddle River, NJ: Pearson Prentice Hall, 2008), 306.
8. Cutlip, Center, and Broom, *Effective Public Relations*, 120.
9. Ibid.
10. Patricia Parsons, *Ethics in Public Relations: A Guide to Best Practice* (Philadelphia, PA: Kogan Page, 2004), 9.
11. Cutlip, Center, and Broom, *Effective Public Relations*, 125.
12. Hoggan, *Do the Right Thing*, 6.
13. Ibid., 7.
14. J.E. Lennertz, "Ethics and the Professional Responsibility of Lawyers," *Journal of Business Ethics* 10, no. 8 (1991): 577.
15. Kathy Fitzpatrick and Candace Gauthier, "Toward a Professional Responsibility Theory of Public Relations Ethics," *Journal of Mass Media Ethics* 16, no. 2/3 (2001): 197.
16. Cutlip, Center, and Broom, *Effective Public Relations*, 126.
17. CPRS, *Pathways to the Profession*, March 2011, http://www.cprs.ca/uploads/education/PathwaytoProfessionEng_Final_11-07-2011.pdf.

18. Juan-Carlos Molleda and Andreia Athaydes, "Public Relations Licensing in Brazil: Evolution and the Views of Professionals," *Public Relations Review*, 29, no. 3 (2003): 271.

19. Ibid., 276.

20. Ibid.

21. Canadian Public Relations Society, "About Us," accessed February 13, 2011, http://www.cprs.ca/aboutus/.

22. Karen Dalton, personal communication, January 2010.

23. Canadian Public Relations Society, "Code of Ethics," accessed February 12, 2011, http://www.cprs.ca/aboutus/code_ethic.aspx.

24. International Association of Business Communicators, "Code of Ethics for Professional Communicators," accessed February 12, 2011, http://www.iabc.com/about/code.htm.

Colin Babiuk

5

LEARNING OBJECTIVES

After reading this chapter you will be able to

- identify and discuss communications theories and models;
- describe the evolution of communications theory and its relevance to public relations planning;
- explain how communications shapes society; and
- apply communications models and theories to identify target audiences, develop appropriate messages, and use appropriate communication channels.

INTRODUCTION

Communication is powerful. It can cause changes in thinking, feeling, or behaviour. Most of what we know and understand of the world around us is shaped by the information we receive through media, which includes all forms of communications.

As a PR practitioner, you will play a lead role in assisting organizations in creating awareness of events and issues and developing messages to support the organization's point of view on these issues. Other organizations will create and distribute their own messages—some in support of your organization's views and others against.

The public debate surrounding all sides of an issue shapes public opinion as people become more aware of an issue. They begin to develop an understanding of the issue and to support the perspective they agree with. Over time, public opinion helps to shape public policy. One example is the growth in support for environmental responsibility.

Societal changes come about from the information communicated through the media by advocates of these issues. By presenting arguments and evidence to support their perspective, advocacy groups convince the public to support their cause and demand social change. Communications is a powerful tool that can have a real impact in a democratic society. As PR professionals, it is essential that we gain an understanding of how communication works and what communication can do.

COMMUNICATION: A DEFINITION

If you were asked to describe what communication is, what would you say? Communication could be described as everything we say, write, or even gesture to another person. But is this truly communication?

You may have sent a text message to a friend saying that you do not want to go to the mall too late. Did he interpret this message to mean you did not want to go to the mall because he did not respond to you in time, or to mean you did not want to go to the mall too late in the day? A message was sent and received, that much is true. But did you both interpret the message the same way? For communication to be effective, the message must be clearly understood by the person sending the message and those who receive it.

With this principle in mind, human communication can be defined as the transfer of information from one person to another that attempts to create a common understanding and generates a response.

THE ROLE OF THEORY IN PROFESSIONAL COMMUNICATIONS

Models and theories help us understand how and why things happen. Models are representations that help us to understand how the communication process takes place. Communications theories seek to explain the effect communication has on the receiver.

The study of communications models and theories provides insight that communicators can apply to improve the effectiveness of their messages and achieve the desired goals of the organization.

RACE: A MODEL FOR PR

As you have read, the role of public relations is to create, maintain, and enhance mutually beneficial relationships between an organization and its many publics through effective communication. PR practitioners use various communication tools and techniques to assist organizations in becoming aware of and understanding the needs and concerns of its publics. PR activities also help to increase the publics' understanding of the goals of the organization.

Communication is also used to correct misunderstanding or misinformation and to change the beliefs, perceptions, and opinions the public may have about an organization. Following a formal, structured process provides a framework that can help to enhance understanding between the two groups and ensure that neither party will be intentionally placed at a disadvantage.

A popular model for the PR process that is recognized by Canadian Public Relations Society (CPRS) and the International Association of Business Communicators (IABC) is based on John E. Marston's RACE formula.[1] The RACE formula begins with conducting research and moves through the stages of analysis, communication, and evaluation:

- **Research** to identify or verify if a perceived problem or opportunity exists, to gain knowledge of the history and scope of an issue, and to identify the publics that may be affected or may have an impact on the operations of an organization.
- **Analysis** of the research findings to identify the potential impact of the issue on the organization and the impact on the publics. Analysis helps an organization identify what it needs communication to do. The "A" in Marston's original formula was "Action." Marston suggested that if something was not already happening, it must be made to occur, such as improving the speed of service if customers were complaining, and then letting people know the change had occurred.
- **Communication** to develop appropriate messages to address the verified concerns of the identified publics and using the most effective media appropriate to each public.
- **Evaluation** to determine if the message was successfully received by the publics and to determine if communication efforts achieved the desired outcomes.

Working through this process, the practitioner can critically examine any issue or opportunity facing an organization. In any given situation, an organization will need to communicate with more than one public. Each group may require different information, and so it is essential that the PR professional is aware of the different communication needs and preferred medium for each group.

For example, if a local food processing plant catches fire, a number of groups will be in need of information:

1. The owner will want to know how the fire started and the amount of damage.
2. The insurance company will also want to know how the fire started; if the damage was limited to the facility or if it spread to other buildings; and if anyone was injured.
3. The fire department will want to know about any chemicals or flammable materials in the building and the layout.
4. Nearby building owners will want to know if their businesses are in any danger.
5. The stores purchasing the products will want to know if their orders will be filled.
6. The employees want to know if they are out of work and what the organization is doing to assist them.

There are numerous publics affected by this incident and each group needs different information. In this case, you would need to develop different messages and provide the information in the most effective way for each group. For example, you could call the stores on the telephone but you would want to ensure you speak to your employees in person.

Narrative Model of Communication

Models that explore the communication process help to explain how communication takes place. The narrative model of communication was developed in 1948 by Harold D. Lasswell. Lasswell saw a pattern to the communication process consisting of five elements:

- Who
- Says what
- In which channel
- To whom
- With what effect?[2]

Lasswell's model aligns with the definition of communication described earlier in this chapter. Information is exchanged to generate a response. Lasswell's model expands on this definition, however, by prompting the communicator to think about the communication channel: how the message was sent.

Who (Source)

All communication begins with a source. This is the person or organization that has a need to communicate something to others. The source must clearly understand the purpose for communicating and who they are communicating on behalf of. To ensure they are accurately representing their organization, they need to be aware of the company's mission, vision, and values, its business goals and its objectives.

Says What (Message)

Depending on the situation, there are a few things to take into consideration. What does the organization want or need the audience to know? What does the audience want or need to know, and why? Because a number of groups may be impacted, the communicator may need to go through this step a number of times to ensure he or she addresses the information needs of each group.

In Which Channel (Medium)

The channel, or medium, refers to the vehicle used to distribute the message, such as a conversation, an advertisement in a newspaper, or a posting on an Internet forum. The choice of medium depends on the audience the communicator wishes to connect with. For example, a "baby boomer" may prefer to watch the television news, while a "millennial" may prefer to get information from a Web-based application on a smartphone.

To Whom (Audience/Receiver)

When developing a message, communicators consider who will be affected by the actions of the organization and how. They need to be aware of the values, stakes, perceptions, and beliefs of the audience they wish to communicate to—and how credible the source is to the audience.

To What Effect (Change in Perception/Belief/Attitude)

The overall purpose of communicating is to have something happen. Once an issue, audience, and communication needs have been identified, what is it that the organization wants the intended audience to do? Does it need the audience

Figure 5.1 Mathematical Theory of Communication

Information Source > Transmitter > Signal > Receiver > Destination

Message   (Channel)   Message

                              ∧
                            Noise

Adapted from Claude E. Shannon, "A Mathematical Theory of Communication," *Bell System Technical Journal* 27 (July, October 1948): 381.

to take immediate action? Or is it seeking to change the audience's perception of the organization? Thinking critically about each of these elements enables an organization to be strategic in its communication efforts.

The Mathematical Theory of Communication

Not all communication models are the result of research into communication. Sometimes studies from other disciplines produce findings that are transferable to communication. This is true of one of the best-known theories in communications—the Mathematical Theory of Communication, or the Shannon-Weaver model.[3]

Claude Shannon and Warren Weaver were electronic engineers at Bell Labs in the United States. In the 1940s, advances were being made in technologies to convert sound into the electronic signals used in telegraphs and telephones. The new technologies would allow a telephone line to transmit more calls simultaneously. This advance, however, also increased the occurrence of electromagnetic interference in the line. Shannon and Weaver were working on solutions to maximize the number of calls a line could handle while minimizing the disruption of static. Shannon and Weaver created a model to help them understand this engineering problem. This model can be applied to communications studies.

The mathematical theory suggests that communication begins with human stimulation or thought. The information source creates a message that is encoded and transmitted to a receiver (such as speaking into a microphone). The message is sent as an electronic signal on a channel (such as a specific radio station's wavelength). The message is decoded from electronic pulse back into speech at the receiver (the music coming through the radio speakers) and heard by the listener (the destination). As the message is being transmitted, it may be subject to interference, which can impact the message getting through clearly.

This model provides a checklist of sorts for the communicator. The following explores the model in communications terms. (See also Figure 5.1.)

Information Source

The source is where communication originates. The source creates the messages to be sent to an individual or a group. The source needs to know who will be receiving the message and how receptive they may be to the information.

Message

The message is the content of the communication. For the message to be effective, it must be relevant to the audience and understood by both the source and the receiver.

If the message is not relevant to the receiver or is not understood, the source will not have achieved the purpose of communicating. The receiver may misunderstand the message or may simply ignore it.

Transmitter

At this stage, the message is transferred into a particular format, such as a speech or a television advertisement.

Channel

This is the medium chosen to send the message to the intended audience, such as a presentation at a conference, or a television station.

Noise

Shannon and Weaver refer to noise as the electromagnetic interference (static) that can disrupt electronic communication. Noise in the communications context refers to anything that interferes with the understanding of a message. Noise can take physical forms. It can be actual noise, such as a shredding machine starting up in the middle of a conversation. It could be environmental, such as a room that is too hot or too cold. Or it could take the form of semantic noise: misunderstanding caused by a poorly worded message.

Noise can also refer to the barriers we create for ourselves based on personal biases and experiences, and our culture and religious beliefs. If the message does not align with our belief system, we tend to block it out.

Receiver

The receiver is where the messages are decoded. In a communications context, it could be listening to the speech, or watching the advertisement on television.

Figure 5.2 Interactive Model

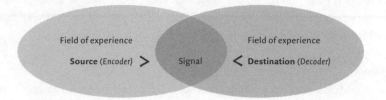

Adapted from Wilbur Schramm, "How Communication Works," *The Process and Effects of Mass Communication* (Urbana: University of Illinois Press, 1954), 54.

Destination

Destination in this model refers to the end receiver of the message: the person or group for whom the message is intended. The receiver "reconstructs" the message. Communication is most effective when the message targets a specific audience for whom the message is both appropriate and relevant. For example, advertising a sports car during a televised sporting event would be more effective than placing the same advertisement during a cartoon program.

The Interactive Model

Wilbur Schramm proposed a deviation to the Shannon-Weaver model. In what he termed the Interactive Model, Schramm emphasized the importance of the relationship between the sender and the receiver. He argued that for communication to be effective, "the sender and receiver must be in tune."[4]

Schramm proposes that the sender and receiver must share a common field of experience. In Figure 5.2, the ovals represent the fields of experience of the source and the destination. The degree of overlap where the fields intersect represents the level of shared understanding of the message. This shared understanding is dependent upon both parties having knowledge of the topic being communicated. Schramm explains that if we have not learned to speak Russian, we can neither code nor decode messages in that language. Similarly, a message written by a physicist cannot be fully understood by a person that has not studied physics.

Schramm also specified that a feedback channel must be present to ensure the meaning was clearly understood. Feedback aids in creating mutual understanding by allowing the source to evaluate if the message was received and how it was interpreted by the receiver.

Figure 5.3 SMCR Model

Source		Message	Channel		Receiver
Source		**Message**	**Channel**		**Receiver**
Communication Skills		Content	Hearing		Communication Skills
Attitudes	*(encodes)*	Elements	Seeing	*(decodes)*	Attitudes
Knowledge		Treatment	Touching		Knowledge
Social System		Structure	Smelling		Social System
Culture		Code	Tasting		Culture

Adapted from David Berlo, *The Process of Communication: An Introduction to Theory and Practice* (San Francisco, CA: Holt, Rinehart and Winston, 1960), 72.

SMCR Model of Communication

Another familiar communication model was introduced in 1960 by David Berlo. Berlo's model consists of the elements of source, message, channel, and receiver (SMCR).[5]

In this model, Berlo contends that effective communication is dependent on a number of variables that affect one's ability to create and to interpret or be receptive of a message. A message may not be understood if the source and receiver have differing levels of skills or experience. Berlo proposed that the closer the match of these variables between the source and the receiver, the more effective communication would be (see Figure 5.3). Like in Schramm's interactive model, communication is enhanced if the source and receiver have a common level of understanding. Berlo extrapolates by also acknowledging the alignment of attitudes, communication skills, and cultural aspects between the source and receiver.

Berlo's model also refers to the concept that different media engage different senses in the receiver. If you are trying to evoke an emotional response, a televised report showing the scope of an event may achieve the reaction you desire. If you are trying to present a logical argument, you may wish to distribute your message in the print news.

MASS COMMUNICATION AND PR

John Merrill, John Lee, and Edward Friedlander define mass communication as institutionalized communication that flows out to large audiences in formal and largely impersonal ways.[6]

Mass communication is characterized by

- large amounts of information;
- formal structure (it is institutionalized—information is produced by an organization in a structured manner);
- anonymity (there is no discernible author);
- disseminatation to a large, diverse audience; and
- delayed feedback.

An example of mass communication would be an advertisement for a new product. The organization, in conjunction with the advertising agency, creates the ad copy and purchases the ad space. The message appears in newspapers and magazines across Canada. The organization does not know who will buy the newspaper and see the ad or how many readers are actually interested in purchasing the product. But everyone who buys the newspaper has the opportunity to see the message.

In turn, the reader has no indication of who actually wrote the ad, and there may be no information to direct the reader on how to contact the organization. Any feedback to the organization usually comes in the form of public discussion and commentary about the message. There is usually no direct link back to the organization to discuss the message.

The news media delivers a substantial amount of the messages created by an organization. News media distributes information quickly to large numbers of people at little to no cost to the organization. The communicator prepares a news release for the media and reporters arrive to ask questions so they can prepare and write news stories.

There is another benefit to using the news media to get your message out. The media hold a vast amount of power in its ability to create or influence public perception of an idea or issue.

Stories covered by the news are subject to an editorial process that ensures the information has been verified and is accurate. This third-party assessment is seen as being less subjective and therefore an issue covered in the news is seen as having more credibility.

Most of what we know about the world around us is formed by what we read, see, and hear through information distributed through news media. Often times we first become aware of an issue through the news.

In fact, the reality we receive through the news is only a reconstruction of reality. The news media cover stories from across the globe. As we cannot possibly be in all places, or present at all events, covered in the newspaper, our sense of the world is shaped by what we read.

As a result, organizations develop messages, choosing their words and the way they are used, in a way that will catch the interest of the news media and make it through the editing process. By carefully crafting messages, an organization can influence the way arguments are presented through the news media. (See Chapter 12 for more on media relations.)

The following theories and models explore how information is distributed and received through media channels.

Direct Effects Theory

The direct effects theory is one of the earliest mass communications theories. This model is also known as the Magic Bullet theory or the Hypodermic Needle theory. It was developed from the findings of Harold Lasswell and Dorothy Blumenstock regarding First World War propaganda and the growth of fascist movements within the United States in the 1930s.[7]

The theory proposed that all individuals exposed to a message sent through the media would be affected the same way. The belief was that the media held great power to influence and that if an organization developed the right message, people would be persuaded to do just about anything.

A common example of the Magic Bullet theory is Orson Welles's radio broadcast of H.G. Wells's *The War of the Worlds* on October 30, 1938 in the United States. The radio play took the format of a series of "news bulletins" informing listeners of an alien attack on Earth. A fictional work had never been broadcast in this manner before, and people did not think they would be purposely misled. The result was widespread panic and confusion. The response was significant enough for the *New York Times* to report, "Radio Listeners in Panic, Taking War Drama as Fact."[8]

The Limited Effects Theories of Communication

As research on the effects of media continued, studies indicated that the direct effects theory was not accurate; there was a limit on the ability for media to influence individuals. The limited effects theories propose that messages sent through mass communication may indeed contribute to actions within society but they do not cause all actions in society. Common limited effects theories are two-step flow of communication, multi-step flow of communication, and the uses and gratification models.

Two-Step Flow of Communication Theory

Paul Lazarsfeld, Bernard Berelson, and Hazel Gaudet studied the reactions of 600 eligible voters to media messages in Erie County, New York during the 1940 American presidential campaign.[9] They had expected the study's results to demonstrate that a voter's intentions would be directly influenced by the messages carried in the media. The results of the study, however, did not support this belief.

Instead, respondents reported that informal discussions with their personal contacts had more influence on their decisions than media coverage. This finding led to the development of the two-step flow of communication theory, which suggests that the power of the media lies more in its ability to inform than to motivate people. The two-step theory was the first theory to recognize the role of intervening publics.

The study revealed that the media had an influence on key opinion leaders in society, who, in turn, influence others in society. In fact, the opinion leaders were found to pay more attention to the media and were more informed about the issues of the day than other members of society to whom they passed on information. The study also discovered that individuals responded more favourably to messages that matched their own beliefs and values.

We now know that people do not automatically follow or believe an organization's messages outright and will seek out opinions from those they find to be knowledgeable about the subject. With this information, an organization can develop a two-step communication approach to facilitate communication when there may be limited acceptance of a message sent by the organization. Certain individuals are seen by the public to be knowledgeable, credible, or objective about a particular topic because of their training, experience, or title. An organization may partner with these individuals to deliver messages that support the organization's initiatives. We see this in action when an external "expert" or a celebrity speaks about an issue that an organization is facing.

Multi-Step Flow of Communication

The multi-step flow of communication model was developed as a result of observations made by John Robinson as he analyzed additional research on factors influencing voting decisions.[10] Robinson discovered that the degree of interaction that took place in these studies was broader than what the two-step model proposed.

Robinson's research acknowledged that while opinion leaders were indeed more engaged in monitoring the media, they primarily followed issues in the news that were of personal interest to them. Therefore, different people were more influential than others depending on the issue. The roles of opinion leader and follower could be interchangeable because a follower could be more informed than an opinion leader on different issues.

Opinion leaders were also found to discuss issues with other opinion leaders more so than with those who were less actively engaged in following the news media. Robinson also found that opinion leaders could be influenced by a less active individual and that less active individuals also talked about issues amongst themselves. Based on these observations, Robinson proposed that the flow of information is more a relay of information between multiple groups than a two-step process.

We can see this model in action today by following a trending topic on Twitter. An individual will post a comment regarding a news article and others will soon join the conversation. People who follow the original sender may reply with their own comments, or they may share the post with others by retweeting it. The message is then made available to people who follow the person who retweeted the message, but they might not follow the original sender. They in turn may retweet the message or create a new tweet referencing the original tweet or the issue.

Uses and Gratification Model

The realization that the media was not an all-powerful force led to further investigations. Elihu Katz introduced the Uses and Gratification theory in 1959. This theory states that the public views and uses messages in the media in relation to their own needs and desires.[11]

Katz observed that much research into media effects at the time focused on the ability of the media to persuade. Yet, the more studies that were conducted, the more media appeared to have less ability to persuade than was previously thought. Katz asked, if the media messages did not persuade individuals, what did? He then rephrased the question, "What does media do to people?" and exchanged it with his own: "What do people do with media?"[12] He believed that exposure to mass communication messages may lead people towards a particular decision, but the message had to be aligned to the receiver's personal values, beliefs, and interests. Our own thoughts, experiences, and beliefs get in the way of taking messages for granted. People are simply not going do something they do not agree with or believe in.

Whereas previous theories regarded the audience as a passive receiver of information, this model suggests that the power belongs to the receiver who picks and chooses from among the information presented. The receiver becomes his or her own gatekeeper, retaining only information of personal use or interest.

Agenda-Setting Hypothesis

By the 1960s, the impression of an all-powerful media was largely debunked. Commenting on the function of the media, Bernard Cohen wrote, "The press may not be successful much of the time in telling people what to think, but it is stunningly successful in telling its readers what to think about."[13]

This observation piqued the interest of Maxwell McCombs and Donald Shaw as they followed the 1968 American presidential campaign in Chapel Hill, North Carolina. McCombs and Shaw tested Cohen's hypothesis as they sought to explain the apparent cause and effect relationship between the degree in which the media emphasized an issue and the extent to which people perceived the issue to be important.[14] The pair was interested in the news production process: how stories originated, how editors chose the stories to publish, and how they determined the priority of the articles selected.

A great deal of our understanding of the world is determined by information we receive through news media. Therefore, there are implications around the stories the media choose to cover, or not cover, and the tone they choose to present the story. Where the story appears in the paper or in the TV news line-up, the amount of "ink" or airtime allotted to the article, and the order in which news items are listed on a web page all work to create a sense of importance to the audience. The manner in which information is presented can influence how an audience feels about an issue and their level of support for it.

Important questions for the communicator to consider include, who brought the issue to the news media's attention? Is the article written in a way that supports the media outlet's views and values?

Grunig and Hunt's Four Models of Public Relations

No resource on communication theory would be complete without mentioning the Four Models of Public Relations developed by James Grunig and Todd Hunt.[15] They propose that there are four main functions of public relations that have developed as the profession has evolved:

1. Press agentry or publicity
2. Public information
3. Two-way asymmetrical communication
4. Two-way symmetrical communication

"Press agentry" or "publicity" refers to one-way communication from an organization to an audience. There is no avenue for feedback; the audience receives only the information the organization wants them to hear, although that message may be inaccurate or incomplete. The intent is to persuade the audience rather than to inform them of something. We see this model in action daily through advertising and promotion.

"Public information" is "for your own good" information: messages sent from an organization that the audience needs to know. For example, Health Canada creates advertisements for influenza vaccination. There may be information directing the audience where they can go for more information, but there is again little or no opportunity for the audience to provide feedback to the organization. These messages are viewed as being less subjective because the intent is to ensure the health and safety of the audience.

"Two-way asymmetrical communication" does provides a feedback channel allowing the audience to respond to the message; however, the information is collected is for the benefit of the organization. While there may be a perception that two-way communication is taking place, the results of the feedback are not shared with the public, and the input may not alter how the organization does business. For example, when a political party asks the public for input on various issues, the party uses the information to its benefit by adjusting its campaign messages and approaches. There is arguably little benefit for the public.

"Two-way symmetrical communication" uses true two-way communication to create a dialogue between an organization and its publics. The organization communicates its goals and asks for input. The feedback is collected, analyzed, and used by the organization to make adjustments. The organization then reports these changes back to the public.

To illustrate this process, we can look at how municipalities communicate new initiatives to residents. For example, if a town is considering the construction of a new recreation complex, it may hold a public information session to introduce the project. At this event, the municipality would display diagrams and models of what the completed project may look like and present information on the benefits of the complex and how it may impact the community during construction. The public would be asked for feedback at these

Figure 5.4 Four Models of Public Relations

Model	Purpose	Feedback channel	Approximate year of development	Role in society
Press agentry	Promote organization	No	1850	Persuade
Public information	Inform public	No	1900	Persuade
Two-way asymmetrical	Research to help organization be more successful	Yes Information used to benefit organization	1920	Inform public of organization's goals
Two-way symmetrical	Create dialogue between organization and publics to help organization meet the needs of its publics	Yes Information used to address needs of public	1960	Create mutual understand-ing between organization and publics

sessions. Based on the collected input, changes to the project may be made. These changes would then be communicated back to the public and feedback requested again.

CPRS and IABC support two-way symmetrical as the preferred communication model for PR practitioners. Depending on the situation, however, all models have a function.

ADVANCED COMMUNICATION THEORIES

When exploring media, there are two areas that have garnered a great deal of study: economic and technological determinism. Economic determinism proposes that the information we receive through the media is controlled by those who own the media. The owners, therefore, control the information we receive. Technological determinism proposes that technology has an effect on society and therefore communication. Technology itself, not money or political power, drives societal change through changes in how we create, distribute, and consume information.

Economic Determinism

Economic determinism in the context of media studies examines the concept of power in media. It looks at the relationship between media owners and the ability to disseminate messages that support the views and values of those owners. In countries with state-controlled media, the media owner is essentially the governing party.

Karl Marx, a reporter himself, believed that the struggle between the rich and the poor created antagonistic forces in society. As landowners and employers, the rich bourgeoisie maintained control through ownership of the means of production, leading to his famous quote, "The class which has the means of material production at its disposal, has control at the same time over the means of mental production."[16]

The growth of the newspaper industry created an opportunity to provide information to many people in a short period of time. Marx feared that a news media controlled by the political and social elite could have only a negative impact on society. Marx believed that powerful media owners would go unchecked while they disseminated their ideals to an uneducated and vulnerable population. This situation would create the opportunity for the elite to also control the minds of the public. The ideology of the ruling class would be disseminated unimpeded, while any commentary to the contrary would be omitted from publication. He also saw a connection to ideological control and economic control—as a means to maintain control through increased profit.

Marx's words have relevance in today's world. Newspapers and other media promote themselves as a source of news and information. Since the 1980s, the number of owners of media has decreased, while the number of media outlets has increased. On top of this, owners are purchasing other forms of media. The result is that one owner may control the local newspaper as well as the television and radio station. While this scenario may save the owner money and increase profit, it also ensures the public receives information from fewer perspectives.

The Political Economy of Media

Edward S. Herman and Noam Chomsky explore the role of communication in society in the book *Manufacturing Consent: The Political Economy of the Mass Media*.[17] Herman and Chomsky assert that the role of the media is not only to entertain and inform audiences but also to shape and support societal beliefs, values, and social codes. Following Marx's philosophy, they argue that money and power influence the news we receive, diminish dissenting views, and provide a platform for government and powerful private interests to get their agendas in front of the public.

Herman and Chomsky caution the public to be critical of the media and to view media messages through a set of filters. The filters most relevant to PR from *Manufacturing Consent* are size, ownership, and profit; advertising; and sourcing news.

Size, Ownership, and Profit

Herman and Chomsky encourage the public to consider that the views of media owners are supported by the messages conveyed their through media companies and the products they distribute. Information that challenges the owners' views does not get presented to the public.

Advertising

Above all else, media is a business. The news and television programs are expenditures. The revenue for these products comes from the sale of advertising. The media create products desired by the public as vehicles to deliver advertising. Companies want their products displayed to as many people as possible. A television station with a larger audience can charge more money for an advertisement than a station with a smaller audience.

Sourcing News

To meet the demand for news items, media prefers to obtain news that is inexpensive and easy to get. Government at all levels and private organizations assist this process by making it easy for the media to get information. The result is these parties enjoy greater visibility through the media. Their information undergoes less editing because it is seen to be more credible, and so their views are made more widely available to the public.

Technological Determinism

As previously stated, technological determinism proposes that technology drives societal change through changes in how we communicate. Before the invention of the printing press, books and manuscripts were written and reproduced by hand. Many of these books were reproduced in monasteries, thus monks were sometimes better educated than royalty. Having greater exposure to written works and knowledge, they engrained themselves as counsellors to the rulers in many cases.

Around 1440, Johannes Gutenberg invented the movable type printing press. This innovation meant that books and other written pieces could be mass produced quickly and economically. Books were not the only product coming off the presses. Leaflets were also mass produced. These leaflets provided information, though highly biased, that could be distributed and shared with the masses and from which they formed opinions of their own. As a result, average people were now able to participate and engage in meaningful debate, regardless of their position in society.

Jürgen Habermas relates to this phenomenon the "public sphere," the theoretical "space" in which individuals discuss current events, criticize the authority of the state, call on those in power to justify their positions and voice their opinion.[18]

Through sharing information and perspectives with others, public opinion is formed. The advent of the printing press gave access to information to the masses and the ability to debate the social issues of the day—a right previously given to the elite.

McLuhan and the Global Village

Dr. Herbert Marshall McLuhan was born in Edmonton in 1911. He was educated as a literary scholar, earning a BA in 1933 and an MA in English in 1934 from the University of Manitoba. He obtained his PhD from Cambridge University in 1946 and taught at St. Michael's College at the University of Toronto from 1946 to 1979. He died on December 30, 1980.[19]

McLuhan had a strong interest in media analysis and mass media technology. In 1962, he created the metaphor of the "global village" to describe the social changes brought about by advances in technology and how electronic media was creating a shift in social organization. He believed that "the electronic media, particularly television, bring people closer together, severing ties of individual nations and making them members of a 'global village.'"[20]

The creation of scheduled times for news and television programs to air allowed people to share experiences simultaneously. McLuhan saw this trend as a "retribalisation" of a village of global proportions. In this technological "village," McLuhan saw people regaining a sense of community. Information from across the world could be shared through a visually and verbally rich medium. This scenario provided the receiver with a sense of participation, of an experience much different from reading a newspaper, at a speed that print media could not provide.

The electronic media of the day brought news of world events into living rooms around the globe within hours of the event occurring. Today, because of the growth of the Internet and wireless communication devices, information from across the globe is accessible almost as it happens. The severing of national ties can now be viewed as an almost total collapse of cultural boundaries as information is available in a 24/7 networked world.

In 1964, McLuhan attempted to describe the effects communication technology has on people thorough the idea that "the medium is the message." By this he meant that the medium used to communicate has as much, or more of, an effect on the receiver than the content of the message itself. Each medium has different unique characteristics that require the audience to engage a different sense. Watching news of a protest turned violent on television, with the associated sights and sounds, has a far different impact than reading about the same incident in the newspaper. Print requires the sense of sight, whereas radio engages hearing. Television requires the senses of sight and hearing combined.

With the changes in communication technologies, the way we consume media has also changed. Where we once listened to the latest news hourly on the radio, watched scheduled TV news, or read the morning paper, we can now visit a website and receive news updates many times per day. The Internet has created another major change: content creation. The advent of Internet tools, such as blogs and microblogging sites, allows anyone the opportunity to create content for public consumption. We can publish our own thoughts and opinions about any subject that we care to. In this twenty-first-century public sphere, there are many perspectives available to the public. Because we can post information directly to the Internet, there is no editorial process that may censor our views and opinions.

CONCLUSION

The role of PR is to create, maintain, and enhance mutually beneficial relationships between an organization and its many diverse publics through communication. The better we are at understanding each audience's concerns and perceptions, the better able we are to identify the messages each specific audience needs to receive and the most effective channel to reach them.

Communications models are representations that help us to understand how the communication process takes place; communications theories seek to explain the effect communication has on the receiver.

Over time, the study of communication has evolved from exploring the concept of an "all-powerful media" where everyone responds to a strong message in the same way to understanding an environment where we are our own gatekeepers and content generators, choosing the media and messages that we want to pay attention to and creating and distributing our own messages.

The development and adoption of new communications technology has changed not only how we communicate but the power structure of communications. Whereas the media owners once controlled the messages they desired the public to receive, the citizen journalist of today transmits photos, videos, and comments about events through social media tools within seconds of an event occurring. Although organizations and news media work to provide facts and accurate data, social media opinion leaders carry influence. The messages they share, however, may be full of bias.

The communications models and theories help us understand the effect electronic media tools have in shaping perception, opinion, and belief and to gain insight into how we need to adapt in this new reality. Our challenge as PR practitioners is to connect with our publics and provide balance to the conversation in a way that we will gain and keep credibility.

KEY TERMS

Communication: The transfer of information from one person to another in an attempt to create a common understanding and generate a response.

Economic determinism: A communications theory that proposes that the information we receive through the media is controlled by those who own the media.

Mass communication: The distribution of a message to a large number of people through media such as television, newspapers, and radio.

RACE formula: John E. Marston's four-step process consisting of research, analysis, communication, and evaluation. RACE is a popular model for the PR process that is recognized by CPRS and IABC.

Technological determinism: A communications theory that proposes that changes in technology shape changes in society. Technology drives societal change through changes in how we create, distribute, and consume information.

FOR REVIEW AND DISCUSSION

1. Which of the communication theories in this chapter do you find most relevant? Explain your answer.
2. Why do PR practitioners have a preference for Grunig and Hunt's two-way symmetrical model of communication?
3. What are the implications of large media companies purchasing new technology platforms such as Skype?
4. What do you need to consider when sending a message to customers that are 60 years of age or older and customers in their late teens?
5. Has the ability for anyone to create and distribute information on the Internet had an impact on the credibility of news? Explain your answer.

6. The Uses and Gratification theory proposes that we act as our own gatekeepers by choosing the media outlets and the articles that are of interest to us. What are the implications of this theory when you need to communicate a message to a specific public?

7. Under what circumstances would an organization use a two-step flow of communication approach? What are the benefits of using this technique?

8. Digital communication devices allow information to be distributed and shared rapidly, whether it is accurate or not. With the speed of information sharing, does the RACE formula still have relevance?

9. Compare Shannon and Weaver's Mathematical Theory of Communication to Berlo's SMCR model of communication. What are the pros and cons of each model? In which situations would each serve a purpose?

ACTIVITIES

1. Scan the news for an emerging issue. Follow the story over the course of its coverage in the news. Create a chart that will allow you to identify any of the communication models in use. Include columns for the name of the model, the description of the model, why you believe this model applies, and whether or not you feel this model is appropriate for the topic you are following.

2. Follow a trending issue on Twitter from as early as possible for a week's time. Who do you and others identify as opinion leaders? What criteria or elements formed your decision?

3. Based on the Twitter topic in Activity 2, locate items from the news (newspapers, TV, radio, news websites). Does the information have a different tone or perspective in the different media? Explain your answers.

4. Read the news over the course of a week and identify articles that interest you. Think about how these issues became news articles—outside of the obvious events that are typically covered by the media, such as fires or accidents. How do you think the media become aware of these issues? If you believe an organization initiated interest with the media, what purpose would they have in doing so?

5. Follow an issue in the news where an organization is receiving primarily negative news coverage. Reflect on the communications activities the organization is using to address the issue. How well is this approach working? What would you recommend they do to communicate more effectively? Think of the various communication models as you prepare your recommendations.

FURTHER READING

Arthur Walter Page Society: www.awpagesociety.com

Broom, Glen A., and Bey-Ling Sha. *Cutlip and Centre's Effective Public Relations*. 11th ed. Upper Saddle River, NJ: Pearson, 2013.

Canadian Public Relations Society (CPRS): www.cprs.ca

Columbia Journalism Review, "Who Owns What": www.cjr.org/tools/owners

Free Press, "Who Owns the Media?" www.freepress.net/ownership/chart

Global Alliance for Public Relations and Communication Management: www.globalalliancepr.org

Guth, David W., and Charles Marsh. *Public Relations: A Values-Driven Approach*. 5th ed. New York: Pearson Education, 2012.

International Association of Business Communicators (IABC): www.iabc.com

Institute for PR (IPR): www.instituteforpr.org

Marshall McLuhan official website: www.marshallmcluhan.com

McLuhan, Marshall. *Understanding Media: The Extensions of Man*. Cambridge, MA: MIT Press, 1994.

Noam Chomsky official website: www.chomsky.info

Public Relations Society of America (PRSA): www.prsa.org

Women in Communications and Technology: www.cwc-afc.com

NOTES

1. John E. Marston, *The Nature of Public Relations* (New York: McGraw-Hill, 1963).
2. Harold D. Lasswell, "The Structure and Function of Communication in Society," in *The Communication of Ideas*, ed. L. Bryson (New York: Harper and Co., 1948), 37.
3. Claude E. Shannon, "A Mathematical Theory of Communication," *Bell System Technical Journal* 27 (July, October 1948): 379–423, 623–56.
4. Wilbur Schramm, "How Communication Works," *The Process and Effects of Mass Communication* (Urbana: University of Illinois Press, 1954), 54.
5. David Berlo, *The Process of Communication: An Introduction to Theory and Practice* (San Francisco, CA: Holt, Rinehart and Winston, 1960).
6. John C. Merrill, John Lee, and Edward Jay Friedlander, *Modern Mass Media*, 2nd ed. (New York: Harper Collins College Publishers, 1994).
7. Harold D. Lasswell and Dorothy Blumenstock, *World Revolutionary Propaganda: A Chicago Study* (New York: Alfred A. Knopff, 1939).
8. "Radio Listeners in Panic, Taking War Drama as Fact" *New York Times*, October 31, 1938.
9. Paul F. Lazarsfeld, Bernard Berelson, and Hazel Gaudet, *The People's Choice: How the Voter Makes up His Mind in a Presidential Campaign* (New York: Columbia University Press, 1994).

10. John P. Robinson, "Interpersonal Influence in Election Campaigns: The Two Step-flow Hypothesis," *Public Opinion Quarterly* 40, no. 3 (1976): 304–19.

11. Elihu Katz, "Mass Communications Research and the Study of Popular Culture: An Editorial Note on a Possible Future for this Journal," *Studies in Public Communication* 2 (1959): 1–6.

12. Ibid., 2.

13. Bernard C. Cohen, *The Press and Foreign Policy* (Princeton: Princeton University Press, 1963).

14. Maxwell E. McCombs and Donald L. Shaw, "The Agenda Setting Function of Mass Media," *Public Opinion Quarterly* 36, no. 2 (1972): 176–87.

15. James E. Grunig and Todd Hunt, *Managing Public Relations* (Belmont, CA: Wadsworth Publishing Company, 1984).

16. Karl Marx and Friedrich Engels, *The German Ideology: Part One* (London: Laurence and Wishart, 2004), 64.

17. Edward S. Herman and Noam Chomsky, *Manufacturing Consent: The Political Economy of the Mass Media* (New York: Pantheon Books, 2002).

18. Jürgen Habermas, *The Structural Transformation of the Public Sphere* (Cambridge, MA: MIT Press, 1991).

19. For more about Marshall McLuhan and his media analysis, see www.marshallmcluhan.com.

20. Kevin Williams, *Understanding Media Theory* (New York: Oxford University Press, 2003), 66.

Marketing

UNIT TWO

Ashleigh VanHouten

6

Marketing: An Overview

LEARNING OBJECTIVES

After reading this chapter, you will be able to

- define marketing;
- understand the consumer buying process and buyer behaviour;
- describe the elements of a market research plan; and
- explain some of the more recent types of marketing, such as direct, social, viral, guerrilla, and mobile marketing.

INTRODUCTION

Marketing, similar to the communications profession, has many definitions. In fact, marketing is often mistaken for communications, thrown in the bucket along with other terms like *public relations* and *sales*, often calling to mind a slick schmoozer selling a product. This image is not accurate, although one can sometimes understand why this misconception exists.

Marketing is about understanding buyer behaviour. It is about understanding target audiences and interacting with them in a way that is beneficial to both them and your company. It is about identifying customer needs, aligning those with what you offer, and attracting and retaining the right customers to profit your organization. The challenge lies in marketing effectively to the right people in a profitable manner. Really, marketing is about researching, understanding, listening, innovating, and communicating. Successful companies and products are built on long-lasting, stable relationships with customers. Knowing who your target audience is and focusing your energy on them is key to establishing and maintaining these crucial relationships. Using your time and resources effectively is important too.

One of the most basic definitions of marketing is "the business of moving goods from the producer to the consumer."[1] Simple definitions can be good, but this one does not tell the whole story. A more current definition from the Chartered Institute of Marketing in the UK defines marketing as "the management process responsible for identifying, anticipating and satisfying customer requirements profitably."[2] Philip Kotler, a distinguished international marketing professor and author, explains that marketing involves "product development, pricing, distribution, and communication" and "continuous attention to changing needs of customers and the development of new products."[3]

Although marketing, in some form or another, has been around as long as people have been trading or selling goods and services, in more recent years it has moved from customer acquisition (simply getting people to buy your product) to customer retention (getting customers to keep buying your product) and now to selective marketing (communicating with the consumers from whom you can benefit the most).[4] With ever-increasing competition, there is also a more concentrated focus on establishing brand loyalty and retaining existing clients before searching for new ones. As the business of marketing, as well as the way in which we communicate evolves, so does the definition of the work we do as marketing professionals.

The "hierarchy of needs" theory developed by Abraham H. Maslow outlines basic human needs in a pyramid form from most basic to most complex.[5] At the bottom of the pyramid are the basic necessities of survival such as water, air, and food. As you travel up the pyramid, you encounter increasingly intangible elements such as social needs (interaction and value in a social setting); ego needs (self-esteem and status); and finally, self-fulfillment needs (whereby you feel you are living happily by meeting your full potential). With this hierarchy in mind, marketing professionals look to align what they are selling with what people need.[6] If you are not addressing one of these human needs, you will have a hard time convincing your audience to buy what you are offering.

THE CONSUMER BUYING PROCESS AND BUYER BEHAVIOUR

Before beginning the process of marketing a product or a service, you need to understand your target audience. Whether you call them buyers, clients, customers, or partners, they are the people with whom you will build a profitable relationship and are your most important (although not your only) audience. Consumer demographics are changing. More young people and women have buying power than ever before, and this is changing the nature of media, marketing, and advertising. Some research points to another important demographic—the baby boomer generation (those born between 1946 and 1964)—as welcoming new technology and social media in growing numbers as well.[7]

Knowing how to market your product or service to your target audience means understanding them—their motivations, life experiences, needs, wants, likes and dislikes, history, and demographics such as race, age, sex, socioeconomic status, and geographic location.[8] Understanding buyer behaviour can be a multi-layered and complex process, where you have to conduct focused research and ask many questions, such as:

- Who is the potential buyer of my product or service?
- Why do they buy or not buy a specific product or brand?
- How, when, and where do they buy?
- What elements influence a buyer to purchase and continue to purchase a specific product?[9]

There are some general principles that will help you understand the decision-making process of buyers. The Diffusion of Innovations theory explains how an innovation (new idea) is spread through a social system over a period of time.[10] The major elements determining an innovation's rate of diffusion and subsequent adoption are:

- **Relative advantage:** the degree to which an innovation is seen as better than the original. For example, how much better is a digital camera than a standard film camera?
- **Compatibility:** whether the innovation is perceived as being consistent with existing values and needs of the consumer. For instance, individuals who pay extra for organic food products do so because they feel it aligns with their values about food, sustainability, and nutrition.

- **Complexity:** the degree of difficulty or complexity of the innovation as understood by the consumer. For example, iPods are largely successful because of their sleek, simple design.
- **Trialability:** the degree to which the innovation can be tested or experimented with before adoption. An example of product testing may be a fast food restaurant that offers free products in order to gauge interest.
- **Observability:** the degree to which the impact of the innovation is observable to those within the consumer group. For example, asking about the mileage on a friend's new hybrid vehicle is a way to observe the results before adopting the innovation yourself.[11]

Next comes the decision-making process by which individuals decide to adopt a new innovation. Consumers use the following five-step process to decrease uncertainty about the innovation and the consequences of adopting it:

1. **Knowledge:** when a person becomes aware of the innovation
2. **Persuasion:** when a person develops an opinion about the innovation (either positive or negative)
3. **Decision:** when a person decides to adopt or reject the innovation
4. **Implementation:** when a person trials or puts the innovation to use
5. **Confirmation:** when a person evaluates the results of the implementation and decides whether he or she will continue to adopt the innovation[12]

According to the Diffusion of Innovations theory, any group to which you are marketing consists of subgroups of individuals who are more or less likely to adopt an innovation. A small percentage are innovators (around 2 per cent), people who take pride in being ahead of the trends. There are slightly larger percentages of early adopters and late adopters (13.5 per cent and 16 per cent, respectively), although the vast majority fall equally into the early majority adopters or late majority adopters groups (about 34 per cent each).[13] Early adopters are individuals who pride themselves on being aware of trends earlier than most, while late adopters often perceive themselves as more shrewd consumers who require an innovation to be tested more extensively before they buy in. Early and late majority adopters make up most of the general population who will eventually pick up on a trend but are slightly more tentative or require more convincing. As we are all individuals, we all have our own set of reasons, understandings, and circumstances that effect when and how we adopt a new product, idea, or trend. The ability to identify your innovators—who are often

Figure 6.1 Diffusion of Innovations Theory: Subgroups of Consumers

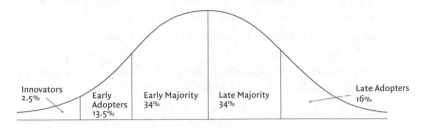

Adapted from Everett M. Rogers, *Diffusion of Innovations*, 4th ed. (New York: Free Press, 1995).

opinion leaders and influencers in a group—and pique their interest is your ultimate goal; most of the rest will likely follow their lead.[14]

Of course, this is an oversimplification of the process. There are always other elements at work that make the buying process complex and sometimes unpredictable, including education, unique motivation and attitudes, and group influence.[15] Consumer groups are more complicated than they may initially appear, which begs the question, how do I really get to know my audience? The answer is research.

MARKET RESEARCH

You have heard the saying, information is power. In no other instance is this more true than in marketing. Relevant, useful information reduces the risk incurred by spending money on untested or under-researched marketing tactics. Today, where the word *google* is now a verb in the dictionary, information is easier to come by more than ever. Rather than seeking out the most information possible, now you must be more selective, making sure your resources are prioritized, categorized, and organized. To begin organizing your information, ask yourself:

· What will I do with this information?
· How will it affect my strategy and tactics?
· What action may result from this information?
· How much is this information worth?
· How much will it cost?
· Do I need it?
· Have I checked secondary sources?[16]

There are a number of different research tactics that are specific to the type of information you are searching for. Examples include market reports, audits, surveys, in-depth qualitative research on consumers, product testing, focus groups, and concept testing.[17] You will learn more about types of research and research methods in Chapter 8.

Effective market research requires a strategic market research plan, which enables you to gather, analyze, and measure your research, ultimately presenting or packaging your information in a way that will assist you in making educated decisions about your marketing strategy. Elements of a market research plan include

- a definition of your problem or challenge: clearly outline what your challenge is;
- a research plan or proposal: layout your overall plan;
- fieldwork/tactics: this is your actual research design;
- data collection and analysis: this is where you actually conduct and collect your research;
- presentation of facts: this is where you clearly present what you've discovered; and
- summary/measurement.[18]

Once you have determined what questions you need answered and what research is best suited to answer them, and have outlined a focused market research plan, it is time to apply what you have learned to actually implementing your goals. When you have gathered all your relevant research and determined who your audience is, you will realize that there are many different ways to market your product or services, according to your particular industry and goals. Armed with the knowledge you have gained through your targeted market research, you can now determine the best marketing strategy to use.

TYPES OF MARKETING

There are different categories of marketing that may be more or less appropriate depending on factors such as your particular organization, budget, goals, campaign, and audience. While there are numerous categories of marketing, ranging from traditional to modern and tailored for every type of goal, campaign, and organization, for the purposes of this chapter, we will focus on a few of the more contemporary types of marketing. The following list is by no means exhaustive:

- direct marketing
- social marketing
- viral marketing
- guerrilla marketing
- mobile marketing

You will find as you read through these categories that many of them overlap and rely on one another for success; it will be reiterated through this chapter that a successful marketing strategy requires a range of tactics that incorporate many different channels and approaches.

Direct Marketing

Direct marketing is concerned with communicating directly to the home, office, or individual, rather than in the general marketplace. The consumer is invited to respond and interact directly. Direct marketing can involve direct mail, telemarketing, door-to-door interactions, home shopping networks, and social networking. Because of the tailored, personal nature of this method, the advantages of target marketing include

- improved customer relationships;
- the ability to build databases and profile specific customers;
- the ability to measure the success of your marketing campaigns;
- cost-effective and smaller-scale marketing tactics;
- increased control and flexibility; and
- the opportunity to test your products and specific marketing tactics.

The disadvantages include the negative connotation associated with direct marketing, which may be seen as intrusive, and the public's increasing disillusion with what they see as unsolicited "junk mail." Further, if no one is familiar with your brand, a basic cold-calling approach may be ineffective. And if your database is not accurate, you could be wasting valuable time communicating with individuals outside of your target audience.[19]

There has been an increase in direct marketing in some industries simply because of increased competition and the subsequent need to be highly responsive and aware of customers' needs.[20] Specific reasons to employ direct marketing may include introducing or testing a new product, establishing brand or product loyalty, identifying new or key relationships, and targeting niche markets.[21] Door-to-door political campaigns are a good example of direct marketing. While some forms of direct marketing (telemarketing, for example) can be seen as intrusive, other types (such as on-the-street, face-to-face promotion of a product) can be a casual, effective way of getting your product or message in front of people. This face-to-face interaction can lead into more unique, innovative methods, such as guerrilla marketing. You will learn more about guerrilla marketing later in this chapter.

Social Marketing

While there are many definitions of social marketing, here is one of the best: "The adaptation of commercial marketing technologies for programs designed to influence the voluntary behaviour of target audiences to improve their personal welfare and that of the society of which they are a part."[22] In essence, social marketing (not to be confused with social media marketing, although these two can work together) involves using various techniques to raise awareness of social issues. Benefiting the end user is the main goal, rather than benefiting the organization.

Social marketing arose as a result of the need for non-profit organizations to have marketing services, as well as to combat the historically negative image of marketing in society.[23] Social marketing is concerned with the dissemination of ideas, anything from environmental sustainability to cancer research to a fundraising party for a friend. The aim is to change attitudes and even behaviours and to promote positive social change. It is based upon providing information and asking target audiences to change their behaviour as a result of the information.[24] An advantage of social marketing is the emotional connection established as a result of selfless promotion for a good cause. The disadvantage is related: if you do not establish that crucial emotional connection, your campaign does not have much (including funds) to go on. Many not-for-profit fundraising campaigns are social marketing campaigns, such as the Terry Fox Foundation's annual international Terry Fox run. Another example is encouraging people from all over the world wear or buy pink products to show their support of breast cancer research. Making your message simple and easily identifiable can benefit your end goal—in this case, raising awareness and changing behaviours.

Viral Marketing

Viral marketing (or social media marketing) refers to the use of social networks to produce an increase in brand awareness or to achieve other marketing objectives. It can be delivered by word-of-mouth and/or the Internet. Viral promotions may include video clips, interactive online games, postings on social media networks like Facebook or Twitter, images, or even text messages.[25]

The goal of viral marketers is to create messages that appeal to individuals with high social networking potential and a high degree of influence within their peer group. These messages have a high probability of being presented and spread by these individuals in their social networks.[26]

Interestingly, viral marketing combines some of the newest forms of marketing with one of the oldest: word-of-mouth marketing. Often, viral campaigns are spread by person-to-person communication. YouTube videos that are obscure one day then have millions of views the next are a great example of viral and word-of-mouth marketing techniques.

Viral marketing has grown incredibly since 2000. Dealing predominantly with the online world, it comes with its own rules and regulations and pros and cons. Viral marketing can be cost-effective and highly interactive and removes the middleman of more traditional forms of marketing. Viral marketing tactics can also be more innovative and exciting than traditional ones.[27]

The downside to an ever-changing medium is that you must be ever-changing to keep up. If you do not use your viral marketing effectively—if you are not constantly updating your information and keeping it fresh—it will be abandoned. The goal of search engine optimization (SEO) is to make your information show up at the top of search engines. SEO is key to the success of any viral campaign.

With the infinite nature of the Web, it is harder and harder to stand out and get noticed. You can probably name a few online viral campaigns, either grassroots or corporate, that were so funny, interesting, or sensational, they became huge successes for the individual, company, or product involved. Have you ever watched a choreographed wedding proposal or perhaps a funny cat video or giggling baby on YouTube? These light-hearted, widely appealing videos explode in popularity simply by being passed among friends and followers via social media sites like Twitter and Facebook until they reach millions of views, sometimes within days. This is viral marketing at its most simple.

What makes social media as a marketing platform so effective—versus traditional methods like television or print marketing—is its reliance on mutual, two-way communication and dialogue between the company or organization and its audience.[28] Its immediacy of message, informal nature, and popularity adds to its effectiveness. Each day, over 20 billion minutes are spent on Facebook.[29] And while social media marketing does seem casual, it is becoming increasingly more strategic, complex, and tailored, as the options and the messages increase and become more diluted. It is now more crucial than ever that your social media channels align with your organization's culture and goals. While a few years ago it may have been a success to create a company Facebook page and Twitter account, these days companies are becoming more strategic about what social media platforms make the most sense for their goals and are hiring trained specialists to help develop strategic, complex, and multi-level social media programs.

Social media is not just about marketing; it can enhance sales, customer support, HR, public relations, brand management, and business intelligence.[30] In fact, even when you are using social media as a marketing function, you must be strategic about how you reach out to your audience. Olivier Blanchard, author of *Social Media ROI* (2011), says that if more than 10 per cent of your online activity via Twitter, Facebook, and other platforms is active marketing, that is too much. At this point, it becomes "talking at" your audience rather than engaging with them, and if you're always trying to sell something, the information gets stale, and ignored, quickly. Mostly, Blanchard says, you should use the lateral, casual, immediate abilities of social media to let people talk and listen to them. You also want to use automation (using social media organization programs to post for you automatically at pre-set times) sparingly and take advantage of the casual, informal nature of online social media to market to your competitor's customers in a way that is entirely ethical. Never before has it been so easy to access information about competitors and their audiences; you can use this knowledge to your advantage when working to grow your own customer base.[31] Jeremy Goldman, author of *Going Social* (2012), agrees with Blanchard that social marketing should be "less marketing, more social," meaning more listening, more collaborating, less direct selling.[32]

A strategic social media marketing plan incorporates research and knowing your audience. For example, "consistent posting" on Facebook and Twitter is no longer enough. Now, you can research and post key messages at specific times to ensure maximum engagement. It's 9 p.m.; do you know where your Facebook friends are? Maybe they're sitting online, waiting for you to send them a message. Analytics like Crowdbooster can tell you when your audience is tuned in. There are also myriad free programs for organizing your various social media sites, enabling you to deliver your message consistently and immediately across a number of platforms, saving the time of logging in and working from each account individually.

Lorrie Thomas, author of *Online Marketing* (2011), explains that knowing your audience boils down to three elements: value, values, and voice.[33] Value relates to the value of the platform to both you and your audience. What do you get out of using these social media sites? What does your audience get or want to get out of it? Second, you must understand the values you and your audience share and how to promote, enhance, and grow these via your social media sites. And third is voice: cultivate, understand, and promote your company's voice and listen to the voices of your target audiences. These voices must be heard in order to achieve anything via social media. If all you want to do is send a message to buy a product, you might as well send an email blast. We have learned, however, that simply "talking at" people instead of engaging with them generally is not an effective way of getting your message across.

Guerrilla Marketing

Jay Conrad Levinson coined and defined the term *guerrilla marketing* in 1984,[34] but with the explosion of social media and new technologies to reach out and connect with each other globally, this form of marketing has taken interesting and surprising new turns. Invented as an unconventional and shocking system of promotion, this type of marketing relies on timing, enthusiasm, and creativity rather than a large corporate budget. With an aim of being interactive and sensational, guerrilla marketing targets consumers in unexpected places or situations. The objective is to create a unique, engaging, and thought-provoking concept to generate buzz and consequently turn viral (see "Viral Marketing"). Successful guerrilla marketing must be

- **Unexpected:** While this usually means new and innovative methods of attention-getting, it can also mean more traditional methods of promotion that may be unexpected for the nature of the campaign or organization, for example, brand ambassadors on the streets promoting an online store.
- **Targeted:** While flash mobs and viral videos can be fun and even popular, if they are not directed towards an intended audience based on research and knowledge, the efforts may never translate into a change in behaviour on the part of the audience. Therefore, the tactic must include some call to action or enticement for its intended audience.
- **Cost-effective:** While new technologies and the grander scale of many guerrilla tactics on the part of larger companies are using more resources, generally a guerrilla marketing tactic is defined by its grassroots, non-traditional approach—that is, little budget for paid workers, advertising, or materials.

- **Profit-driven**: The ultimate goal of any marketing campaign is to raise awareness of a product, service, or company, with the ultimate goal of creating revenue. Even if your tactics are virtually cost-free, it is a waste of time if your efforts do not translate into more business. Always relate every tactic, even subtly, back to your bottom line: Do you want people to subscribe to you? Buy a product? Refer you to others? Make sure that whatever your bottom line may be, you make it easy and clear for your audience to accomplish it. To do this, it helps if your messaging is clear, consistent, personal, distinct, and easy to share (think text message, Facebook alert, or tweet).[35]
- **Newsworthy**: Often, people can get caught up in the fun and excitement of guerrilla tactics and not think about how it will be received by others. Again, a flash mob or demonstration might be fun, but if there is no connection between the event and its intended audience—if there is no discernible message that is of value—it will not get far. When creating guerrilla marketing tactics, you must look at the event from the point of view of the intended audience: What did this event teach me, give me? What will I do and how will I change as a result of this event?

Some unusual guerrilla marketing tactics include flash mob encounters in public places, street giveaways of products, or stunts—any unconventional tactic intended to get maximum results using minimal resources. More innovative approaches to guerrilla marketing now use cutting-edge mobile digital technologies to engage the consumer and create a memorable brand experience.[36] Mobile technologies will be discussed further in the section on mobile marketing later in this chapter.

Guerrilla marketing is most often used by smaller businesses and entrepreneurs such as non-profit organizations and startup companies with little to no marketing budget—although unique guerrilla-type marketing efforts are increasingly being used to catch people's attention in promoting movies, music, and other larger-scale campaigns. Today, there are even agencies dedicated to this specific, think-outside-the-box form of marketing.[37] These efforts generally tend to be less expensive and more creative, using volunteer manpower rather than large budgets; the ability to be creative, cutting-edge, and the perception of viral, real-time guerrilla marketing as "fun" makes it a marketing tactic for which it is relatively easy to recruit unpaid assistance. Of course, with a targeted, unusual, and often one-off method of marketing, you run the risk of being ineffective, not knowing your audience well enough, or even getting into trouble when your tactics fall into deceptive or upsetting territory. For example, at the 2004 Olympic Games in Athens, a Canadian man (dressed only in a tutu and sporting his sponsoring company's website, an online gaming company, across his bare chest) dove from the diving board of the Olympic pool, which resulted in his arrest and significant upsets and delays for the divers.

Mobile Marketing

The prevalence and popularity of mobile technology is indisputable. According to a 2012 article in the *Huffington Post*, Canadians sent an average of nearly 2,500 mobile messages every second in 2011, for a total of about 78 billion.[38] Increasingly, text messages are being used more frequently than actual phone calls to deliver concise, useful information. Even better, these messages are received immediately: some 97 per cent of all marketing text messages are opened.[39]

Mobile marketing is the use of mobile phones to deliver marketing campaigns and strategies, largely through the use of text messages and smartphone applications. It is a legitimate and increasingly popular way to reach target audiences, as evidenced by global companies like McDonald's and Nike making use of such technologies. Because a person's mobile phone is kept on them at virtually all times and is usually only used by the owner, it is an immediate, constant, and intimate way to communicate with audiences. The key to mobile marketing, however, is that for it to be legitimate, it relies on obtaining informed permission from the users—that is, individuals willingly provide their phone numbers and contact information because they see value in doing so.[40] This permission is, in essence, what differentiates mobile marketing from anonymous mass advertising or "spam," those unwanted texts and emails that audiences have grown to despise and ignore. Furthermore, the ability to customize and personalize the information and messaging adds value to the user and helps reduce the negative association many people have with receiving unwanted messages in their personal accounts. The social media element of mobile communication is also an asset; a viral effect can develop when users forward messages to others who were not in the initial target group for the messaging, thus widening exposure and potential clients.[41]

Mobile marketing can be used in a number of ways: to promote a new product or service; to provide information; to request feedback or participation; to offer incentives and encouragement for interacting. And mobile marketing strategies are evolving as quickly as the technology being built to support them.

For example, one of the latest ways to market a product or service via mobile phone is to incorporate geolocation technologies, which enable companies to locate the user and customize results to the user's location.[42]

As you will see in the case study on Barack Obama's 2008 presidential campaign, mobile marketing can be a fast and highly effective way to "mobilize" a group to act or behave in a way that is beneficial to a company or group—but only if the marketing strategies provide value to the user. Overwhelmingly, studies on mobile marketing campaigns have shown that strategies must be creative, entertaining, informative, and provide value for the user to be effective. Here are a few major criteria for a successful mobile marketing campaign:

- **Make it simple; make it authentic**: You must provide users with real value; determine what they would want, rather than simply what you need, and determine how to make these points intersect. Deliver real value rather than treating your mobile marketing efforts as another broadcast platform like email or direct mail.[43] Studies also show that being professional and showing restraint is better received, regardless of the audience; using texting slang can be seen as pandering or unprofessional.[44] Whenever possible, shorten and simplify all messages.
- **Offer incentives**: Asking people to buy campaign t-shirts via text message, for example, is a more rewarding and creative way than asking for 25 dollars because the individual receives a tangible reward in the process. Awards, gifts, exclusive rewards, and memberships are great incentives but, often, successful adoption of a mobile marketing campaign is as simple as providing information or resources. Ultimately, a mobile marketing campaign is a two-way communication and your audiences must get something from the exchange other than requests for their time and money.
- **Encourage user interaction and feedback**:[45] This could be the toughest part but it is how you actually get people engaged and determine if they're interested. Interaction and feedback, such as requesting individuals to visit a website and vote or comment, can also provide measurement for the effectiveness of a campaign.
- **Be consistent**: While it is equally as problematic if you overwhelm your audience with too many messages, being sporadic and inconsistent with your messaging will also result in your audience failing to recognize, anticipate, and desire this information channel. Certain missteps in consistency that seem small—for example, sending text message alerts from varying

individuals, or from people whose names are not recognizable—can still make a huge imprint on the overall effectiveness of your message.[46]

- **Connect your mobile marketing strategy across a range of platforms:** Nearly every campaign post, mobile website, and app released during the 2008 US presidential election asked its readers to share the news across other social media platforms such as Facebook or Twitter.[47] This request will attract other followers, generate buzz, and assist with measuring the success of your campaign. A mobile marketing campaign that mirrors and complements more traditional forms of marketing, such as in-person, print, or television, strengthens and lends credibility to your messaging.

- **Generate tangible ROI (return on investment):** As you will see in the case study on Barack Obama's 2008 presidential campaign, his team's mobile marketing strategy succeeded in increased attendance at volunteer events and rallies as well as raising funds.[48] Having individuals provide their information is a crucial first step, but unless they change their behaviour (such as subscribe to your service, buy your product, or attend an event), the goals of your mobile marketing campaign are not being met.

CASE STUDY: MOBILE MARKETING IN BARACK OBAMA'S 2008 PRESIDENTIAL CAMPAIGN

Perhaps nowhere are the stakes higher in a mobile marketing campaign than in the race for the office of President of the United States of America. After all, in this case, recipients are not being asked to try a new latte flavour or sign up for a yoga class; they are, as Katie Kuehner-Hebert says in an article in *Target Marketing Magazine*, "convincing Americans to respond with their money, time, contact information and opt-in, and ultimately nurturing those relationships into long-term supporters who will have a high lifetime value as donors and be reliable party voters in elections to come."[49]

Mobile Marketer, an online publication for mobile marketing practices, named Barack Obama mobile marketer of the year in 2008 for his mobile marketing campaign.[50] Obama, at the time a presidential hopeful, used a number of tactics to provide what some say was a "textbook" mobile campaign to win votes in the 2008 election. With two mobile websites, text alerts from an easily recognizable shortcode (62262, or OBAMA), mobile video and banner adds, and a smartly thought out communications approach to winning people over, Obama's team conducted one of the most well-received mobile marketing strategies to date.

There are a number of reasons mobile marketing can be a highly effective and persuasive tool in changing people's behaviours. Mobile marketing engages with audiences in a direct, personal way because mobile phones themselves are personal; the owner is generally the only user, and the phone is virtually always on or near their person.[51] As such, you also have the opportunity to send less formal, highly personalized messages, which Obama's team succeeded in doing—the messages were crafted to appear more like communicating than marketing or selling. With mobile marketing messages, you also have the ability to time them strategically in order to remind or encourage. For example, Obama's team send out reminders to attend meetings, volunteer, or vote directly before these events.

It is important, however, that marketers do not take advantage of this constant, instant connection with their followers by overwhelming them with messages or orders. For a mobile campaign to succeed, it must offer incentives for the user (such as free campaign paraphernalia), but even more importantly, the communication must be perceived as genuine. Take for example this text message sent minutes after Obama was elected on November 4, 2008: "We just made history. All of this happened because you gave your time, talent and passion to this campaign. All of this happened because of you. Barack."[52] As more proof that Obama's mobile campaign was a success, he was able to get 2.9 million voters to opt-in (by willingly giving over personal information, including their phone numbers) to receive a text announcing his pick for vice-president—an exchange that ranks as one of the largest single mobile marketing messages to date in terms of number of recipients.[53]

In the short time between the 2008 and 2012 elections, mobile technology (and subsequently, our standards for its use) rose dramatically. During the 2012 presidential election, almost 38 per cent of mobile users reported looking up news and information on the election on their phone.[54] In a 2012 article on the presidential election, Alex Campbell wrote that neither candidate (President Obama and Mitt Romney) fully used the mobile marketing tactics available to them to capitalize on the unique characteristics of mobile use—time, location, and interaction.[55] While in 2008, simply sending personalized messages to subscribers was enough to leave a good feeling, this time around, Campbell notes, "I was usually sent a message that asked me to donate or enter a contest. There was very little effort by either candidate to understand who I was."[56] He added, "Mobile is two-way, yet neither candidate is using mobile to make it easier for me to communicate with him."[57] Campbell's statements reiterate the need to create meaningful exchanges via this personal channel rather than taking advantage of the immediate connection by simply blasting one-way messages and sales pitches. As the world's comfort and familiarity with mobile marketing increases, so will it's expectations. To avoid frustration and the ultimate failure of a marketing campaign (that is, when audiences ignore it entirely), mobile marketing campaigns must be genuine and consistent and provide real value to their audience.

CONCLUSION

Marketing is the exercise of fulfilling the needs of your target audience in a profitable and ethical manner, and it is one of the more quickly growing and evolving business segments. One of the potential barriers in some organizations is marketing's perceived "intangibility"—that is, if marketing is not presented as directly and positively effecting a company's bottom line, it can be hard to convince that marketing as a "support" function is truly needed in these lean economic times. Yet, increasingly, a company's marketing department is becoming more visible in the discussions and decision-making operations of many companies, and it is incorporated in every element of business, from business development to advertising, public relations, and human resources recruitment.

Marketing, including innovative social, mobile, and guerrilla marketing tactics, is also being used increasingly in unique and fresh ways to gain attention, change behaviours, and spur change. There are many different types of marketing, which can be used selectively depending on the various goals and details of your specific campaign, and it is becoming apparent that a strategic mix of both traditional and contemporary marketing tactics, used to complement one another in reaching the companies' goals, is an effective use of marketing resources.

In many cases, marketing professionals must be a "jack of all trades," able to work closely with every department, understand and communicate with various audiences, conduct research and implement tailored, strategic, and integrated marketing programs to help companies achieve their objectives. As our technological and social worlds continue to grow and develop, so too will the nature of marketing.

As you can see, many types of marketing complement each other and are used in tandem to maximize results. One type of marketing, whether direct, social, viral or guerrilla, is rarely used on its own but rather is combined with complementary strategies to maximize effect.

Now you have a better idea of what kinds of tactics are at your disposal to market your product to your target audience. But what exactly do marketing professionals do to accomplish their goals? In the following chapters we discuss the key aspects of a marketer's job in greater detail: integrated marketing communications (IMC) in Chapter 7; advertising in Chapter 11; and media relations in Chapter 12.

KEY TERMS

Diffusion of Innovations theory: A theory explaining how, why, and at what rate new ideas and technology spread through cultures. Developed by Everett Rogers, the Diffusion of Innovations theory is the process by which an innovation is communicated through certain channels over time among the members of a community.

Direct marketing: A strategy whereby marketers communicate directly to the home, office, or individual rather than in the general marketplace. The consumer is invited to respond and interact directly. Direct marketing can involve direct mail, telemarketing, door-to-door interactions, home shopping networks, and social networking.

Guerrilla marketing: A marketing strategy in which generally low-cost, unconventional means—such as flash mobs—are used to convey or promote a product, service, or idea to a specific group.

Marketing: While often confused with public relations and sales, marketing is concerned with understanding target audiences through strategic research and interacting with them in a way that is beneficial to both them and your company. It is about identifying customer needs, aligning those with what you offer, and attracting and retaining the right customers to profit your organization.

Maslow's hierarchy of needs: A theory posed by Abraham Maslow in his 1943 paper "A Theory of Human Motivation," it outlines the stages of growth necessary to all humans from meeting physiological needs to self-actualization.

Mobile marketing: Using mobile phones or devices to promote or market to customers through wireless networks.

Search engine optimization (SEO): Enhancing the visibility of a website through a search engine's search result. The product of research and knowledge about what your audience is looking for will assist in creating wording around your website that results in a high ranking on a search engine's results list, so more readers will see it and, ultimately, visit your site.

Social marketing: Commonly used by non-profit or charity organizations, social marketing aims (through both traditional and modern marketing tactics) to influence the voluntary behaviour of target audiences to raise awareness of social issues with the aim of benefiting the user or audience and the larger community, rather than the organization.

Viral marketing: Using social networks to promote a company, product, or service with the aim of increasing awareness and achieving other marketing goals. The word *viral* refers to the self-replicating nature of online promotion, similar to the way a virus spreads throughout the body. Messages are shared, forwarded, reproduced, and replicated to spread information quickly, cheaply, and easily.

FOR REVIEW AND DISCUSSION

1. If you had to define marketing in one sentence, what would it be?

2. What type of marketing interests you the most? Explain your answer.

3. List real-life examples of campaigns for each type of marketing listed in this chapter. Explain your rationale for how you have categorized each example.

4. Predict how the nature of guerrilla marketing may change along with Internet technologies and our increasingly desensitized consumer outlook.

5. Have you had a personal experience with mobile marketing? Discuss your experience and whether the campaign worked. For example, did you buy the product or change your behaviour as a result of the mobile marketing campaign?

6. Think of an organization or company you respect that you think uses one of the following types of marketing well: guerrilla, viral, or mobile. Explain your example and why it works.

7. Think of an organization or company you respect that is lacking in any or all of the types of marketing mentioned in this chapter? Suggest a method or tactic you think might improve their operations and why.

ACTIVITIES

1. Research and present a brief case study on a recent marketing campaign that resonated with you. What types of marketing were implemented? Was the campaign successful? In what ways? In what ways could it have been improved?

2. Imagine you have just launched a company that sells a tangible, affordable, trendy product (such as a cool new pair of shoes). Your task is to develop a mobile marketing strategy to increase awareness of and revenue for this product. Outline your strategy, including at least three mobile marketing tactics you will employ. Explain how these tactics will benefit your company in terms of increased awareness, revenue, and/or customer retention.

FURTHER READING

Advertising Age: www.adage.com

Canadian Institute of Marketing: www.professionalmarketer.ca

Canadian Marketing Association: www.the-cma.org

Fern, Edward F., and James R. Brown. "The Industrial/Consumer Marketing Dichotomy: A Case of Insufficient Justification." *Journal of Marketing* 48 (1984): 68–77.

Guerrilla Marketing: www.gmarketing.com

Li, Charlene, and Josh Bernoff. *Marketing in the Groundswell*. Cambridge, MA: Harvard Business Press, 2009.

Marketing Profs: www.marketingprofs.com

Marketing Terms dictionary: www.marketingterms.com

Mobile Marketer: www.mobilemarketer.com

Word of Mouth Marketing Association: www.womma.org

NOTES

1. P.R. Smith and Jonathan Taylor, *Marketing Communications: An Integrated Approach* (Philadelphia: Kogan Page Limited, 2006).

2. Chartered Institute of Marketing, homepage, accessed November 2012, http://www.cim.co.uk/Home.aspx.

3. Philip Kotler and Sidney J. Levy, "Broadening the Concept of Marketing," *Journal of Marketing* 33 (1969): 10.

4. Smith and Taylor, *Marketing Communications*.

5. Abraham H. Maslow, "A Theory of Human Motivation," *Psychological Review* 50 (1943): 370–96, reproduced at *Psych Classics*, http://psychclassics.yorku.ca/Maslow/ motivation.htm.

6. Dennis L. Wilcox, *Public Relations Writing and Media Techniques*, 4th ed. (New York: Addison Wesley Longman, 2001).

7. Jamie Carracher, "How Baby Boomers Are Embracing Social Media," *Mashable*, April 6, 2011, http://mashable.com/2011/04/06/baby-boomers-digital-media/.

8. Smith and Taylor, *Marketing Communications*.

9. Ibid.

10. Everett M. Rogers, *Diffusion of Innovations*, 4th ed. (New York: Free Press, 1995).

11. Ibid.

12. Ibid.

13. Ibid.

14. Ibid.

15. Smith and Taylor, *Marketing Communications*.

16. Ibid.

17. Ibid., 127.

18. Ibid.

19. Ibid., 147.

20. Tony Yeshin, *Integrated Marketing Communications: The Holistic Approach* (Burlington, MA: Butterworth-Heinemann, 2000), 386.

21. Ibid.

22. Alan R. Andreasen, "Social Marketing: Its Definition and Domain," *Journal of Public Policy and Marketing* 13 (1994): 108–14.

23. Ibid.

24. Ibid.

25. Jure Leskovec, Lada A. Adamic, and Bernardo A. Huberman, "The Dynamics of Viral Marketing," *ACM Transactions on the Web* 1, no. 1, article 5 (May 2007), doi:10.1145/1232722.1232727.

26. Ibid.

27. Smith and Taylor, *Marketing Communications*.

28. Olivier Blanchard, *Social Media ROI: Managing and Measuring Social Media Efforts in Your Organization* (Boston: Que Publishing, 2011).

29. Ibid., 7.

30. Ibid., 19–24.

31. Ibid.

32. Jeremy Goldman, *Going Social: Excite Customers, Generate Buzz, and Energize Your Brand with the Power of Social Media* (New York: AMACOM, 2012), 13.

33. Lorrie Thomas, *The McGraw-Hill 36-Hour Course: Online Marketing* (McGraw-Hill, 2010).

34. Jay Conrad Levinson, *Guerrilla Marketing: Easy and Inexpensive Strategies for Making Big Profits from Your Small Business*, 4th ed. (New York: Houghton Mifflin, 2007).

35. Jay Conrad Levinson and Shane Gibson, *Guerrilla Social Media Marketing: 100+ Weapons to Grow Your Online Influence, Attract Customers, and Drive Profits* (Irvine, CA: Entrepreneur Media Inc., 2010).

36. Levinson, *Guerrilla Marketing*.

37. Jonathan Margolis and Patrick Garrigan, *Guerrilla Marketing for Dummies* (Hoboken, NJ: Wiley Publishing, 2008).

38. *Huffington Post*, "Text Messaging Canadians Sent an Average of 2,500 Texts Every Second in 2011, Total of 78 Billion," April 13, 2012, http://www.huffingtonpost.ca/2012/04/13/text-messaging-canada_n_1424730.html.

39. Mark Cohen, "Text-Message Marketing," *New York Times*, September 24, 2009, http://www.nytimes.com/2009/09/24/business/smallbusiness24t.

40. Hans H. Bauer, Stuart J. Barnes, Tina Reichardt, and Marcus M. Neumann, "Driving Consumer Acceptance of Mobile Marketing: A Theoretical Framework and Empirical Study," *Journal of Electronic Commerce Research* 6, no. 3 (2005): 181–92.

41. Ibid.

42. Ibid.

43. Chantal Tode, "Obama, Romney Rely on Mobile Apps for Votes," *Mobile Marketer*, August 1, 2012, http://www.mobilemarketer.com/cms/news/content/13431.html.

44. Cohen, "Text-Message Marketing."

45. Tode, "Obama, Romney Rely on Mobile Apps for Votes."

46. Katie Kuehner-Hebert, "Cover Story: The Direct Marketing Election," *Target Marketing Magazine*, November 2012, http://www.targetmarketingmag.com/article/election-2012-barack-obama-mitt-romney-microtargeting-retargeting-mobile-marketing-social-media-voter-databases/1.

47. Shuli Lowy, "Voting, Politics and Mobile," *Mobile Marketer*, November 8, 2012, http://www.mobilecommercedaily.com/voting-politics-and-mobile.

48. Mickey Alam Khan, "Why Barack Obama is Mobile Marketer of the Year," *Mobile Marketer*, January 15, 2009, http://www.mobilemarketer.com/cms/news/advertising/2462.html.

49. Kuehner-Hebert, "Cover Story: The Direct Marketing Election."

50. Alam Khan, "Why Barack Obama is Mobile Marketer of the Year."

51. Ibid.

52. Ibid.

53. Lowy, "Voting, Politics and Mobile."

54. Ibid.

55. Alex Campbell, "Why the Presidential Campaign Was Not a Case Study in Building a Mobile Strategy," *Mobile Marketer*, November 6, 2012, http://www.mobilemarketer.com/cms/opinion/columns/14149.html.

56. Ibid.

57. Ibid.

Marsha D'Angelo

7

The Changing World of Marketing Communications

LEARNING OBJECTIVES

After reading this chapter, you will be able to

- define marketing communications;
- identify and describe the components of the marketing communications mix;
- explain the role of marketing communications in promoting organizations and their products;
- identify the key characteristics of today's consumer and their media consumption habits; and
- discuss the evolution of integrated marketing communications (IMC) and its impact on campaign planning.

INTRODUCTION

Marketing messages are everywhere. Research tells us the average person living in a city sees up to 5,000 ads per day.[1] Advertisers who once focused their budgets exclusively on TV billboard ads are now using every opportunity to get in front of us. In 2007, the *New York Times* reported the CBS network was stamping supermarket eggs with the names of its television shows. Meanwhile, a

Toronto-based company, with the help of custom software, installed advertising behind public washroom mirrors in cities such as Toronto, Montreal, and Vancouver.[2]

Less traditional marketing strategies are growing in popularity as the average person—more technologically distracted, informed, and skeptical—is harder to reach. It takes a lot for a company to break through the messaging clutter and get noticed these days. It takes even more for them to earn consumers' trust and love.

As you read in Chapter 1, marketing communications is the "combination of the elements, activities, and techniques an organization employs to connect with or persuade the target market to engage in a particular action or response, such as buying a product, using a service or accepting an idea."[3] This chapter will explore the seven promotional disciplines that comprise the marketing communications mix, including public relations, advertising, sales promotion, personal selling, sponsorship, direct response communications, and digital communications.[4]

Note: Because this chapter has a marketing focus, the definition of marketing communications mix includes PR as a component. PR professionals, however, consider PR to be outside the marketing communications mix.

THE CHANGING CONSUMER

In the 1960s, a "creative revolution" was underway in American cities like New York and Chicago. Led by the original "Mad Men" of advertising, including Bill Bernbach, Leo Burnett, and David Ogilvy, these individuals created some of history's most memorable advertisements.[5]

At the time of the creative revolution, the average North American household had one television with only a few channels. Audiences, unable to fast forward commercials or channel surf remotely, watched TV ads and sponsored programming with greater attention. Today, getting an individual to stop, look, and remember any aspect of a marketing campaign is a monumental task. There are hundreds of television channels, endless magazine titles, and millions of websites vying for our attention. With the explosive rise of social media, the medium is as important a consideration as the message. Organizations are working overtime to be in the right place at the right time—on our televisions, in our news stories, on Facebook and Twitter, in our mailboxes, and on our mobile devices.

In an interview with *Marketing Magazine*, a senior executive from Cossette, one of Canada's largest communications agencies, addressed the challenges of reaching today's consumer: "What works today will not necessarily work tomorrow. Means of communications can be pertinent one day, and outdated the next...The time when we used to create a communication plan for a year is past. We are on high alert every day."[6]

WHAT IS THE MARKETING COMMUNICATIONS MIX?

As you read earlier, the marketing communications mix is comprised of these seven promotional disciplines:

- public relations
- advertising
- sales promotion
- personal selling
- sponsorship
- direct response communications
- digital communications

Which of these promotional disciplines (or group of disciplines) an organization chooses to implement depends on the campaign objectives, target markets, and budget. Given the high cost and managerial challenges, it is rare the entire marketing communications mix would be used in a single campaign.

Public Relations

In 2002, Vancouver health food grocer, Capers, found itself at the centre of a media storm when an employee working in its deli tested positive for hepatitis A. With the health of thousands at risk, the company had little time to determine the best course of action.

Capers turned to Hoggan and Associates, a public relations agency in Vancouver to create an information campaign. In partnership with Hoggan and Associates, Capers set up a website about the hepatitis A situation, launched a 1-800 number that people could call with questions, distributed media updates, and apologized for the incident via a radio and print campaign.[7] Soon after the campaign launch, customers were back shopping at the popular grocer. As one customer told a media reporter at the time, "They've looked after it, so we move on."[8]

In business, reputation is everything. How a company handles a crisis, treats its customers, and develops its products all impact how it is perceived.

And with so much choice in the marketplace, companies use public relations to maintain the respect and goodwill of their customers and prospects. As you read in Chapter 1, the Canadian Public Relations Society (CPRS) defines PR as "the strategic management of relationships between an organization and its diverse publics, through the use of communication, to achieve mutual understanding realize organizational goals, and serve the public interest."[9]

PR practitioners rely heavily on traditional and digital media to disseminate messages. In fact, one's success as a public relations professional relies greatly on the ability to navigate and grab the attention of reporters. Traditionally, PR campaign messaging was distributed via a blanket press release—a one- to two-page announcement detailing the who, what, when, where, and why of a particular story or announcement—to encourage any and all journalists to cover a particular story. This practice, while still done, has been expanded to respond to a media landscape that is increasingly fragmented, specialized, and taking up more room online. To keep up with these changes, PR professionals now deliver more targeted, concise, visually driven, and online-friendly communication pieces that better capture the attention of specific journalists, bloggers, and social media outlets (all while managing the increased risk that comes with promoting messages online and in real time) than a blanket press release. This approach better respects the individual interests and backgrounds of journalists, which can result in a higher rate of coverage. With media opinions still carrying more influence and credibility among the public than advertising alone, it serves most campaigns well to be seen in leading news publications, websites, and broadcasts. (See Chapter 12 for more on media relations.)

Sometimes, as with Capers, a PR team will find itself managing unsolicited media attention. In these situations, they work overtime to answer media questions and ensure their client's messages are heard and audiences' concerns are addressed.

But, like all marketing communications disciplines, PR is changing. The Internet and social media have changed the pace of reporting. In a crisis, companies have only minutes to implement a PR strategy before the world weighs in online via blogs, Facebook, and Twitter. Perceptions become reality. (See Chapter 16 for more about crisis communications.)

Advertising

Advertising is "any paid form of non-personal message communicated through the media by an identified sponsor."[10] Good advertising is creative, memorable, and persuasive. It boosts awareness and creates a desired response in a particular audience. Advertising (the good and the bad) is everywhere—on our televisions, radios, online, and in the streets we inhabit.

Companies spend a lot of money to advertise their products, viewpoints, and brands. In 2010, the Associated Press reported British Petroleum (BP) spent US$93 million on advertising following the Gulf coast oil spill.[11] The total amount spent for advertising in Canada in 2008 was C$13.3 billion.[12] While nearly a quarter of this amount was on television commercials, the budgets for online and mobile advertising are fast catching up.

Mobile advertising—advertising messages delivered to target audiences via mobile devices like smartphones and tablets—is a growing segment of the advertising business. Its growth makes sense given that Canadians are using mobile technology at a significant rate. A 2012 Ipsos Reid poll reports that the average Canadian uses his or her smartphone 222 times per month, for an average of 2.8 hours per day.[13] While most companies recognize the importance of reaching consumers increasingly "on the go," many are still trying to determine how to deliver marketing messages that resonate on tiny mobile screens.[14]

As of September 2013, approximately 49 per cent of Canadians use a personal video recorder (PVR) to tape television programming.[15] With PVRs, television audiences can record their favourite television shows and movies and skip the commercial breaks entirely. Leading brands, fearful the impact of a 15-second commercial may be waning (particularly among the younger demographic), are also competing for spaces within television programs and movies. In 2010, BrandChannel.com revealed that Apple products were in 10 of the year's number one films, while in *Iron Man 2* various branded products appeared 64 times.[16] (See Chapter 11 for more about advertising.)

Sales Promotion

If you have ever used a coupon to make a purchase, sampled a new product in the grocery store and then bought it on impulse, or if your wallet is bursting with loyalty cards from retailers and airlines, then you have participated in a sales promotion strategy. Sales promotion is defined as "those marketing activities that provide extra value or incentives to the sales force, distributors, or the ultimate consumer and can stimulate immediate sales."[17]

Sales promotion activities target two audiences—consumers and retailers—and include tactics like coupons, rebates, contests, and in-store sampling. Costco Wholesale Corp., an American company founded in Kirkland, Washington, is the seventh largest retailer in the world and sells thousands of products by sampling them in-store to customers.[18]

The influence of retailers and wholesalers on customer purchasing decisions makes sales promotion a critical marketing strategy. Consumer goods manufacturers like Procter & Gamble, who own brands including Gillette, Pampers, and Tide, rely on grocers and retailers to promote their products. By offering price deals, these firms regularly negotiate more and better shelf space for their products.

Sales promotion tactics, such as coupons, are also finding a home online. Websites like Groupon.com promote hundreds of discounted gift certificates a week. By offering time-limited deals, delivered direct by email, they entice people to try a new brand or revisit an old one. These sites, in addition to brand exposure, offer companies a highly measurable tool to promote their products.

Personal Selling

Personal selling is the person-to-person interaction between a company's sales staff and a prospective buyer. While other promotional disciplines, such as PR and advertising, heighten brand awareness, personal selling involves direct contact between a customer and a salesperson with the aim of making a sale. It is a marketing discipline most effective in industries where the purchaser requires detailed consultation and advice. Automotive, financial, and cosmetics industries, for example, all rely heavily on personal selling techniques to influence purchase decisions and to close sales.

Personal selling can occur between individual customers and businesses at the point of sale, over the phone, or from one business to another (known as B2B sales). A key objective of personal selling is to deliver an exceptional sales experience that leaves the customer feeling comfortable to make a purchase. In some instances, particularly when a product is complex or expensive, the personal selling process may require several exchanges to result in a sale. A longer-term, gentler sales process is sometimes referred to as relationship selling. In relationship selling, the sales team works hard to cultivate connections and build long-term loyalty among their customers or clients. Effective relationship selling can contribute to boosting brand image and loyalty. For example, a senior manager at Hudson's Bay directly attributes the expertise of the sales team, called beauty experts, with customer loyalty to the store.[19]

For many customers, the sales experience represents the face of a brand. How customers are treated during a transaction can form their opinions of a company and its products. It can, in fact, make or break their loyalty to the brand. For this reason, and because there is so much choice in the marketplace, companies invest in personal selling.

Sponsorship

For companies looking to reach a specific demographic or target audience, sponsorships can provide an effective way of getting noticed. In exchange for a cash or in-kind fee, an organization can be closely associated with a sporting, entertainment, or charitable event that often already had significant reach with a particular audience. For example, Bell Canada invested millions of dollars to become the telecommunications sponsor for the 2010 Olympic Games in Vancouver. The Canadian bank CIBC sponsors the CIBC Run for the Cure to raise money for the Canadian Breast Cancer Foundation.

Few sponsorships are as high-profile as those mentioned above but organizations of all sizes are seeing the benefit of supporting charities, sporting teams, and even venues in exchange for the right to promote the relationship, use event logos, and have a visible presence at the sponsorship property. It is an opportunity for them to get in front of current or prospective target audiences at times and places where their brand might not normally be visible.

How does a company decide which cause or property is worth investing time and money? There are several criteria an organization must consider before signing on to host an event or sponsor a third-party property, including the ability of the sponsorship deal to

- attract the attention of the target audience;
- boost brand awareness;
- offer category exclusivity; and
- be measured.

For an organization looking to increase exposure among target audiences, sponsorship can be a highly effective. Companies want to maximize exposure to customers and prospective clients and reach these groups even in their free and recreational time. In fact, it is now hard to think of any major charity, event, or professional sporting venue or team that does not have some level of sponsorship. Across North America, stadiums have been renamed and decorated with corporate logos, such as Air Canada Centre in Toronto and Staples Centre in Los Angeles. Sports teams wear jerseys with corporate logos. Fundraising events like the Vancouver Sun Run and the CIBC Run for the Cure greatly boost sponsors' brand loyalty and exposure. Even media outlets regularly partake in sponsorship deals. For example, CBC is a sponsor of the 2014 Winnipeg Comedy Festival.

As with all disciplines discussed in this chapter, the Internet is impacting how companies promote their sponsorship arrangements. Eager to do a good thing and be seen doing it, companies turn to Facebook and Twitter to talk about their support of third-party causes and to boost brand recognition. For example, in 2010, Telus Corp. launched a six-week promotion called "Go Pink." Telus asked Facebook users to turn their profile pictures pink. In exchange, the telecommunications giant donated $1 to breast cancer prevention for every individual who opted in, to a maximum of $50,000. Within 72 hours of the campaign (a campaign slated to last six weeks), the company had reached its target. "We had an ad campaign prepared," says Anne Marie LaBerge, the company's vice-president of marketing communications, "but we never released it. We didn't have to. It was like a brushfire."[20] By the end of the campaign, more than 800,000 Facebook users had joined "Go Pink," resulting in a donation of $200,000 for digital mammography machines at Canadian hospitals.[21] Following "Go Pink," Telus saw a significant increase in traffic to its Facebook page.

Unlike other marketing disciplines, the translation to sales is not quick, but sponsorships contribute greatly to a brand's reputation and creation of long-term, meaningful relationships among key communities and customers.

Direct Response Communications

Direct response communications refers to strategies and tactics that target a single customer or prospect to generate an immediate and measureable response. If you have ever received a catalogue or email from a store you regularly shop at, a free product sample in your mailbox, a call from your bank about a new financial product, or bought a product after watching a late-night infomercial, then you have experienced a direct response campaign.

In direct response campaigns, customer information is everything. With the rise of database management systems, companies have access to the contact information and buying habits of their existing customers. This information allows companies to engage effectively in direct response strategies whereby they send material and messages to our doorsteps and email inboxes that are relevant and enticing.

Direct mail, the distribution of promotional brochures or flyers, for example, accounts for $1.5 billion or 13 per cent of net advertising revenues in Canada.[22] With the success of direct response communications, companies are working overtime to track consumer data and spending habits. Retailers offer loyalty programs where, in exchange for contact information, a person receives points and or discounts at the till. These programs offer companies a vast database of contact information and buying habits so they can market in a more tailored and direct way.

The Internet, and in particular companies like Google and Facebook, have allowed advertisers an unprecedented means of targeting consumers with messages that match their specific interests and lifestyles. By using wall posts and status updates on Facebook, advertisers can directly deliver ad messages tailored to appeal on a specific level to individuals. For example, users who mention a craving for pizza on their Facebook wall might immediately receive an ad or coupon from a nearby restaurant chain tempting them to order.[23]

Digital Communications

Digital communications refers to the ways by which people connect using technology. According to an Ipsos Reid poll, Canadians are now spending more time online than in front of the television.[24] No single force, in recent years, has more greatly influenced marketing communications than the Internet. It has changed everything: how we buy products, how we communicate with each other, and how marketers reach us.

There are many ways to reach consumers in the online space. Historically, online advertising included banner and pop-up ads or website takeovers where a single company brands a site like Yahoo.com for a day. While fifteen years ago some companies argued the merits of a website, there is no room for debate today. A company without a website is irrelevant in the marketplace.

In addition to a website, countless companies have a Facebook page. According to the *Globe and Mail*, every day about 50 million connections are made between businesses and users on Facebook.[25] For example, Tim Hortons has millions of fans on Facebook. Even massive brands with national advertising budgets turn to Facebook to enhance brand exposure and start conversations. For example, Knorr, during its 2010 campaign to promote sodium-reduced rice dishes, used Facebook and other social media to promote the central character in its TV and magazine ads: Salty. Knorr's agency created a Facebook page for Salty, written in the character's own voice, and invited consumers to follow his life. Salty collected thousands of Facebook fans.[26] The company also posted a series of commercials clips starring Salty, which aired only on YouTube.

Social media is becoming a mainstream tactic for most companies. However, social media campaigns are only as effective as the messages they send out. There are hundreds of companies building Facebook pages that hold little interest for any external audience. The success of digital communications, like all disciplines in the marketing communications mix, still relies on its ability to distribute messages that engage the target audiences. Marketing communications specialists must now follow digital media carefully for new trends and changes. (See Chapter 13 for more about digital communications.)

CASE STUDY: CANADIAN TOURISM COMMISSION[27]

In 2008, Canada's economy was slowing down and the country's tourism industry was losing tens of billions of dollars. As part of the Canadian government's Economic Action Plan, a two-year investment strategy designed to protect jobs and economic prosperity, the Canadian Tourism Commission (CTC) received stimulus funding to help address the significant decline in domestic tourism. In the hopes of encouraging more Canadians to vacation at home, the CTC approached the advertising agency DDB Canada.

The CTC's objectives for the communications campaign included three elements: (1) convince 240,000 Canadians, by the end of 2009, to vacation within Canada; (2) stimulate Canada's economy by encouraging Canadians to travel domestically; and (3) create a sense of urgency among the target audience via tactical offers. (Essentially, convince Canadians to book their domestic travel right away.)

Research for the Canadian Tourism Commission revealed that for many Canadians an interesting or "exotic" holiday experience could only be had abroad. To overcome this idea, DDB Canada created an intrigue-based campaign intended to change Canadians' perceptions about Canada and to get them talking about the unique destinations and experiences available in their homeland. Using a combination of advertising, public relations, and digital communications, the campaign creative teased the audience with some surprising discoveries about Canada's potential as an interesting holiday destination.

The CTC campaign, called "Locals Know," kicked off with a series of print ads. Full-page colour advertisements, in both French and English, were placed in Canadian newspapers during the summer and winter of 2009. The images included photographs of sand dunes in Saskatchewan and swimmers in a tropical looking Georgian Bay. Each ad was accompanied by the simple question: "Where is this?" and an invitation to visit www.localsknow.ca to learn more.

The campaign's television advertising, which was also bilingual, premiered during the 2009 Stanley Cup finals. The TV ads, consisting of a series of 15-second clips, were composed of user-generated content discovered on YouTube and other social networking sites. The visuals for the campaign included a man surfing the Lachine Rapids near Montreal, and a zip-liner rushing through tree tops in British Columbia—all real experiences captured by travellers and posted online.

The campaign website was built with the clear intention of creating an online community. It was to be a place for Canadians to come together, share their stories, and upload their favourite images and videos of their corner of Canada. The results were overwhelming. In total, over 715,000 people visited the "Locals Know" website and more than 5,000 individuals uploaded clips and commentary, which resulted in a content-rich library of Canadian travel tips.

"Locals Know" brought together traditional and digital communications strategies with phenomenal success. All campaign targets were exceeded. As the campaign reached its half-way mark, Forbes.com named "Locals Know" one of "The 10 Best Travel Campaigns," and media coverage, thanks to a strategic public relations effort, was picked up across Canada's largest daily newspapers on the last day of the campaign. "Locals Know" also far surpassed the original business objectives and resulted in 404,605 trips that would otherwise have been taken to foreign destinations.

Marty Yaskowich, managing director of DDB Canada, the integrated digital and social marketing arm of DDB Canada, commenting on "Locals Know," stated his strong belief in the importance of an engagement strategy: "These days, everyone is talking about social media strategies. The truth is even the most sophisticated online tools won't help an organization if they don't determine how to get their audience to participate in, play with and pass along the communications. The consumer is the most influential and cost-effective way to reach new audiences. It is the essence of effective marketing today."[28]

INTEGRATED MARKETING COMMUNICATIONS

For years, companies relied on advertising to deliver their messages. Other promotional disciplines like PR and direct marketing, if used at all, were designed separately from the advertising effort. Organizations requiring a multidisciplinary campaign would hire an advertising firm for TV and magazine ads, a PR agency to talk with the media, and a direct marketing team to create promotional mail pieces.

In the 1980s, businesses started to question this disjointed approach and demand more integration. The co-ordination of the marketing communications mix is known as integrated marketing communications (IMC). In Keith Tuckwell's book *Integrated Marketing Communications: Strategic Planning Perspectives*, he defines IMC as the "co-ordination of all forms of marketing communications in a unified program that maximizes impact on consumers and other types of customers."[29]

By the 1990s, IMC had taken off. Large advertising agencies had acquired PR, direct, and promotional teams to provide clients with "one-stop" shopping for their communications needs. But according to Don Schultz, whom many consider the father of IMC, true integration would require more than co-ordinating strategies and tactics across the promotional mix. In *The New Marketing Paradigm*, Don Schultz, Stanley I. Tannenbaum, and Robert F. Lauterborn assert that a "major difference between the new integrated marketing communications planning programs is that the new focus is on the consumer, customer, or prospect, not on the organization's sales or profit goals."[30] Businesses had for too long focused on their own needs and objectives. Schultz, Tannenbaum, and Lauterborn argue that marketers had to provide customers and prospects with what they wanted to know about products.[31]

While nearly all marketing communications specialists agree about the need to integrate, the reality of how this actually happens is still being worked out in many agencies. Traditionally, the advertising team, the group with the largest budget, would take charge of a campaign, but now it is also common for the PR or the digital communications team to take the lead.

Simon Francis, a communications specialist in London, England, believes that integration requires a more creative planning structure. He says,

> The challenges for integrated campaigns are how to organize an agency structure and how, within an overall success measure, to strip out the contribution of individual channels/disciplines. We've operated a policy of a "rolling lead agency" where, depending on the desired outcome of the campaign phase, PR, digital, direct, media buying and advertising all took the lead at different times in co-ordinating the agencies' response.[32]

Ultimately, the results will speak for themselves. While there are certainly challenges to co-ordinating an effort across distinct marketing disciplines with people of different backgrounds and talents, a co-ordinated approach is the only thing that makes sense for the target audience. As Ashleigh VanHouten's case study of the 2010 Olympic Torch Relay Campaign demonstrates below, as long as companies choose to prioritize consumers' needs and responses to marketing campaigns, they will move towards an integrated approach that delivers greater impact and clarity.

CASE STUDY: 2010 OLYMPIC TORCH RELAY CAMPAIGN

By Ashleigh VanHouten

The 2010 Olympic Torch Relay Campaign is a Canadian example of a high-profile, successful, and complex campaign that relied on an integrated marketing and communications mix for its success. The 106-day campaign ran from October 30, 2009 to February 12, 2010 in advance of the 2010 Winter Olympic Games, making it the longest domestic torch relay in history at the time. Over 1,000 communities across Canada and 12,000 torchbearers participated. According to the Vancouver Organizing Committee (VANOC), the campaign's goal was to raise excitement and build momentum for the Olympics throughout Canada and around the world—and keep that momentum for a full 106 days. Their focus on accessibility for and inclusion of all Canadians was an ambitious one: their aim was for the relay to be within an hour's drive of 90 per cent of all the homes in Canada.

VANOC began organizing the campaign in 2006. Built over time, the communications team consisted of ten people (one director, two managers, six specialists, and an assistant) and the marketing team consisted of three (one manager and two co-ordinators). Overall, a dozen individuals handled the communications and marketing for an event that touched millions.

While the communications team was responsible for media relations, community engagement, communications and promotional materials, and issues and crisis management, the marketing team managed the sponsors and related marketing campaigns. Andrew Greenlaw, torch relay marketing manager, was responsible for developing and executing the overall marketing plan for the Olympic and Paralympic torch relays and collaborated on developing the integrated campaign plan for the Red Mitten initiative (an integral part of the overall campaign) along with Suzanne Reeves, director of communications for VANOC and torch relays.

The major sponsors of the torch relay were Coca-Cola (an international brand and a long-time Olympic supporter) and RBC (a highly recognizable Canadian brand). The campaign was also supported by the Government of Canada. Each of these groups required tailored, direct attention, and support. Both corporate sponsors ran public contests for individuals to win the right to be a torchbearer. To manage the volume of marketing and promotional materials that the sponsors were producing, VANOC used a software program through which sponsors would submit marketing materials for approval to ensure they were following the appropriate rules and guidelines.

Because the campaign moved so quickly and required so much material, from print to online communications and promotional materials, being proactive was necessary. To ensure consistent messaging reached the widest number of Canadians, the communications team provided pre-written Q&A sheets, press releases, radio spots, advertisements, posters, and other promotional materials to the various communities through which the torch travelled.

Interaction between the communications and marketing teams was consistent and symbiotic. The teams conducted weekly meetings that included a diverse cross section of internal stakeholders, including licensing or permissions, community relations, and creative services. In these meetings, the teams discussed any communications challenges, new developments, current initiatives, and the status of the campaign. An important element in their success was having clearly defined roles and lines of responsibility as well as a clear project plan; there was no overlap or ambiguity with respect to each individual's duties.

As with any effective integrated marketing and communications campaign, there were many moving parts, communications channels, and tactics to raise awareness, understanding, and support for the torch relay. Social media played a part in the campaign: with a Twitter account, Facebook page, blogger, and an interactive website, the communications team set out to stay as interactive, accessible, and current as possible. Just keeping the massive, enthusiastic audience up to date on the various event locations and status of the torchbearers was more than a full-time job.

The greatest communications challenge of the Torch Relay Campaign was one that most campaigns would be happy to have: rather than struggling to drum up attention and support for their event, the heritage and historical significance of the Olympics held the entire country's (and the world's) attention from the beginning. Thus, the communications and marketing teams' work was in getting the volume and type of information that was needed to the people who needed it in a timely and efficient manner. Certainly, another obstacle was the sheer logistic challenge of managing 12,000 torchbearers and the necessary entourage, media, fans and well-wishers, and any other groups (including protestors) that make an appearance along the route. For a seven-week event that was completely reliant on strict adherence to schedules, the ability to think quickly and be flexible was paramount.

The Red Mitten initiative was an integral part of the overall Torch Relay Campaign. It was established based on feedback from the community who wished to physically show their support for the torchbearers during their run. The now-famous red wool mittens (created in partnership with the Hudson's Bay Company, an iconic Canadian brand) were given out en route and eventually sold in stores. The mittens, the proceeds of which went back to the athletes, were quintessentially Canadian with their iconic maple leaf on the palm. They became part of the torchbearer's uniform and one of the most memorable and far-reaching elements of the campaign. The red mittens worked where conventional advertising didn't because they created an emotional, tangible attachment, and this part of the campaign came about by listening to what the public wanted by providing people with a way to "join the celebration." As Mr. Greenlaw put it, "The Red Mitten campaign is a great example of how you can use existing assets (athletes, torchbearers, etc.) and resources to create a compelling and effective campaign—without a traditional budget and marketing mix."[33]

Canadians weren't the only target audience: different communications tactics were established for targeted international groups. VANOC partnered with the Canadian Tourism Commission to identify 10 countries that were important for Canada tourism. Then they set to work identifying celebrities or key influencers in those jurisdictions and invited them to participate as torchbearers in the relay, knowing that they would help spread the message of the games and excitement in their own communities. To help spread the word and tell Canada's story, media from each country were invited to follow the celebrity selected from their part of the world.

With a campaign of this—or any—size, it is not a question of whether there will be challenges to face; it's what those challenges will be and, most importantly, how you react to them. VANOC had to contend with issues related to timing and weather, but this was just the start. They also had to deal with protesters, whom they handled proactively by setting aside a free speech area for groups to respectfully voice their concerns. Brand consistency was also an issue, which involved balancing the desire to share the brand with every community while still adhering to the International Olympic Committee's strict guidelines for brand usage. Finally, the committee had to manage the myriad channels through which to communicate, including media, TV, print, broadcast, and social media channels. With a campaign of this magnitude, budget and staff resources were a reality, which created a necessary dependence on the campaign's partners—be they sponsors, media, or community members—to help broadcast the message and generate excitement.

Handling the volume of media inquiries and questions from the public was another constant challenge. But even for the notoriously negative media, there was not much to criticize; there were no major organizational snafus, debt problems, venues that were not ready, or other scandals. Even for Canadians, who are known for being positive, polite, and hospitable, the reaction to this campaign was overwhelmingly positive. "There was a level of Canadian engagement unlike anything seen before," said Jenée Elborne, the communications manager of the torch relays.[34]

Although the campaign was a great success and the iconic red mittens remain a staple of Canadian patriotism to this day, Suzanne Reeves suggested that there were, of course, areas that could have been improved upon. When asked what elements of the campaign could have been better, she responded,

> From the time the campaign started in around 2008 to when it
> concluded in 2010, social media technologies changed drastically. Knowing what was possible in social media in 2010, we
> would have allowed the public more freedom to help us tell
> the story from the beginning. Instead of the communications

team documenting the entire experience, we could have had the public do that for us. There is the added risk associated with less control over the messaging, but it's a much more interactive experience for the community, and totally appropriate considering the goals of raising excitement and involvement.[35]

The major key to the campaign's success, according to Reeves, was

collaboration with communities and sponsors. Collaboration really is the "Canadian way"—we wanted to work closely with local governments and make sure that the experience was unique for each community while still keeping the major messaging and branding consistent, which required a lot of thinking on our feet. We required a close, positive collaboration with our sponsors to ensure that they were happy and their brands were also being protected.[36]

Andrew Greenlaw explains how the team measured their success:

Success was measured with quantitative, tangible benchmarks. One such measurement was overall Red Mitten sales: with a target of 500k units sold and $2.5 million raised, the campaign ended up selling more than 3.5 million units and raising more than $14 millon. A public and media relations measurement involved collecting media clippings to assess how many impressions the campaign was securing, along with the overall attitude and positivity in the clippings. Yet another measurement rubric involved the Community Recognition program, where marketing tools were provided for communities, and their level of usage was monitored.[37]

The 2010 Olympic Torch Relay Campaign is a prime example of a multi-layered and large-scale marketing communications campaign. The ubiquity of those red mittens in Canadian culture today is certainly one of the most tangible measurements of success of this uniquely Canadian project.

CONCLUSION

There has never been a more exciting time for the marketing communications industry. The marketing communications mix has been significantly impacted by the Internet and specifically social media. Every discipline is navigating today's Information Age and adapting to stay relevant. Consumers have an unprecedented power base in promotional activities—they can seek out answers on their own time, express their viewpoints online for anybody to read, and demand much more from the companies with which they choose to deal. The world is changing quickly, and marketing communications experts are working overtime to keep up and stay in front of the consumer.

KEY TERMS

Advertising: A paid form of marketing communications from identified sponsors offered through the media that is designed to influence the thought patterns, attitudes, and behaviour of target audiences.

Digital communications: The various means by which people connect using technology. Digital communications include text, photos, audio, and video distributed through electronic devices, including computers and mobile telephones whether to individual users (for example, through email or text message) or groups of users (for example, on social networks). This definition is intentionally broad as it must account for not only today's products and services that enable these connections but those of tomorrow as well.

Direct response communications: The strategies and tactics used to target a single customer or prospect to generate an immediate and measureable response. Examples of direct response communications include flyers, promotional emails, and infomercials.

Integrated marketing communications (IMC): IMC is the practice of co-ordinating various marketing communications disciplines in a single campaign to heighten the impact of a campaign on a particular target audience.

Marketing communications: The various marketing and communications disciplines (e.g., direct response and advertising) that organizations use to engage a particular target market and/or persuade them towards a particular action or purchase. Each discipline may be used on its own or in conjunction with others (integrated marketing communications).

Mobile advertising: A form of advertising delivered to target audiences via mobile devices such as smartphones and tablets.

Personal selling: The face-to-face process whereby a company's sales team encourages purchases by retailers and other buyers.

Sales promotion: A series of techniques used to increase immediate sales and consumer demand for a product, including in-store contests, coupons and rebates.

Sponsorship: A financial or in-kind fee paid by a company in exchange for having their brand associated with a particular event or cause (typically sports, entertainment events or a charitable cause).

FOR REVIEW AND DISCUSSION

1. What are the various elements of the marketing communications mix? Explain the role each plays in the promotional process.
2. Describe the influences that are changing how consumers respond to advertising and marketing campaigns.
3. What is integrated marketing communications? Do you agree that IMC is necessary today? Defend your answer.
4. What are your thoughts about advertisers using Facebook and Google to reach consumers? Do you feel your privacy is being invaded, or do you appreciate the targeted messages based on your personal interests? Explain your answer.

ACTIVITIES

1. The chapter points out that the average individual see thousands of advertisements per day. Discuss with your classmates all the places you saw advertisements today. Describe the techniques advertisers are using to reach you in your daily life. Evaluate the effectiveness of these techniques in influencing decisions you make each day.
2. You work for a large marketing communications agency. A client approaches your firm to develop a campaign to increase donations to a local food bank. The client has a limited budget but wants innovative and unique ideas that can be applied throughout the year. Work in small groups to brainstorm which disciplines from the marketing communications mix you would recommend for the campaign. Describe some tactics that you would use for each discipline. Be prepared to present and defend your choices.

FURTHER READING

Art & Copy. Directed by Doug Pray. 2009. Art & Industry, Granite Pass, and The One Club, 2010. DVD.

Belch, George E., Michael A. Belch, and Michael Guolla. *Advertising and Promotion: An Integrated Marketing Communications Perspective*. 3rd Canadian ed. Toronto: McGraw-Hill Ryerson, 2008.

Forsyth, Patrick. *Marketing: A Guide to the Fundamentals*. New York: Bloomberg Press, 2009.

Godin, Seth. *All Marketers Are Liars*. New York: Portfolio, 2005.

Mazur, Laura, and Louella Miles. *Conversations with Marketing Masters*. West Sussex, UK: John Wiley and Sons, 2007.

Neumeier, Marty. *The Brand Gap*. Indianapolis, IN: New Riders Publishing, 2003.

Seitel, Fraser P. *The Practice of Public Relations*. 10th ed. Upper Saddle River, NJ: Pearson Prentice Hall, 2007.

Schultz, Don E., Stanley I. Tannenbuam, and Robert F. Lauterborn. *The New Integrated Marketing Paradigm: Integrated Marketing Communications*. Chicago: NTC Publishing Group, 1993.

Shiffman, Denise. *The Age of Engage: Reinventing Marketing for Today's Connected, Collaborative, and Hyperinteractive Culture*. Ladera Ranch, CA: Hunt Street, 2008.

Sullivan, Elizabeth A., ed. *Marketing News*. [Magazine]. Chicago: American Marketing Association.

Upshaw, Lynn. *Truth: The New Rules for Marketing in a Skeptical World*. New York: AMACOM, 2007.

Tuckwell, Keith J. *Canadian Advertising in Action*. 8th ed. Toronto: Pearson Prentice Hall, 2009.

———. *Integrated Marketing Communications: Strategic Planning Perspectives*. Toronto: Pearson Prentice Hall, 2007.

NOTES

1. Louise Story, "Anywhere the Eye Can See, It's Likely to See an Ad," *New York Times*, January 15, 2007, http://www.nytimes.com/2007/01/15/business/media/15everywhere.html.
2. Susan Down, "Mirror Ads Are in Your Face," *Toronto Star*, March 29, 2010, http://www.thestar.com/business/smallbusiness/article/786751--mirror-ads-are-in-your-face.
3. Norman A. Govoni, *Dictionary of Marketing Communications* (Thousand Oaks, CA: Sage, 2004), 123.
4. The selected seven disciplines used in this chapter are adopted from Keith J. Tuckwell, *Integrated Marketing Communications: Strategic Planning Perspectives* (Toronto: Pearson Prentice Hall, 2007).

5. In the mid-twentieth century, advertising executives working in New York's Madison Avenue ad agencies coined the term *Mad Men* to describe themselves. For more on this period in advertising history, see the documentary *Art & Copy* by Doug Pray (2009).

6. Caroline Fortin, "Mélanie Dunn Becomes Head of Cossette Montreal," *Marketing Magazine*, January 31, 2011, http://www.marketingmag.ca/news/agency-news/melanie-dunn-becomes-head-of-cossette-21952.

7. Kevin Chong, "Mr. Green Spin," *Vancouver Magazine*, July 1, 2008, http://www.vanmag.com/News_and_Features/Mr_Green_Spin?page=0%2C1.

8. "Vancouver, Victoria Residents Line up for Hep A Shot," *CBC News*, March 29, 2002, http://www.cbc.ca/news/canada/story/2002/03/29/hepa020329.html.

9. CPRS, "What Is Public Relations?" accessed April 9, 2014, http://www.cprs.ca/aboutus/whatisPR.aspx. The 2009 CPRS definition of public relations was developed by a team of academics and communications professionals, including Terence (Terry) Flynn, Fran Gregory, and Jean Valin.

10. Keith J. Tuckwell, *Canadian Marketing in Action*, 8th ed. (Toronto: Pearson Education, 2010).

11. Associated Press, "BP Spent $93M on Advertising after Gulf Spill," *CBS News*, September 1, 2010, http://www.cbsnews.com/stories/2010/09/01/national/main6827683.shtml.

12. Keith J. Tuckwell, *Canadian Advertising in Action*, 8th ed. (Toronto: Pearson Prentice Hall, 2009), 3.

13. "Canadians Maturing as Mobile Users, Still Love Their Smartphones, Tablets, e-Readers, but Spending Less Time Using Them," *Ipsos.ca*, August 20, 2012, http://www.ipsos-na.com/news-polls/pressrelease.aspx?id=5724.

14. Susan Krashinsky, "Kiip Looks to Make Mobile Advertising More Rewarding," *Globe and Mail*, November 22, 2012.

15. TVB Canada, "BBM Media Technology Trends," accessed April 9, 2014, http://www.tvb.ca/pages/BBM_MediaTechnologyTrends_htm._

16. Abe Sauer, "Announcing the Brandcameo Product Placement Award Winners," *BrandChannel.com*, February 22, 2011, http://www.brandchannel.com/home/post/2011/02/22/2010-Brandcameo-Product-Placement-Awards.aspx.

17. George E. Belch, Michael A. Belch, and Michael Guolla, *Advertising and Promotion*, 3rd Canadian ed. (Toronto: McGraw-Hill Ryerson, 2008), 9.

18. Omar Akhtar, Erika Fry, Anne VanderMey, and Kurt Wagner, "Costco" in "World's Most Admired Companies," *CNN Money*, March 18, 2013, http://money.cnn.com/magazines/fortune/most-admired/2013/snapshots/2649.html.

19. Dave Lackie, "The Bay Celebrates Beauty Mentors with New Program," January 17, 2011, http://www.cosmeticplatform.com/2011/01/the-bay-celebrates-beauty-mentors-with-new-program.html.

20. Simon Houpt, "Tapping Social Media for a Cause," *Globe and Mail*, December 6, 2010.

21. Simon Houpt, "Mustaches on Your Face (book)," *Globe and Mail*, November 19, 2010, B7.

22. Tuckwell, *Integrated Marketing Communications*, 167.

23. Irina Slutsky, "A New Kind of Facebook Advertising," *Marketingmag.ca*, March 28, 2011, http://www.marketingmag.ca/news media-news/a-new-kind-of-facebook-advertising-25027.

24. Michael Sachoff, "Internet Use Surpasses TV Viewing in Canada: Canadians Spending More Time Online," March 25, 2010, *WebProNews.com*, http://www.webpronews.com/internet-use-surpasses-tv-viewing-in-canada-2010-03.

25. Houpt, "Mustaches on Your Face (book)," B7.

26. The fan number was checked on March 28, 2011. The Salty Facebook page is no longer active, but for information on the campaign, see "Salt Reduction Campaign Creates Internet Star: A Canadian Campaign to Encourage Salt Reduction in Food is a Worldwide Success," *Guardian Sustainable Business Partner Zone, Sponsored by Unilever*, October 5, 2011, http://www.theguardian.com/sustainable-business/salt-reduction-campaign-internet-star.

27. Information in this case study appears courtesy of the Canadian Tourism Commission (www.canada.travel) and DDB Canada (www.ddbcanada.com).

28. Marty Yaskowich, email to the author, January 3, 2013.

29. Tuckwell, *Integrated Marketing Communications*, 3.

30. Don E. Shultz, Stanley I. Tannenbaum, and Robert F. Lauterborn, *The New Marketing Paradigm: Integrated Marketing Communications* (Chicago: NTC Business Books, 1993), 55–56.

31. Ibid., iii.

32. Simon Francis, email to the author, March 21, 2011.

33. Andrew Greenlaw, interview with Ashleigh VanHouten by email, April 6, 2011.

34. Jenée Elborne, interview with Ashleigh VanHouten by telephone, April 12, 2011.

35. Suzanne Reeves, interview with Ashleigh VanHouten by telephone, March 25, 2011.

36. Ibid.

37. Greenlaw, interview.

David Scholz and Carolyne Van Der Meer

Research Methods

8

LEARNING OBJECTIVES

After reading this chapter, you will be able to

- describe the types of research available to marketing and PR professionals;
- explain which types of research are appropriate for which marketing and PR tasks; and
- understand how research is an important part of the research, analysis, communication, and evaluation (RACE) formula.

INTRODUCTION

Research is a critical component for marketing and public relations professionals. It adds a level of professionalism and provides a means to demonstrate return on investment (ROI). ROI is the benefit a marketing or PR professional can receive based on the marketing or PR effort that he or she has made. Research provides marketing and PR professionals with a means to measure and define what has happened based on their activities. Through measurement of customer attitudes, behaviour, or emotions, marketing and public relations professionals are able to see if they have effected positive changes on the target audience. When we talk about ROI, we are really talking about the marketing and PR industry's ability to demonstrate the effectiveness of its actions. When a company executes a marketing or public relations strategy, the only way we can tell if that activity is effective is through these measures of ROI. This chapter is an introduction to research and will describe ways to collect information that helps marketing and public relations professionals make informed decisions.

WHAT IS RESEARCH?

Research is a broad category and can include everything from experiments on the strength of the outer fabric in space suits to an analysis of a baby's awareness of its mother through sound. At its simplest level, research is a form of measurement. While other forms of measurement may focus on centimetres, degrees Celsius, or litres, opinion research uses measures of awareness, desirability, acceptance, and intention. Opinion research is collected through conversations, surveys, and observation and provides the basis for evaluating marketing and public relations campaigns because it can show how the campaign has changed these measures in the audiences who participate.

TYPES OF RESEARCH

There are several types of research. In its purest form, research is about collecting and analyzing observations and/or information. Many people automatically think of opinion research as surveys or polling. In both instances, researchers use a questionnaire to ask a series of questions to gather opinion. Research, however, does not have to require *any* interaction with the stakeholders about whom you wish to learn more. Depending on the need, there are a number of ways to collect and analyze observations and/or information. These information collection techniques include

- observational research;
- secondary research;
- media content analysis;
- qualitative research; and
- quantitative research.

Observational Research

In his book *Why We Buy*, Paco Underhill demonstrates that we can learn from simple observational techniques.[1] Underhill, for example, used cameras or human observers to watch how people shopped in stores and interacted with store merchandise.

We can learn from people's behaviour. For instance, a client of one of the authors of this chapter—a food association—was concerned with how people selected canned goods. The client wanted people to look for country of origin on the labels. The hypothesis was that people preferred products from the client's country, in this case the United States. In-store sales, however, did not support this viewpoint. By employing "watchers" in the canned goods aisle, the client was able to watch shoppers as they selected canned food products. These watchers were researchers employed by the author's firm to stand at the end of the aisle with a shopping cart and appear to be actual grocery shoppers themselves. By looking like they were simply other shoppers and not researchers recording behaviour, the researchers were able to observe how the shoppers interacted with the product in a "real" manner, not one influenced by the research approach. After recording the behaviour of several shoppers, the researchers learned, much to the client's surprise, that shoppers were selecting products without turning the cans around to see where they were from. Not reading labels could mean one of two things: consumers already knew where the product was made, or their choice was not based on country of origin.

Additional research involved having consumers come to one of the author's offices to taste the product and tell us more about what made them purchase one product over another. This strategy demonstrated that consumers actually preferred the taste of the client's product and preferred purchasing it over other products. In the store, however, the decision was made based on price and brand name first. The client used this research to develop a marketing campaign that encouraged shoppers to discover where the product was grown, using a vacation contest as incentive. The result was greater product knowledge among customers and increased sales for the client.

Observational research allows you to consider real behaviours in real time and in a natural setting. It helps you to understand what people do and how they interact with various stimuli, such as informational posters, floor plan designs, or other forms of communication.

But be careful. As researchers, we must always be aware of how we can bias research findings. When you are studying behaviours, often the person you are observing is also observing you. If you are doing a study on seatbelt use and you are standing in a parking lot with a clipboard watching people get into their cars, there is a significant likelihood that they may put on their seat belt only because you are watching. Without intending to, you have created a situation where your presence has affected the responses observed and your results are, therefore, biased. When you are conducting observational research, be as unobtrusive as possible. That does not mean you have to hide behind trees or only use cameras to record behaviour; some observational research actually allows you to be part of the scenario.

A company where one of the authors is employed once completed research for a major international airline. The goal was to assess the comfort level of first-class passengers without them knowing. Researchers, acting as regular passengers, travelled between cities in the first-class cabin and were told to look for certain potential behaviours exhibited by the passenger in the next seat. The research team had to be careful not to influence the person being observed but could respond to conversation if engaged. At the same time, researchers could not take any notes or record any of the behaviours they were observing until the flight was over, which, in some cases, was several hours later. This type of research requires extreme discipline. The researchers must be close enough to the person they are viewing to record their behaviour but not influence it in any way.

Observational research tells you the *what* but not the *why* of behaviour. Researchers must be careful not to allow personal biases and experiences colour how they view behaviour. If everyone walks up to a sign that advocates the need for as many Canadians as possible to get flu shots at the start of flu season and stands there for a few minutes, it does not necessarily mean that they are reading the sign or processing the information. All it tells you is that they stopped there (which is the first goal of all information posters: to be where they have the time to see it). Additional research would have to be done to see if the sign also increases awareness or desire to receive a flu shot.

Secondary Research

In secondary research, researchers are not gathering information directly from human subjects. Rather, they are using other pieces of previously conducted research or previously written analyses or commentary. This type of research uses information that already exists to learn more about a topic. The analysis can include government census data, previously published academic studies or white papers, newspaper or magazine articles, and social media. In the academic world, this research is often referred to as a "literature search." A great place to start your literature search is at your library. Librarians can be a great aid to you if this is the type of research you are conducting.

The benefit of secondary research is that the costs can be minimal. If you are designing a new campaign or creating a business case for a new product or service, much of the information you need may be already available through these public resources. From a cost standpoint, it is often more beneficial to use these historical records than reinvent the wheel every time you start to design a marketing or PR plan.

Media Content Analysis

Media content analysis, also called news content analysis, is a method of measuring the outcomes of marketing and public relations programs through tracking their coverage in the media. In the past, practitioners tended to measure production rather than results, or outputs rather than outcomes, which did not provide a valid measurement of the success of campaigns. For example, issuing 100 press releases in a year is not an *outcome* but an *output*. An outcome is the number of media stories that were generated by those press releases—and the number of positive, negative, or neutral stories generated by the releases. These are measureable results, and media content analysis provides a concrete and reliable way of measuring and tracking them.

Essentially, media content analysis is undertaken to measure the success of marketing or public relations campaigns, or as a tool for reputation management. In other words, if we understand what the media (print, broadcast [i.e., radio and television], and Internet) are saying about our campaign or our organization, we will have a better understanding of how our organization and its actions or behaviours are perceived by the public. If we discover that our organization is poorly perceived, or our organization's reputation requires even a minimum amount of bolstering, we can use what we have learned through media content analysis to devise media relations strategies that will massage or alter the perception of our organization in the public arena.

How do we do achieve this goal? First, we need to understand what is being said about our organization. To do this, we look to six main types of metrics for media content analysis, some of which provide more data than others:

- clip counting
- audience impressions
- qualified volume measures
- media analysis indices
- share of media coverage[2]
- social media analysis

Clip Counting

Also called media monitoring, clip counting is a measure of sheer volume of media coverage.[3] How many articles were written about your organization? This metric does not consider whether the coverage was positive, negative, or neutral or the size or duration of a story. As a result, it is not an accurate measure of the success of a marketing or PR campaign. For example, you may discover that 50 articles have been written about your organization's campaign or product, but if all of them are negative, your program, campaign, or launch has not been a success. Clip counting is not "analysis" but merely a measure of volume.

Audience Impressions

This metric considers the audiences reached in terms of print circulation, broadcast gross impressions (number of mentions in broadcast coverage), and daily Internet hits.[4] These impressions are tabulated to provide an estimate of the number of people who read, heard, or watched the coverage. Again, this metric is a measure of volume that does not consider the size or duration of a story or whether the coverage was positive, negative, or neutral.

Qualified Volume Measures

Qualified volume measures tabulate and compare the news items (print, broadcast, and Internet) that have been analyzed to determine tone (positive, negative, or neutral); story prominence; whether the story contains key messages that were accurately expressed and within the correct context; and whether the story reached the initially targeted audience.[5] These metrics also look at the size and duration of the story and if and how it dominates the general news coverage.

Clip counting and audience impressions provide an overview of volume coverage, whereas qualified volume measures get into the specific analysis of media attention and how it can advance your outputs towards true measureable outcomes. To truly appreciate the media's delivery of your message, you must understand whether coverage is positive, negative, or neutral. This understanding is the cornerstone of using media content analysis and can then be used to develop media relations strategies to further enhance public perception of your organization if the coverage is good, or work to change public perception if the coverage is negative. (See Chapter 12 for more about media relations.)

Media Analysis Indices

Firms who undertake media content analysis develop media analysis indices: a scoring system that combines quantitative measures (clip counting and audience impressions) with qualitative measures,[6] such as tone; prominence (this refers to the quality of the mention; for example, whether your organization is mentioned in the first paragraph of the article or the last); key messages; context; quotes from company spokespeople; third-party endorsements; article placement (on what page the article is placed and where on the page); headline mention; initial mention; extent of mention; dominance (how dominant is the coverage); visuals; mention of the competition; and the extent of these mentions.[7] These criteria are used to determine a score that considers prominence and reach: how many people are likely to remember news about a company for how long.[8] This score gives clients a general idea of their organization's treatment by the media. The score is usually presented in quarterly reports or more frequently if a particular issue is being tracked.

Share of Media Coverage

It is also important to look at the share of media coverage achieved by your organization versus the share achieved by your competition.[9] This metric is particularly useful for comparative analysis and can be used to determine whether you should consider media strategies to get your company more in the news. This metric also helps you to determine what other news is competing for the spotlight, not just in terms of the competition.

All of these methods of media content analysis can be undertaken by hiring a firm that specializes in it or by contracting out certain indices and undertaking the rest in-house. For example, clip counting or media monitoring can be done manually if your media sample is small enough to manage. Counting manually means you read and track the clips and simply count them up yourself; the danger with this method is that you may miss some articles. If you want to track national or international coverage, employing a firm that runs powerful media monitoring software to gather coverage is probably the best route and will ensure that you understand the true breadth of coverage, since the software that is used will pick up every mention of your organization. Qualified volume measures can be undertaken by a firm or by a qualified individual on staff if your company is willing to find the expertise and dedicate the resources.

Social Media Analysis

Beyond evaluating traditional media through content analysis, techniques of measurement have been developed to allow marketing professionals to understand and research content on social media. Through the use of software that tracks conversations and online discussions, communicators have a means to gather information from social media sites. This type of analysis can give communicators an understanding of what words are being discussed, who is discussing the topic, and how much volume is being generated. All the media content analysis techniques previously discussed can be applied to the information gathered from these social media sites.

To conclude, media content analysis can help identify trends and the ever-changing tide of public opinion.[10] Figuring out what is driving media coverage is critical. The media's focus provides the pulse of the marketplace—and this can be essential to your business strategy. Media content analysis can also help you make other decisions. For example, during a moment of crisis, how do you get media attention *off* of something? How do you get into a journalist's head in a positive way? Which journalists are in your camp, which are not, and how do you get them there?[11] Media content analysis provides a way to understand these issues and can then be used to strategize media relations programs that lead to more positive coverage. Positive coverage is akin to a third-party endorsement; your company's credibility can skyrocket in public opinion. This kind of endorsement is worth more than any advertising you can buy or marketing strategy you can devise.

Qualitative Research

Much of the research used in marketing and public relations involves asking questions to gather information from people. Qualitative research involves asking questions of small groups or individuals. It is different from other research in its use of a conversational style or group discussion. Researchers use a guide or question outline that helps them lead the discussion, but present themselves to the group or individual from whom they are collecting the information in a way that is seen as open and encourages dialogue and disclosure.

This type of research allows investigators to explore a topic or issue through a structured conversation with a stakeholder. It is less structured than other techniques, however, which allows the potential for unique learning that investigators may not acquire in other research. By asking questions that encourage a conversation between the researcher and the stakeholder, you can learn much more than you usually anticipate before undertaking the research. This method allows for a broader range of response than a survey would, for example. In fact, many research programs will start with qualitative research to help the researchers understand more of the range of possible responses; they will use this knowledge to create a larger research program that can go to more respondents and validate or add support to the results found in the qualitative component.

Nevertheless, it is important to be aware that the information gathered in qualitative research is not representative of the larger population because it is a discussion that does not involve a random selection of respondents from the larger population. The group or individuals interviewed may not be similar to the population at large. To be a truly random study, everyone selected to take part would have to agree to provide information. Unfortunately, that is not possible since some people who are contacted will not wish to participate at all or may be unavailable at that time, so we are left including those who are available when the research is being done. The potential for bias is also high in this type of research. With the interaction between the researcher collecting the information and the respondent, the potential for the researcher to affect or influence the responses from the interviewee increases substantially.

Focus Groups

The focus group is a special form of qualitative research. This research approach usually includes eight to ten individuals engaged in a round table discussion. A moderator helps to keep the conversation on topic and expertly guides the discussion of the issue at hand. Focus groups exemplify qualitative research in that the group members are asked to provide their viewpoint and comment on the viewpoints of others in a non-combative style. The findings are not presented as representative of a population; instead, they are viewed as a way to show how people may feel but are related to the group in the room only.

Focus group research has become an industry unto itself with some researchers specializing in this approach and dedicated focus group facilities being created.

Focus groups can be used to

- test messaging for a marketing or PR campaign;
- brainstorm new product ideas;
- modify existing products;
- understand why one product is preferred over another;
- provide a more in-depth understanding of survey results; or
- test packaging concepts.

One of the authors' clients uses this technique to test all their advertisements before they release them to the media. By allowing focus group participants to view the ads and discuss them in a group format, researchers can learn if there are parts of the ad that may be confusing or offend the viewer. In this way, the client creates an advertisement that has the most potential to impact the intended target.

Focus groups add a new dimension to the list of potential factors that can affect your research: the other participants in the group. The benefit of focus groups is that they allow for group discussion among participants. Moreover, within the group discussion, ideas often are presented that an individual in the room may have not expressed without some other participant speaking up first. While this interaction is a good thing, it is also the main reason that researchers should complete a minimum of two focus groups for each stakeholder category of their research. Although it is the moderator's role to ensure the group works in a way that allows all participants to discuss their views, some participants may have such entrenched beliefs that they overly influence (bias) the whole group discussion. A second group becomes a must if you wish to be safe and protect against potentially biased results.

The person who moderates the focus group must be able to guide the group participants through the session with an empathic, attentive, and firm manner. The moderator has a great deal of influence and needs to be in control of his or her group. A moderator should be a good listener with an ability to use verbal and nonverbal cues to sustain a conversation and to delve deeper and uncover insights. At the same time, the moderator must be firm and guide the group through the sessions with the right amount of emphasis placed on each section of the discussion, or the research objectives may not be met.

A moderator must also be an actor: he or she must have the ability to maintain the same expression regardless of whether he or she agrees or disagrees with a respondent's point of view. The goal is to get the information without one or more participants taking control of the group.

Quantitative Research

While focus groups are great for exploring the qualitative nature of a topic, one must consider quantitative research to understand how attitudes or behaviours have changed or to benchmark an actual issue among a population of stakeholders.

Surveys

Surveys use a larger number of respondents and collect information in a way that allows one to extrapolate to the larger population. The end goal is to achieve results that meet the standards of both reliability and validity:

- **Reliability:** This refers to the ability of the researcher to achieve the same (or very similar) results every time he/she conducts the research, assuming that no major factor has affected the results.
- **Validity:** This refers to the ability of the research process to measure the actual behaviour, attitude, or other issue that it is intended to measure.

Surveys use a large number of respondents who have been randomly selected. For example, if you wanted to get a representative survey of Canadians, you could do so by randomly surveying 1,000 Canadian households as long as you give every household the potential to be included in the study. In this way, the results will approximate the results of all 35 million Canadians. This method allows you to estimate real responses within a specific margin of error.

By allowing every individual the chance to participate in your study, you have the greatest likelihood of achieving a survey that is representative of the larger population. However, unless you survey everyone and achieve a census, the data will never completely represent the views of that larger population. For this reason, researchers describe the data using a "margin of error." Most surveys and polls that are published will have this statistic included as a way to show the reliability of the data. For example, assuming we have 1,000 surveys from a representative Canadian population, and we find that 75 per cent of Canadians say they trust Company A, we can say that the score of 75 per cent on trust is accurate within ± 2.8 per cent, 19 times out of 20.

The 2.8 per cent indicates a range of possible responses into which the actual response is likely to occur. In this case, the actual trust score could be between 72.2 per cent and 77.8 per cent. This point is important. Let's say we have two trust scores: Company A achieves a score of 50 per cent on positive trust, and Company B receives a score of 57 per cent on positive trust. One may conclude that Canadians trust Company B more than they trust Company A. However, the margin of error must be taken into consideration. Let's say we conducted only 100 surveys. The margin of error for 100 surveys is at 10 per cent for the Company A result and 9.9 per cent for the Company B result. That means Company A could have had a score of 40 per cent to 60 per cent in reality, and Company B could have had a score of 45.1 per cent to 64.1 per cent. There is a distinct possibility that Company B is the more trusted company, but, given that we have only 100 surveys in our analysis, it is impossible to tell at this level.

In an ideal world, we would collect as many surveys as possible. The reality is, budgets and timing come into play, and, for these reasons, we try to complete as many surveys as we can within these two factors.

So how many surveys should you conduct? The answer lies in who you are surveying and what you want to do with the results. There was a time when many researchers preferred research studies that had 1,000 or more respondents, but this is not always practical. If you were completing a survey of endocrinologists in Canada, you would be hard-pressed to get 100 respondents; 1,000 would be simply impossible because there are not that many in Canada to begin with. The rule to follow is that for an easy-to-reach population, you should aim for a minimum of 400 to 500 surveys.

Sometimes, you may wish to conduct more than 500 surveys. Let's say you are doing a survey across Canada of a representative sample of Canadians and you do 500 surveys. You may have difficulty when you analyze your results if you want to compare people from Manitoba or Saskatchewan with other provinces because you will have completed very few surveys in these low-population density areas. At this time, it may be appropriate to go to 1,000 or 2,000 survey respondents to allow for greater depth in analysis and reporting.

One current industry trend is to use social media populations to complete surveys. Researchers can post surveys on Twitter or Facebook and have their contacts and extended contacts complete the survey. While you will receive filled-out surveys from these social media contacts, it is important to understand that because of the nature of this population, you cannot generalize to a larger Canadian population. It is highly likely that the respondents will be similar to each other given the way we network within social media, which thus reduces the representative nature of the survey. While these are easy populations to reach, the results are indicative of these populations only and should not be extrapolated to the larger population.

The RACE Formula

As you read in Chapter 5, RACE is an acronym for *research, analysis, communication, and evaluation* and is the protocol endorsed by the Canadian Public Relations Society and many other organizations for any professional who wants to do exceptional work. The concept is used in marketing communications and public relations planning. This chapter focuses on only the R and the E of the formula because these are the two categories that potentially involve research.

Research in RACE

The research component of the RACE formula concerns understanding the client and understanding who the stakeholders are and how to reach them effectively. Many PR and marketing professionals will use survey research as a means of identifying these characteristics. For example, by using readership data, we can learn who reads particular newspapers, watches certain television shows, drives past spaces where a billboard can be placed, listens to the radio, or uses social media. This information can be crucial to a campaign if you are targeting a particular group of people.

In addition, this phase of the campaign can use research to understand words or phrases that are important to the stakeholder group in question. These words or phrases can be used to develop the advertising or communications efforts for the actual program's tools. Focus groups and secondary research are often employed for this purpose.

Evaluation in RACE

Evaluation is all about assessing the potential effect of the marketing or PR campaign. This level of analysis can take the form of media content analysis, survey research, sales data, or other forms of behavioural measures, such as measuring if an individual reduces foods that are high in sodium based on being exposed to a healthy lifestyles campaign.

Let's look at an example of a well-measured campaign from an evaluation standpoint. A heart research team at a hospital in Canada led a campaign that would indicate whether marketing and communications efforts could increase sodium-reducing behaviours among a targeted community. The communicators identified a specific community as their target area and proceeded to create a plan, which included television, radio, and newspaper ads, press releases, social media discussion, and a website. Prior to launching the plan, the hospital conducted surveys in the targeted community as well as in another community that resembled the test community. The goal was to measure residents' sodium consumption behaviours and attitudes toward sodium and healthy eating. The marketing and communications plan was launched in the test community only and follow-up research was completed in both communities again to show the potential impact of the campaign. The second location was measured both pre- and post-campaign but did not see the campaign. In this way, it was a control group to compare against any potential changes from the test area. The inclusion of a control group allowed the communicators to understand how their program influenced people who live and work in an area that is not in a sterilized lab. What this means is that at the same time that the communicators were running their program, other news stories and events were happening that could have influenced sodium consumption. With a control group that was potentially affected by these other discussions, but not the PR campaign specific to the test community, an important comparison against which to analyze the results was established.

VENTURING INTO A NEW MARKET: FRANCOPHONE QUEBEC

Francophone Quebec offers a unique example of some of the advantages and limitations of using market research to enter a market. Cultural differences and sensitivities in a multicultural country are significant and must be taken into account. However, market researchers can help the communicator and marketer sort out what is unique in a target market and what is consistent with standard practice and usage.

Leger conducted and assembled a variety of research on Quebec in January 2013. Through analysis of more than 3,600 consumer indices (behavioural, perceptual, and opinion questions) over five years, a comparison between Quebec and Canada outside Quebec shows the following:

- Quebeckers obtain identical results to Canadians on 81 per cent of indices; and
- Quebeckers vary significantly on 19 per cent of the indices.[12]

The challenge is not to know if we are different, but to know how we are different, why we are different, and what impact these differences have on consumer behaviour.

In Leger's opinion, "Quebeckers are probably not as different from other Canadians as they think they are and probably more different than other Canadians think they are." Some differences are sociological. Quebeckers, for example, have the highest number of single-parent households, 40 per cent more than Ontario and 55 per cent more than the Prairies. Quebeckers are more likely to be renters than homeowners and have lower incomes (on average) and lower savings. As consumers, Quebeckers statistically tend to be impulse buyers, sensitive to lower prices and open to advertising. Quebeckers, like most people, prefer a spokesperson to be from their community. They spend more on food and dress than other Canadians and prefer stylish clothing.

In terms of media, 9 out of 10 television programs are produced in Quebec; in Canada 9 out of 10 are produced in the US. Conventional television was the market leader in the early part of the century, with 70 per cent of francophones watching prime time television (and TVA, the privately owned French language television network in Canada, is the go-to market, reaching nearly 40 per cent of television viewers in prime time.) According to research, francophones tend to be late adaptors to new communications technology. For example, whereas 42 per cent of Canadians say "yes" to the statement, "The development of new technologies excites me," only 25 per cent of Quebeckers agree.

This is a simple summary of many scientific, statistically accurate surveys of Quebec demographics and consumer and media preference. The larger picture is much more sophisticated and can be explored in some depth. Don't, however, be so entranced or intimidated by the details of delving into new markets that you forget that the fundamental principles of public relations and marketing communications still apply. As our colleague Michel Dumas from Quebec explains,

I conducted some research when I was president of the Worldcom Group of international independently owned PR agencies. I submitted the same case to six of our partner agencies on five continents to verify to what extent their solutions would be more or less the same. It appeared that in all cases, the same strategies and in good part the same tactics were applied, no doubt because all firms today use the same best practices. The differences were mostly linguistic (to address the audience in its language) and cultural (some cultural traits that have to be taken into account). As an example, when a Toronto firm once asked us to make a press conference locally in Montreal at the same time as other partners in Canada in the framework of a national public relations campaign, we had to decline because it was on the 24th of June, the Saint-Jean Baptiste Day, the most significant holiday in Quebec, when newspapers do not publish that day and even the day before or the day after. It was a strategy which had been developed apparently without consultation on the appropriate day for a public relations event nationwide.[13]

Nevertheless, the Quebec case illustrates some of the values of market research:

1. Do market research into your market, even if you think you know it. Public opinion and attitudes are constantly changing, as is communications technology.

2. While the specifics of your target market may vary, the principles of marketing and communications still apply, as Mr. Dumas notes above—and they apply internationally.

3. If you don't know your market, work with someone who does. This can be either a national PR/marketing firm, or it can be a local agency that you take on as a partner or subcontractor. They may be able to point out some of the nuances of the market you're trying to enter.

4. Once you've developed your communications materials, test them out. Focus groups can be skewed, bad questions can make for bad research, and there's always something that looked good in principle but that simply doesn't work.

5. And if you're going to be working in that market for some time, as opposed to doing a one-time campaign, keep researching and keep on top of your market as it grows and changes.

CONCLUSION

Whether observational, secondary, qualitative, quantitative, or a combination of these, research lays the groundwork to develop successful marketing and PR campaigns. Research also provides the means to demonstrate the effectiveness of these campaigns.

As we find more ways for companies to communicate with stakeholders, and as more products enter the market, research becomes critical to understanding the target audience and how that audience is influenced by marketing and PR activities. Ongoing evaluation will help marketing and PR professionals to understand what works and what does not work, and to continue to learn and grow within the profession.

KEY TERMS

Impressions: Generally, the number of eyeballs or ears reading, watching, or listening to a given media outlet. Some call this *reach*. Impressions are more than just circulation numbers, as is the case of print media, since a given newspaper or magazine is often read by more than one person in a household or office.

Media content analysis: An analysis of media stories to help companies understand how they are portrayed by the media and, by extension, how they might be perceived by the public as a result of this coverage.

Media relations: The art and science of reaching your target audience with key messages through the news media. This public relations practice area focuses on interfacing with the news media, both proactively (through news releases and other tools) and reactively (providing information and facilitating interview requests).

Observational research: Collecting information through watching how people interact with each other and with products.

Opinion research: The collection of stakeholders' opinions and attitudes using research techniques.

Qualitative research: A means of collecting information that uses conversations and interactions as the main data collection tool. This type of research generally asks questions that create a flow of dialogue rather than closed-ended questions. It is not representative of the whole population but a great tool to understand how a group of people may feel about your product or company.

Quantitative research: Structured research that provides a statistically representative portrayal of a stakeholder audience.

RACE formula: John E. Marston's four-step process consisting of research, analysis, communication, and evaluation. RACE is a popular model for the PR process that is recognized by the Canadian Public Relations Society and the International Association of Business Communicators.

Return on investment (ROI): The benefit a marketing or public relations professional receives based on the marketing or PR effort that he or she has created.

Secondary research: The use of previously published materials as a form of data collection.

Stakeholder: Any individual, corporation, or entity that you wish to impact with your marketing or public relations campaigns.

FOR REVIEW AND DISCUSSION

1. How might you bias results in an observational study? List as many ways as possible. For each of the possible ways, what could a good researcher do to lessen the effect of the bias?
2. If you only had access to Twitter or some other publicly accessible form of social media, how could this social media tool be used to evaluate what people think of a new product? In what way is this type of research limiting?
3. How would social media have to change for it to be an accurate research tool that predicts consumer behaviour?

4. Explain the differences between qualitative and quantitative research. Is one better than the other? Defend your answer.
5. What are the advantages and disadvantages of using focus groups? Surveys? Explain your answers.

ACTIVITIES

1. Pick a product and collect copies of TV, print, and online ads. Look at how the product is portrayed in each of these areas and see if there is consistency in the messaging. How do you think research was used to develop each of these ads and the overall messages about the product?
2. Qualitative research is about asking questions in a way that solicits a conversation. Write a series of questions that ask only for a yes/no response. Then, rewrite the questions in a way that allows the person answering the question to add to his or her answer. For example, instead of asking, "Do you like eating potato chips for a snack?" try asking, "What do you think about potato chips as a snack food?" Ask the questions of a few people. Assess which type of question gives you more information.
3. Imagine you are designing a campaign for a new candy product. What research methods could be used at various points in the campaign? Include in your discussion the type of research that would be most appropriate at product design, product launch, during the campaign, and post-campaign. What would each piece of research tell you, and how could you use the information for the next candy product to be designed and launched?

FURTHER READING

Altheide, David L. *Qualitative Media Analysis.* New Delhi, IN: Sage Publications, 1996.

Berger, Arthur Asa. *Media Analysis Techniques.* New Delhi, IN: Sage Publications, 2005.

Global Alliance, ICCO, Institute for Public Relations, Public Relations Society of America, and AMEC U.S. and Agency Leaders Chapter. "Barcelona Declaration of Measurement Principles." Presented at the 2nd European Summit on Management. Final version July 19, 2010. http://amecorg.com/wp-content/uploads/2012/06/Barcelona_Principles.pdf.

Krueger, R.A. *Focus Groups: A Practical Guide for Applied Research.* Newbury Park, CA: Sage Publications, 2009.

Jim Macnamara, official website: www.jimmacnamara.com

Macnamara, Jim. *Jim Macnamara's Public Relations Handbook*. 5th ed. Sydney: Archipelago Press, 2005.

News Group International. *The Measurement Standard: The Newsletter of Public Relations and Social Media Measurement*. http://kdpaine.blogs.com/themeasurementstandard/.

Stacks, Don W. *Primer of Public Relations Research*. New York: Guilford Press, 2010.

NOTES

1. Paco Underhill, *Why We Buy: The Science of Shopping* (New York: Simon and Shuster, 2008).

2. Angela Jeffrey, David Michaelson, and Don W. Stacks, "Exploring the Link between Volume of Media Coverage and Business Outcomes," White Paper published by the Institute for Public Relations, Gainesville, FL, November 2006, 4–5.

3. Ibid., 4.

4. Ibid.

5. Ibid., 5.

6. Ibid.

7. Carolyne Van Der Meer, "Understanding Media Analysis," *Communication World*, May–June 2005, 34.

8. Ibid.

9. Jeffrey, Michaelson, and Stacks, "Exploring the Link," 5.

10. Van Der Meer, "Understanding Media Analysis," 35.

11. Ibid.

12. Information in this section is based on Leger's "Quebec Differences 101" (PowerPoint presentation, 2013) as well as internal information and research Leger conducted in 2013. Further research on Quebec consumer behaviour is forthcoming from Leger. All information is used with permission.

13. Michel Dumas, email to William Carney, April 29, 2013.

Ange Frymire Fleming

9

The Communications Plan

LEARNING OBJECTIVES

After reading this chapter, you will be able to

- explain the need to develop a communications plan for communications and marketing campaigns;
- describe the role that research, analysis, communication, and evaluation (RACE) can play in developing a communications plan;
- describe the components of a communications plan; and
- explain how communications plans can fail.

INTRODUCTION

The communications plan is the guide to an organization's internal and external communications needs. It forms the blueprint that guides communications and marketing campaigns, initiatives, special projects, and annual planning. (For the purposes of brevity, further references will use "campaign" to mean any campaign, project, or initiative.) As well, a communications plan leads the organization through the implementation and evaluation stages of the campaign, which can involve multiple departments. The plan should identify audiences, messages, strategies, tactics, activities, resources, time frames, and evaluation metrics to be incorporated into each campaign. These are determined by thorough analysis of research, which is critical to establishing foolproof strategies.

The plan is a living document that is updated as needed. Aligned with corporate or campaign objectives, it guides departments through the principles of the communications process (see Figures 5.1, 5.2, 5.3 in Chapter 5). In this communications process, success occurs when the receiver interprets (decodes) the message exactly as the sender had intended it. By addressing these steps of communications, the communicator can convey the right message to the right audience through the right channel at the right time.[1] (See Chapter 5 for more about communications models and theories.)

The organizational hierarchy will dictate whose department is responsible for developing the communications plan. The plan can also be created by many departments, including communications and marketing. In some cases, head office or corporate staff will write the plan. Some plans will also incorporate sponsorship action items, such as finalizing sponsorship contracts, obtaining logos and other sponsor-driven collateral materials (e.g., posters, brochures, handouts, postcards, etc.), signage, and other materials that may be required for wrap-up reports, month-end reports, and the like. It is important for all departments to establish and maintain communications with each other to ensure that planning requirements are not duplicated or omitted.

The benefits of written communications plans include

- establishing priorities;
- creating organized, appropriate messages for all audience levels;
- guiding all stakeholders in managing responsibilities, creating and implementing key messages, and executing oral/written communications;
- providing day-to-day focused activities;
- building stronger control over barriers and gaps that can hinder success;
- informing employees and executive staff on their responsibilities, start times, deadlines, and day-to-day needs;
- responding proactively to last-minute changes and reactive requests from management, staff, sponsors, and primary stakeholders;
- assisting with smoother implementation of campaign elements;
- determining strengths and weaknesses of current campaigns to improve future campaigns; and

- evaluating the effect of all communications (actions, written, spoken, electronic) upon audiences.[2]

THE ROLE OF RACE

Preparing communications plans requires organizational knowledge, comprehensive research, accurate audience analysis, and precision with the written word. The RACE model, used by many agencies and PR practitioners, plays a significant role in the development of communications plans.[3]

As you read in Chapter 5, RACE focuses communications through rigorous application of

- **Research** that combines fact-finding and feedback from primary and secondary data collection;
- **Analysis** of planning and programming to develop high-level, achievable strategies and develop budgets;
- **Communication** and action through tactical implementation, production, and execution; and
- **Evaluation** using metrics that determine elemental successes, such as achieving goals and objectives, audience acceptance, media coverage, sales, third-party services, and meeting budget requirements.[4]

Some organizations prefer well thought-out plans that are succinct and shorter. Others produce larger documents that contain vast amounts of research information to support analysis.[5] Both styles should include action plans that identify week-by-week or day-to-day duties that assist the organization (e.g., budgeting, follow-up) or that support the communications strategy (e.g., booking speakers, event logistics).

COMPONENTS OF COMMUNICATIONS PLANS

The following sections describe the components of a typical communications plan. These components are listed in the provided template. This template contains all possible categories that are found in communications plans used in agencies, corporations, sports organizations, retail businesses, or not-for-profit organizations. Explanations of each section follow the template.

See Appendix A for an example of a communications plan by Arts Umbrella, a not-for-profit organization based in Vancouver, BC. Appendix A also has a template for a communications plan for government.

TEMPLATE: COMMUNICATIONS PLAN FOR AGENCIES

Front Pieces:
- Title Page
- Table of Contents
- Executive Summary (where applicable)

Communications Plan Sections:
- Introduction
- Background
- Approval Protocols (optional)
- Goals
- Objectives
- Product or Service Description (optional)
- Research Tools (optional)
- Situation Analysis
  - Environmental Scan (political, technical, economic, social, environmental, ethical)
  - SWOT Analysis (can be a table rather than subsections)
    - Strengths (Internal)
    - Weaknesses (Internal)
    - Opportunities (External)
    - Threats (External)
- Risks Summary (extended from SWOT Analysis)
- Audience Analysis
  - Primary Stakeholders
  - Secondary (optional)
  - Tertiary (optional)
- Key Messages
  - Overarching
  - Issue-specific (where applicable)
    - Primary (optional)
    - Secondary (optional)
  - Audience-specific (where applicable)
    - Primary (optional)
    - Secondary (optional)

Strategies

Tactics Summary

Action Plan

Budget

Evaluation

> Tools (optional)
>
> Metrics
>
> Recommendations

End Pieces/Appendices:

Research Data (optional and varied)

Collateral Material (optional)

Previous Budget (optional)

Other Appendices (optional and varied)

Introduction

The Introduction provides a brief synopsis of the campaign, organization, or purpose.

Background

This section provides an overview of facts, statistics, and historical data accumulated from current knowledge and/or research. It provides additional context essential to understanding the organizational culture.

Approval Protocols

All parties who are included in the approval process are identified in this section. Their sign-offs will be required for news releases, letters to high-ranking officials, community engagement strategies, and the like. Some plans ask for sign-off in the document itself, which will have a table identifying each person's name, position, signature, and signing date.

Goals

Goals are broader, longer-term indicators that define corporate direction. What are the organizational and communications goals of the initiative? Are there changes in opinion, behaviour, or product sales that need to be achieved? What must be accomplished for the plan to succeed?

Figure 9.1 SMART Objectives

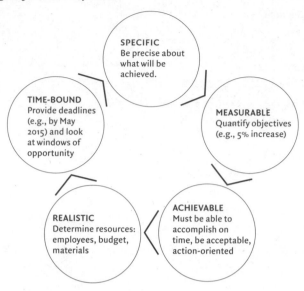

Objectives

The communications objectives should be measurable, precise statements that clearly outline the expected outcomes of the campaign. The Integrated Marketing Communications (IMC) model often uses the SMART acronym to establish critical deliverables (specific, measurable, achievable, realistic, and time-bound).[6] Figure 9.1 outlines SMART objectives. Using these objectives in the communications plan helps to ensure successful execution and implementation.

Specific metrics should be included in each objective to measure the level of success attained for each one. Such metrics can include

- market-share objectives to achieve within a certain time frame;
- increase of profit (such as percentage, dollars, units sold);
- growth in the business for a specific period (such as sales, customers);
- increase in brand awareness over an indicated period of time; and
- maintenance of the plan, which is a survival objective during difficult financial times.

For example, a SMART objective for a computer firm may be to achieve a 5 per cent market share over an eight-month period.

Objectives, which play a crucial role when determining strategic planning, are developed carefully. They should inform and educate a specific audience about

- decisions regarding projects, services, plans;
- directions and policy, either existing or proposed;
- methods, processes, and techniques;
- the impact of changes on the target audience; and
- the value and necessity of the project.

They must build and maintain support for a given direction by determining the level of support needed from the organization and from external stakeholders. Objectives should also manage resistance to change by assessing the

- willingness or ability to change;
- risks to implementing change; and
- disruptive factors, such as angry employees, managers not on board, lower return on investment (ROI), and customer challenges.

Product or Service Description

A description is included that identifies the product(s) or services supplied by the organization. Although this section does not appear in all communications plans, it is important to include it when dealing with umbrella organizations that oversee a number of not-for-profits, especially when those agencies provide different services. It can also be helpful for a committee reporting to more than one organization.

Research Tools

Research tools are divided into primary or secondary categories. As you learned in Chapter 8, primary research is data that is conducted for the first time, whereas secondary research is data that already exists or has been published. Research can also be formal or informal as well as quantitative or qualitative.

Many communications plans do not list research tools. The advantage of listing them is to ensure that they are integrated into the action plan where appropriate. For example, if audience behaviours are to be measured, surveys or other appropriate tools will need to be created and distributed strategically to measure the levels of change against the first survey. The first survey acts as a baseline for comparing results of future surveys and other tools.

Figure 9.2 Situation Analysis

Internal Areas to Analyze	External Areas to Analyze
E-news, newsletters	Competition
Technology readiness and needs	Economy
URL content, dark site preparation and usage (see Chapter 16 for more about dark sites)	Political situations with municipal, regional, provincial, federal, and First Nations governments, legislation (current and proposed)
Budgets, timelines, management models (top-down or bottom-up)	Industry trends
Manuals, memos, email directives	Social issues
Media protocols for management and staff	Public-at-large opinions and trends
Employee relations and ownership	Technological considerations
Labour issues	Environmental concerns
Meetings (face-to-face, webinars, video conferencing, etc.)	Industry and societal best- and next-practices recommendations

Situation Analysis

A situation analysis is an environmental scan that contains information about the organization's internal and external environment. A number of factors can be dissected, including target audience data, stakeholder beliefs, assumptions, attitudes, behaviours, and issues faced by the organization or industry. The intention is to address constraints and take advantage of opportunities that will increase the organization's success, growth, awareness, and ROI.

This section should analyze the situation that currently exists, both internally (inside the organization) and externally (all factors and issues outside of the organization). Some plans include a SWOT analysis as one of the components in a situation analysis. SWOT means strengths (internal), weaknesses (internal), opportunities (external), and threats (external). A critical note in conducting a SWOT analysis is finding strategies that turn the weaknesses into strengths and the threats into opportunities. If a turnaround is not possible, strategies can then be developed to minimize negative fallout from the weaknesses and threats. See Figure 9.2 for internal and external areas to focus on in a situation analysis.

The amount of time spent on internal and external analysis, which is collated from the research, will depend on the campaign's objectives, available time, issues, previous similar campaigns, management objectives, resources, previous media coverage, employee capacity, manpower availability, budgets, and desired outcomes.

Risks Summary

A risks analysis assesses both external and internal dangers. The intention is to understand, monitor, minimize, and control potential dangers on resources and the campaign in order to maximize the opportunities. Examples of risks include

- negative media coverage;
- lawsuits;
- loss of sponsors;
- decrease in sales;
- loss of goodwill;
- store closures/layoffs;
- reduced research and development opportunities;
- slashed budgets;
- salary or wage cuts;
- downsizing;
- high staff turnover; and
- bankruptcy.

Risks are usually found in the SWOT analysis. For plans that require risk as a stand-alone component, this section will summarize the critical risks found in the research stage. In some cases, plans will provide additional analysis or background information, depending on the severity and probability of the risk. Strategies will then be created to mitigate or reduce risks. Tactics to support those risk management strategies will be included in the action plan.

Audience Analysis

This section is so critical to developing strategies that both Canadian Public Relations Society (CPRS) and the Public Relations Society of America (PRSA) insist on strict audience analysis for accreditation. In-depth information on audience lifestyles, education, age, and attitudes better prepares the practitioner to develop strategies that guarantee success.

If audience analysis is weak, inaccurate, or rushed, there is a real possibility that the objectives cannot be accomplished. Incomplete audience analysis also can result in increased risk management, dilution of the brand, inability or refusal to understand or accept the key messages and, ultimately, failure of the campaign or plan.

Audience analysis can be intimidating, as there are so many options to look at. Stakeholders can include proponents, opponents, the uncommitted, those who don't know, don't care, or are still undecided.

It is wise to break down audiences into primary (key people and organizations you must communicate with) and secondary (less important audiences who may influence the organization or primary audiences), especially when dealing with crisis or issues management. A helpful tip is to identify their demographics, psychographics, and geographics, which will help to craft more targeted, focused, and persuasive messages. Demographics include physical traits such as age, gender, race/ethnic origin, income, education, occupation, social class, marital status, and dependents. Psychographics identify lifestyle preferences (how they spend their time), activities, personality, interests, and values and opinions. In some cases, behavioural attitudes are also included. Geographics identify preferences and distinctions in sample or total populations. Differences include rural versus urban, one province versus another (such as British Columbia versus Ontario), or neighbourhoods within a city. These regional neighbourhoods almost always have marked differences in political views, discretionary income, interest level in urban affairs, educational differences/choices, and shopping. Strong analysis of the applicable geographical regions can help uncover critical aspects that can influence or damage the campaign. Stakeholder analysis can contain numerous categories, such as

- boards of trade, chambers of commerce;
- business improvement associations (BIAs), merchant associations, industry associations (supportive and adversarial);
- business owners, employees, customers, investors;
- competition, community action groups, service clubs (e.g., Kinsmen, Rotary);
- educators, such as school boards, trustees, superintendents, principals, teachers, parent-teacher groups, professors and instructors (especially those who contribute to academic journals, those in communications, and those who speak to the media);
- government, police officials;
- minority group leaders, special-interest groups, unions;
- traditional media (print editors, key reporters, radio and TV news directors, key reporters, relevant columnists, freelancers, broadcasters, program producers, weather reporters); and
- social media (bloggers, thought leaders, citizen/netizen journalists).

Stakeholder analysis should answer the following questions:

- What do the stakeholders know about this issue/organization/event?
- What are their needs and wants?
- Are they proponents or opponents?
- What factors influence them (demographics, geographics, psychographics)?
- How and why will they react to your messaging?
- What are their sources of information (traditional media, social media, e-news, newsletters, etc.)?

For an example of audience analysis, see the Sidney Health Fair in Appendix A.

Key Messages

Key messages are primary points that must be communicated to targeted audiences. They are clear, succinct main statements about the organization, event, situation, or issue that are used consistently in the communications plan. These core messages educate, advocate, brand, enforce, promote, or explain the salient aspects of a campaign. The savvy communicator will create key messages that employ distinct language and grade levels for each segmented audience.

There are advantages—and dangers—in creating and using key messages. One is repetition. Audiences must clearly identify with, understand, and accept the messages. If, however, the receiver feels overexposed to the same wording or talking points, he or she may dismiss, block out, or disbelieve the message, the organization, or both.

Another advantage—and danger—is answering questions. Practitioners should expect to communicate orally to employees, media, government inquiries, neighbourhood residents, and the business community. This communication can occur through a number of channels, such as meetings, telephone conversations, emails, social media dialogues, news conferences, guest presentations, and video conferencing, many of which include live question-and-answer periods. Skilled usage of key messages can solidify an organization's position and help stakeholders to understand clearly the situation and context of an event or issue.

However, there is also a risk of sounding repetitive in written and oral one-way or two-way communications. When a person answers questions only by using key messages in his or her answers, some receivers sense that the person is not telling the truth, avoiding the question, or not answering directly. A sense

Figure 9.3 CAPS² Model

Acronym	Explanation
Concise and Credible	Avoid jargon and acronyms. Provide examples, facts and statistics to back up the message. Use the KISS principle of "keep it simple and straightforward."
Audience and Active	Write to the tailored audience using an active voice wherever possible.
Positive and Proactive	Tell what one can do, not what one cannot do.
Short and Specific	Write it in one memorable sentence of 10 to 20 words or 10 to 20 seconds. Address a particular challenge so that the audience can identify with the main points.

of mistrust and disbelief can develop. As a result, the key message delivery can fail because the audience did not understand the communication as the sender had intended it.

Developing key messages that deliver impact and credibility takes practice. When creating them, aim for crisp, precise statements. Use the acronym CAPS² (pronounced "CAPS squared") to help create engaging, memorable messaging; see Figure 9.3.

Some campaigns have a maximum of four messages. Others have multiple messages, depending on the complexity of the issues, the receptiveness of the audiences, and the level of knowledge regarding the subject material. In some cases, communicators create three to eight messages and then wordsmith each one for segmented audiences.

Questions should be asked, such as

- What does the audience already know about this issue/event/organization?
- What does it need to know?
- What doesn't it want to know? (often helpful in creating messages for crisis planning)
- How will it benefit from knowing this information?
- What are the principal facts and issues that need to be communicated?
- Will there be primary and secondary messages?

Use these steps to create messages:

1. Identify the various issues that need to be communicated.
2. List all facts, statistics, and figures that are positive and make the organization into a champion. (e.g., More than 85 per cent of students are hired within one month of graduation.)
3. Create a response for each issue that reflects your organization's mission, value statements, and code of ethics. (Hint: Sometimes it also is important to identify what is not to be said for each issue, which helps to create a clearer, more relevant message addressing the issue at hand.)
4. Write all the aspects of the key message, no matter how long it is, and then break it down to a short, concise, clear statement. Sometimes this strategy will produce two or three key messages when you keep each sentence to one subject.
5. Repeatedly ask "why" and "how" to get to the core messages.
6. Use everyday language. Substitute industry lingo for clear language that will be understood by all. Ensure the messages are understandable, uncomplicated, jargon-free, and simple to grasp. Write at a grade 8 to 10 level to ensure it is understood immediately.

The key messages below were two of dozens created for the Sidney Health Fair, owned by the Sidney Integrated Wellness Community Society (SIWCS). SIWCS's mission is to cultivate opportunities that foster the development of relationships between all health-related fields.

- The fair provides an opportunity for the public to learn about alternative and mainstream choices to maintain health and wellness.
- By reducing admission to $5 for adults, the health fair can educate the community on the changes and evolution of personal health and wellness choices.

INTERVIEW: DANIELLE CÔTÉ

Danielle Côté co-owns BKT Health Promotion and Communications, which is located in Ottawa, Ontario. A bilingual communications practitioner with 20 years of experience in the health sector, she provides strategic communication advice and project management services to a variety of clients. She is an accredited expert in public relations, community relations, and media relations who has developed, implemented, and evaluated numerous comprehensive health communication campaigns and has worked with the Health Communication Unit at the University of Toronto, building capacity among francophone Ontarians. She has worked with clients such as the Canadian Cardiovascular Society, the Heart and Stroke Foundation of Canada, the Canadian Nurses Association, and the Canadian Produce Marketing Association. Ms. Côté's interview provides advice on developing effective communications plans. What follows is a summary of her responses to interview questions.

Communications plans written for not-for-profit organizations are concise and focus on supporting business objectives. They are used as a guide and include a clear action plan.

Assets of developing a strong communications plan include

- buy-in from the organization and support for a plan to be written and implemented;
- solid research of the organization, its objectives, and its audiences;
- a thorough audit;
- input from all organization departments;s
- measurable objectives to make sure the plan is on the right track and can be adjusted over time; and
- resources to implement the plan's key activities and strategies.

Barriers to developing a strong communications plan include

- lack of support for a plan;
- lack of organizational data;
- lack of resources;
- a plan that no one buys into or doesn't understand;
- lack of buy-in from senior management; and
- lack of measurable objectives to determine if you are successful or not.

Côté recommends as the following as the first critical steps in creating a plan:

1. Look at best practices in other strong communications plans to get a sense of what they include. If you are a novice writer who

has not written many plans, consult experts and review excellent examples of communications plans from recognized sources.

2. Have a thorough understanding of your organization's own business plan.

3. Outline what your process will be to create the plan and a timeline so that those you consult understand what you are trying to achieve.

Challenges that can negatively impact the success of a communications plan include the following:

- The writer takes too much time necessary to complete it.
- There is a lack of understanding from senior management or from the client on the role of a communications plan and the value it brings to the organization.
- Plans are not tied to business objectives.
- Plans lack evaluation metrics to determine success and failure attributes.
- The written plan is not followed up or used as a regular guide by practitioners.

Strategies

This critical section of the communications plan guides the organization on how to achieve the campaign's objectives. A strong communications strategy will define substantive and operational priorities that reflect the organization's culture. Strategies can include a vast range of possibilities, such as programs, public education, positioning, stakeholder or community outreach, and advocacy.

Strategic thinking enables the organization to be proactive in using resources that position the campaign positively with proponents. It can also create shared opportunities with supporting businesses and other advocates, resulting in overarching support from primary and secondary audiences.

There can be multiple strategies presented, depending on the organization, issues, problems, events, and barriers. Some practitioners develop themes with linked messages and tactics in order to develop more co-ordinated results-based campaigns.

Tactics Summary

The tactics section is sometimes considered the "guts" of the communications plan because it provides an action plan that dictates who will do what when. Of

Figure 9.4 Action Plan, Sample 1

Start	Deadline	Action	Lead person	Notes
Sept. 5	Mar. 15	Confirm partnership and financial contribution with Northern Lights	AF	Agreed to participate for $X,XXX investment. Invoice in Oct. XX.
Oct. 1	Feb. 28	Develop awards criteria	AF	Liaise with MB and use research collected last year on awards in North America.
Oct. 1	Feb. 28	Finalize name of award	AF MB	Completed June 20XX, after discussions with NJ June 25 and MB June 27.
Oct. 1	Mar. 15	Determine date of event	AF	Christmas parties for each chapter. Market each as gala or awards dinner or presentation, rather than Xmas party.
Nov. 1	Feb. 28	Develop judging criteria	AF MB	Use research collected last year on awards in North America. BR assisting.

note should be baseline measurements and milestones. John Barry (formerly of BC Assessment Authority) describes tactics as a "multi-pronged tactical approach that involves using several kinds of communications tools."[7]

Action Plan

Tactics are placed into an action plan, which acts as a day-by-day or week-by-week planner of the various duties that must be completed.

Multiple choices exist to create the action plan. See Figures 9.4 and 9.5 for samples. This format shows all tactics in chronological order. The Notes column in Figure 9.4 can be used to identify information needed to begin the tactic or to summarize results once that tactic has been completed.

In the second sample action plan (Figure 9.5), each tactic lists the communications tools to be developed.

Determining which tactics to include requires a solid knowledge of event planning, administrative needs, organizational objectives, and excellence in scheduling and project delivery. It is best to list all activities that will occur during the campaign, such as preparing mailing lists, sending out invitations, creating media kits, writing sponsorship proposals, arranging licensing, buying supplies, and leasing equipment. Many event planners and agencies work backwards from the final day of the campaign to determine what needs to happen when; this type of action plan is called a workback.

Ensure that the evaluation tools designed to measure the campaign's success are also integrated into the action plan. As discussed during the research stage, baseline surveys may be required in campaigns that act as a measuring

Figure 9.5 Action Plan, Sample 2

Tactic	Audience	Delivery date	Responsibility
Internal communications e.g., e-news article	Organization's staff	Nov. 15	Jane Smith
Stakeholder information and education e.g., PowerPoint presentation	Local government, managers, associations	Nov. 28	Jane Smith John Doe Sue Black
Government relations e.g., Ministerial briefing	Minister Jones	Nov. 1	John Doe
Public information and education e.g., fact sheet posted to organization's website	Public	Nov. 15	Sue Black
Media relations e.g., news release	Media/public	Nov. 15	Sue Black
Issues management e.g., briefing note, issue note	Ministry, organization's executive	Nov. 28	Jim Brown

guide to determine changes in opinions, attitudes, and behaviours. For long-term plans, checkpoints should be created at regular intervals to monitor progress and aid adjustments.

Budget

The budget is yet another important component of the communications plan. Monitoring and keeping on budget will be a critical success factor throughout the entire campaign. In many cases, quotations will need to be obtained during the analysis and planning stage to ensure that the strategies and tactics are affordable. For communications consultants, budget becomes a risk factor for reputation and for contracts; some consultants and agencies can be held liable for budget overruns.

When designing budgets, look for opportunities to use the organization's current internal resources to reduce costs, especially when the budget is tight and there is little or no "wiggle room" for shortfalls.

Evaluation

Evaluation applies best practices to the communications plan. Evaluation should have three components:

- **Planning:** Evaluation tools and techniques (how they will be administered) must be determined in the analysis and planning stage so that appropriate tools are built into the action plan for measuring and evaluating what is working and what needs adjusting.

- **Implementation:** Metrics must be collected during implementation that show successes, strengths, weaknesses, gaps, barriers that can stop success and negative responses. By evaluating success on a constant basis, stopgap measures can be introduced when the intended communications outcomes are showing distress or are in danger of being reached.
- **Post-campaign:** Analyze all metrics and evaluation results to determine what worked, what did not, and areas where there were no changes when change had been anticipated.

Unfortunately, evaluation is often one of the areas that is omitted, neglected, or rushed through by practitioners. The reasons are varied and can include

- lack of time to finish that portion of the campaign because of a host of other responsibilities or new campaigns that must be managed;
- failure to include a critical evaluation tool in the action plan;
- sloppy or late implementation of the evaluation tool;
- misinterpretation of how the tool will assist in objective evaluation;
- organizational management's reluctance or inability to give appropriate budget or time to the evaluation process; and
- inappropriate, misleading, or poor criteria to measure outcomes.

Evaluation results can be quantitative (numerical or statistical data for comparative purposes), such as the number of customer complaints, number of media stories, or the number of people who attended a town hall meeting. Measures can also be qualitative (understand reasons that govern human behaviour, compiled from primary sources such as audits, focus groups, or surveys), such as the tone, context, and framing of the discussions by the neighbours at the meeting.

Some plans provide sections in which practitioners can record recommendations throughout the campaign. This is particularly helpful during campaigns or initiatives that span several months. In many cases, this kind of observation allows revision of the strategies or tactics if the plan is not going well. Interim reporting can include

- daily, weekly, or monthly reports on work in progress;
- formalized department reports for presentations;

- periodic briefings for department meetings, chief staff executives, department heads; or clients; and
- year-end summary for the annual report.

VULNERABILITIES OF COMMUNICATIONS PLANS

The list below—used by Fortune 500 firms and found in the CPRS Accreditation Handbook—lists recommended steps to developing strategies and solving problems, using the RACE model once again:

- **Research/Analysis:** Identify the issues and contributing factors.
- **Analysis/Planning:** Choose the top critical factors, identify top possible solutions.
- **Communication:** Apply solutions through the campaign or sprogram.
- **Evaluation:** Evaluate the campaign using appropriate metrics.

The effectiveness of communications plans is based on proven corporate strategy used by leading businesses, retailers, and not-for-profits. It is a top-down model that begins with the organization's goals and integrates them with the objectives of the communications plan, as illustrated in Figure 9.6.[8]

This section will dissect the vulnerabilities that communications plans are subject to, using the RACE model.

Figure 9.6: Top-down Planning Model

Organizational Goals

Campaign Objectives

Strategies

Tactics

Research

Identifying risks with the organization and the environment is the cornerstone of strategy development. Critical success factors must be built into the research strategy. The practitioner should possess a strong understanding of the organization, its brand, and how others perceive the brand through ongoing primary and secondary research.[9]

The communicator must ensure that integrity and objectivity are maintained throughout, regardless of beliefs, suspicions, affirmations, and current behaviours of the public or organization. Management, employees, and external stakeholders rely on the communicator's suggestions, counsel, and strategies because they assume that the communicator has done her homework, weighed the consequences of all strategies, and presented the best possible plan to guarantee success.[10]

Research is one of the starting points in preparing the communications plan. The practitioner cannot provide reliable analyses and recommended strategies until he or she has completed research that is current, accurate, and relevant. When research data seems incomplete, appears to be agenda-driven, indicates poor quality control, uses inappropriate sample populations, or does not provide sources or dates of information collected, the astute practitioner will find more reliable, objective sources. Faulty research can mar success because it is often

- biased (by the communications planner, the organization or the research itself);
- difficult to measure return on investment (ROI);
- inaccurate, dated, or wrong;
- incomplete (situation analysis is too brief or not in-depth);
- inadequate (poor sample population sizes or not enough data);
- inappropriate (poor audience selection or research sources);
- rushed (critical factors overlooked, not included or only surface research);
- time-consuming; and
- unreliable (sources not credible, inappropriate, unknown, not "proven," or not subject-matter experts).[11]

Even with thorough research, it is important to note that the contents of the plan must be based on the results of the analysis and planning stage rather than a template model that does not factor in critical research findings.

Analysis and Planning

Identifying problems and opportunities is a core management principle that produces solutions. However, effective analysis and planning is only as good as the research compiled in stage one of RACE. When the breadth and depth of research is faulty, the analysis of the problem or issue will be weak. This impairs the accuracy of risk analysis, producing further problems, such as layoffs, strikes, bankruptcy, or legal action. As a result, integrity is a salient characteristic of the PR professional, who must be non-biased and objective.

Developing trustworthy analysis and planning takes time. For the beginning practitioner, maintaining objectivity through high-level analysis is sometimes overwhelming and can be regarded as a burden rather than a necessity. One may find it easy to scrutinize the strengths. However, accurately assessing the weaknesses and threats requires complete honesty and thoroughness. Some organizations are adverse to hearing and digesting this type of "bad news" in strategic planning. Failure to articulate all weaknesses and threats can endanger the plan, its budget, the department and the organization, as well as its customers, its goodwill, and its supporters (sponsors, government liaisons, regulators, etc.).

There is often fuzziness around developing goals, objectives, strategies, and tactics, so ensure that the objectives align with the goals of the organization. Consider each as parts of a whole that must work in unison to achieve success.

Goals are broad, general intangible intentions. Objectives are precise, concrete, tangible, or shorter-term measureable outcomes that accomplish the goals. For example:

Organization:	The Riverboat Festival Society
Goal:	To develop an annual event that fosters goodwill, champions citizenry, and increases summer visitors to the city.
Objective #1:	To obtain community support for the 1st Annual Riverboat Festival.
Objective #2:	To enlist the support of two city councillors.
Objective #3:	To obtain $50,000 (in-kind or cash donations) from businesses or To obtain four new local sponsors.
Objective #4:	To achieve attendance of 500 people in Year 1.

Strategies are broad statements or "ideas" that conceptualize how specific objectives will be achieved. Many organizations find it challenging to create well-formulated strategies that can be successfully executed. According to a study published by the online thought leader Global Village (a resource organization that specializes in business practices and transformational leadership), less than 5 per cent of employees understand their organization's strategy.[12] Only 9 per cent of organizations claim success in executing initiatives or delivering strategic results.[13] As a result, care must be taken in the analysis and planning stage to ensure clarity, concision, precision, and high-level thought processes that follow from research. They can be multi-layered, showing how objectives can be reached through a number of approaches, such as changing people's opinions, swaying attitudes, or creating allies to facilitate change.

Tactics are specific actions that enable strategies to succeed and are incorporated into a timeline called an action plan (see the description of "Tactics Summary" and "Action Plan" earlier in this chapter). They are task-driven and should be assigned to individuals or teams to undertake, lead, or complete that tactic. The example below demonstrates the strategies and tactics used for Objective #2 for the Riverboat Festival Society:

Organization:	The Riverboat Festival Society
Goal:	To develop an annual event that fosters goodwill, champions citizenry, and increases summer visitors to the city.
Objective #2:	To enlist the support of two city councillors.
Strategy #1:	To develop an ongoing, permanent, proactive relationship between the society's board of directors and city councillors.
Tactic #1:	Assign each director to a city councillor by matching portfolios, interests, and connections.
Tactic #2:	Directors to contact their assigned city councillor by Month 2 to discuss relevant portfolio issues (parking, licensing, vendors, policing, exhibitors, etc.)
Tactic #3:	Directors to track councillors' websites, blogs, comments during council meetings, public appearances; report on developments and fallbacks at each society board meeting.
Tactic #4:	Invitations to all society events for the year to be issued to each councillor, with follow-up from society staff.
Tactic #5:	Finalize advertising needs for radio, TV, print, and online. (Note: This tactic could be broken down further to determine copy deadline dates, ad content, costs for each media outlet, ad frequency, media reach, etc.)

Tactics must be realistic, achievable, and included in the action plan.

Budgeting is also part of the analysis and planning stage. After determining strategies and accompanying tactics, the budget should be created to match departmental spending allotments.[14] This requires projecting costs for all expenses, such as design, printing, outsourced specialists, licensing, etc. (see

"Action Plan" earlier in this chapter). Budget preparation includes obtaining timely quotes on costs of products or services, as well as comparing this year's anticipated revenues and expenses to past years' budgets. If the budget is over the allocated amount for that campaign, the practitioner must determine what cutbacks are needed.

Many organizations create budgets that are unaffordable and unrealistic, resulting in under-resourcing or cost overruns, with severe consequences. If budget allocations cannot support the firm's financial objectives, the practitioner must re-strategize or modify expectations to ensure success.

When building the plan, ask these sets of questions to reduce barriers and gaps:

- What are the organization's goals and the campaign's SMART objectives?
- What length of time is required to accomplish those objectives? Are there multiple phases to the campaign?
- What strategies will support each short-term, mid-term, and long-term objective?
- What tactics are needed to achieve those strategies?
- Are there tactics not attached to any strategies and objectives?
- What can compromise campaign success?[15]

Communication

Effective communication needs an action plan that lists all tactics basis. The action plan is a critical infrastructure timeline that identifies tasks, leads, and deadlines.

For instance, when organizing a community event, awareness tactics need to be executed strategically: the practitioner must know the what, when, and why well in advance to meet attendance targets or obtain sponsorship dollars. This involves numerous requirements, including arranging food vendors, obtaining street performers, leasing tenting needs, advising the media, arranging advertising, and inviting the public.

Some communications specialists do not use formally written plans, which is common in busy organizations. These practitioners rely on experience and communications knowledge of staff to guide the department on the day-to-day tactics. The risk factor increases exponentially, however, especially in larger, more tactic-driven campaigns. Missing deadlines can result in delayed results, postponing other tactics, or compromising the success of the campaign.

Evaluation

This is another area that is often overlooked or put on "the back burner" due to time constraints, a lack of resources or shifting priorities. Measurement tools are critical for this stage and include a plethora of choices, such as

- surveys (telephone, face-to-face, Internet, drop-off) and focus group results that measure attitudinal or behavioural changes;
- Delphi panels, communication audits, readability assessments, polling, trend tracking;
- social media monitoring, traditional media monitoring, content analysis, MRP (media relations rating points) analysis, content analysis; and
- number of phone calls, number of complaints, number of goodwill letters, which should identify and measure context (proponents, opponents, neutral).

When measurement tools are not built into the tactical action plan, lost opportunities are created. Remember: success is not just determined by the volume of media coverage or by the number of people in attendance.

For example, Service Canada needed a communications agency to "find solutions to homelessness." The agency was to work with the Sustaining Communities Partnerships Committee, which represented over 170 not-for-profits in the social services sector (food banks, housing agencies, emergency shelters, crisis lines, drop-in shelters, etc.). When Vocal Point Communications was hired to determine the assets, gaps, and barriers that divided and united residents on homelessness issues, it conducted an environmental scan in eight different communities throughout British Columbia and Yukon. It recommended launching pilot projects in each city to demonstrate assets, gaps, and barriers to residents, businesses, and governments; in other words, the projects were to show what was working and where help was needed, whether financial, community, or business resource support (e.g., volunteering accounting assistance, training new employees, etc.).

The first city to launch its "demonstration project" was Kelowna. Its 2004 event—called Homelessness Awareness Week—involved tours of multiple social service agencies, a street fair, and influential guest speakers. One of the objectives was to measure behaviours and attitudes of residents. However, there was no credible, relevant research conducted prior to this event that accurately portrayed citizens' viewpoints on homelessness, other than anecdotal references, which should always be regarded as unreliable and unproven. As a result, surveys were created for the week's events. The results became the established baseline against which to compare future surveys. These types of metrics must be developed in the analysis and planning stages of the communications plan. Evaluation must be determined in advance of rolling out the campaign. Measurement tools must be designed and then administered at various intervals of the campaign, which the action plan should identify.

Kelowna's evaluation of its Homelessness Awareness Week resulted in significant results-based achievements, which included

- more accurate, credible, and objective media coverage;
- increased business partners and supporters;
- increased volunteer support from business and residents;
- proactive interest and responses from elected government officials; and
- multiple cities throughout BC organizing their own annual homelessness awareness week.

It is important to note that evaluation is not just an end-of-campaign requirement. Effective evaluation is an ongoing process to accurately measure attitudinal changes and campaign successes or failures. Many campaigns have been saved because early evaluation determined that certain strategies or tactics were not appropriate. Changes can be introduced quickly and strategically into the plan to steer it successfully towards intended outcomes.

To sum up, poor communications planning results in missed opportunities and negative audience response. Reasons for failure can include

- absence of risk-mitigation strategies;
- aiming for perfection (being too rigid, not having enough flexibility);
- capacity challenges with people, resources, knowledge, or budgets;
- changes in organizational goals;
- changes in the marketplace;
- failure to execute tactics;
- information that seems too complicated to assess;
- missed deadlines;
- no time to think through possible adverse reactions;
- omission of critical steps;
- poor research; weak audience and impact analysis;

- communications design is too complicated or complex;
- overwhelming amount of prose or complex terminology used in the communications tools; and
- too many or not enough tactics.

INTERVIEW: JOHN BARRY

The BC Assessment Authority is a provincial Crown corporation with British Columbia's provincial government, with over 640 employees in the organization and 1.9 million properties. John Barry was its manager of communications from 2002 to 2013. He has over 29 years of experience as a PR professional and oversaw all internal and external communications with the Crown. His interview with Ange Frymire Fleming, which was conducted during the research phase of this writing, demonstrates the different elements of communications protocol in government relations. Following are some excerpts taken from that interview.

Ange Frymire Fleming: *How long does it take for you to develop a communications plan?*

John Barry: I've written over 300 strategic, comprehensive plans and have become quite adept at writing them within two to three hours. It typically takes several days or weeks to finalize a plan. The time-consuming portion is working with the client back and forth with revisions.

AFF: *How are government communications plans different from the private sector and/or not-for-profit sector?*

JB: We need to be very transparent in our communications, as we serve the public and taxpayers. We must take great responsibility in developing the most cost-effective communications strategies that are in the public interest and that may be subject to Freedom of Information requests.

AFF: *How often is your organization's communications plan revised?*

JB: Each year, BC Assessment publishes a strategic plan and corporate business plan. The Communications Department publishes its own annual strategic plan. Furthermore, each individual employee in the department writes an annual Performance Development Plan (PDP), which links back to the corporate plans and performance goals.

AFF: *What are the advantages of developing a strong communications plan?*

JB: Identifying and knowing your audience is the key piece to address first. Talk to your client, face to face if possible. Things can get lost in translation if you solely rely on email going back and forth. It is prudent to always do a quick risk analysis or SWOT analysis to anticipate what issues your audience may raise. The follow-through and tracking progress are also critical to ensuring success. It's critical that all the parties track key dates and deliverables to ensure the tactics are being carried out and that people take responsibility for the actions they signed up for. Every communications plan should be evaluated at its conclusion to determine future improvements.

AFF: *What makes a plan fail?*

JB: I've seen plans be written and then filed away in a cabinet, to never see the light of day again. Sometimes, other competing priorities surface; suddenly, the plan becomes less urgent compared to its beginning point. Someone has to champion the plan to keep it alive and relevant so it doesn't get lost in the enormous amount of other information that is flowing through the organization. The biggest challenge is convincing project managers to bring Communications into the planning process at the onset. Usually, Communications is informed at a very late stage, particularly after key business decisions may have been made related to a project. Sometimes, it's even too late for our department to add any value, as there is simply no time to adequately launch any tactics that will have meaning.

AFF: *How heavily do you rely on social media in the plan?*

JB: Social media channels are more tools in our toolbox for getting information out. We've seen success with Twitter, Facebook, LinkedIn, and YouTube since 2010. Our plans will now always look at how social media could be used in the tactics, but it is not a sole communication tool.

AFF: *What measurement tools do you use for evaluating the impact of social media?*

JB: We track our YouTube "views" and have targets for increasing followers on our Twitter and Facebook sites. We also use social media for human resources recruitment; the job-interview process measures if social media was a factor.

AFF: *What other measurement tools do you use for evaluating success?*

JB: Annual customer survey results, the number of public inquiries received during a specific inquiry period, the number of formal appeals received during a specific inquiry period and volume, tone, and type of media coverage.

AFF: *What tips you have for people developing a communications plan?*

JB:

1. Develop a consistent "template" to work with, one that guides the user how to complete it.

2. Ensure you have the project manager and project sponsor (often an executive) sign off on the final plan so there is consensus on the high-level objectives.

3. Keep it as brief as possible without losing the meaning. Most people are bombarded with information on a daily basis, so a brief plan makes it easier for them to digest it.

CONCLUSION

Preparing a communications plan requires vision, thought, and savvy preparation skills. It can take a week to a month to create your first few. As you learn to think more strategically and increase your expertise, you will create higher-level plans that showcase your analytical powers. It is a constant wheel in motion, a creation that changes as the challenges and opportunities shift.

Practitioners can extend their professional reputation by creating communications plans of excellence. Understanding the cycle of communication, using the RACE formula and developing SMART objectives will ensure that all critical details are included.

In today's busy climate, many professionals do not actually write down the communications plan; instead, they rely on their many years of expertise and execute a plan in their heads. Communications expert John Barry, however, has three words of advice: "Write it down!" There is more individual and team accountability when actions are assigned to people in writing. "If it isn't recorded, it probably won't get done," Barry notes, "and what gets measured gets done."[16]

KEY TERMS

Communications plan: A guide to an organization's internal and external communications needs that directs communications and marketing campaigns, initiatives, special projects, and annual planning.

Demographics: Segmenting audiences by age, gender, race/ethnic origin, income, education, occupation, social class, marital status, and dependents.

Geographics: Audience analysis that identifies preferences and distinctions in sample or total populations. Differences include rural versus urban, one province versus another, or neighbourhoods within a city.

Key messages: Primary, succinct statements about an organization, event, situation, or issue.

Psychographics: Audience analysis that identifies lifestyle preferences (how audiences spend their time), activities, personality, interests, values, and opinions. In some cases, behavioural attitudes are also included.

RACE: A CPRS-endorsed model that describes the order that effective communications should follow: research, analysis, communication, and evaluation.

Six-step communications process: A model that describes the process of communications: sender, encoder, message, receiver, decoder, and feedback.

SMART: A marketing communications term to describe creating objectives that are specific, measurable, achievable, realistic, and time-bound.

Strategy: Broader, overarching methods that guide the organization on how to achieve the campaign's objectives that looks at programming, public education, positioning, stakeholder, or community outreach and advocacy.

SWOT: An assessment tool that identifies internal strengths and weaknesses, as well as external opportunities and threats.

Tactics: Day-by-day or week-by-week actions and duties that must be completed to achieve baseline milestones and meet objectives, which show how the strategies will be accomplished.

FOR REVIEW AND DISCUSSION

1. Label each statement as a goal, SMART objective, strategy or tactic.
    a. Obtain stakeholder feedback during the campaign.
    b. Reduce paper consumption by 5 per cent during second quarter.
    c. Reduce our ecological footprint.
    d. Increase trust from customers by 75 per cent by December 20XX.

e. Book presentation with Chamber of Commerce on email scams.

f. Provide value to customers.

g. Use blog to show authority, build trust, and obtain feedback.

h. Write blog entry on new product launch party.

2. What is the purpose of a risks summary? List some examples of internal and external risks.

3. What is audience analysis and why is it important?

4. What are the critical sections headings of a communications plan prepared by a PR agency?

5. What dangers can compromise the effectiveness of a communications plan?

ACTIVITIES

1. In groups of three, search online for two to three communications plans. Each group should discuss the differences and similarities between each and determine why the differences exist. Rate each plan in terms of audience analysis, the RACE formula, issues management, and evaluation metrics used.

2. Using your educational institution, identify the top five primary audiences that would be used in a communications plan for developing a new degree or program in communications. Rationalize your choices for each stakeholder.

3. The mayor and council of your municipality have passed legislation to improve recycling services throughout that electoral district. Give an example of the type of service (objective), then determine an effective strategy for that program and identify at least three tactics to implement that strategy.

4. Using the mini case study identified in Activity 3, determine the types of evaluation metrics that must be built into the communications plan to measure the effectiveness of the improved recycling program. Rationalize your choices for each selection.

5. In groups or as individuals, interview a PR/communications agency to determine the salient points that agency uses when creating communications plans. Present your findings to the class and discuss the various approaches, strategies, and challenges agencies encounter.

FURTHER READING

Arthur W. Page Society: www.awpagesociety.com

Brian Solis, Thought Leader: www.briansolis.com

Burnett, John, Sandra Moriarty, and E. Stephen Grant. *Introduction to Integrated Marketing Communications*. Toronto: Prentice Hall, 2001.

Canadian Business for Social Responsibility: www.cbsr.ca

Canadian Public Relations Society (CPRS): www.cprs.ca

Carney, William Wray. *In the News: The Practice of Media Relations in Canada*. 2nd ed. Edmonton: University of Alberta Press, 2008.

Center for Media and Democracy, Public Relations Case Studies: www.source-watch.org/index.php?title=Case_studies

Cutlip, Scott M., Allen H. Centre, and Glen M. Broom. *Effective Public Relations*. 9th ed. Upper Saddle River, NJ: Prentice Hall, 2006.

Czarnecki, Al. *Crisis Communications: A Primer for Teams*. iUniverse Inc., 2007.

Ethics Resource Center, Ethics Toolkit: http://www.ethics.org/page/ethics-toolkit

Giannini, Gaetan T., Jr. *Marketing Public Relations: A Marketer's Approach to Public Relations and Social Media*. Upper Saddle River, NJ: Prentice Hall, 2010.

Hanson, Les, and Darryl Hammond. *Business Communication: Contexts and Controversies*. Toronto: Pearson Canada, 2011.

Harris, Robert. "Evaluating Internet Research Sources." *Virtual Salt*. December 27, 2013. www.virtualsalt.com/evalu8it.htm.

International Association of Business Communicators (IABC): www.iabc.bc.ca

Longenecker, Justin G., Leo B. Donlevy, Victoria A.C.Calvert, Carlos W. Moore, J. William Petty, and Leslie E. Palich. *Small Business Management: Launching and Growing New Ventures*. 4th Canadian ed. Toronto: Nelson Education, 2010.

Public Relations Society of America (PRSA): www.prsa.org

Seitel, Fraser P. *The Practice of Public Relations*. 11th ed. Upper Saddle River, NJ: Prentice Hall, 2011.

Society for New Communications Research (SNCR): http://sncr.org

Wilcox, Dennis L., and Glen T. Cameron. *Public Relations: Strategies and Tactics*. Toronto: Pearson, 2010.

Word of Mouth Marketing Association (WOMMA): www.womma.org/main

NOTES

1. Six Disciplines, "Six Disciplines Strategy Execution Coaching," accessed February 6, 2012, http://www.sixdisciplines.com.

2. John Barry (former director, communications, BC Assessment Authority, Victoria, BC), interview with the author, June 2, 2011; Danielle Côté (principal, BKT Communications, Ottawa, ON) interview with the author, May 27, 2011; Susan Smith (director, programming, Arts Umbrella, Vancouver, BC), interview with the author, May 30, 2011; Morlene

Tomlinson (Executive Consulting Services Inc., Victoria, BC), interview with the author, June 6, 2011.

3. Scott M. Cutlip, Allen H. Centre, and Glen M. Broom, *Effective Public Relations*, 9th ed. (Upper Saddle River, NJ: Prentice Hall/Pearson, 2006).

4. Fraser P. Seitel, *The Practice of Public Relations*, 11th ed. (Upper Saddle River, NJ: Prentice Hall, 2011). John E. Marston is the originator of the RACE formula.

5. Côté, interview.

6. John Burnett, Sandra Moriarty, and E. Stephen Grant, *Introduction to Integrated Marketing Communications* (Toronto: Prentice Hall, 2001).

7. Barry interview with author, June 2, 2011.

8. I created Figure 9.6 based on information that I have known for years and is also contained on the CPRS website, http://www.cprs.ca.

9. Burnett, Moriarty, and Grant, *Introduction to Integrated Marketing Communications*.

10. CPRS, *The National Council of Accreditation Accreditation Handbook*, accessed March 15, 2012, http://www.cprs.ca/uploads/Accreditation/2012_Accreditation_Handbook_English.PDF, 22–28.

11. Burnett, Moriarty, and Grant, *Introduction to Integrated Marketing Communications*.

12. Sharon Weinberg, "Leading Collaborative Decision Making Processes," *Global Village Academy*, July 19, 2013, http://gvillage.org/gv/index.php/management-tips-21/21-management/96-collaborative-decision-making.

13. Project Management Institute, *The High Cost of Low Performance*, 2014, accessed April 23, 2014, http://www.pmi.org/ffi/media/PDF/Business-Solutions/PMI_Pulse_2014.ashx.

14. Dennis L. Wilcox, and Glen T. Cameron, *Public Relations: Strategies and Tactics*, 9th ed. (Toronto: Pearson, 2010).

15. Ibid.

16. Barry, interview with the author, May 17, 2011.

Elements of Public Relations and Marketing Communications

UNIT THREE

Writing for Public Relations

Sandra L. Braun

10

Bad writing makes bright people look dumb.
William Zinsser, "On Writing Well"

LEARNING OBJECTIVES

After reading this chapter, you will be able to

- explain how public relations writing is different from other kinds of writing;
- describe the goals and purposes of public relations writing;
- describe the writing process and the hallmarks of good public relations writing;
- analyze the writing formats that public relations practitioners use; and
- understand the ethical considerations in public relations writing.

INTRODUCTION

Many readers have likely heard the phrases, "You are what you eat" or "You are what you think." The same thought can be applied to writing: You are how you write. People often form opinions of others based on how they write. A person who writes well can be regarded as intelligent, articulate, and knowledgeable, and person who cannot write well can be judged negatively.

Writing is a core skill for public relations practitioners. A public relations professional who cannot write well is somewhat of an oxymoron. This realization has posed some dismay to many public relations students who are anxious about their own writing abilities. But learning how to write well is not a huge mystery. People can improve their writing skills by attending to just a few simple but key strategies, which this chapter will cover. Additionally, learning to write well is more of a journey than a destination. Everyone can improve and seldom few ever arrive. There's always something new to learn. We are all students of the writing process and even the most seasoned public relations professional can be seen sporting a copy of Strunk and White's *Elements of Style*, or other writer's resource.

PUBLIC RELATIONS WRITING AND THE GREAT SHIFT

The first and most important step in this journey toward good public relations writing is realizing that this is a different, and often new, genre of writing for many people. It is not essay writing and it is not novel writing. It is business writing. Throughout grade school, students are taught to develop their writing skills by expanding vocabulary, lengthening sentences, adding descriptive words, and creating imaginative conclusions—that is, they are well-trained in the genre of composition and essay writing.

Public relations writing, however, demands a different set of skills. For starters, it requires conciseness and clarity. It requires short sentences, fewer words, more precise words, and frequent use of the inverted pyramid method of organization. In a regular pyramid, the most important information for the reader goes at the end of a communication piece. This is illustrated as the pyramid being "heavier" at the bottom. The inverted pyramid method of organization requires that the conclusion or main point, and/or most important information, go closer to the beginning of the piece rather than at the end. The pyramid is heavier (or larger) at the top. That is, when writing using the inverted pyramid method of organization, information should appear in more or less descending order of importance to the reader. This requires an understanding of your audience and their information needs.

Figure 10.1 illustrates the difference between the pyramid and the inverted pyramid method of organization. The figure demonstrates this difference within the context of an email communication between a professor and a student. In

Figure 10.1 Methods of Organizing Information in a Communication Piece

Triangle A: PYRAMID

Dear Professor:
When I got up this morning, I wasn't feeling
well. Then, I got a call from a friend who said he
needed a ride to the emergency room because
he cut his hand on a glass. For these reasons,
I will be unable to attend class today.
Sue Rogers
Comm 1281

Triangle B: INVERTED PYRAMID

Dear Professor:
I will be unable to attend class today. When I
got up this morning, I wasn't feeling well, and
I need to drive my friend to the emergency
room because he cut his hand.
Sue Rogers
Comm 1281

Triangle A, the student emails her professor to let the professor know that she will not be in class. The most important piece of information for the reader appears at the end of the communication and, to illustrate, the largest and weightiest part of the triangle appears at the bottom of the figure. Triangle B shows the same piece of communication using the inverted pyramid method of organization. The most important point for the reader appears at the beginning and, to illustrate, the larger portion of the triangle appears at the top of the figure.

Business, public relations, and journalistic writing rely heavily on the inverted pyramid method of organization. Learning to flip your thinking and writing to an inverted pyramid style is perhaps the biggest shift in thinking for public relations students when it comes to writing, since they have been more exposed to composition and essay writing where the piece of writing builds to a climax and the "punch line" usually comes at the end. The key to success with this transition is to put yourself in the reader's position. Once you understand your reader (or audience) and his/her needs, it is relatively easy to organize your communication pieces for greater effectiveness.

THE PURPOSES OF PUBLIC RELATIONS WRITING
Writing to Create Goodwill

Public relations writers write, ultimately, to "broker goodwill between an institution and its publics."[1] The creation of goodwill is important because goodwill
turns into public acceptance and public acceptance turns into social permission for the organization to continue operating. Without public acceptance
and social permission, the organization is eventually doomed. Let's take the
example of tobacco companies. Over the years, as the dangers of smoking have
become apparent, and as people have embraced the option to be smoke-free,
public opinion toward tobacco companies has become less favourable, with
some questioning even the right of such companies to exist. Some would also
challenge tobacco growers about their choice of profession, and tobacco farmers are experiencing decreased revenues in a growing culture of non-smokers.
Reduced need in the marketplace is challenging the economic success of the
tobacco industry, and lack of public acceptance of the habit of smoking is
gradually turning into reduced social permission for the industry in the marketplace. Ongoing social disfavour has produced legislative bans on smoking
in certain public areas. Continuing disfavour can possibly lead to even more
restrictions and an entire legislative ban, which would mean tobacco companies will have lost all public permission to continue. Without some measure of
public acceptance, companies simply cannot exist or continue to function in
the marketplace.

Writing to Persuade

Not only is public relations writing concerned with brokering goodwill; it is
also concerned with persuasion. Public relations messages are often created to
persuade audiences to change behaviours, beliefs, or attitudes through "tailor-
ing messages for particular media and publics."[2] A public relations person in the
tobacco industry, to continue with our example, could sometimes be called upon
to produce communication pieces that reinforce the positive role of tobacco in
society. Imperial Tobacco Canada illustrates such communication on a web page
targeted at the general public.[3] The communication piece argues for a bright
future for the tobacco industry and then discusses the reasons why, including
a relatively strong market in Canada, and the threat of illegal and underground
activity if tobacco is banned. The writer presents an argument, which he or she
hopes is persuasive, for allowing the tobacco industry to be in business.

Where Can We Find Examples of Public Relations Writing?

Public relations writing can appear in many formats from web pages, news releases, feature articles, public services announcements (PSA) for print or broadcast, op-eds, and brochures, to speeches, briefs, annual reports, emails, and blogs, to name just a few. The formats in which a public relations practitioner may write are numerous. There are many public relations writing books that have chapters dedicated to many of these formats (see Notes and Further Reading at the end of this chapter). Therefore, the goal of this chapter is not to re-hash all the great information already available about each of these formats, but simply to focus on the actual writing process and to provide an overview of tips for successful writing in the most common formats.

Assessing the Audience

So, how do we write to inform or persuade target publics in order to build and broker positive relationships?

Before any writing takes place, we must first understand the audience. A quick, but careful, assessment of the audience's needs, goals, desires, and preferred methods of communication must first be conducted to tailor our messages for maximum effectiveness. Ask questions such as the following:

- What do I think my message is?
- Who is the audience I am trying to reach with this message? Where are they? How do they think? What are their needs and desires?
- What might they want or expect from my organization and from this particular message?
- How do they feel about my organization?
- What do I want them to know, think, or do as a result of being exposed to this message?
- What specific behaviour, attitude, or action of theirs am I trying to influence?
- Is this the right message for this audience at this time, or does this message need to be altered or changed in any way?

It can also be helpful to consider the concept of persona. Once you have identified your target public, you can build a persona of a typical audience member, consider the needs of that member and write for that member. For example, if you are writing a speech for a politician who will address a group of fishery workers in Newfoundland, a possible persona of that audience could look something like this:

Ned is 35 years old. He was raised in Newfoundland in a fishing family that goes back generations. He is a hard worker and spends long days out at sea during the season catching fish for a living. He has a tenth grade education and is the smartest guy around when it comes to the fishing industry and how it works; he knows a falsehood when he hears one. He and his buddies often gather at the local pub for a pint after a long day at work, and they talk a lot about what's going on in the industry and how their families are doing. He really does not have a lot of time to read, but he gets his news from evening television at the local pub. He and his buddies talk about the news when it is on and as they watch it together. He is a little hostile toward politicians right now because of government regulations that are adversely affecting the fishing industry.

Now, write your speech.

Here is another example. Perhaps you are preparing a public relations ad with the message "do not text and drive." Here is a persona you could create to help with the writing process:

Stephanie, aged 21, college student, part-time job at a bar 20 hours per week, lives in an apartment with a roommate, tends to burn the candle at both ends with an extremely busy life, has an active social life, uses her phone a lot, always gets the latest gadgets and apps, "lives" on her phone, drives a white Pontiac Sunfire, shops at Abercrombie & Fitch for clothing and IKEA for furniture.

Now, write for this specific person.

By using the concept of persona to create a representative audience member in your mind before and as you write, you will see your writing become much more targeted and alive.

Only after you have carefully considered who your audience is and what they are like, and possibly even built a persona, should you begin the actual writing process. This process will help you write more efficiently and more effectively.

WHAT IS GOOD WRITING?

> When something can be read without effort, great effort has
> gone into its writing.
> —Enrique Jardiel Poncela, *Obras completas, vol. 3*

How will you know if, or when, you have produced a good piece of public relations writing? Like all great skills, the best writing appears effortless. Just like an ice dancer who performs a three-minute routine that looks effortless, flawless, and beautiful, but has taken months or even years to prepare, good writing is a skill that takes work and, in the end, reads well. Good writing does not just happen. It grows out of experience, knowledge, and practice with the writing process and writing skills. Writing well requires an understanding of the writing process.

After you have researched your audience and are ready to write a communication piece, you can conceptualize the following steps as the process of good writing:

- idea formation and planning
- supporting research (such as preparatory research, topical research, content research, or background research)
- drafting and organizing
- revising
- copy editing
- proofreading
- feedback

These steps, however, do not usually happen one at a time in a linear fashion. It is more helpful to view writing as a recursive, not linear, process.[4] Writers are likely to jump between steps, or may even go through the steps a few times in a circle. For example, you may start with idea formation and planning, go through some research, then go back to the idea stage if it becomes apparent that the idea is not strong or could be better. Or you may go through the idea formation and planning stage, conduct research on the idea, produce a draft that is fairly well organized, revise and edit it, and then go back to the drafting

Figure 10.2: The Recursive Nature of the Writing Process

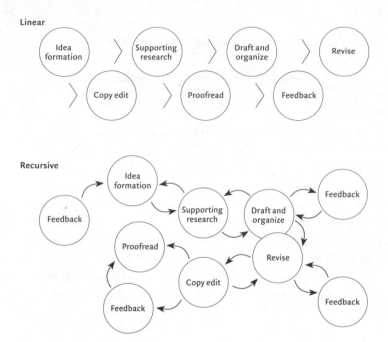

stage if it becomes clear that major changes would improve the document. You may also go through all the steps to a finished draft only to find major flaws in the work and have to go back to the first step of refining your idea and starting the document over again. A significant number of order combinations that you could go through to get to a finished piece exist. So, do not be timid—just plunge into the process, knowing that it is not necessary to go through the steps in a linear fashion and that you will likely jump between steps toward your finished product. The important thing is that all steps are done at least once, and some steps, like feedback or editing or proofing, should definitely be done as often as possible.

Idea Formation and Planning

This is the idea and brainstorming stage. What is the main idea of the piece and what information will go into your piece of communication? This is often the most difficult part of the creative process since everything to follow depends on how well you have conceptualized the basic idea and main message of the project or the work. You will find that if the basic idea or main message is not clearly defined, and if you have not done adequate audience research, you will be coming back to this basic step.

The best ideas for what goes into a communication piece are those that are *focused* and *specific*. For example, if you need to write a public service announcement that encourages the public to practice safety while in vehicles, it is more powerful to focus the message on *one* aspect of the topic (to buckle up and use a seat belt, for example) than many aspects of the topic (use a seat belt, be alert, don't drive tired, and don't drive under the influence). The latter idea has too much information to cover in the few short seconds of a traditional public service announcement, and you can have a much more powerful message by focusing on one, or perhaps two, specific aspects.

One method of idea formation is mind mapping (also known as concept mapping, mental mapping, or concept webbing). Mind mapping was developed in 2006 by researchers at Cornell University.[5] A mind map identifies a central word or concept or message or idea and then maps out other words associated with it. Once you have your idea and have done a bit of topical research, start in the centre of the page with the main idea (thesis). This keeps you focused on your core message or idea. Then write down the supporting points of the main idea. Near each supporting point, put additional information and supporting points to each of the supporting points. Work outward in all directions to produce a structure of related thoughts, words, or images (see Figure 10.3). Ideally, you want to know what your main points are to support your main idea and have those as the first set of branches coming out of the centre. These will become your sections or main paragraphs. Each branch could then have supporting information coming from each of them. What you will have is an outline, of sorts, in visual form. You can prepare a written outline from this or simply use the mind map as your outline.

If you do not feel quite so clear about things and are not sure what are the main points or supporting points, you can just put the central idea (thesis) in the middle of the page and then jot down all the points on your mind all over the page. Then, take a step back and note patterns and relationships. Cluster the related items together (which will become your main sections or main paragraphs). Then, after items are clustered, think of a general order that you think the clusters of information should follow. At this point, you could do your written outline or use the mind map to guide you as you begin to start writing.

Mind maps do not need to be neat and pretty. They can be crazy and lots of fun and colourful and filled with doodle art—whatever it takes to get ideas

Figure 10.3: Mind Map

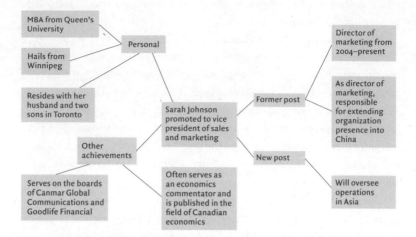

out of your head and onto a piece of paper. There is also specialized software designed to help create mind maps.

To illustrate, Figure 10.3 is an example of mind map created in preparation to write a fictional newsletter article about an employee, Sarah Johnson, who has been promoted.

Supporting Research

Researching any preparatory information, background information, or content information needed for the planning, preparation, and dissemination for your public relations piece is important. Every piece of communication will have a different set of research needs. A news release will require proper research, among others, for a proper media list. A ghostwritten speech may require that you properly study the presenter for his or her word choices or expressions. A feature story may require some topical research on the content of the piece and also research for the best sources for quotations to support your story. You may be writing a public service announcement with the message "get a flu shot" and so may want to research some statistics to put in your public service announcement that would help persuade your audience to take the action you are suggesting.

Without proper research, you can have the most cleverly written piece of communication that totally misses the mark because it contains errors, is unsuited to the audience, went to the wrong media contact, is unpersuasive, or has weak content.

Drafting and Organizing

Once you have developed the core idea, mapped out the related ideas and supporting points you wish to include, and gathered the necessary supporting research, it is time to start committing your work to paper. Remember: writing is recursive. You can go back and change your draft later if you need to—just get started. You may go back and change your core concept. You may organize it a bit differently than you initially thought before you started the draft. You may add items to your mind map. You may take some points away. Anything can happen. Just go ahead and start writing. You can start writing at any point in the document you wish. You may wish to start at the beginning, the middle, or even the end. Work in the section in which you feel currently inspired. (It will likely be the section(s) in which you feel most clear about what it is you wish to say.) You will be able to see the mind map structure start to come alive in Figure 10.4, showing a sample of a rough first draft of a newsletter article developed from the mind map in Figure 10.3.

Figure 10.4: Sample First Draft

New vice president of sales named

Sarah Johnson has been promoted as the new vice president of sales. As our director of marketing since 2004, Johnson led the company through expansion into the Asia-Pacific region, so she is very deserving of this promotion!

She has certainly prepared well for her sales and business career and we know she'll go a long way. She studied Business and Economics at Queen's University. She resides in Toronto with her husband and sons Tyler and Sean, aged 14 and 12. She is from the city of Winnipeg.

Johnson is very well known and is a very positive thing for our company. She often serves as an economics commentator and is published in the field of Canadian economics. She serves on the boards of CanMar Global Communications and GoodLife Financial.

In her new job, she will continue monitoring the growth and development in the Asia-Pacific region. We wish her all the best!

Revising

Once you have become focused on a core idea, mapped out related ideas, done any necessary supporting research, and have written a first draft, it is time to revise. Revising is not editing. Please don't go comma hunting! Editing is focused on the smaller and local details like spelling and punctuation while revising is a broader process concerned with the larger and more global elements such as the core idea, the organization of the piece, the supporting points, the beginning, the ending, or the transitions. This is not the time to edit because you may determine, as a result of the revising process, that you will delete an entire section of your document. So, you don't want to spend time doing fine editing too early in the process. Think of revisions in terms of elements and waves. Revise for big things first (global), and take one element at a time. Leave the fine revising (local), such as changing commas and correcting spelling, for later. Global elements include the following:

- **Main concept:** Is this concept holding up well? Is it something you can successfully write about, and that is relevant to the audience?
- **Development of ideas:** Do the subsequent points support the main idea well?
- **Organization:** Is it organized in a manner that is easy to follow and that makes sense to the reader or listener?
- **Style and tone:** Is it the appropriate writing style and tone for the format and for the purpose of the document? Is it concise, with no jargon? Is it written in active voice, with short sentences and paragraphs, and no long, complex sentences?

Go through the entire document for each element in waves. After you have completed your waves of global revisions, read your draft aloud. You may discover that the public service announcement you just wrote may read well on paper but does not sound good to the ear. Or you may discover that the letter to the editor you just wrote is filled with too much emotion and needs to be re-worded. A simple read-aloud can help you spot major problems if you take the time to do it. You can also ask others for their input (feedback in the recursive process).

An additional way to revise your communication piece is to review other similar pieces—preferably good ones! You can gauge your document as "in the ballpark" or not. The key here is to review good ones, or exemplars. Just because something has been written or produced does not mean it is of high quality,

Figure 10.5 Sample Revision

Johnson promoted to vice president of sales

Sarah Johnson has been promoted as the new vice president of sales. As our director of marketing since 2004, Johnson led the company through expansion into the Asia-Pacific region. In her new job, she will continue monitoring the growth and development in the Asia-Pacific region.

Johnson is has a public profile as an economics commentator and is published in the field of Canadian economics. She serves on the boards of CanMar Global Communications and GoodLife Financial.

She studied business and economics at Queen University. She resides in Toronto with her husband and sons Tyler and Sean, aged fourteen and twelve. She is from the city of Winnipeg.

or that it is of any quality at all. You will always want to compare your creation to the standards of excellence for that creation. There are hallmarks for good speeches, good news releases, good creative briefs, and good public service announcements. It is your job to know what the basic standards of excellence are for each format, some of which will be covered in this chapter.

Figure 10.5 shows a revision of our promotion announcement for our newsletter article. It has been revised for a more specific headline, stronger organization of information in inverted pyramid method of organization, and better business tone by taking out overly informal words.

Copy Editing

Once your draft has undergone the waves of global revisions, you can now start a more localized process. You are close to your finished product. Now you can start to copy edit. This means checking for the finer details. Local elements can include:

- **Spelling and grammar:** Does the piece hold to standard rules of basic English?
- **Punctuation:** Does the piece follow proper punctuation?
- **Format:** Does it hold to the fundamentals and conventions of style for the format? That is, if it is a news release, is proper news release format followed? If it's a television spot, does it use television production format?

Figure 10.6 Sample Copy Edit

Johnson promoted to vice-president of sales

Sarah Johnson, former director of marketing, has been promoted to
vice-president of sales. As director of marketing since 2004, Johnson
led the company through expansion into the Asia-Pacific region. In
her new post, she will continue monitoring the growth and development in this area.

Johnson has a public profile as an economics commentator and
is published in the field of Canadian economics. She serves on the
boards of CanMar Global Communications and GoodLife Financial.

Johnson studied business and economics at Queen's University.
She resides in Toronto with her husband and two sons, Tyler and
Sean, aged 14 and 12 respectively. She hails from Winnipeg.

Does it meet the requirements for your organization/boss
with regard to spacing, page numbering, etc.
- **Style:** Is it in proper style (CP, AP, MLA, APA) as required?

These are the finishing touches on your document.

Now for a word about spell-check and grammar-check in your word processor. Computer programs are very helpful with the spell-check tool. First of all,
please use it! Second, do not rely on this as your only source to check spelling
and grammar. It catches many errors, but it does not catch all errors. A public
relations professional is often judged by the quality of his or her writing: it is in
your best interest to copy edit carefully, even enlisting the aid of others.

Figure 10.6 shows the newsletter article after copy editing. There are spelling, grammar, punctuation, and CP style corrections.

Proofreading

Once you have edited, proofread your work. Then proofread it again. Now,
again. Now get someone else to proofread it. Get another. You can never
proofread enough. A good rule of thumb is to proofread as many times as you
can in the time that you have. Have as many others as possible proofread it as

well. It is helpful to have as many sets of eyes view the document as possible because you will be too close to the document to catch all the errors that may be obvious to others. Another way to proofread is to read your document aloud to someone else, or have someone read it aloud to you. Clerical and administrative support personnel can be particularly helpful at this stage, as they are usually constantly proofreading in the course of their work. Check your ego at the door and learn to take constructive criticism. High quality pieces are seldom created in isolation.

Feedback

Because good writing rarely occurs in isolation, taking your work to respected peers for ongoing feedback is important. Feedback can occur at any stage in the writing process, from planning, to revising, to copy editing, or during the proofreading stages.

Feedback may come from a professional editor. Editors are experts, either in the content of the material and/or in the editing process. An expert editor can make your piece or your book go from okay to fabulous by providing a critical eye, making suggestions for changes and enhancements, challenging you to be more clear, or helping you to express yourself more fully and accurately. Excellent writing rarely (if ever) occurs accidentally, and a good editor will bring out the best in you. Your editor may be your supervisor who has more writing experience than you do or may be a professional editor. If you want to improve your writing, and if you are serious about your literary journey, you will gladly work with editors at all levels.

Additionally, you will need to accept that there is an approval process for all your work in the course of your job. Public relations people, or any business people, rarely write without requiring at least one approval somewhere along the way by a supervisor or executive. This means that your work will be constantly subject to critiques. You must learn to be the gracious recipient of feedback and come to an understanding of how the approval process can be helpful, and how it can also ruin perfectly good copy (too many cooks can spoil the stew). The best purpose for approvals is for subject knowledge and fact checking. As the public relations person, you really should be one of the best, if not the best writer in the vicinity, and your copy should not need a whole lot of revisions; however, it is possible that it will need more feedback and more supporting research in the areas of content and subject expertise. Once again, check your ego at the door and be willing to do whatever it takes to produce a good end product.

BEST TIPS FOR EFFECTIVE PUBLIC RELATIONS WRITING

> A scrupulous writer, in every sentence that he writes, will ask himself
> at least four questions, thus: What am I trying to say? What words will
> express it? What image or idiom will make it clearer? Is this image fresh
> enough to have an effect? And he will probably ask himself two more:
> Could I put it more shortly? Have I said anything that is avoidably ugly?
> —George Orwell, "Politics and the English Language"

There are volumes dedicated to what makes effective writing (see Notes and Further Reading at the end of this chapter). When it comes to acquiring a strong command of the English language and learning to communicate well through the written word, there are a myriad of elements to consider; and there is always something more to learn. This section will highlight some of the most important elements of effective public relations writing and the most common issues faced by students.

Effective public relations writing means writing effectively and efficiently.[6] This means writing with attention to comprehension, clarity, and conciseness.

Writing for Comprehension

Public relations writers want their messages to be attended to and understood. Writers need to draw in audiences by first gaining their attention at the beginning of a piece. There are whole fields of study devoted to attention-getting techniques but some of the main ways include the following:

- Engage as many senses as possible.
- "Hook" the audience by showing how something will benefit them.
- Have a strong opening or engaging lead (by asking a question, providing a quote, telling a story, making a shocking statement, etc.).

Once the audience is engaged, the public relations writer must keep their attention throughout. Body copy should be readable, understandable, and relevant. One way to achieve this goal is to consider the grade level at which you are writing. When writing for the general public, it is advisable to aim for about a grade 9 level.

There are many formulas available to test for readability and comprehension. The most common is the Flesch-Kincaid Grade Level formula, based on a calculation of sentence length and the number of single-syllable words in a text of 100 words. Fortunately, many computer programs will automatically calculate this and other comprehension formulas for you. For example, you can simply paste a portion of your text into a website such as Online-Utility.org to get instant readability results.[7] This site provides scores for many readability tests, including the Flesch-Kincaid Grade Level, the Gunning Fog index, the Coleman-Liau index, and the Automated Readability index. You can also run readability tests in various word processing programs such as Microsoft Word.

Writing for Clarity

Effective communication means writing clearly. Nothing is more frustrating for readers than to spend a considerable amount of energy into reading something and then come away saying, "Huh?" Words, sentences, and paragraphs are intended to be the vehicles by which to communicate meaning. They are not meant to confuse or obfuscate. They also have purpose. For public relations, the purpose of words is to inform, create goodwill, or persuade. These goals cannot be achieved unless the communication is clear to the target audience.

Two of the most important ways to achieve clarity in writing is to

- write in active voice rather than passive voice, and
- write in plain language.

Active Voice or Passive Voice?

Sentences can be written in either active or passive voice. Active voice is more direct, concise, and vigorous. It is the preferred language of business because it is the easiest to understand and keeps the engines of business moving forward. In active voice, the main subject of the sentence is doing the verb and acts upon something/someone else (the direct object). For example:

The applicant will provide an updated resume.

In passive voice, the subject is the one being acted upon and/is on the receiving end of the verb. For example:

An updated resume will be provided by the applicant.

How do you tell the difference? A good test is the "grandma" test, according to Tim Burnett, a communications officer for FedEx. Burnett says if you can add "by my grandma" to the end of a phrase or sentence, then you have probably written in the passive voice.[8] For example:

- The book was written...by my grandma.
- The study was conducted...by my grandma.
- An updated resume was provided...by my grandma.

You can also tell if something is written in active or passive voice by going through the following steps:

1. Identify the main verb (using the above example: "written," "conducted," "provided").
2. Ask yourself who/what is doing that action; who is the actor? That is, "my grandma."
3. Find where the subject is in relation to that main verb. (Is it before or after the verb?)

If the subject of the verb (the actor) appears *before* the verb, the sentence is in active voice. If the subject of the verb (the actor) *appears* after the main verb, the sentence is in passive voice. You can change a sentence from passive to active voice by putting the subject of the verb in front of the verb and re-writing as necessary. For example, both of the following are in active voice because the subject/actor appears before its verb:

My grandma wrote the book. (The subject/actor "grandma" appears before its verb "wrote.")

My grandma conducted the study. (The subject/actor "grandma" appears before its verb "conducted.")

Many businesspeople and bureaucrats use passive voice (whether knowingly or unknowingly) to obscure responsibility. For example, "It was announced that there will be layoffs" (passive voice) is easier to hide behind than, "The chief operating officer announced that there will be layoffs" (active voice).

Sometimes passive voice is the best choice and is the most appropriate. Use the passive voice when you want to focus on who or what is on the receiving end of the main action (the direct object). For example:

A study was conducted by Ipsos Reid to examine the effectiveness
of the public relations campaign.

The main verb of the controlling idea here is "conducted." The subject doing
the "conducting" was "Ipsos Reid." But the main purpose or main idea is not
about Ipsos Reid; the main fact is that a study was conducted (it could have been
done by anyone). So, when you want to emphasize the direct object, and de-
emphasize the subject, choose the passive voice.

Passive voice is also good to use when describing generalized actions, beliefs,
or results. For example:

The style of music created by musicians today is significantly different
from the style created by musicians of the 1800s.

If this sentence was active voice, it would read, "Musicians of today create
significantly different styles of music from musicians of the 1800s." But we want
the emphasis to be on "style of music" (the direct object), not "musicians" (the
subject/actor). Passive voice helps us to communicate that emphasis.

Whichever voice you choose in each of your communication pieces or
paragraphs, just remember to be consistent within the entire piece or entire
paragraph, as appropriate, to communicate clearly and retain cohesion.

Plain Language

Another way to achieve clarity is to avoid jargon and write in plain language. On
January 5, 2010, the Congress of the United States enacted the Plain Writing Act
of 2010.[9] The purpose of the act is to improve communication between federal
agencies and the public by promoting clear communication that the public can
use and actually understand. As of 2010, any US government document that
is produced for the general public to provide information about a government
agency or service, or that explains how to comply with any federal regulation,
must be written in plain language.

In other words, the US government was telling itself, "Enough already—
if we want people to understand what we do and what we want them to do,
write so they can understand it." At the Plain Language website, the US federal
government offers tips, guidelines, and examples of how federal agencies
can simplify their documents so that ordinary people can understand them.[10]
For example:

Whereas, the Division of Business Conduct, upon receipt of a complaint, shall appoint an officer from within the department to investigate such complaint. The investigation shall focus on the actions of the named business to determine if said business had complied with all the policies, guidelines, and regulations under the Small Business Act.

Instead, write:

Once the Division of Business Conduct has received a complaint, an officer from the department shall be assigned to the case to investigate for compliance with the Small Business Act.

In Canada, there has been a plain language section in the Communications Policy of the Government of Canada since 1988. The Communications Policy states, "an institution's duty to inform the public includes the obligation to communicate effectively. Information about policies, programs, services and initiatives must be clear, relevant, objective, easy to understand and useful."[11]

Plain language does not mean to condescend to your audience or "dumb down." Its purpose is to write at the audience's appropriate level of understanding. What constitutes plain language for one group may not necessarily constitute plain language for another group. The concept of plain language has been studied since the early part of the twentieth century when scholars in education and psychology began to research how people read and process text. Writing in plain language is simply choosing appropriate vocabulary for the target public, using appropriate sentence constructions (usually simple and direct), arranged in easy-to-manage sentence lengths and paragraphs. Its purpose is to facilitate efficient and effective communication and reduce the possibilities for miscommunication, which, in turn, saves time and money.

Other terms and phrases used to describe the absence of plain language are "gobbledygook," "it's all Greek to me," "double speak," "double Dutch," "written in hieroglyphics," or "bafflegab." Whatever you choose to call it—avoid it. Choose simple, direct, and plain language for effective communication.

Writing for Conciseness

Not only should good public relations writing be *effective*, it should also be *efficient*. In other words, say what you want to say powerfully in an easy-to-understand manner considering the audience, and also in the most concise way possible. We live in an attention-deficit society. People do not want to spend or waste time wading through pontifications and fluff. People want to be communicated with directly and succinctly. People like brevity. When you think about it, so do you.

Brevity can be achieved in a number of ways but some of the most important involve

- sentence length;
- word choice;
- use of the verb to be; and
- redundancy.

Sentence Length

To achieve brevity, aim for sentences of up to 20 words, and no more than 40. If you can say it in few words without sacrificing meaning, then do so. Additionally, avoid trying to pack too much into one sentence. Say one thing at a time, and do not overload your sentences with too much information or a number of different thoughts.

For example, the sentence below has a number of different thoughts strung together, which are better communicated by using more sentences:

> Nick Sorenson, CEO, will take his new post at BAT Corporation next spring after he completes his obligations to TransWest Airlines, where he led the company to record profits in the face of recession and he is also a well-respected leader in the industry.

Better to divide this into two or three sentences:

> Nick Sorenson, CEO, will take his new post at BAT Corporation next spring after he completes his obligations to TransWest Airlines. Sorenson experienced great success at that company, leading it to record profits in the face of recession. He is well-respected in the industry.

Word Choice

Attending to word choice can fulfill a number of functions. For one, it can provide specificity and paint a picture.

For example, you may write the following for a newsletter article:

Since the campaign, donations have *increased* by 125 per cent over last year.

Or:

Since the campaign, donations have *skyrocketed* by 125 per cent over last year.

While both sentences are technically accurate, the second sentence captures the drama of the increase. Just be careful that there is truth in your word selections. Certainly, in this case, a 125 per cent increase is large and warrants use of a strong word like "skyrocketed."

One mistake you want to avoid is using words inappropriately. Build your vocabulary so that you avoid this trap. Know words: know what they mean and how they are best used and in what context. For example:

We are hoping that through this awareness campaign, we will *elicit/ illicit* a favourable public response.

"Elicit" is a verb that means to "provoke," "bring about," or "evoke." "Illicit" means "illegal."

The journalist was unable to elicit any information from the politician about possible illicit campaign activity.

Some of the most commonly confused words by college and university students have been captured in Diana Hacker's *A Canadian Writer's Reference*, which is listed in the Further Reading section.

Overuse of the Verb *to be*

Another strategy to achieve conciseness is to eliminate use of the verb *to be*. This is a particularly common offence in young or first-time writers. Overuse of the verb *to be* drains sentences of energy. See Figure 10.7 for examples of how to replace the forms of the verb *to be*, such as *am, is, are, was, were, being, been, be.*

Redundancy

Writers can achieve conciseness by avoiding redundancy within sentences. sIf one "co-operates together with" someone else, how is that different from "co-operating with"? Or if "the members of the Progressive Conservative Party

Figure 10.7 Replacing the Verb *to be*

Wordy	Strategy	Revision
I am going to send you the brochure layout tomorrow.	Identify the form of the verb *to be*. Substitute it with another verb to make a more specific statement.	I will deliver the brochure layout tomorrow.
This plan could be of benefit to the residents of Moncton.	Turn a noun, adjective, or prepositional phrase following the verb *to be* into a verb.	This plan could benefit the residents of Moncton.
It is necessary for lawmakers to address this problem.	Watch for sentences that start with "It is," "There are," or "There could be..." These phrases are non-specific.	Lawmakers need to address this problem.

voted today," how is that different from "the Progressive Conservative Party voted today"?

How can we be free of pontifications, jargon, clutter, redundancy, and repetition? What can we do as writers to avoid the temptation to inflate? The answer is simply to clear our heads. Strip a sentence down to its most basic elements. Clear thinking becomes clear writing.[12]

PUBLIC RELATIONS PRODUCTS: WHAT DO PRACTITIONERS WRITE?

The following section describes the most common public relations formats or products and includes some tips for best practices for each. (This section is not meant to be a detailed treatise of public relations formats. Please consult the public relations writing guides in Notes and Further Reading at the end of this chapter for more descriptions and exemplars.)

Public relations writing often falls into three categories of writing styles:

- journalistic and media writing
- responsive writing
- business writing

Journalistic and Media Writing

Very often, the bulk of the writing done by a public relations person is writing for media such as newspapers, magazines, television, radio, and the Internet. There are many formats applicable to media writing, but here are some of the most common.

News Releases

Practitioners particularly find themselves writing many news releases. A news release is an article that the public relations practitioner has written for the journalist in the hope that it will make its way into the news. It will be written in standard news release format, and in inverted pyramid method of organization, meaning the information is arranged from the most important to least important to the journalist. The inverted pyramid method of organizing information for journalists developed out of a need for news editors to cut the length of stories because of space limitations, without sacrificing the main meaning and important information.

All news releases have a lead, or introductory paragraph. Sometimes, the lead has all the important information in the first few paragraphs—namely, the who, what, when, where, why, and/or how. This is called a 5W lead, straight lead, or summary lead. Other leads can include the anecdote lead, where you start with a story or anecdote. Other types of leads are the shocking statement lead or the question lead. The purpose of a lead is to get the reader's attention. There are many kinds of leads from which to choose and they are well covered in journalism textbooks or online sources. The following are possible leads for a news release.

Example of a 5W lead (sometimes called a straight lead, or a summary lead):

> Canadians will be able to take advantage of free admission to national parks during the month of July, according to Parks Canada. This is in effort to boost park attendance by Canadians.

Example of an anecdote lead:

> Ian and Rachel Macdonald of Calgary say they have long complained, along with many of their friends, of not being able to find family-friendly activities to do in and around Calgary. It was only recently, when challenged by a friend, that they say they even thought of spending a weekend camping in nearby Banff National Park.

Examples of a shocking statement lead or statistics lead:

> According to a recent survey, 25 per cent of Calgarians with children under 12 have never visited nearby Banff National Park as a family.

Example of a question lead:

> Are you a family looking for something to do? Have you ever taken
> your family to a nearby national park? Canada Parks and Recreation
> will offer free admission in July to boost attendance by Canadians to
> national parks.

When you write a news release, your primary audience is the journalist, so your lead must capture him or her. If you don't capture the journalist with your news release and your lead, your story will not get past him or her to see the light of day in a publication. Therefore, write your leads with the journalist in mind. Journalists want to be engaged and caught up in your story. Be aware of the many different kinds of leads at your disposal.

The other important part of a news release is the headline. Many journalists will not get past the headline, and if they do, they may not get past the lead. Good headlines are ones that have a strong verb, are less than 10 words in length, and provide a good idea of what the story is about. For example, good headlines might read:

- "Calgarians 'wake up' to Banff";
- "Parks Canada offers free admission in July"; or
- "Looking for family fun near Calgary? Think Banff."

News releases are trending toward digital. The social media release is fast becoming popular. The social media release has the main story but also provides links to outside sources for more information, MP3 files, and links to videos or podcasts. It incorporates the traditional news release with all the support of communication technology. Shift Communications created one of the first social media templates.[13]

Media Alerts

The media alert or media advisory is similar to a news release, but it is much more succinct and is more of a list. It is a simple listing of the who, what, when, where, why (and sometimes how) of a story. The media alert is particularly useful when advising news media about events, such as a press conference, fundraiser, speech or statement, or an appearance. See Figure 10.8 for an example of a media alert.

Figure 10.8: Sample Media Alert

University of the Northwest
123 University Drive
Anytown, Province T2T 8L7
. (123) 456-7890

Sept. 3, 2014
FOR IMMEDIATE RELEASE

MEDIA ALERT

Best-selling author and British-Canadian journalist, John Lawrence, will speak at the University of the Northwest this month. He will be promoting his new book, *Capitalist Culture and the Dulling of Social Conscience.*

Who: John Lawrence, best-selling author

What: Lecture, "Capitalist Culture and the Dulling of Social Conscience," followed by question/answer period

When: Thursday, September 12, 1 p.m.–3 p.m.

Where: Leacock Theatre, G-487

Lawrence will be available for questions and photos by media at 3:30 p.m. following the lecture. Members of the media should call for a press pass, which will give them a parking permit, media kit, dedicated seating at the event, and access to the speaker after the event.

Contact: Sylvia Lee, Media Relations
(607) 365-1458
slee@unw.ca

Additional Information: John Lawrence is a staff writer for the *Toronto Herald* and the best-selling author of five books, including *Canadian Sport and Culture,* and *The Brotherhood: The Story of the Canadian 1st Battalion Royal Newfoundland Regiment.*

University of the Northwest, established in 1912, is located in Anytown, Province and is ranked among the top 50 universities in the world. Its 400-hectacre campus is home to 30,000 domestic and 10,000 international students. It features Prince Albert Hospital, one of Canada's leading teaching and medical facilities.

Media Kits

Public relations practitioners often assemble and distribute media kits. A media kit is a packet of information containing a news release and a selection of appropriate supporting material. This material, depending on the reason the kit was prepared, can include, but is not limited to, the following:

- a fact sheet about the issuing organization
- a biography about a subject in the news release or any members of an organization's leadership
- a backgrounder article that provides additional information about the topic in the news release, or
- background information that may provide context to the news release in the kit
- product information if the news release is about a new product

There could also be organizational brochures or booklets in the media kit. An accompanying CD could include audio and video files, such as logos, artwork, pictures, photos, diagrams, or interviews. Some practitioners put the entire media kit on a CD. Although printed media kits have been popular in the past, with the advent of digital media, many organizations have also posted their media kits on their websites in sections designated for journalists (often called press rooms or media rooms). Journalists cannot always attend your event, even though they might like to; so, when you send out your media alerts and news releases, be sure to also post plenty of information on the Web for journalists to access. Public relations practitioners need to consider carefully the needs of the journalist and to provide appropriate materials.

Public Service Announcements

The PSA (public service announcement if broadcast, or public service advertisement if in print) is a tool for the public relations practitioner to get some print or broadcast exposure for little to no cost. Radio, television, and newspaper outlets will often devote a certain amount of space or time for PSAs. The Canadian Radio-television and Telecommunications Commission (CRTC) requires radio and television outlets to devote a portion of their airtime toward public service announcements. Stations must log their PSAs and present them to regulators when they go to renew their broadcast licences.

Radio, television, and newspaper outlets all welcome PSA submissions. Non-profit and government organizations traditionally qualify for these spots

Figure 10.9: Sample PSA

CLIENT: Mental Health Association	TIME: 30 seconds
TITLE: I'm still the same person	DATE: July 8, 2014

FEMALE VOICEOVER: When I told my friends I had been diagnosed with bi-
polar disorder, suddenly, they changed. They began to look at me funny...
avoid me...treat me differently. Just because I have a mental illness,
doesn't mean I'm not the same person.

MALE VOICEOVER: When I told my co-worker I had started taking medica-
tion to treat my depression, I noticed I got passed up for a promotion I
was expecting. It really hurt. I'm the same person I always was and I can
still do my job.

MALE VOICEOVER: When I casually mentioned to my landlord that I was
doing a lot better these days since I'd got some help for my post-traumatic
stress disorder, he found a way to not renew my lease. I don't understand.
I've always paid my rent on time. I'm still the same person.

ANNOUNCER: Mental illness is not a reason to shun people. It is a condition that affects some two million Canadians. Let's break the stigma.
Get informed.

based on their mission of serving the public good. Naturally, the competition among groups for this free space is often fierce, so it is imperative that public relations practitioners take every advantage available to get their public service message accepted and create PSAs that are as beneficial, relevant, well-written, and as appealing as possible.

PSAs can be event-centred (inviting the public to an event) or behaviour-centred (challenging people to adopt, modify, or quit a behaviour). Some examples of behaviour-centred PSAs include: *stop smoking, don't drink and drive, recycle, don't litter,* and *exercise more.* PSAs tend not to be about political or highly controversial topics, such as gun control or abortion. They are more about information that is widely agreed to be in the public's best interest, such as *don't text and drive,* and *wear a helmet.* Figure 10.9 is an example of a radio PSA whose purpose is to change people's thinking and behaviour about mental health. A public relations practitioner might write such a PSA for a mental health organization that is trying to deal with the issue of mental health and stigma.

Newsletters

Often, organizations have newsletters (printed or online or both), which public relations practitioners must write. Newsletters can be for internal audiences, like employees, or external audiences, like customers. They are often created to inform the audience and are comprised of a number of short articles of interest to the reader. Public relations practitioners must create content, conduct interviews, write articles and headlines, and work with the graphic artist for a suitable layout. Newsletter articles can be comprised of news items or feature stories. News articles will take on the inverted pyramid style of organization, with the 5Ws in the lead or close to it. Feature stories will tend to have other types of more creative leads such as anecdote, irony, contrast, or conflict.

Digital Media

More and more, public relations practitioners are called upon to write for digital media, including websites, blogs, or even social media releases (such as digital news releases with links for video and podcasts). Writing for digital media is predicated on the fact that users of digital media tend to scan more than they read. Hence, any writing for digital media should be concise with short sentences that are easy to scan, easy to read, and written at about a sixth to eighth grade reading level. Easy reading levels facilitate scanning and increase the chances that your message will be attended to by readers. Other techniques that help readers to scan material include boldfacing, underlining, bulleting lists, and using hyperlinks. If you highlight or draw attention to keywords and themes, you have more control over what the reader scans and can ensure that your intended message is communicated. When writing for digital media, make sure web pages are easily navigable. If readers cannot navigate pages easily, they will move on and read something else, likely leaving your site.

As you read earlier, organizations often will set up a media room on their websites. Journalists will use a media room like a media kit. They will use it to get background information and photos to write news stories. For that reason, media rooms should be current, informative, and easy for journalists to navigate. Media rooms must also contain the public relations person's contact information so that the journalist can contact him or her for more information. According to research, some of the most common frustrations that journalists have with media rooms is that public relations people do not put contact names in them and the links do not work.[14] These are all easy things to fix. None of these problems should exist on the websites of companies that have attentive public relations personnel.

Responsive Writing

Aronson and Spetner define responsive writing as "the act of correcting or capitalizing on a situation by writing to fill in omitted details or otherwise add information that better explains a subject, points out an error or promotes your client."[15] For the public relations practitioner, this may include writing letters to the editor, guest editorials, op-eds, crisis news releases, and/or official statements. They are writings that have come about out of necessity to respond to an issue, problem, or situation.

Letters to the Editor

A letter to the editor is a public relations tool that can be used in various ways to achieve public relations purposes. Letters to the editor can be used to (a) correct misinformation, (b) respond to negative coverage or tell another side to a story, (c) bring an issue into the spotlight, and (d) gain publicity. The kinds of information that might need to be corrected could be misinformation such as incorrect sales figures or the misquoting of a company representative. You can respond to negative coverage or tell your side of a story by offering new information, telling the story from a different viewpoint, or challenging a reporter if you think the reporting was imbalanced. Letters to the editor are also opportunities to bring an issue to people's attention or to remind people about an issue. For example, if you are a communications person for a non-profit organization whose mission is to decrease brain injuries, when news stories start appearing about athletes and hockey players experiencing concussions, you could write a letter to the editor drawing even more attention to the issue to keep it in the spotlight. You can use a letter to the editor to gain positive publicity for your organization. For example, if a competitor has new leadership, you could write a note of congratulations, demonstrating goodwill and drawing attention to your industry and organization. You could also congratulate someone in your own organization (depending on the level of public interest), thus affirming the employee and showing the public the quality of your organization's workers. It is not inappropriate to "toot your own horn" as long the situation and context warrant! See Figure 10.10 for an example of a letter to the editor that takes a legitimate opportunity at self-promotion.

Op-Eds

Newspapers (printed or online) have sections called opinion pages. Opinion pages include letters to the editor, an opinion piece by the newspaper's editor, and sometimes other opinion pieces called op-eds. *Op-ed* means "opposite the

Figure 10.10: Sample Letter to the Editor

Dear Editor:

I was pleasantly surprised by the number of Canadian designers whose work was worn by celebrities at the recent Juno Awards. Some 45 per cent of the outfits displayed were from our own domestic talent. I was never so proud to be a Canadian designer.

Canadians can expect to see a new line of accessories from Mona Charon Designs gracing the red carpet of next year's Country Music Celebration Awards in Branson, Missouri, as we have just solicited Miranda Richardson to wear our new line starting at the awards show.

Canadian designs and designers are having their work noticed both here and abroad. The Canadian design industry is alive and well!

Mona Charon, Designer
Vancouver

editorial page," referring to the page adjacent to the other editorials. Newspaper editors will often solicit guest writers to write opinion pieces to fill that space, or they may get personalities or figures of the day to write in response to a news story. If the writer of the op-ed is a CEO or manager or an industry expert (that is, not a public relations person), he or she will often consult with a public relations practitioner on the writing of the piece, have the public relations practitioner write the piece, or run his or her piece by a public relations person for input. Sometimes, the newspaper will ask a public relations person to write a piece on a certain topic or issue. For example, a public relations person may be asked by a newspaper to write an op-ed about crisis communication during the time of a crisis incident, such as the sinking of the *Costa Concordia* cruise ship in 2011 or the E. coli outbreak at XL Foods in 2012.

The job of writing op-eds often falls to the public relations department in an organization because it is a communications need in the marketplace, and no other department is as well-suited for this task. The public relations practitioner must consult with relevant organizational representatives, gather topical research, and write intelligently on the issue. The piece is often circulated and approved by appropriate organizational authorities since it is coming from the organization.

Op-eds are often about a subject that is timely, significant, unusual, or controversial. For example, a newspaper may ask a representative of an oil company to write an op-ed about why a particular pipeline project should be approved; it may also invite an environmentalist to write an op-ed about why it should not. A premier of a province may be invited to write a piece on an issue facing the province and affecting the nation. A union leader may be asked to write an opinion piece about why union workers should stay on the picket lines.

An op-ed should have a strong and engaging lead and a thesis or main controlling idea. The opinions or points espoused in the piece must be supported with good examples and evidence (such as polling data, interviews, research, case studies, personal experience) and sound logic. It should be written clearly and concisely, with short sentences and paragraphs, in plain language, and should be under 1,000 words. A strong conclusion should drive the main point home. When writing an op-ed, always check with the newspaper regarding their particular writing policies.

Crisis News Releases and Official Statements

A crisis news release is a news release written in response to a company or organizational crisis. The public relations practitioner, on behalf of the organization, will write a news release on the latest happenings of the crisis to inform news media and the general public. Similarly, a public relations practitioner may need to write, or assist the CEO in writing, a prepared official statement in response to the crisis. This statement may be made by the CEO or another representative of the organization, including the public relations representative.

Business Writing for Public Relations

This section will discuss the reality that public relations practitioners are called upon to engage in routine business communication, including the preparation of

- business letters and memos;
- reports;
- electronic communication;
- speeches and public presentations; and
- marketing and promotional materials.

Business Letters and Memos

Business letters are pieces of correspondence sent to external audiences. They should follow standard letter format. Every letter should contain

- sender's name and address;
- recipient's name and address;
- date;
- salutation line;
- body text (introductory paragraph, body paragraph(s), and concluding paragraph); and
- signature block (including any enclosure information).

Optional elements include a subject line after the salutation. Sometimes, business letters also contain the initials of the sender and the typist.

In contrast, the memo is for internal communication. The memo is comprised of

- *Memo* or *Memorandum* (title across centre of the page)
- Date:
- To: (recipient's name)
- From: (sender's name)
- Subject line
- Body text

Memos can be formal or informal, long or short.

The writing style of letters and memos is similar to journalistic writing in the sense that it follows the inverted pyramid method of organization—that is, the most important information for the reader goes first. The most important item in a business letter or memo is often called "the bottom line," and it should go in the first paragraph, with supporting information following in the subsequent paragraphs. The bottom line is the one or two main things the audience needs to know as a result of reading this communication.

For example, if you are writing a letter to a client and the main purpose of the communication is to send a copy of an annual report, the bottom line and the first few sentences of a cover letter should say something like, "Enclosed is a copy of our latest Annual Report." Or, if the purpose of a memo is to let employees know that the company has added a new employee benefit, the first few sentences should state, "XYZ Corporation is pleased to announce that employees may now add vision care to their list of benefits." (The exception to this is when the letter or memo is of a sensitive nature or would have an emotional impact on the reader. It may require an extra paragraph to lead up to the difficult main point.)

After the introduction of the bottom line, the body of both letters and memos should be comprised of the supporting details to the bottom line. The final paragraph of either letters or memos should contain the "call to action," or "what happens next," such as, "Please call me if you have any questions," or "I look forward to seeing you at the next meeting," or "I will call you next week to follow up."

Memos move organizations. It is the standard form of communication for businesses and organizations. Public relations practitioners, as communication managers, will find themselves writing a lot of memos, both in print and as emails. Note: Whatever you write in memos and emails is considered to be public and is subject to legal considerations and consequences. You will want to be careful not to write things that open you to litigation or cast shadows on your or your company's reputation.

Public relations practitioners often write specific kinds of letters called pitch letters and query letters. Part of the practitioner's job is to gain publicity by having favourable stories appear in various media. A practitioner may write feature stories suited to targeted media and ask editors to publish the stories (making the request in a query letter), or they may write editors and suggest that a publication write its own story on the suggested topic (making the request through a pitch letter). Query letters and pitch letters should follow all the rules of good letter writing; that is, they should be written on letterhead, have a date, an address block, a salutation, an introduction in which the request is made (that is, stating the bottom line), a body of supporting details, a conclusion that indicates what happens next, a signature block, and an enclosure line (if applicable).

Reports and Proposals

Public relations practitioners are often called upon to write reports and proposals. For example, these could be communications plans (see Chapter 9), status reports on a project, annual reports, or communication audits. Reports, depending on their size, typically contain a title page, a table of contents, an executive summary, body, summary/conclusion, and possibly appendices.

The most important part of a report is the executive summary. Busy executives and managers tend to read the summary, and sometimes only the executive summary, so the executive summary must be as complete, yet concise as possible, and should, ideally, be no more than one to two pages in length. (Of course, some reports are hundreds of pages long and so, a one-page summary is impossible; use discretion.) The executive summary can be the most challenging part of the report to write because one must distill the project down to its most important points as well as write completely and accurately. This task requires skill, time, and effort to write concisely. As Blaise Pascal (1623–1662), the seventeenth-century French philosopher and mathematician, once said of a letter he wrote, "I have written this letter longer than usual, only because I have not had the time to make it shorter."[16]

A communication audit is a report to a boss or client about the results from analyzing the communications tools and/or processes of an organization. It can be as simple as auditing the effectiveness of a certain piece of communication all the way to evaluating the effectiveness of all formats and channels of communication of an organization (such as brochures, website, intranet, training manuals, policies and procedures manuals, newsletters, telephone procedures, system of meetings, avenues of client/employee/customer appreciation). Such audits, depending on their scope and complexity, are usually conducted by the senior public relations professionals of an organization or can be contracted out. The structure of a communication audit would likely be a title page, table of contents, executive summary, introduction, description of the audit project and process, audit findings, recommendations, conclusions, and any appendices.

Backgrounders are reports that supply background information on an issue and are often used in media kits or accompany news releases. The purpose of a background is to address any anticipated questions on a subject.

Position papers are reports that explain an organization's position on a relevant topic or issue. A scientific organization may write a paper about its position on genetically modified foods. A pro-life group may have a position paper on when life begins, as might a pro-choice group. Government agencies often have position papers that outline the government's position on policy issues.

The creative brief is a specific type of report. It is a synopsis, overview, or summary of the understanding between an agency and a client, about the creative direction and roles and expectations of both the agency and client with regard to an event, project, or communications campaign. It can include information such as the client contact information, agency contact information, statement of the project, background or overview, target audience with major motivations and characteristics, major themes and key messages, goals and objectives, tone, focus, purpose, or vision, scheduling and budgeting considerations, and desired results of a communication effort. The purpose of a creative brief is to provide a clear understanding of the project to other members of your creative team who can take that information and execute their particular portion of it, whether it be to produce a creative work (e.g., advertisement, web page, etc.)

or execute an action (e.g., specifics of an event). The particular challenge in preparing the creative brief is distilling it in a *brief* form—generally two pages.

Sometimes, public relations practitioners must prepare briefing notes, attachments, and enclosures. Briefing notes are to help decision makers keep informed of the issues. A briefing note is, in essence, a short paper or report. It can be on any topic, policy, situation, issue, or project that the recipient needs. The recipient can be an individual (CEO, manager, government official) or a group (committee). Recipients look to communicators for their ability to discern and inform them of the core and key concepts.

Briefing notes are prepared for decision makers and for senior-level people to

- help make decisions or consider courses of actions;
- examine options;
- stay abreast of a matter;
- become informed or examine an issue;
- become more clear on an issue;
- prepare for an event or speech;
- provide context, background, information; and
- distill and encapsulate matters (some people may have to track multiple issues/projects and so their time is limited. Or the content of the issues may be extremely complex and/or voluminous).

Briefing notes should be clear, concise, easy to read, accurate, and, like its name implies, brief (one to two pages). There is no standard structure, but they all traditionally have a statement of the issue or topic, a discussion of the necessary information, and a conclusion that may include recommendations.

Electronic Communication

Writing emails is often overlooked in the discussion of public relations writing. This discussion is important, however, because so much communication occurs via email. When writing emails, senders will want to keep in mind that, even though emails can be quick and informal, they are not the same as texting. Emails are permanent business records.

Business communication using email should be in full sentences, with appropriate salutations. Special care should be paid to the possibility of miscommunication because emails cannot transmit for tone. Communications should be brief and focused. Do not use emoticons in business communication.

Figure 10.11: Unacceptable Workplace Email

Hey john–just got here (traffic's a bear :(and i wonder what u wanted again on
research for the dairy campaign (?????)....can't remember since we didn't finish
our meeting should we meet later?...hopefully we can do lots better than that last
agency with that crazy campaign idea. No wonder the dairymen jumped ship -
dont get me started - LOL.
Me

Figure 10.12: Acceptable Workplace Email

Good morning John:

I'm ready to start the research for the milk campaign. I'll do what I can and then
I'll likely need to consult with you further, since we didn't get to finish our meeting yesterday. Shall we meet later today?

Looking forward to working on this new account!

Regards,
Joe Kincaid
Research Assistant
XYZ Agency

Figures 10.11 gives an example of an unacceptable workplace email. The
example is exaggerated but it serves to highlight a number of issues. Figure
10.12 shows a better approach. Specifically, it uses full sentences, proper spelling, punctuation, and grammar, a salutation and signature line, and appropriate
business tone.

For all these forms of writing, the letter, memo, or any report, practitioners
will want to follow the rules of good business writing. Writing should be clear,
concise, devoid of jargon, written in plain language, and with predominant use
of active voice. Sentences and paragraphs should be short. Additionally, writing
will need attention to visual elements that help readers digest copy. Generous use
of bold face, underlining, bullets, charts, tables, graphs, and appropriate use of
colour, show a writer is audience-sensitive and audience-centred.

Speeches and Public Presentations

Often, public relations practitioners write speeches (for themselves or others) and make public presentations. President Barack Obama's speechwriter, Jon Favreau, was in his twenties when he was recruited by the Obama campaign to weave words. It was Favreau's words that helped Obama rise to the top during the early days of his presidential campaign. Favreau said his strategy was to spend time with Obama, getting to know his nuances, his vocal patterns, ideas, and phrases. Favreau also spent a lot of time reading great political speeches.[17]

Christopher Buckley, speech writer for the first President Bush says, "The trick of speechwriting, if you will, is making the client say your brilliant words while somehow managing to make it sound as though they issued straight from their own soul."[18] Scott Feschuk and Scott Reid, business partners and former speechwriters and political advisors to the Rt. Honourable Paul Martin during his time as prime minister write, "A speech can influence the course of events and careers. It can alter the future of an organization—and shape the reputation of the speaker."[19] Obama, Bush, and Martin were attuned to the connection between speech writing and relationship building (or public relations).

Marketing and Promotional Materials

Public relations practitioners may be involved in writing marketing and promotional materials such as brochures, advertisements, specialty advertising items, and direct mail products or advertisements. While these materials are not specifically public relations writing, public relations practitioners may be involved in their production. In this case, a public relations practitioner's role should be to serve as an advocate for the target audience with regard to truthfulness, accuracy, fairness, transparency, and ethical considerations, while serving organizational goals. (See Chapter 11 for more on developing advertising materials.)

WRITING ACROSS BORDERS

Although English is spoken the world over and is an international language of business, there are different nuances in usage and style of the language. British English is used by the United Kingdom and its influence extends to many of its former colonies and Commonwealth countries, including Canada. American English is used mainly in the United States. Even though the United States is only one country out of some 200 in the world, it is a country of significant population and global influence; hence, American English is an important language for global communication and trade. Between British English and American English, there are differences in vocabulary, inflection, grammar, terminology, punctuation, and grammar.[20] For example, in British English, to "table" an item in a meeting, is to discuss it; in American English, it means to delay the discussion for future. In British English, one sits on a chesterfield; in American English, one sits on a sofa or couch. In a financial news release written in British English, one might write of "turnover," but if written in American English, one is writing about revenue.

There are also some common spelling differences. For example, British English uses–re and American English uses–er, as in *centre/center* or *metre/meter*; l's are often doubled on conjugated verbs in British English, but not in American English, such as *travelling/traveling*. In British English, people write cheques, but in American English, they write checks.

To help sort through these differences, Canadian public relations writers and journalists largely use the *Canadian Press Stylebook* (CP style), while those in the United States use the *Associated Press Stylebook* (AP style). Public relations practitioners should be aware of the more common style rules in the *CP Stylebook* and be proficient enough with the book to know how to look up the rest, as needed. A quality public relations course of study should offer some exposure and training in CP style.

What does a Canadian public relations practitioner do if he/she is preparing materials for audiences of American English? There are varying views. Some feel one should simply prepare the materials in the style of the originating country and allow the recipient country to edit for their own market(s). Others feel that practitioners should prepare materials in the form and style of the recipient country. Some materials are meant to be posted online on the company website. Websites can be accessed globally and it would be impossible to accommodate all audiences, so, naturally, post in the form of the originating region and allow others to modify for their own market. But note that some companies do have alternate versions of their websites, particularly companies that conduct business in both Canada and the United States (such as Ally Financial and Sears), and so materials are prepared respectively for each website.

ETHICAL ISSUES OF WRITING

As you read in Chapter 4, public relations practitioners need to make ethical decisions about how and what they write. Ethics are not about the law, because practitioners must follow the law. (See Chapter 3 for law related to communications.) Ethics are about what *should* be done versus what is legal or illegal. Ethics are standards of conduct that help you decide what to do. A practitioner can be operating within the guidelines of the law but still be unethical.

Figure 10.13: The TARES Test for Ethical Writing

T—truthfulness of the message. Is the message accurate and complete? Am I creating a truthful, and not false, impression?

A—authenticity of the writer. Can I stand by the information, both personally and professionally?

R—respect for the audience. Is the message written in such a way that the target audience can understand it? Have I given the audience enough information to make an informed decision? Have I appealed to the audience's higher good, or have I simply pandered to their base inclinations? Does my message help them make responsible decisions for their lives?

E—equity of the appeal. Have I communicated fairly and justly? Is the audience properly informed by this message? Are the senders and receivers on a level playing field with regard to this message? Have I exploited the receivers in any way or selected them based on some predisposed vulnerability?

S—socially responsible. Does this message serve the public interest? Is it helpful to the audience and not harmful to another person, company, or organization?

Adapted from: Sherry Baker, and David Martinson, "The TARES Test: Five Principles for Ethical Persuasion," *Journal of Mass Media Ethics* 16, no. 2/3 (2001): 148–75; Donald Treadwell and Jill B. Treadwell, *Public Relations Writing: Principles in Practice*, 2nd ed. (Thousand Oaks, CA: Sage, 2005), 71–72.

The field of public relations has undergone a sea change with regard to ethics. Under increasing pressure, practitioners have developed codes of ethics to govern many aspects of practice. (See Chapter 4 for more about the CPRS and IABC codes of ethics.) These codes have implications for writing. For example, practitioners are called upon to be truthful and accurate. By implication, what a practitioner writes should be the truth and it should be accurate information. Practitioners are called upon to be transparent. By implication, that means that the true source of a communication should be clear. Practitioners are called upon to be honest. By implication, when writing, a practitioner should be careful to give proper credit whenever he/she uses other people's materials— sources should be properly credited, and plagiarism should be avoided.

Plagiarism is a very important issue for students of public relations to become aware of. Students are often confused about what constitutes plagiarism. Basically, do not copy other people's words without putting those words in quotations and properly citing the source. Also, do not cut and paste from the Internet. This is a simplistic explanation and it warrants further and appropriate study from college and university learning centres and professors. Plagiarism is a little different than copying other people's logos and creative logo (that's trademark infringement and is also illegal), and the topic is a serious one that students need to attend to as they enter a career in public relations.

Baker and Martinson have developed an ethics self-test for public relations writers. They call it TARES—an acronym for *truthfulness, authenticity, respect, equity,* and *social responsibility.*[21] TARES encourages writers to ask themselves questions about each piece of communication. See Figure 10.13 for more about TARES.

The presumption is that public relations writers have a responsibility in public relations ethical decision making with regard to their writing.

CONCLUSION

Public relations writing is a specific skill. It is unlike essay writing or academic writing and students should be aware that this is another skill they can add to their public relations toolkit. Unlike essay writing, the main point or "bottom line" of any piece of writing usually appears at the beginning of a piece rather than at the end. Public relations writing skills can be developed and mastered through understanding some key principles, such as the importance of writing for a specific audience, using active voice, and employing good grammar.

KEY TERMS

Crisis news release: A crisis news release is a news release written in response to a company or organizational crisis. The public relations practitioner, on behalf of the organization, will write a news release on the latest happenings of the crisis to inform news media and the general public, continually keeping media updated.

Email pitch: A short, punchy email address to a journalist or blogger, suggesting he or she write about and publish a story on a certain topic. A news release with all the information appears below it.

Inverted pyramid method of organizing information: A method of organizing information that requires the conclusion or main point to go at the beginning, not the end of the piece. Information appears in descending order of importance to the reader.

Letter to the editor: Sometimes referred to as LTEs, a letter sent to a publication by a reader or a public relations person on a topic or issue of concern. The intention is for that letter to be published in the publication so that other readers can read it.

Media alert (media advisory): A simple notice of the who, what, when, where, why (and sometimes how) of a news story, usually a simple or single event, such as a public appearance or a press conference.

Media kit: A packet of information prepared for journalists, containing a news release and a selection of appropriate supporting material, such as a fact sheet, biography, or backgrounder article.

Media room (press room): The designated section on an organization's website for journalists to access a media kit, an archive of current and past media releases, public relations contact information, photographs, and anything else an organization wishes to make accessible specifically to journalists.

Mind mapping: A visual brainstorming technique that identifies a central word or concept around which other related words or concepts are arranged. Once you have your main idea and have done a bit of research, start in the centre of the page with the main idea (thesis), and then work outward in all directions to produce a structure of related thoughts, words, or images. You can group like items together to produce a sort of visual outline.

News release: An article that the public relations practitioner has written for the journalist in the hope that the story will make its way into the news either as written or used as an idea by the journalist for his/her own angle or story.

Official statement: Planned and prepared information supplied to reporters by an organization on a timely, significant, unusual, or controversial matter, or in a crisis.

Op-ed: An opinion piece that appears in the editorial pages of a newspaper (most often "opposite the editorial" article of the newspaper's editor) and is written by someone outside the newspaper staff and editorial board. Sometimes newspapers ask experts and relevant members of the public to write on a certain topic, and sometimes people will simply send an op-ed unsolicited in hopes it will be printed. It is also sometimes referred to as "opinion editorial." The topic or subject will likely be on a major news issue of the day that is timely, significant, unusual, or controversial.

Pitch letter: A letter written by a public relations practitioner to an editor, asking him or her to write a story on a suggested topic.

Plain language: Writing in plain language is simply choosing appropriate vocabulary for the target public, using simple and direct words and sentence constructions arranged in easy-to-manage sentence lengths and paragraphs.

Position Paper: A publication prepared by an organization, most often the public relations person, that outlines the organizational perspective on a topic or issue related to the organization.

Public service announcement (PSA): A proposed script for a broadcaster (television or radio broadcast) to read on-air that announces or discusses items of public concern and benefit (such as "stop smoking," "wear a helmet," a fundraiser, etc.). PSAs are usually 10 seconds or 30 seconds in length, although they can be up to 60 seconds.

Query letter: A letter written to ask an editor to publish a feature story or article that he or she has written. Freelance writers often query publications to accept their works, as do public relations practitioners. Public relations practitioners, however, are writing stories that will in some way enhance the reputation and image of their organizations.

TARES: A self-test developed by Baker and Martinson (2001) that can be used by public relations people to guide them in ethical considerations about a piece of writing. It is an acronym that calls upon the writer to consider *truthfulness, authenticity, respect, equity,* and *social responsibility* in the preparation of communication pieces.

FOR REVIEW AND DISCUSSION

1. What is public relations writing? Describe how the inverted pyramid method of organizing information is different from other ways of organizing information that you have used in the past.
2. Explain some guidelines for good public relations writing.
3. Which formats are used in public relations writing and which do you think you will enjoy writing the most? Explain your answer.
4. Assess what some of your biggest strengths are and what your challenges will be with regard to producing good pieces of public relations writing.
5. Predict how it may feel to have your writing critiqued during the approval and/or feedback process. How might you handle criticism?
6. Propose how you will integrate ethical considerations into your writing.

ACTIVITIES

1. Think of your favourite company, brand, product, service, or organization. Go to the corresponding website and enter the media room (also called a press room).

Imagine you are a journalist and evaluate the usefulness of the media room. Consider the following:

- How current are the news releases?
- Do the news releases include a contact name?
- What other types of documents are available here?
- Are there photos and logos?
- Does the media room appear to be maintained and updated regularly?

2. Pick up a copy of a major daily newspaper. Look for the opinion pages and note the articles that appear here. Find an article from the editor. Find the letters to the editor and find an op-ed.

Note the topic of the op-ed and the writer. Evaluate whether the op-ed is written according to the best writing practices outlined in this chapter. Consider the following criteria in your assessment:

- Does the op-ed state a position early in the piece?
- Is the opinion supported with good evidence?
- Is the tone professional and respectful? Explain.
- Is it persuasive? Defend your answer.

3. Imagine that the Public Relations Department at your school produces a print and online publication that provides short biographies of each student, telling who they are, where they come from, any past education, their favourite part of public relations, and what they want to do with their degree. The intended audience is fellow students.

a. Interview a classmate to get the information you need to write a short biographical article for this publication.
b. Write the article (about five paragraphs). Create a simple mind map if you need to.
c. After you have written the article, run a readability test using your word processor or a website.
d. Go through the article to check the use of active voice. How many sentences are in active voice? How are many in passive voice? (Hint: Microsoft Word will tell you what percentage of your article is in passive voice.)

e. Go through the article for word choice. Are the words strong, appropriate, and truthful?

f. Go through it again for sentence length. Are there any long, cumbersome sentences?

g. Go through it again for paragraph length.

h. Look at it again for spelling and grammar.

i. Have a peer read the article and provide feedback. How did it feel to have your work critiqued?

FURTHER READING

Berry, Jeremy, Richard T. Cole, and Larry Hembroff. "US-Canada Study of PR Writing by Entry-level Practitioners Reveals Significant Supervisor Dissatisfaction." *Journal of Professional Communication* 1, no. 1 (2011): 57–77.

Bivins, Thomas H. *Public Relations Writing: The Essentials of Style and Format.* 8th ed. New York: McGraw-Hill Higher Education, 2013.

Davies, Christopher. *Divided by a Common Language.* Boston: Houghton Mifflin Harcourt, 2007.

Diggs-Brown, Barbara. *The PR Style Guide: Formats for Public Relations Practice.* 3rd ed. Belmont, CA: Thomson Wadsworth, 2012.

Felker, Daniel B., Frances Pickering, Veda R. Charrow, V. Melissa Holland, and Janice C. Redish. "Guidelines for Document Designers." Washington, DC: American Institutes for Research, 1981, http://files.eric.ed.gov/fulltext/ED221866.pdf.

Foster, John. *Writing Skills for Public Relations.* 5th ed. London: Kogan Page, 2012.

Government of Canada. *Successful Communication Toolkit: Literacy and You.* May 2003. http://www.nald.ca/library/learning/successe/successe.pdf.

Hacker, Diana, and Nancy Sommers. *A Canadian Writer's Reference.* 5th ed. New York: Bedford St. Martin's, 2012.

Kimble, Joseph. "Writing for Dollars, Writing to Please." *The Scribes Journal of Legal Writing* 1996–97. http://www.plainlanguagenetwork.org/kimble/Writing1.pdf.

Phillips, David, and Philip Young. *Online Public Relations.* 2nd ed. London: Kogan Page, 2009.

Strunk, W. Jr., and E.B. White. *The Elements of Style.* 4rd ed. New York: Allyn and Bacon, 2000.

Treadwell, Donald, and Jill B. Treadwell. *Public Relations Writing: Principles in Practice.* 2nd ed. Thousand Oaks, CA: Sage, 2005.

Walker, Robyn. *Strategic Business Communication: An Integrated, Ethical Approach.*
Mason, OH: Thomson South-Western, 2006.

Wilcox, Dennis L. *Public Relations Writing and Media Techniques.* 7th ed. Upper
Saddle River, NJ: Pearson Higher Education, 2012.

NOTES

1. Doug Newsom and Bob Carrell, *Public Relations Writing Form and Style,* 6th ed. (Belmont,
   CA: Wadsworth Thomson Learning, 2001), 4.

2. Ibid., 9.

3. Imperial Tobacco Canada, "The Future of the Canadian Tobacco Company," last updated
   June 26, 2012, http://www.imperialtobaccocanada.com/groupca/sites/imp_7vsh6j.nsf/
   vwPagesWebLive/D07VVQQN?opendocument&SKN=1.

4. D. Roen, G. Glau, and B. Maid, *The McGraw-Hill Guide: Writing for College, Writing for Life,*
   2nd ed. (New York: McGraw-Hill, 2009).

5. Joseph D. Novak and Alberto J. Canas, "The Theory Underlying Concept Maps and How
   to Construct and Use Them," Technical Report IHMC Cmap Tools 2006-01 Rev 01-2008,
   Institute for Human and Machine Cognition, Florida, 2006, http://cmap.ihmc.us/publica-
   tions/researchpapers/theorycmaps/theoryunderlyingconceptmaps.htm.

6. Kathryn Riley, Kim Sydow Campbell, Alan Manning, and Frank Parker, *Revising Professional
   Writing in Science and Technology, Business, and the Social Sciences,* 2nd ed. (Chicago: Parlay
   Press, 2007).

7. The readability calculator is at http://www.online-utility.org/english/readability_test_
   and_improve.jsp.

8. Sue Horner, "My Grandma Helps Avoid the Passive," *Get it Write* (blog), December 10,
   2010, http://getitwrite.ca/2010/12/10/grandma-helps-avoid-passive/.

9. Plain Writing Act of 2010, Pub. L. No.111-174, 124 Stat. 2861 (2010). See http://
   www.gpo.gov/fdsys/pkg/PLAW-111publ274/pdf/PLAW-111publ274.pdf.

10. See www.plainlanguage.gov.

11. Communication Policy of the Government of Canada, "Policy Requirements, 3. Plain
    Language," last modified November 27, 2013, http://www.tbs-sct.gc.ca/pol/doc-eng.aspx
    ?id=12316&section=text#sec5.3.

12. William Zinsser, *On Writing Well* (New York: Harper, 1998).

13. Shift Communications social media template is available at http://www.shiftcomm.com/
    downloads/smprtemplate.pdf.

14. Coy Callison, "Media Relations and the Internet: How Fortune 500 Company Web Sites
    Assist Journalists in News Gathering," *Public Relations Review* 29 (2003): 29–41.

15. Mary Aronson and Don Spetner, *The Public Relations Writer's Handbook* (Toronto:
    Maxwell Macmillan Canada, 1993), 199.

16. Blaise Pascal, from Letter XVI: To the Reverend Fathers, the Jesuits, accessed
    March 4, 2014, http://oregonstate.edu/instruct/phl302/texts/pascal/letters-c.
    html#LETTER%20XVI.

17. Ashely Parker, "What Would Obama Say?" *New York Times*, January 20, 2008, http://www.nytimes.com/2008/01/20/fashion/20speechwriter.html.

18. Ibid.

19. Feschuk.Reid, "Why Feschuk.Reid?" accessed March 5, 2014, http://feschuk-reid.com/whyfeschukreid/.

20. A helpful resource is Jeremy Smith, *The American-British, British-American Dictionary For English Speaking People* (Corvallis, OR: CodeSmith, 2004).

21. Sherry Baker and David Martinson, "The TARES Test: Five Principles for Ethical Persuasion," *Journal of Mass Media Ethics* 16, no. 2/3 (2001): 148–75.

Cynthia Wrate

Advertising: A Primer for Public Relations

11

LEARNING OBJECTIVES

After reading this chapter, you will be able to

- define advertising;
- describe the creative and business roles in advertising;
- explain the difference between paid media space and unpaid media space;
- describe the criteria for selecting different types of media for advertising;
- explain the advantages and shortcomings of the different types of media;
- describe the components of a creative plan; and
- identify media vehicles that are particularly useful to public relations.

INTRODUCTION

If you asked several strangers what "PR" is, chances are very good many of them would reply "free advertising." Yet one of the defining characteristics of public relations is that PR is not advertising. As you have read in previous chapters, the role of public relations is to build mutually beneficial relationships with a wide range of stakeholders, audiences, and publics.

The role of advertising is to promote products, services, and ideas to what is usually a clearly defined stakeholder—customers. Most PR professionals will benefit from some understanding of advertising and its role in corporate communications.

DEFINING ADVERTISING

Tuckwell defines advertising as "a paid form of marketing communications through the media that is designed to stimulate a positive response from a defined target market."[1] Let's look at important points in this definition:

- **Advertising requires payment.** If an exchange or payment is required for a message or endorsement to appear in any media, it is a form of advertising. Payment typically is monetary but can also include other forms of exchange, including trade for services and barter.
- **Advertising is designed.** Every element of advertising is within the direct influence or control of the advertising organization. The precise words, design, schedule (defined in the advertising industry as "trafficking"), size, specific page ranges or times, calls to action, links, and even paid Internet search rankings can be specified by the sponsoring organization.
- **Advertising is directed at defined target markets.** The choice of media, the creative strategy and execution, specific messages, and timing of messages are developed by the sponsoring organization to match the interests and viewing and reading habits of the specific audiences that the sponsoring organization is trying to reach.

Advertising, then, is any message, in paid media space, where the sponsoring organization has control over content, placement, and timing in order to influence target markets and audiences to view a product, service, or idea favourably and motivate them to purchase, use, or support it. You will learn more about paid media space later in this chapter.

As you have read in previous chapters, many organizations view communications as an interdependent and complementary group of activities. As the distinction between the disciplines disappears, public relations experts, advertising, event marketing, and digital communications specialists often work together to provide their organizations with an optimal blend of integrated marketing communication (IMC) services.

A BRIEF OVERVIEW OF THE ADVERTISING INDUSTRY IN CANADA

Although it is impossible to provide an in-depth understanding of the advertising industry in one chapter of a public relations text, it is important for public relations professionals to understand advertising as a communications medium, especially the elements of advertising that work particularly well to build relationships and influence opinion.

Advertising is a $7.1 billion industry in Canada (2012) and employs an estimated 71,000 people.[2] The advertising industry includes

- advertisers (retailers, industry, manufacturers, service firms, all levels of government, and non-profit organizations that invest in advertising);
- advertising agencies that develop advertising;
- the media that carry advertising (e.g., newspapers, websites, television, magazines, billboards);
- media associations that conduct measurement and represent industry interests (such as Numeris; the Canadian Circulation Management Association);
- research firms that study public attitudes and behaviour; and
- production companies that film, edit, and design video, web pages, and print and broadcast advertisements.

UNDERSTANDING DIFFERING ROLES IN ADVERTISING

Advertising is usually managed within the marketing departments of most organizations, although it is not uncommon for advertising and public relations functions to be part of an integrated marketing and corporate communications structure. In the agency realm, public relations and advertising firms tend to focus on specific areas of expertise.

If public relations is about relationships, then advertising is about ideas. Advertising experts work in diverse specialized roles that generally fall into two streams:

- creative development and services, and
- business development and services.

The people who come up with ideas and turn them into actual advertisements work in creative services as writers and designers. Creative roles include copywriting, graphic design, Web design and print, video, audio, and online production and other creative functions involved in conceptualizing, creating, and implementing advertisements. Together, people in these positions are responsible for developing ideas that effectively communicate a message, as well as refining and producing the final creative material.

Roles in business services include

- account and client relationship management;
- account planning;
- media planning and media buying to help clients select the right blend of media without overspending;
- production management;
- purchasing outsourced services, materials, and supplies; and
- research.

Account and client relationship management staff are the people who are responsible for overall management of the advertising process, acting as a bridge between the client's advertising, product, or brand managers and the agency's creative team.

Account managers within advertising and public relations agencies have similar responsibilities—developing marketing and advertising strategies that meet clients' objectives, preparing project briefings that guide the creative development process, and project managing the completion of the many components of a campaign. Successful account and relationship managers have a sound understanding of business strategy, marketing and communications strategy, and consumer behaviour. Senior account management staff provide strategic counsel to clients, build client relationships, and manage the business of the agency.

ADVERTISING COSTS

Advertising budgets are significantly higher than public relations budgets. Public relations budgets must account for research, time (the salary or hourly cost for the time public relations people spend working on projects), event production, and the costs of materials. In public relations, time is generally the highest cost. In advertising, however, media space and creative production represent the significant costs. Major national advertising campaigns can run in the millions of dollars. A small regional campaign that includes purchasing advertising on a few regional broadcast stations and print publications can cost tens of thousands of dollars. Even small local campaigns will require thousands of dollars.

Nevertheless, advertising provides public relations practitioners with important support to media relations and relationship building. (See Chapter 12 for more about media relations.) When you need to control the timing, specific expression, audience reach, and distribution of a message, advertising is an important part of your public relations plan.

Defining Paid Media Space

As described earlier in this chapter, advertising appears in paid media space. Distinguishing paid media space from unpaid media space is not always easy. If you are uncertain if a message in any media might be advertising, ask these questions:

- Is there a clear "sponsor"—an organization or individual—affiliated with the message content?
- Is the message clearly placed into defined space in the media in which it appears, such as a particular section of a newspaper or web page, a 30-second commercial on television or radio, a pop-up or banner advertisement on a web page, or a poster?
- Is the message controlled by the sponsoring organization? Does it feature a way to respond directly to the sponsor organization?
- Does the same message and creative expression appear in many different media?
- Did the sponsor organization pay a fee or exchange something of value for the message to appear?

If the answer is "yes" to any of these questions, you are likely dealing with advertising, and some form of payment was made to appear in that media. (See Figure 11.1)

CHARACTERISTICS OF ADVERTISING

Public relations and advertising work most closely together in two broad situations: when public relations is an integral part of the introduction or revitalization of a product, service, or idea by generating news coverage—sometimes referred to as "buzz"—and when advertising is an integral part of image building or advocacy—influencing public opinion toward an issue, need, or idea.

Figure 11.1 Comparison of Paid and Unpaid Media Space

Paid media space (Advertising)	Unpaid media space
Paid space; can be expensive	Earned presence; is unpredictable
Controlled content and timing; message is defined; requires creative strategy	Uncontrolled content and timing; message is interpreted, requires news value
Message is defined by the advertiser	Message is interpreted by media
Message sponsor is clearly identified	Message sponsor is usually unclear
Creative media strategy is of primary importance	News value is of primary importance
Audience perceives message as "sell"; lowers credibility	Audience perceives message as "news"; heightens credibility
Focus is on customers	Focus is on multiple stakeholders and influencers
Primary focus is to generate sales	Primary focus is to create goodwill
"Sales" orientation is not as effective in social media	Relationship, listening orientation is strong in social media

When advertising deals with controversial subjects or contains provocative content, the campaign itself can become the source of positive—or negative—attention from news media. The Atheist Bus Campaign generated significant media attention in Canada and the United Kingdom when it launched a moderately expensive transit advertising campaign regarding atheism on transit media. In some locations in Canada, the advertising was refused. There is no question the subject of religious advertising elicits strong views, but from an organizational awareness perspective, the attention from news media played a highly positive role in building awareness and support among target supporters of the sponsoring organization. At the other end of the spectrum, two companies that advertised in the 2011 Super Bowl—the most expensive single advertising vehicle in North America—issued apologies following public backlash against advertising messages that were seen as insensitive and violent. Groupon apologized for advertising that was perceived as insensitive to issues in Tibet and HomeAway issued an apology for what some perceived as promoting violence in its depiction of a doll being smashed against a wall.[3]

Incorporating advertising into public relations plans requires an understanding of the particular conditions that shape the suitability and success of advertising as part of an overall PR plan.

Media Selection and Timing

Before the broad availability of the Internet in the late 1990s, effective advertising media selection required determining which of an established selection of media choices best matched the listening, reading, and viewing habits of specific target markets and audiences. Media plans would usually include a selection of newspaper, magazine, television, radio, billboard, poster, transit, and direct mail choices that supported the creative approach developed for a campaign, reached the target audience, and could be purchased within budget. Advertising agencies and their clients placed highest importance on the creative "idea" while media buyers (experts who specialize in buying and placing messages in media) focused on successful acquisition of, and negotiation for, an optimal blend of time and space to support the timing of the campaign and the creative execution of the advertising. You will learn more about creative execution later in this chapter.

Today, the media consumption patterns of audiences are highly fragmented and the range of advertising opportunities is almost limitless. Making the right choice about media is critical, and the role of media planners has taken on greater importance. Media planners determine the media strategy that will meet specified organizational or campaign objectives, select specific media that will best support the strategy, and evaluate how effective different media are at reaching and interacting with audiences. Media selection and buying is now equally important to the creative development of a campaign (and sometimes more important than creative development) for three reasons: media costs are usually the most expensive part of a PR program; there are so many media options available; and audiences have become very fragmented.

Added to traditional media are newer, interactive, and emerging media choices that include Internet banner advertising, paid search engine results and search-driven advertising, branded YouTube channels, cinema advertising, location-based ads on mobile devices, and product placements in television programs and movies. Advertising options exist in almost every location and in every format where people use communication tools, consume media, or can be exposed to a message. In fact, it is estimated that consumers are exposed to more than 3,000 commercial messages every day.[4] To make sure their organizations stand out in such a crowded environment, media buyers make selections using a specific audience profile. You will learn more about audience profiles later in the chapter.

When choosing specific media, media buyers will look at

- media performance;
- media type; and
- media timing.

Media Performance

When rating performance, media buyers evaluate the reach, frequency, and impact a particular message must achieve in order to meet advertising objectives. Reach is a quantitative measure that determines how many people in a target audience are exposed to a message, while frequency measures how often the average person in that target market is exposed to the message. Impact is a qualitative measure of the degree to which an audience is likely to respond to an ad, the distinctive way audiences consume specific media, and to what degree audiences are likely to engage with that media.

For example, a message in one newspaper may be viewed as more authoritative and trustworthy (for example, the *Globe and Mail*) than it is in another (a supermarket tabloid). Television and Internet video have more impact for messages that must be seen or that depend on emotion, while radio has greater impact for local and immediate messages or those that spark the imagination through sound. Website banner ads invite detailed comparisons; ads on mobile phones encourage spontaneity; while direct mail, including email, can be highly personalized.

Strategic media buying requires selecting an optimal mix of media types to ensure the message is seen by enough people, often enough and with enough impact to generate the desired response.

Media Type

The types of media available fall into several broad categories and subcategories:

- traditional media
- digital media
- alternative media
- new media

Television, newspapers, magazines, direct mail, radio, and out-of-home media (such as billboards and transit posters) are all examples of traditional media. Digital media includes electronic messages appearing on screens that are operated by a computer, such as Web banner ads, electronic billboards, and

Figure 11.2: Strengths and Shortcomings of Various Media Types

Media	Strengths	Shortcomings
Alternative (niche media, often short-term and created for specific campaigns to draw press attention)	High impact; has news value	Reaches a narrow audience; audience exposure is short term; media has a short lifespan
Digital (focused on digital devices such as tablets and smartphones)	Messages can be customized for different locations; can buy media on national or international telecommunication networks; animation, sound, and visual design add impact	Banners can be viewed as annoying; audience skews to high Internet users; audience is usually focused on something else; recipients may have to pay for text messages on mobile phones
Direct mail (including email)	Messages can be personalized and highly targeted; messages are flexible and measurable; supports detailed message; is a controlled media with no competitors/other advertisers; timing is flexible	Print has high cost per audience contact; spam has reduced how willing audiences are to open direct email; can be viewed as "junk"; response rates are often low; has a short lifespan
Internet	Message can be interactive; advertising can be produced almost immediately for low cost; messages are easily shared; is highly targeted to specific audiences	Audience can control whose messages reach them; messages have low impact
Magazines	High reader engagement; strongly targeted; advertising can be highly compatible with the publication's editorial content; media has a long life span; magazines have a high share "pass along" rate	High cost per audience contact; requires advance planning as there is a long lead time (2–3 months) between when an advertisement is produced and when it appears
Newspapers	High trustworthiness; timely; local, typically good local distribution; flexible; visual	Short life; print editions not easily passed along; negative environmental perceptions
Out of home (billboards, transit shelters, posters)	Strong local presence; very low cost per audience contact; can target specific routes/locations on transit/billboards; message has a long life	Messages must be very short; billboards can be cluttered on highways; difficult to reach specific audiences
Radio	Highly localized; low cost; reaches broad audience; excellent for messages that draw on imagination; timing can be tied to radio programming	Must buy time on multiple stations to reach wide audience; audience tends to listen as "background" noise, which can mute message
Social media	Highly targeted; timely; measurable response	Audience rejects overt promotion
Television	Very high impact image and awareness; mass market reach; good local market/program targeting	Very high cost per ad placement and production; creative production must be excellent; short lifespan

Web pop-ups. Alternative media refers to niche and non-traditional out-of-home media, such as posters in bathrooms, building murals, and shopping cart posters. New or emerging media refers to various social and digital media that are gaining in use but not well established.

Strengths and Shortcomings of Various Media Types

Each type of media encompasses many media vehicles. A media vehicle is a specific product within a media type. For example, print media vehicles include

- display advertisements (a full page or less) in printed newspaper and magazines;
- advertising features (can be multiple pages);
- free-standing or tipped-in inserts (stand-alone single or multiple page booklets, loose or bound into the publication); and
- advertorials (a combination of an advertisement and editorial used primarily to promote ideas by an identified sponsor in paid media space).

Broadcast media vehicles include

- specific television programs (such as *Mad Men*);
- sponsorships (such as *Hockey Night in Canada*);
- public service announcements for local community events; and
- live on-site broadcasts at a store opening or special event.

Interactive and online communication has multiplied the media vehicles available to advertising. Non-traditional media vehicles offer new ways to reach audiences with highly targeted, low cost, high impact communications. Online and interactive vehicles can include pop-up advertising, banner ads, paid search engine results, interactive content, games and contests on social media sites. Examples include location-based advertisements or social network-based advertisements sent to mobile devices such as smartphones and tablets.

Media buyers consider a combination of traditional, alternative, and new media to reach audiences effectively. Consumers have many communication options available to them, and some browse many media at once. For example, it is the norm more than the exception for someone to check in with social media or read the paper while watching television, or surf social media or download apps while using mass transit. It is not surprising, then, that the emergence of media multitasking is a major trend influencing media buying. Media buyers must take the number (such as multiple radio stations), type (such as broadcast, print, or digital), and combination of media into account when selecting the media they will use.

Media Timing

Advertising allows organizations to determine what their messages say, where they will appear, and when. Timing of advertising influences cost, reach, frequency, and impact. Advertisers match their advertising plans to their major sales, fundraising, or membership cycles. For example, high demand seasonal periods like back-to-school and the Christmas holiday period increase the cost of advertising on television and radio. The Canadian Cancer Society ties its advertising to a spring daffodil campaign, while auto-club membership drives are often tied to the winter driving or summer holiday season.

Media planners must also consider the overall schedule of the advertising. Because media is a significant investment, advertisers must decide how frequently they need to run their messages in order to effectively reach an audience. Media planners may choose to run advertising continuously (schedule advertising evenly within a specified time); flight their ads (run periodic waves of advertising separated by periods of inactivity); or pulse their ads (run a base level of ads, supplemented with intermittent higher level of advertising in an on-off, on-off pattern similar to flighting).

Advertising continuously allows organizations to establish a strong foundation for message awareness. Flighting allows organizations to extend the length of their campaigns by establishing baseline message awareness that is then carried over the period with no activity to the next scheduled advertising flight. Pulsing allows organizations to achieve an impact similar to continuous advertising but at a lower cost.

The strategy media planners select depends on how great an impact the advertiser must make, how cluttered the media environment is, how long the campaign must run, and what budget is available for the campaign.

CREATING AN AUDIENCE PROFILE

As you have read in previous chapters, to reach and motivate audiences successfully, organizations need a highly detailed understanding of those audiences. One tool many organizations use is an audience profile.

A comprehensive profile that considers demographics, psychographics, and location allows media buyers to choose options that have the greatest potential to reach the right audience, with the right medium at the right price. Advertisers develop detailed descriptors of target markets and audiences based on common characteristics that include demographics, psychographics, and location information.

Demographics

Demographics are quantifiable and measurable attributes such as age, gender, income, education, ethnicity, occupation, marital status, and family composition. Although demographics provide a starting point for grouping people who may have common interests due to life stage and spending power, they do not distinguish between interests, values, and influences. Attitudes and influences are quantified through psychographics.

Psychographics

Psychographics refer to ways of thinking and behaving. Individuals of the same age, income, and gender can have starkly differing values and interests. For example, people with similar views on environmental issues, social justice, or economic development are likely to represent all genders and a broad range of ages, education, and income but share common opinions and motivations.

The psychographic profile of target audiences significantly influences what media the audience tends to read, listen to, watch, or interact with and how the audience responds to messages. Understanding the psychographic profile of target audiences is critical to both media buying and creative execution.

Location

Canada is a geographically diverse country, with significant regional, urban, and rural differences. Eighty per cent of Canadians live in urban environments (cities) where media clutter is the norm. In many locations in Canada, geography can limit access to technology. Some rural Canadians cannot readily access high-speed Internet service or media common elsewhere. But regardless of region or size of their community, Canadians do tend to have one thing in common. Canadians tend to value local news, and it is the news that directly influences and is influenced by PR. When using advertising to support PR, it is important to match media buying decisions with local news media.

CREATIVE EXECUTION

If media buying and strategic planning are the science of the advertising business, creative execution is its art. Writers, designers, photographers, animators, videographers create everything from simple display advertisements in the local newspaper to big-budget television or audio-visual productions that can rival the movie industry and often employ the same talent.

In 2009, London advertising agency BBH London blurred the boundaries between advertising and film even further when they created the world's longest cinema advertisement for client Johnny Walker. Shot in a single, continuous six-minute take, The Man Who Walked Around the World is a short film, and long advertisement, with all the characteristics of a blockbuster.[5] The ad features a notable star (Scottish actor Robert Carlyle), a production house studio director (Jamie Rafn), a substantial credit roll, and distribution through movie theatres. Add a list of industry awards for creativity and technical achievement, and it is difficult to tell where the advertisement stops and the entertainment feature begins.

Regardless of format, or the size of the budget, advertising follows a creative plan that considers

- the problem or opportunity that the advertising is intended to solve;
- the characteristics identified in the audience profile;
- the distinguishing advantages and positioning of the product, service, or idea that is the focus of the advertising; and
- the media that will best reach the target market.

Public relations programs that include advertising components are often trying to accomplish a communication goal that

- creates or increases awareness of a company, product, or idea;
- creates or changes perceptions of a product, idea, or organizational image;
- introduces a new product, opportunity, or idea;
- presents information regarding an issue; and
- promotes a positive organizational image.

Based on the specific communication goal(s) for the advertising, the creative plan specifies a message theme, tone and manner, and a specific appeal method that supports the plan's strategic objectives. A theme is the overarching idea that carries across all media and all target groups. Tone and manner refers to the attitude, personality, and style of an advertisement or advertising campaign. For instance, a few examples of tone and manner could be humorous, irreverent, factual, understated, youthful, mature, or authoritarian. Tone and manner are based on the positioning and personality of the sponsoring organization. Appeal methods are based on the type of approach that is most likely to be most influential in provoking the desired response from the intended audience.

An emotional appeal is frequently used in corporate-image advertising, by non-profit organizations, and by social organizations. Emotional appeals have strong impact and successfully influence changes in attitudes, perceptions, and behaviour. Tim Hortons is well known for its use of appeal advertising, such as its "Proud Fathers" hockey ad and "Welcome Home" immigration ad.

A positive appeal puts the emphasis on an enjoyable benefit the target audience will experience from the advertised product or idea. The overall impression is pleasurable, so the audience feels good about the subject of the ad. Home Depot Canada's former slogan "You can do it, we can help" is an example of a theme that carried a positive appeal in their advertising.

A negative appeal plays on fear or discomfort. The target audience is motivated to act in order to avoid an unpleasant experience, decision, outcome, or development. Buckley's Cough Syrup's famous "tastes awful, but it works" theme uses a double negative. Most people would avoid something that tastes awful (a negative), but even worse is suffering through a cold and sore throat (another negative).

A factual appeal taps into reason and rational thought. It is effective when there are clear facts to support a decision, whether the decision is to buy a product, support a development, or understand a decision.

One set of facts can lead to an opposing set of facts. A comparative appeal is commonly used when an organization wants to draw attention to the specific benefits of a decision, purchase, or behaviour if directly contrasted against its closest alternative. Comparative appeals are common when there are two clear competitors or sides to an issue. Comparative appeals can result in strong divisions among the intended audience and can provoke a response from the compared organization. Well-known examples of comparative advertising include the Pepsi Challenge and the humorous Mac versus PC campaign sponsored by Apple.

Examples of advertisements that draw attention to an idea rather than a product are MADD Canada's public service advertisements. One long-running and well-known television advertisement replicates the perspective of a driver behind the wheel of a vehicle as a succession of drink glasses is stacked in front of the viewer. An equally progressive loss of vision occurs until the viewer/driver's vision is literally and figuratively impaired and the viewer drives into a streetcar, and the advertisement ends with the message, "Each drink you have before driving impairs your judgement." This high impact ad follows MADD Canada's "don't drink and drive" theme. Its tone and manner is suspenseful. The viewer's vision blurs with as each glass is set in front of the one before. An unspoken message linking the empty glasses to deteriorating vision is well communicated. The ad uses a factual appeal with negative consequences—the presumed death or injury to the viewer—to deliver a high impact message.

A new media example of an online ad campaign that generated a lot of media attention was a campaign for Old Spice body wash in 2010. The campaign used a positive appeal and was designed to revitalize the Old Spice brand, which was viewed as a stodgy men's cologne your grandfather might wear. The campaign was targeted toward the male and female 12- to 34-year-old market with a theme of "smell like a man, man."[6] The tone and manner were irreverent and played on manly stereotypes. The humorous appeal was a hit with the target audience, and the campaign became an Internet and social media sensation. The campaign also became the focus of media attention on a changing advertising landscape, resulting in total combined paid and unpaid media impressions of over 1 billion.[7]

RECOMMENDED MEDIA VEHICLES FOR PUBLIC RELATIONS

Media vehicles that work particularly well with public relations include

- newspaper special features;
- advertorials;
- print inserts;
- broadcast announcements and vignettes; and
- Internet, mobile, and emerging media.

Newspaper Special Features

In 2014, there were 94 paid (subscription-based) and 24 free daily newspapers in Canada. In 2012, daily circulation for paid newspapers was 4.2 million, and for free newspapers was 1.8 million, for a total daily circulation of 6 million.[8] Despite the perception that print is passé, newspapers still provide tremendous reach.

Newspaper special features tend to focus on issues, special events, and achievements of interest to readers, but are supported through additional advertising. For example, a real estate developer who wants to draw attention to the environmental qualities of a new housing development may pitch a special feature on "green building techniques." The developer would feature prominently in the content of the feature, while encouraging suppliers and other stakeholders to purchase the advertising that funds the feature. Special features are common for businesses achieving a milestone, fundraising activities for community buildings such as recreation centres and libraries, or tourism destinations.

Although a printed newspaper is still the main way Canadians read newspapers and magazines, print readership is dropping as newspapers attract new readers via the Internet. In 2012, 80 per cent of Canadians read a newspaper every week, either online or in print.[9] E-readers and tablets are giving Canadians more ways to access newspapers, including through apps.[10]

Internet news makes it easy for readers to link to similar stories that interest them, connect to organizations referenced in the body of a news story, and refer media stories to others (either directly to individuals or to broader networks through social media). Online news also provides easy access to background information or other material of interest.

Print also plays an important role with social media. At least 77 per cent of Canadian social media users read a print or online newspaper every week, while only 7 per cent access online versions exclusively.[11] The strong relationship between newspapers and social media present opportunities for PR professionals to use the timing, control, and placement benefits of advertising to encourage audiences to engage in social conversations online.

Advertorials

Advertorial is a coined word that blends *advertising* and *editorial*, so it is not surprising that advertorials work well for public relations professionals. Advertorials are paid advertisements written in the form of news editorial, which provide the combined benefit of a controlled advertising message with the detail and interest of a news story. Used in print publications for over 60 years,[12] advertorials are also a common vehicle in digital space, particularly in the form of paid blogs.

Advertorials are written and designed to mimic the format of news content in the publications in which they appear, and the publisher will assign one of its own writers to the advertorial to maintain editorial consistency. Since news and third-party opinion is considered less self-serving than advertising, an advertorial provides the benefit of increased credibility. Because advertorials are written and designed to resemble news coverage, many readers may not realize they are reading sponsored content. In order to maintain the trust of readers and journalists, public relations professionals who use advertorials as a promotional tool must clearly identify the advertorial as an "advertisement," "advertorial," "paid supplement," or other term that clearly designates the advertorial is paid content.

Print Inserts

Print advertising media include newspapers, magazines, leaflets, flyers, and other forms of direct mail. Print is still considered the most reliable source of information, and advertising in print publications provides the opportunity to present detailed content to audiences with an interest in local, current, and newsworthy events. The online versions of print publications are also highly credible and provide opportunities to add interactive elements to advertising. Print inserts include any print publication that is inserted into another print publication, such as flyers or leaflets inserted in newspapers or information cards inserted into magazines.

Broadcast Announcements and Vignettes

Television and radio advertising are media that work particularly well for emotional, positive, and negative appeals designed to reach large audiences. Public relations tends to use broadcast media only for corporate image advertising and for crisis communications.

For example, when Maple Leaf Foods shut down one of its meat processing plants in 2008 and initiated a national recall of products due to Listeria,[13] the timely and heartfelt broadcasts of national television ads featuring CEO Michael McCain played an important role in demonstrating the company's commitment to resolving the problem and protecting consumers. The company purchased ads after the crisis as well to outline the steps the company had taken. The actions of the company, expressed through its advertising, played an important role in restoring Maple Leaf Food's reputation.

Broadcast advertising is expensive. However, it is possible for non-profit organizations to use interstitials, also called vignettes, which are as long as regular 30- or 60-second advertisements but are treated as mini information segments. They are less expensive because there are rules that prevent overt promotion, but they are an excellent information source when tied to highly relevant programming. Public service announcement time is a fraction of the cost of regular advertising, though production costs remain an important consideration.

Although broadcasters are not required to carry paid advertising messages or broadcast public service announcements or advocacy ads,[14] the Canadian Radio-television Telecommunications Commission (CRTC), which regulates the industry, does expect broadcasters to contribute to the creation and presentation of Canadian programming.[15] Because broadcasters are motivated to air Canadian programming, public relations professionals who can provide interesting, well-written messages and produce good quality, informative public service announcements with strong Canadian content are highly likely to gain the support of local and national Canadian broadcasters.[16]

The CRTC regulates the broadcast industry but it does not regulate advertising, except for messages directed to children and ads featuring alcohol. Broadcast advertising content is self-regulated by the Television Bureau of Canada (TVB), and in almost all cases ads that air on television, including public service announcements, are sent to the TVB for content clearance. According to the TVB, over 55,000 ads were approved in 2010, confirming that television continues to be an important advertising medium.[17]

Non-profit organizations can also become their own broadcaster. For example, YouTube provides free branded YouTube channel services to qualified non-profits in Canada. A branded YouTube channel has distinct advantages that are quite different from the open YouTube site. The channel is designed to reflect an organization's image and identity; the organization can control the content; site visitors are not distracted by other videos; and comments can be moderated.

Internet, Mobile, and Emerging Media

Online, mobile, and emerging media opportunities are multiplying rapidly and changing just as quickly. No matter the specific vehicle, however, all new opportunities share some important common characteristics: they are timely, they are targetable, and they reach a highly mobile, "always-on" audience, and they can be tracked and measured.

Internet and mobile communication networks provide the means to pinpoint online advertising tied to audience interests, audience location, and search patterns. A service such as Google Adwords is a method of search engine optimization that permits advertisers to draw audiences to corporate websites and other communication tools. For example, a public relations manager for an organization that supports student loan reform may choose to purchase the words and phrases that students, policy makers, lenders, post-secondary admission planners, and other key stakeholders use when searching for information about student loans. As a result, the organization would appear near the top of the search results list of anyone using those words in a Google search.

Advertising on mobile devices can specify delivery of messages to precise addresses, a significant advantage for public relations efforts geared toward encouraging people to support specific initiatives, visit local landmarks, or modify behaviour. For example, if a cellphone user was hiking near a park that was subject to development, the public relations representative of a conservation group could send an advertising message using a text message to solicit support for a "save the park" campaign.

The ability to pinpoint communication so precisely has raised concerns regarding privacy. For public relations professionals, these legitimate concerns demand that organizations protect, respect, and use information ethically in order to guard the privacy of individuals and uphold the reputation of the organization. Privacy is an emerging reputation issue, from which public relations professionals can anticipate new interpretations of Marshall McLuhan's famous expression, "the medium is the message."[18] Perceptions of traditional, new, and emerging media impact how a message is received as well as how the media changes perceptions.

CONCLUSION

Public relations and advertising professionals are both experts in supporting organizational goals through the effective planning, development, and implementation of communication programs. Public relations and advertising generally differ regarding the audience to which communication is directed, and whether the media space where a message appears has been compensated for carrying the message. The audience for advertising is typically target consumers, who are reached through a controlled message deliberately placed in specific media that have been paid for. In comparison, public relations develops relationships with many different audiences. News media interest in messages generated from PR activity is based on the news worthiness of the message.

There are times when public relations programs and campaigns benefit from the use of controlled messages in paid media. Organizations are increasingly integrating their corporate communications activities to ensure consistent messages across numerous media and to multiple audiences. Public relations professionals who understand how advertising and PR complement each other, the planning and implementation of advertising, and the strengths and weaknesses of specific media are well prepared to ensure that their organizations develop effective communication programs.

KEY TERMS

Advertisers: Individuals, organizations, governments, associations, and others who sponsor (buy) advertising.

Advertising: A paid form of marketing communications from identified sponsors offered through the media that is designed to influence the thought patterns, attitudes, and behaviour of target audiences.

Advertising agencies: A service business composed of creative people and business people who plan, create, produce, and place advertising messages in advertising media for clients seeking to find customers for their products, services, and ideas.

Advertorial: A combination of an advertisement and editorial used primarily to promote ideas by an identified sponsor in paid media space.

Alternative media: A variety of media that reach audiences when they are engaged in specialized activities. Alternative media can include movie theatre advertising, subway stations and tunnels, and other niche items designed to attract news media attention.

Audience profile: Economic, demographic, and social characteristics of the specific readership, viewership, and listenership of a particular advertising medium.

Creative plan: A document prepared by an advertising agency that outlines the creative theme, message, tone, manner, and appeal method to guide the development of the writing and design of an advertising campaign.

Digital media: Digitized words, pictures, audio, and video that can be delivered over the Internet or telecommunications networks. This type of media can be directed toward mobile phones, smartphones, and tablets. Digital media can also refer to *new media*.

Frequency: The number of times that each person in an audience is exposed to an advertiser's message over a specified period of time.

Impact: The effectiveness of the match between media and message to ensure the greatest potential audience will be exposed to the message, remember it, and be motivated to acquire the good or service or act on the idea.

Media buyer: The person who selects, negotiates, and monitors specific media space as necessary to place messages in media.

Media planner: The person responsible for developing the overall strategy of a media plan by assessing the strengths, weaknesses, cost efficiencies, and communication potential of various media.

Media space: A specified allotment of time or space in various categories of media, broadcast, print, Internet, digital, and direct mail available to sponsors who wish to purchase advertising.

Media vehicles: Specific print, broadcast, digital, or other media used in an advertising campaign.

New media: Media that are not yet fully established. Most new media has been developed since the advent of the Internet. This phrase is sometimes used interchangeably with *digital media*.

Paid media space: Specified allotment of time or space in various categories of media for which an identified sponsor has paid a fee, or exchanged a service of value, in order to place advertising.

Reach: The number of different (unduplicated) people exposed to an advertiser's message over a specified period of time.

Traditional media: Established media, usually referred to as media introduced before the advent of the Internet, such as magazines, direct mail, newspapers, and broadcast television and radio.

Unpaid media space: A specified allotment of time or spaced in various categories of media in which a product, service, or idea is mentioned as a result of news media interest. Also called *earned media*.

FOR REVIEW AND DISCUSSION

1. Why is it important for public relations practitioners to understand advertising?
2. In your opinion, what are the similarities and differences between roles in public relations and advertising?
3. Describe the three criteria that media buyers use to choose specific media for a campaign.
4. Describe examples of communication you have seen that made it difficult to tell if it was advertising or public relations.
5. What are some questions you can ask to distinguish between paid and unpaid media space?
6. Why do you think many people think to public relations as "free" advertising?
7. In your opinion, which advertising appeal would be particularly effective if:

   a. You were developing a public relations campaign for a food bank.
   b. You were introducing a new product or service.
   c. You were wishing to expand an industrial site near a city. Near a small town.

8. In your own words, describe the components of a creative plan.

ACTIVITIES

1. Imagine you are introducing a new video game. Compare and contrast the media choices you would make for public relations and advertising. Explain the reasons for your choices.

2. Review a section of a local newspaper. Identify advertisements you think are affiliated with a public relations campaign. What appeal are they using? Is there any editorial content in the paper related to the campaign? If so, how does this content support or detract from the public relations message? If not, what might you suggest to the sponsoring organization to improve the effectiveness of their public relations campaign?

3. Visit the websites of three media industry associations, such as the Canadian Newspaper Association, the Interactive Advertising Bureau of Canada, the Television Bureau of Canada, or the Out-of-Home Marketing Association of Canada. Review any information you find on the websites regarding the strengths of the media the associations represent. Imagine you are a media buyer. What recommendations would you make to a public relations professional about the specific media you have chosen?

FURTHER READING

Canadian Media Directors' Council: www.cmdc.ca

Institute of Communication Agencies: http://www.icacanada.ca/aarc/assetDetail.aspx?id=24.

Interactive Advertising Bureau (IAB Canada): www.iabcanada.com

Magazines Canada: www.magazinescanada.ca

Newspapers Canada: www.newspaperscanada.ca

Television Bureau of Canada: www.tvb.ca

NOTES

1. Keith Tuckwell, *Canadian Advertising in Action*, 8th ed. (Toronto: Pearson Education, 2008), 502.

2. Statistics Canada, *Annual Survey of Services Industries: Advertising and Related Services*, CANSIM (63-257-X), released January 14, 2014, http://www5.statcan.gc.ca/olc-cel/olc.action?objectId=63-257-X&objectType=2&language=0&limit=0.

3. Tim Calkins, "Learning from Groupon and HomeAway," *Super Bowl Advertising Review*, Kellogg School of Management, February 11, 2011, http://kelloggsuperbowlreview.wordpress.com/2011/02/11/learning-from-groupon-and-homeaway/.

4. Louise Story, "Anywhere the Eye Can See, It's Likely to See an Ad," *New York Times,* January 15, 2007, http://www.nytimes.com/2007/01/15/business/media/15everywhere.html.

5. To view the ad online, search for "Johnny Walker Man Who Walked around the World" video.

6. Eleftheria Parpis, "Spice It Up," *Ad Week,* July 26, 2010, http://www.adweek.com/news/advertising-branding/spice-it-102895.

7. P&G, "Old Spice," Latest Innovations Factsheet, accessed March 6, 2014, http://www.pg.com/en_US/downloads/innovation/factsheet_OldSpice.pdf.

8. Newspapers Canada, "FAQ," accessed March 6, 2014, http://www.newspaperscanada.ca/about-newspapers/faq-about-newspapers/faq.

9. Newspaper Audience Databank Inc., "Toronto Report," accessed March 31, 2014, http://www.nadbank.com/en/studies/2012.

10. "Postmedia Network Launches 10 Canadian Newspaper Apps for iPad," *Business Wire,* December 7, 2010, http://www.thefreelibrary.com/Postmedia+Network+Launches+10+Canadian+Newspaper+Apps+for+iPad.-a0243728768.

11. Newspaper Audience Databank, "Why Newspapers? Social Network Users: A New Conversation?" September 2009, http://www.nadbank.com/en/system/files/Social%20Networking%20Users.pdf.

12. Merriam-Webster dictionary cites the first use of the word in 1946.

13. CBC News, "How Maple Leaf Foods is Handling the Listeria Outbreak," August 28, 2008, http://www.cbc.ca/news/business/story/2008/08/27/f-crisisresponse.html.

14. CRTC, "Broadcast Advertising Basics: Revenue, Limits and Content," last modified December 11, 2013, http://www.crtc.gc.ca/eng/info_sht/b300.htm.

15. CRTC, "Reinvesting in the System," last modified December 2, 2013, http://www.crtc.gc.ca/eng/cancon/t_reinvest.htm.

16. See, for example, CBC Radio-Canada Public Service Announcement Policy, accessed March 31, 2014 http://www.cbc.radio-canada.ca/en/reporting-to-canadians/acts-and-policies/programming/public-service-announcements/1-4/.

17. TVB, "FAQ," last modified February 13, 2014, http://www.tvb.ca/pages/just+the+faqs_htm/.

18. For more about Marshall McLuhan, see http://marshallmcluhan.com/.

Mark Hunter LaVigne

Proactive Media Relations

12

LEARNING OBJECTIVES

After reading this chapter, you will be able to

- define media relations;
- explain the difference between reactive and proactive media relations;
- describe the principles that govern successful media relations;
- identify criteria that makes a story newsworthy;
- list the steps to create a media relations plan;
- describe how to monitor media coverage of your PR campaign; and
- explain the importance of media training.

INTRODUCTION

Media relations is the art and science of reaching your target audience with key messages through the news media.[1] Media relations is one of PR's main practice areas and, arguably, one of the most difficult. It is one of the only marketing communications disciplines that goes through a gatekeeper—news media—to reach the end audience. The media relations strategy that enables key messages to pass through the gatekeeper intact is easily applied to other marketing communications disciplines. Finding the newsworthiness in a message necessarily removes non-essential information. It focuses organizations intellectually to get down to their brass tacks: to keep their messages simple, to the point, and honest.

Media relations can be very effective when its key messages are adopted by advertising and sales promotions and are rolled out in an integrated manner. Key messages can also be adopted by other divisions of a company, from sales to human resources and from the reception desk to shipping and receiving.

PROACTIVE AND REACTIVE MEDIA RELATIONS

There are generally two types of media opportunities: reactive and proactive.

Reactive media relations generally involves the media coming to you, usually within a negative context, such as layoffs, product recalls, reorganizations, poor stock performance, specific industry regulatory issues, fires, and illegal activity within the organization. This kind of media relations is often called crisis communications or deliberate response communications because you should be ready to deal with these kinds of situations when they arise. (See Chapter 16 for more about crisis communications.)

Proactive media relations generally involves going to the media proactively, usually for positive stories, but sometimes for negative ones as well. Reasons for such contact run the full gamut, including new product or service launches, product re-launches, appointment announcements, mergers, lobbying efforts, and reorganizations. Methods of media contact can include news releases, special events, news conferences, video and audio news releases, conventional and satellite or Internet media tours, and telephone or personal meetings with journalists with whom you have developed professional or personal rapport. With proactive media relations, you are in the driver's seat. You go to the media when you are ready, on your schedule, and generally to your agenda.

MEDIA RELATIONS PRACTICE

The five basic principles that govern successful media relations are

- content;
- context;

- organizational access;
- proactive response; and
- relationships with the news media.

Content must be tightly written, with a focus on the facts and an avoidance of hyperbole and half-truths. It must be constructed in an electronic format and delivered to the news media on an electronic platter. The inundation journalists suffer, plus continued merger mania in the news business, means they have little time to research or sift through useless information to find your news.

Context is placing your organization's news within the ebb and flow of the daily news. It also includes timing, especially in relation to what else is going on.

Organizational access is very important. The news media operate on a much tighter schedule for everything compared to the regular business world. A radio journalist, news agency, or website needs the information or interview requested that hour, not the next day. Television needs it the by the same afternoon, at the latest. So does print since they too are trying to match the 24-hour news cycles on their websites and through digital media.

Proactive response is essential in creating a two-way flow of information between your organization and news media. The more proactive an organization is over time, the less severe the reaction by the media if there is a crisis. If the news media know your organization as open and honest through years of access, then the worst part of a crisis ("what are they hiding?") may be mitigated or at least minimized.

Relationships with the news media goes hand in hand with access. Over time, if your organization and PR practitioners have been open and honest with the media, that access and honesty go a long way in raising your organization's credibility and position on a journalist's priority list. You must keep in perspective the amount of information bombarding the news media today.

THE STATE OF THE MEDIA IN CANADA

One of the first rules of media relations is to know the type of media you are working with. When you know something about the environment in which journalists have to work, you appreciate their deadlines and their perspectives, all of which helps to improve your skill in reaching them with your story or news release.

Since the 1980s, the news media, particularly private sector newspapers, magazines, radio and television outlets, have suffered from the same economic turmoil as other private sector organizations. Globalization, recessions, national and multinational mergers, and technological revolution have significantly affected the business side of the news media, which has caused upheaval in newsrooms across the country.

Since the turn of the millennium, computers and computer networks have enabled the same news reporting functions to be performed by fewer people, while the same technology has exponentially increased the amount of news available for reporting. Consequently, there is more news to be processed by fewer people.

Many journalists, those who survived recessionary and technological downsizing, have stayed in their positions longer than in the past. The rate of staff turnover in the news business traditionally is high, and still is to a certain extent, but in major news markets such as Toronto (or Chicago, New York, Los Angeles) there is far less movement than ever before, partly because there are fewer jobs available.

Although it still takes the average journalist ten years to reach major markets such as Toronto (moving from minor market to medium market to finally to this news mecca in English Canada), economic conditions have kept these reporters in their same jobs, rather than the typical movement from general reporter to beat reporter to editor. Progression up the news ladder is much slower than it has been in the past.

Because of these factors, journalists are older, smarter, better educated, and more cynical than they were in the past. That cynicism breeds distrust (a traditional journalistic trait anyway), which makes reporters and editors alike a lot more suspicious in general. When it comes to reactive media relations (when the news media come to you, usually within a negative context), they are more formidable than they ever have been.

Combined with relatively low pay (compared to other industries) and the uncertainties of most private sector jobs (downsizing continues as a trend), tabloid journalism has risen in popularity in a quest for greater audience numbers (to attract dwindling advertising dollars) as well as a justification for what journalists do both for the news owners and to satisfy their own increasing cynicism. Tabloid journalism tends to be sensationalistic, unbalanced, and controversial. It has spread from weekly newspapers to television and is anticipated eventually to infect radio news and daily newspapers. Technological advances have made research easier and more precise, so when a news story is placed on official record, it can be accessed by more news media than ever before, for a much longer period of time.

The News Hole

Furthermore, a dramatic shift in advertising revenues from mass advertising to much more targeted marketing communications has drastically reduced advertising revenues available to the majority of private sector mass news outlets. The rise of direct mail, promotions, and social media has spread marketing communications revenues across a much broader plane of media. The consequence for anyone submitting a news story or media release is that the traditional news hole (the space in which proactive news can be placed) has dramatically shrunk because advertising revenues for traditional news media have been diverted to other marketing communications vehicles.

The News Fence

A news fence has always existed between advertising (those that sell advertising) and editorial (the news gatherers—reporters, editors, producers) in most news media organizations. Journalists are trained literally to bite the hand that feeds them—that is, to be distrustful of the very advertisers who ultimately pay their salaries. Journalists must not let advertising influence the news.

Public broadcasters, such as TVO (Television Ontario), generally do not rely on advertising (CBC TV is an exception) for the bulk of their revenue and, therefore, have an even more entrenched anti-private sector bias than their media counterparts in the private sector. Some of the most critical programs (to private sector organizations) are broadcast on public networks. The economic and demographic forces influencing news media in the private sector described earlier are even more profound in the public media sector. Government cutbacks have turned public broadcasting on its ear and will likely continue to do so for years to come.

In smaller media outlets in the private sector, such as some trade magazines or broadcast outlets, the news fence is thinner than in major markets. In bigger or more established media outlets, however, the fence can be as thick as a bomb shelter wall. The width of the news fence indicates to what degree advertising can influence editorial decisions.

Nonetheless, proactive media relations in the private sector (for example, a product launch) is often suspected by many of the news media as veiled advertising. A common, if not subconscious, media response is, "if you want to buy advertising, you should go down the hall to the advertising department to buy it." In reactive situations, the media generally suspect private sector representatives are lying. You are considered guilty until proved innocent in the court of media opinion. The point is that if you are using multiple means of reaching your audience, including advertising, you cannot expect to get any special treatment from reporters just because you are advertising in their medium. They will judge each case on its journalistic merits, not your ad budget. This independence is even reflected if that medium has agreed to be a sponsor of yours. If you have obtained media support to sponsor your special parade, for example, and a car blows up, reporters will cover the car explosion, regardless of how negative it is to your campaign.

Newsworthiness

Usually within the realm of proactive media relations, a newsworthiness checklist has been developed to help determine whether a story you propose taking to the media, yourself or through a public relations practitioner, is newsworthy.

Reporters and editors are essentially storytellers. Newsworthy means good story. There are general criteria for what constitutes news, discussed below. However, each media outlet's choice of news is affected by its understanding of what its specific audience wants.

Out of all the activity happening everywhere, reporters and editors choose what is news. They decide what is worthy of the front page of the paper or the cover of the magazine and what is worthy of being one of the 15 stories that makes it on a local television newscast.

Their decisions are based, to a certain extent, on practical considerations. When a television station has video of a fire, for instance, that story is much more likely to get covered in the newscast than if the camera crew did not get to the blaze in time to record it.

There are seven criteria that determine whether an idea is newsworthy. For any story to make the news anywhere, the media must believe it will affect the public's mind or heart because of these elements:

- **Impact:** What impact will the story have on society or one of its facets?
- **Proximity:** Is it locally important? Nationally important?
- **Timeliness:** Is it happening now?
- **Prominence:** Does it speak for itself?
- **Conflict:** How many sides are involved in an issue? How contentious is it?
- **Novelty:** Is this new or simply a regurgitation of something from the past?
- **Human interest:** How much of the focus is on people?

If none of these criteria is prominent, what you have is information, not news.

HOW TO REACH THE MEDIA

Spend the research dollars and time to research your target audiences carefully. Know your audience and know what news media they follow so that you can reach them through it.

Mainstream news media such as daily newspapers and network television will often reach many of your target audiences. But don't overlook the many relevant media outlets for the target audience, such as magazines, cable TV shows, email newsletters, and blogs that can reach your target audience(s) more directly. As well, make sure your media messages can be adapted to more than one medium (e.g., television, radio, print, and online) so that your message gets to your target audiences in a variety of ways.

Often, an integrated campaign that provides news editorial can be augmented later with advertising. Display advertising (small print or tile Web ads) in smaller circulation media outlets need not be expensive. If another media outlet picks up the story, follow up by placing an advertisement in that outlet.

After you have clearly defined who your target audience is, determine which media outlets you would like to use to reach those target audiences. Now it is time to create your media list (list of media contacts). There are a variety of suppliers that sell media lists in electronic form and can customize them to your needs. These suppliers offer one-time purchase of lists and subscriptions to Web-based list services that are constantly updated. Both options are expensive but invaluable to a successful media relations campaign because they will save you the time spent on researching this information yourself. Non-profit organizations can build their own lists through the Yellow Pages, Web searches, and library searches and build their own databases.

It is always a good idea to purchase media lists from a number of different suppliers, especially if you are starting out in a new media niche. To ensure your media list is as complete as possible, plan to email or call and confirm information at key media outlets. When purchasing media lists, make sure they contain phone and fax numbers, email addresses (the best are those that go directly to the journalist and not to general inboxes), and snail mail addresses (for sending product samples if relevant).

Once you have your media list, aim to hit the target media in at least two ways, such as via direct email (from your own service provider, with your name on the email) and via paid newswire services available to the PR industry (such as Marketwired and the CNW Group). Using as least two methods will ensure the targeted news media have seen your message.

You should update your media list constantly. Use email bouncebacks as a warning that you have the wrong information. Keep up with the list services and never underestimate the power of an old-fashioned phone call to the media outlet's reception desk: they know everything.

MEDIA RELATIONS PLANS

PR practitioners should get into the habit of writing plans as early in their careers as possible. (See Chapter 9 for more on preparing communications plans.) Steps for creating a media relations plan include the following:

1. Create or gather as much research as possible about the relevant target audiences.
2. Develop your key message.
3. Establish which news media to target and create your media list.
4. Create the communications to send through the target media to the target audiences. Be sure to get your budget parameters from your internal and external clients.

The McCormick case study, taken from a wrap-up report, shows the structure of a media relations plan.

CASE STUDY: MCCORMICK® GOURMET SUPER SPICES[2]

Preamble
- The Gourmet Super Spices campaign was launched in March 2010. Media relations tactics included an English and French matte article (material prepackaged to look like print-ready news articles) with article, sidebar, and recipes distributed via News Canada; English and French news releases distributed via Marketwire (rebranded as Marketwired) and direct email; and a Chinese news release distributed via Dyversity PR.
- Product sample kits went to an A-list of about 100 media contacts.

PR Objectives
- Through proactive media relations, the objective was to generate positive media coverage in both the consumer and trade food news holes to help drive awareness and sales. At least 10 million total

impressions generated, a 75 per cent overall score (Media Relations Rating Points–MRP) with a cost per contact of $0.05 or below.

Target Audiences
The target audiences for the campaign included

- primary purchaser, female aged 35–54 with 2+ kids at home; children under 18 at home, predominately maturing families (kids aged 6–12); and established families (kids aged 13–17);
- relatively affluent households with income of over $70K; and
- health-focused homes.

Target Markets
The target markets for the campaign included

- Toronto (extended Golden Horseshoe area from Hamilton through Toronto to Oshawa in southern Ontario): 6.5 million;
- Montreal, Quebec City (Laurentians/Eastern Townships) corridor: 3.6 million;
- Vancouver and Lower Mainland, BC, including Whistler: 2.6 million;
- Calgary/Edmonton Corridor: 1.9 million;
- Maritimes and Atlantic Canada: Halifax, NS, St. John's, NL: 500,000;
- Prairies: Winnipeg, Saskatoon, Regina: 250,000;
- Smaller towns and cities in between covered by News Canada distribution; and
- Chinese Canada focused in major urban areas including Vancouver, Calgary, Edmonton, Toronto, and Montreal.

Target Media
The target media for the campaign included

- major market daily newspapers and wire service contacts (mainstream food);
- consumer magazines (mainly women targeted, food editors and writers);
- trades and business magazines (food, packaging, grocery);
- electronic media (radio and TV where relevant);
- websites/E-zines (food);

- freelancers (mainly food); and
- community newspapers and small dailies (through News Canada distribution channel).

Tactical Summary

Tactics utilized included

- English Canada media relations, campaign design, and co-ordination: Hunter LaVigne Communications Inc., Aurora, ON;
- French Canada media relations: ACJ Communication, Montreal, QC;
- Chinese Canada media relations: Dyversity PR, Markham, ON;
- Paid wire: Marketwired;
- Matte article/recipe distribution: News Canada;
- Media monitoring: Cision, News Canada, Marketwired;
- Media evaluation: MRP, News Canada.

Budget

- Fees of $8,000 and disbursements of $15,890 for a total of $23,890

Results

- Total impressions captured: 47,444,820 (10 million was the target)
- Cost per impression: $0.001 ($0.05 was the target)
- MRP: 87.28% (75% was the target)

Highlights included pickup of the Super Spices story by Rita Demontis in her nationally syndicated "Eat" column, sourced from her *Toronto Sun* full-page article in 30 Sun Media dailies and 28 corresponding online media outlets. Major daily pickup included the *Sun* newspapers in Toronto, Winnipeg, Ottawa, Edmonton, and Calgary. Total impressions were 5.3 million impressions. Other major news portals in English and French that picked up the story verbatim from the news release included Yahoo, Google, Altavista, Reuters, Congoo, Findarticles, Topix, MSNBC, with reviews in *Canadian Packaging*, *24 Heures*, *Hamilton Spectator*, *Grocer Today*, *Ontario Restaurant News*, and *Pacific/Prairie Restaurant News*. Total impressions were 31.7 million impressions. Articles and recipes distributed by News Canada netted 8.1 million impressions, with Chinese media relations bringing in 1.8 million impressions.

Impressions

Impressions relate to circulation or audience numbers as determined by an objective agency like the Audit Bureau of Canada (ABC) for newspapers, or Numeris for television and radio. For example, the *Globe and Mail* has approximately 300,000 readers a day; a story placed there could claim 300,000 impressions. Some practitioners add a multiple factor of two or three times to reflect pass-along readership, such as in an office subscription. (See Chapter 8 for more on impressions.)

Media Relations Rating Points (MRP), developed by CPRS, aim to provide a scientific basis for measuring media coverage. See Figure 12.1 for an excerpt from the MRP report for the McCormick® Gourmet Super Spices Campaign of 2010.

The continued evolution of Web and social media hits will also help to measure all means of media in the future.

Goals and Sales

Equating sales to impressions is difficult to predict and should not be tied together. Sales results depend on a number of factors, such as a client's sales resources, including the strength of its sales force; its placement at retail outlets (such as prominent displays versus mid-shelf); and other elements of the campaign. Equating sales to impressions also comes too close to conflicting with the eighth point of the CPRS Code of Professional Standards: "A member shall not guarantee specified results beyond the member's capacity to achieve."[3] Your job is to get the right number of media hits from the right media that reaches your audience.

MEASURING AND EVALUATING MEDIA COVERAGE

MRP is "Canada's standard for earned editorial media coverage."[4] (Earned editorial coverage is media coverage that the company or PR firm has not paid for.) MRP is "designed to make it easy for communications professionals to measure, evaluate and report the results of media coverage generated by media relations campaigns."

The MRP system was developed as a "simple, standardized reporting system that is easy to use and...widely accepted by the PR industry and utilized to measure any type of editorial coverage whether that be print, broadcast, or online. The MRP system includes a media report template, rating system and a tool

Figure 12.1 Media Coverage and Analysis Report Sample Page

Publish Date	Media Outlet	Location	Prov	Type	Reach	Positive	
2-Mar-10	Yahoo.ca	National	CA	Website	2,805,802		
8-Mar-10	www.lisaliving.ca	National	CA	Website	10,000		
3-Apr-10	Worldjournal.com	National	CA	Website	50,000		
11-Mar-10	Worldjournal.com	National	CA	Website	50,000		
11-Mar-10	Worldjournal.com	National	CA	Website	50,000		
3-Apr-10	World Journal: Vancouver Edition	Vancouver	BC	Daily	148,200		
11-Mar-10	World Journal: Toronto Edition	Toronto	ON	Daily	136,500		
21-Apr-10	Woodstocksentinelreview.com	National	CA	Website	7,100	✓	
21-Apr-10	Winnipegsun.com	National	CA	Website	246,422	✓	
2-Mar-10	Wikio.com	National	CA	Website	248,462		

Report Totals:	47,444,820	20%
Number of Stories:	279	
Budget:	$23,890	
Total Reach:	47,444,820	
Cost Per Contact:	$0.001	
MRP Quality Score:	87.28%	

The information presented here was compiled in September 2010 for a campaign held in March 2010. Adapted with permission from McCormick Canada/Hunter LaVigne Communications.

Balanced	Negative	Bonus / Demerit Point	Company / Brand Mention	Key Message(s)	Website /1-800 Mention	Call to Action	Notes
✓			✓	✓	✓	✓	News release verbatim
✓			✓			✓	Mango-Blueberry Cobbler
✓			✓	✓	✓	✓	News release verbatim & photo
✓			✓	✓	✓	✓	News release verbatim & photo
✓			✓	✓	✓	✓	News release verbatim & photo
✓			✓	✓	✓	✓	News release verbatim & photo
✓			✓	✓	✓	✓	News release verbatim & photo
		✓	✓	✓		✓	Rita Demontis, full page, 3 McCormick mentions, B&W, sidebar
		✓	✓	✓		✓	Rita Demontis, full page, colour, 3 McCormick mentions, sidebar
✓			✓	✓	✓	✓	News release verbatim
80%	0%	21%	98%	70%	62%	98%	

for obtaining up-to-date accurate reach numbers."[5] The development process took almost four years to complete, and MRP was launched in 2006. Because of CPRS's involvement in the development of the system, MRP is a registered trademark of the CPRS.

The MRP system analyses editorial media coverage by tone (positive, balanced, or negative), customized criteria, and cost per contact (derived by dividing the cost of the campaign by the total impressions). Key to the MRP system is the reach data, which is provided by News Canada via a subscription Internet service. News Canada is the authorized supplier of reach data for the MRP system.

Figure 12.1 contains excerpts from the MRP report for the McCormick® Gourmet Super Spices Campaign, compiled in September 2010.

MRP is a subscription-based tool that helps those practicing media relations to

- analyze and score media coverage;
- evaluate their media coverage (e.g., clips, airings, etc.) for tone and criteria;
- attach clips, proof of coverage into the report template;
- enter an audience reach number using the media outlet database provided by MRP data.com;
- produce comprehensive reports; and
- demonstrate return on investment (ROI) through the cost per contact tool in the online template.

The reach data provided by News Canada is "gathered from top Canadian media research companies and provides data regarding Canadian audiences," which is particularly useful when a news website that is based in the United States or elsewhere is being evaluated.[6] One key advantage of this system is MRP provides data on Canadian Internet traffic to websites around the world. These companies survey the general public to "determine what Canadians are listening to, surfing, watching or reading."[7] The companies include News Canada, provincial newspaper associations, comScore, NADbank, and Numeris. The cost of subscribing to these companies individually is prohibitive for many PR firms. Hence, this gathered data is an immense value-added part of the MRP service.

Generally, an overall MRP score of 75 per cent is considered a good campaign. A score of 80 per cent or above is considered excellent.

Another aspect of this measurement system, besides providing consistent measurement data, is that smaller, low budget campaigns can compete at the awards level with the million-dollar campaigns. In fact, MRP measurement is required by the CPRS for its national award entries.

To understand how valuable this media relations measurement paradigm is, look at how media relations evaluation had been conducted previously. Generally, it started with the gross audience numbers, such as circulation for newspapers. Then a multiple was applied to arrive at impressions, such as two to ten times for print, depending on the evaluator's or the public relations firms' protocol. (For example, the *Daily Planet* would have a circulation of five million but could have a multiple of 15 million.) For broadcast data, if you called an outlet and asked different people who work there on both the editorial and sales sides, you would probably get different answers on the "reach" because those numbers depend on how that department reports the numbers, which could be total show reach, quarter-hour audience reach, or even total station reach.

What MRP does not do is provide advertising equivalencies, and rightfully so. Traditionally, advertising equivalency was arrived at by measuring column inches and then inserting the newspaper's line advertising rate. Therefore, an article generated by a media relations campaign could be reported to be worth $5,000 because that is what it would cost to place an ad in the actual space occupied by the article. This form of measurement has at least a few problems. First, news content cannot be purchased and therefore cannot have an advertising equivalency. Second, editorial often has far more third-party word-of-mouth generation power than does advertising.

MRP provides a standard reach number now for a vast number of media outlets. If the data is not in the system, MRP staff will find it for you. However, please note, MRP does not give measurement numbers for news aggregators or most blogs.

MRP does not provide a media monitoring service; the actual articles have to be captured by other methods and suppliers. However, it does provide the consistent and universal measurement data for that media captured, whether it be print, broadcast, or Internet editorial. MRP provides data that PR can trust.

MEDIA MONITORING

Monitoring media coverage generated by your campaign is of critical importance. It is essential to provide proof of article or broadcast generation through trusted suppliers as well as your own search means. The task has never been more difficult and time-consuming. Here are some tips:

- Subscribe to as many media monitoring services as budget permits.
- Train in-house staff and clients to seek and report coverage accurately as a team effort. The more eyeballs looking for coverage, the better because no media monitoring system captures everything.
- Build in inherent tracking systems to chase as much coverage as possible. Develop detailed media logs so all involved in the media relations task know which media asked for what, and when and where they intend to publish or broadcast the article or story. Get on as many complimentary lists as you can. Many media outlets will place key PR representatives for a given client on free distribution if asked.
- Subscribe to all key media within the client's category if you can afford it.
- Deliberately build in keywords and use a named quote (ideally with an uncommon name) in news releases to help with electronic monitoring. For example, search for the name of the person being quoted to find where the news has disseminated.
- Beg every journalist who has promised coverage to send you tear sheets (hard copy coverage), URLs, MP3s, MP4s, DVDs, and give them your courier account numbers to send hard copies at no charge to them. Be sure to thank the journalist for their trouble.
- Some chains, such as Sun Media, offer an in-house media monitoring service, where they will get the hard copy coverage and send it to you for a fee. This service can be expensive, but it is worth every penny because they can dig internally for the coverage as a part of the fee.
- Constantly research which search engines are best, such as Google, Yahoo, and Bing.
- Subscribe to the MRP system to use its measurement data for all media outlets (including a plethora of online news sites) and for its qualitative measurement paradigm.

MEDIA TRAINING

In the planning stage of every media relations campaign, media training should be provided by a PR practitioner or a seconded media training specialist to prepare the key spokesperson for media interviews. Media training helps the spokesperson to prepare strategic key messages and practise that messaging on camera. Most media training sessions occur at the client's location and last a half to full day.

Media training offers intangible benefits. The theory portion of a good media training course helps reduce news media illiteracy, which manifests itself in either trainees being terrified of the news media, or too arrogant with them, treating them just like another marketing communications function for hire. Teaching these executives the difference between advertising and news editorial, and the inherent danger of underestimating the power of the news media, tends to promote more humility. Explaining that buying advertising does not guarantee media coverage, a common misconception, is fundamental for many executives to understand.

Conversely, once trainees understand the "information as commodity" concept, they tend to relax more when they fully understand their role in that two-way relationship. If properly developed, clients provide news that specific news media need to develop their stories. News media "sell" their product to their specific audiences. Although PR offers up a client's news for free, the resulting coverage, if positive, is valuable indeed.

Practising key messages and answering general questions in front of a camera reduces the fear and/or promotes humility and increases media literacy. Also allowing trainees to interview their colleagues, to play journalist, helps them to better understand the role the news media does play and the challenges on that side of the fence. It can also better identify potential information quagmires, since no one generally knows their business better than the trainees and all the areas that are problematic.

Media training can also greatly enhance the reputation of in-house media relations functions and officers by teaching potential spokespersons how difficult the art and science of media relations really is—that successful media relations is a complicated mix of newsworthy content, access, timing/context, and delivery of the messages. The training can become a useful opportunity to explain media relations protocol and how breaching this protocol can become career limiting. It also introduces the in-house media relations team to the executive/spokesperson team and provides a full day where they can work together and get to know each other and respect each other's roles and responsibilities, opportunities, and challenges.

One of the greatest frustrations of media relations specialists, and news media, is the slow response to requests for information or interviews. Executives in the private or public sector are inundated with information via email, voicemail, and hard copy. Often, however, executives do not understand the rapid timelines that the news media operate under—they do not understand how quickly something ceases to be "news," or how quickly the media may lose interest in a proactive media relations venture. Studies dating back to the 1970s show that slow response times are the media's biggest complaints about dealing with potential subjects.[8]

The media training experience, when done in a proactive, co-operative style, can also serve as a team-building exercise. Practising in front of a camera, when done as a group, can pull a group together since it can be as frightening as climbing a wall or scaling a rope bridge, which were popular team-building exercises in the 1980s and 1990s. Media training often brings together product managers from different divisions who only see each other at sales conventions or work-related social gatherings.

As a general training tool, media relations theory and practical training can also form a healthy foundation of knowledge so that an organization is better prepared for a deliberate response to a crisis. Then more focused, reactive media training can take place quickly for rapid but proper response to the crisis.

Handling a Media Interview

Here are some general tips for handling media interviews:

1. Be media trained and have your key messages and response statements memorized.
2. Never say anything "off-the-record" or say "no comment." Try saying something like, "When I have more information, I will be in a better position to respond."
3. Review recent news coverage on the interview topic so you are as well-informed as possible.
4. Take your time before answering questions. Pauses can be used as a tool to your advantage.
5. Adhere to the "under 10-second quote rule": a broadcast or print quote should be under 10 seconds in length.
6. Record your interview if possible. Listening to the interview afterwards will help you engage in continuous learning and refinement of the interview process. In some circumstances, this recording can also be used in legal proceedings.
7. If you do not know the answer, admit it. Promise to get back to the journalist later with the answer if possible.

8. If a question is negative, do not repeat the negative; always counter with a positive.
9. Correct any erroneous or misleading information in a question without repeating the negative before you go on to answer the question.
10. Keep your cool, no matter what.
11. Listen carefully to the interviewer. If you did not understand or hear the question, ask to have it repeated.
12. Keep eye contact.
13. Let the situation dictate your demeanour (and keep that demeanour throughout).
14. Do not answer in monosyllables such as "yes" or "no."
15. Do not speculate on hypothetical questions.
16. Do not use trade speak or marketing jargon or get too technical.
17. *Do not ever ask to review an article or broadcast story in advance of publication.* Media will view this request as disrespectful of their professionalism and an indication of your desire to control the story. It is their story, not yours. If you are not comfortable with the notion, pick another means of communication.

Telephone Interviews

Telephone (and taped) interviews can be the most dangerous because you can be too relaxed in your own environment, not focused enough on the interview or distracted by computers, phones, or other interruptions.

Avoid the temptation of doing the interview upon immediate request, unless you have directly approached the media and are hoping for coverage. If possible, tape the interview (using a telephone bypass jack found at most electronic stores).

Ask the interviewer if you are being recorded. In Canada, although journalists must inform you if you are being taped for broadcast, they can record you without telling you if it is not to be broadcast. In other words, everything is "on the record." In some US states, both parties to a taped program must agree to its release, even if the contents are just to be transcribed and not broadcast.

See Appendix B for tips on how to handle more types of interviews (television, radio, print).

Scrum

Scrum is trade slang that describes when a number of journalists gather around you for comment. It is an informal news conference, where you do not have the luxury of prepared statements, a room you control with Internet or satellite media feed, or experts by your side. The scrum is common after court appearances or in politics, for example, after Question Period. The media may also scrum you at public appearances such as speeches, panel discussions, or regulatory meetings. Often scrums are held to get specific answers to specific questions and to get better sound bites from you.

Reporters will often ask questions all at once. Choose the question you like. If you are in the middle of answering an undesirable question and another more positive question is asked, turn to that reporter and answer his or her question.

Take your time to answer and remember your key messages. If you do not understand a question, ask for it to be repeated. Because scrums are a form of pack journalism, you can use pauses to elicit other questions; other reporters will always fill in pauses with questions. Do not forget the competitive nature of the journalists surrounding you.

CONCLUSION

Media relations is a two-way information flow process. The newsmaker (the client; the organization where the news originates) and the journalist (the news media gatekeeper) are closely linked. The client wants to see his or her organization, product, or service treated positively in the news media. The journalist wants to provide news of interest to his or her audiences. Sometimes this relationship is positive. At other times, it is negative.

This chapter has provided some context and tools to help you understand the practice area of media relations. Media relations involves researching target audiences; developing key messages; creating a media list; training spokespeople; and capturing and evaluating media coverage. As with all other practice areas, it is crucial that you follow the CPRS Code of Ethics. Specifically, tell the truth to the best of your knowledge and ability.

If a conflict arises between what your client is doing, and what the news media wants, remember that you work for the client, whether you are outside or inside PR counsel. This principle is also part of the CPRS Code of Ethics. Media relations ostensibly puts the practitioner between the client and the journalist. Hence, it is always important to remember that the PR practitioner represents the client, not the journalist.

KEY TERMS

Impressions: Generally, the number of eyeballs or ears reading, watching or listening to a given media outlet. Some call this *reach*. Impressions are more than just circulation numbers, as is the case of print media, since a given newspaper or magazine is often read by more than one person in a household or office.

Media list: A detailed and time-consuming exercise to determine specifically which media will receive an organization's news. The media list comes from many sources, including media list brokers, and should include the contact name, media outlet, email and courier address, phone, cell, and fax numbers. The list can also include the media outlet's reach numbers and the contact person's preference for receiving news by email, fax, or not at all!

Media relations: The public relations practice area that focuses on interfacing with the news media, both proactively (through news releases and other tools) and reactively (providing information and facilitating interview requests).

Media relations plan: A formal plan that provides the detail for a media relations campaign, including details for researching target audiences, developing key messages, establishing which news media to target, creating a media list, and creating communications to send to the target audiences.

Media relations rating points (MRP): Created by an industry panel of PR experts, and owned by the Canadian Public Relations Society, MRP provides both a qualitative and quantitative media relations measurement paradigm that not only provides a media report template, but metrics including reach data and an overall MRP percentage score.

Media training: The process in which spokespersons are trained in both theory and practice on how media relations works, with a specific focus on developing and delivering key messages. Ideally, everyone on the media relations team, including the support staff, should receive media training too.

News fence: The barrier that exists between editorial and advertising in commercial news media outlets. The width of the news fence indicates to what degree advertising can influence editorial decisions.

News hole: The space in which proactive news can be placed. For example, business stories go into the business section of the news. Technology news can go into the technology section of the business area of the news, but also can fit into other categories.

Proactive media relations: The part of media relations where PR actively seeks out media participation and coverage through a variety of tools, including news conferences, interviews, news releases, photos, audio, video, and articles.

Newswire: Refers to a variety of services that will transmit a news release to a predetermined category of news media. Generally, newswires charge by the word.

Reactive media relations: The part of media relations where the news media comes to PR seeking information, photos or video, or interview requests. The circumstances can be positive or negative.

Scrum: When a group of reporters surround a spokesperson to get news. Often scrums occur in a crisis situation, but can also be a fast news gathering technique as opposed to a more formal news conference. Scrums are often visible in the political arena, when press gallery reporters gather news quickly from a number of individuals. These are also common for media covering the courts or police beats, where subjects are surrounded for news gathering.

FOR REVIEW AND DISCUSSION

1. Compare and contrast proactive and reactive media relations.
2. Describe the five principles of successful media relations. Which principle do you think is the most important today? Defend your answer.
3. What is the news fence? What challenges does the news fence pose for media relations practitioners?
4. Describe what makes a story newsworthy. Examine three recent stories in the news media and describe which criteria made them newsworthy.
5. In your opinion, what is the biggest barrier to successful media relations? What stops a good campaign from succeeding?
6. Explore the merits of media training. Describe recent news stories in which the spokesperson appeared to have media training or was lacking in it.

ACTIVITIES

1. Working in small groups, choose an organization that you know well.

- Create three key messages that you would use in media training and your news materials.
- Categorize the news media you would target with your news.
- Create a brief plan for your media relations campaign, using the McCormick Case Study for ideas.
- Draft a media advisory or news release that would generate interest in the organization, being sure to include the key messages you have

developed. (See Chapter 10 for descriptions of media advisories and news releases.)

FURTHER READING

Carney, William Wray. *In the News: The Practice of Media Relations in Canada.* 2nd ed. Edmonton: University of Alberta Press, 2008.

Columbia Journalism Review, Columbia University, New York: www.cjr.org.

Debarats, Peter. *A Guide to Canadian News Media.* Toronto: Harcourt Brace, 1990.

Hannaford, Peter. *Talking Back to the Media.* New York: Facts on File, 1986.

Hunter LaVigne Communications Inc.: www.hunterlavigne.com

LaVigne, Mark Hunter. *Making Ink and Airtime: How to Conduct Proactive Media Relations in Canada.* 2nd ed. eImpressions, 2011. http://www.hunterlavigne.com/book.html.

McKercher, Catherine, Allan Thompson, and Cumming, Carmen. *The Canadian Reporter News Writing and Reporting.* 3rd ed. Toronto: Harcourt Brace and Company, 2010.

Mediacaster Magazine: www.mediacastermagazine.com

Media Magazine, Canadian Association of Journalists: www.caj.ca

Ryerson Review of Journalism: www.rrj.ca.

Tasko, Patti, ed. *The Canadian Press Stylebook.* 17th ed. Toronto: The Canadian Press, 2013.

NOTES

1. Mark Hunter LaVigne and William Wray Carney, "Media Meltdown: How to Generate News Coverage in Both Traditional and Online Media," presentation at CPRS National Conference, Regina, SK, June 2010.
2. Adapted with permission from McCormick Canada.
3. CPRS, "Code of Professional Standards," in "Code of Ethics" accessed March 9, 2014, http://www.cprs.ca/aboutus/code_ethic.aspx.
4. CPRS, "Media Relations Rating Points (MRP)," accessed March 9, 2014, www.cprs.ca/membership/mrp.aspx.
5. Ibid.
6. CPRS and News Canada, "Canada's Role in MRP," 2010, www.mrpdata.com.
7. Ibid.
8. William Wray Carney, *In the News: The Practice of Media Relations in Canada* (Edmonton: University of Alberta Press, 2008), 157.

Jeff Scott

13

LEARNING OBJECTIVES

After reading this chapter, you will be able to

- explain the concept of digital communications;
- correct common assumptions made about digital communications;
- explain the similarities and differences between traditional and digital communications;
- understand how public relations practitioners and journalists use digital communications;
- describe the skills and tools needed for effective digital communications;
- explain the key elements of a digital communications plan; and
- understand the risks associated with digital communications.

INTRODUCTION

Simply put, the phrase *digital communications* refers to the various means by which people connect using technology. This definition is intentionally broad as it must account for not only today's products and services that enable these connections but those of tomorrow as well. Consider that tools such as email newsletters and services like Twitter were almost unimaginable in the 1990s, yet today both are important tools for public relations practitioners. The speed and reach of digital communications makes them attractive to organizations that want to connect with their stakeholders around the world in real time. In response to increasing demand, public relations practitioners, advertisers, and marketers have each claimed to be the best at creating and managing organizations' digital communications campaigns. This chapter focuses on the use of digital communications by the public relations industry.

THE EVOLUTION OF CONVERSATION

For decades, organizations employed public relations practitioners to communicate their stories to target audiences. Traditionally, public relations practitioners have worked with organizations to craft stories and pitch them to media for distribution to target audiences. Occasionally, stories would be offered to media under embargo in exchange for exclusivity or to ensure that the news was made public only at a specified time. After the story appeared, the organization, public relations practitioner, and journalist would all move on to the next one.

This process describes the one-way asymmetric communications model. Under this model, public relations practitioners are relatively sure that the story they pitch to media will be represented in the desired way to their target audiences by the journalist. In turn, journalists nurture regular and reliable sources for their work, and audiences consume the types of stories they find interesting. In short, the one-way asymmetric communications model describes the process in which a message travels from its source (the public relations practitioner), through an intermediary (the journalist) and, hopefully, reaches its intended target (various audiences). A drawback to this model is that other than a letter to the editor or customer service call, there is almost no way for the organization to receive feedback from the audience. While the organization could commission a survey, that process can be lengthy and costly.

Technology has always played a critical role in communications: the printing press, the ballpoint pen, the personal computer, and the Internet have each enabled more people to create and share more information with greater ease. The increasing speed of technological advances combined with rapidly diminishing costs since the 1980s have led to the democratization of communications. Today, the rich, the poor, the free, and the oppressed can all use digital communications to communicate with others instantly using text, audio, images, and

Figure 13.1: Traditional, One-way Asymmetric Communications Model

Adapted from NATIONAL Public Relations, used with permission.

video. Thanks to public libraries and open-access Wi-Fi hotspots, more people than ever before can get online and communicate with others. Digital communications have shifted the flow of communications from the one-way asymmetric communications model, where messages travel from a public relations practitioner to targeted audiences through an intermediary such as a journalist, to the multi-directional interactive communications model, one that more closely resembles a conversation. In this model, messages move between official sources of information, such as public relations practitioners, and the audiences they have targeted and possibly beyond. In short, digital communications enable audiences to communicate messages back to the organizations targeting them. This model affords public relations practitioners, organizations, media, and the public the means to communicate with anyone, including each other, in real time. Since digital communications tend to take place in public, these conversations can be monitored and analyzed for explicit or implicit feedback. This means that public relations practitioners must now be prepared to move beyond crafting and communicating messages exclusively for media: they must now engage directly with target audiences as well. Doing so effectively requires new skills. (See "Important Skills for Effective Digital Communications" later in this chapter.)

In their analysis of transparency laws and interactive public relations, Searson and Johnson use Twitter to show how organizations can now connect with stakeholders without needing to go through the media, a process known as disintermediation. This disintermediation is made possible thanks to digital communications and can be both helpful and problematic:

Twitter [allows] for multi-directional interactive communication between an organization and its stakeholders and among the members of the stakeholder group(s), without organizational intervention. For example, a university that establishes an Alumni Facebook page

Figure 13.2 Multi-Directional Interactive Communications, as Exemplified by Digital Communications

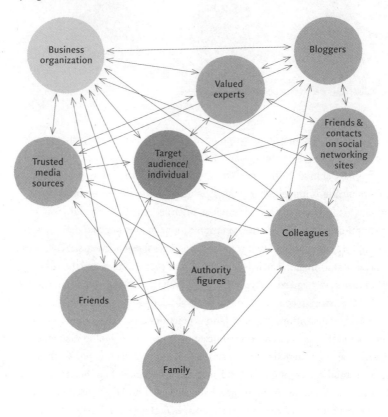

Adapted from NATIONAL Public Relations, used with permission.

can be dismayed to see posts criticizing the university along with bolstering posts.[1]

Many organizations are still wary of the multi-directional interactive communications afforded by digital communications, particularly as they struggle with the issues of control and risk. (See "Risks Associated with Digital Communications" later in this chapter.) However, it is important to note that using digital communications does not guarantee multi-directional conversations. Conversations between and within stakeholder groups must be nurtured and managed, and thanks to their expertise, public relations practitioners may be better suited to do so than advertisers or marketers.

Assumptions about Digital Communications

Organizations are increasingly asking public relations practitioners to include digital communications in their campaigns since the allure of leveraging services that offer access to global audiences in real time at virtually no cost sounds too good to be true. Unfortunately, in many cases, it is. In particular, little evidence exists to support the effectiveness of social media in public relations campaigns. Here are six common assumptions about digital communications and the realities behind each.[2]

Assumption 1: Digital communications and social media are the same thing.
Reality: Some confusion surrounds the difference between social media and digital communications. Simply put, the difference is that social media are a subset of digital communications. The term *social media* is typically used to describe the means by which people electronically create and share content including text, images, audio, and video. Whereas *digital communications* can include email campaigns, electronic newsletters, text messaging campaigns and more, the phrase *social media* typically refers to social networking websites (Facebook, LinkedIn); image, video, and bookmark sharing websites (Flickr, YouTube, Delicious); and public blogging platforms (WordPress, Twitter). In short, all social media are a form of digital communications, but not all digital communications are social media.

Assumption 2: Most services are free, and those that charge are inexpensive.
Reality: With digital communications, as with so many other things in life, you tend to get what you pay for. While some services are free to use, many employ a "freemium" model whereby the features most important to organizations require payment. Many sites charge for such things as metrics (performance, user and/or other types of data), user-level accounts, offline use, backups, or enhanced security, among others. Even services that are completely free generally require a considerable amount of time to configure, customize, optimize, and manage properly according to an organization's needs. In other words, the actual cost to the organization is usually substantial.

Assumption 3: It takes little time to get started with digital communications.
Reality: As with traditional public relations campaigns, digital communications campaigns require serious preparation if a successful outcome is to be expected. Developing a solid strategy; choosing, customizing, and building

the right tools; developing relationships with influencers and other stake-holders; and keeping abreast of changes in the digital world all take time. Proper planning is crucial to a campaign's success, so even though it is often possible to get started quickly, it is important to spend an appropriate amount of time preparing.

Assumption 4: Results can be seen almost instantly in a digital communications campaign.

Reality: While digital communications allow for unprecedented speeds in reporting campaign performance, the truth is that most campaigns need time to generate measureable results. Metrics are typically easy to come by, but without access to a massive budget and a lot of good luck, the odds are very much against any one campaign noticeably "moving the needle" overnight. Despite the speed at which digital communications can travel, it takes time to build enough momentum within and across target audiences to generate measurably meaningful impact.

Assumption 5: Digital campaigns often "go viral."

Reality: Some campaigns generate so much excitement it seems like everyone on the planet knows about them. Images and videos from digital communications campaigns appear daily in mainstream media. Virality, the process whereby a message reaches a much larger audience than the one initially targeted, occurs when a number of factors combine to attract the attention of many users in a short time. While it is possible for this to happen with any campaign, it is much more likely to happen with a campaign that is well financed and reaches the right influencers early on. Content that goes viral tends to be short, catchy, funny, and/or emotionally moving. Even content that is crafted with all these attributes can fail to go viral for no good reason. Rather than trying to create viral content, organizations should focus on using the best possible strategy and tactics to achieve their goals. While it is natural to want a viral hit, it is extremely important to manage expectations.[3]

Assumption 6: All digital communications are global.

Reality: Insofar as the Internet is a global network, anything on it is theoreti-cally available globally, but it is important to keep a few things in mind. First, public relations campaigns are most effective when they resonate profoundly with their target audience. Given the diversity of audiences around the world (let alone from region to region, even within Canada), it should come as no surprise that a good digital communications campaign probably should not be global even if it can be. The disproportionate amount of attention Western media currently give to sites such as Facebook and Twitter misses the fact that in other parts of the world, local audiences are more active on other platforms. Remember too that the Internet is monitored, restricted, and censored in many countries, making the reach of certain campaigns illegal or impossible.

THE RELATIONSHIP BETWEEN TRADITIONAL AND DIGITAL COMMUNICATIONS

The ubiquitous nature and speed of digital communications are having a profound impact on the role of public relations practitioners. Here are a few ways in which instant, global access to information is changing the profession:

1. At any time, almost anyone anywhere can consume, create, and respond to messages about an organization. This has forced public relations practitioners to develop ways to monitor and manage conversations in an "always-on" environment that differs considerably from traditional communications.

2. Because digital communications make it easy to join or create a conversation about organizations, more and more content is being created daily. Organizations therefore need to monitor and analyze this content to decide whether and how to respond. Managing this increasing volume of information from digital sources can make the role of public relations practitioner extremely challenging.

3. Stakeholders' expectations are changing as a result of digital communications tools: many express frustration at organizations that do not use digital communications to listen or respond to them at all or in a timely manner. Organizations need to have the resources, infrastructure, and procedures in place to monitor and respond to mentions of their brands, and it is important for organizations to communicate their response guidelines to stakeholders in order to manage their expectations.

4. Filtering irrelevant conversations ("noise") from relevant conversations ("signal") is becoming increasingly more difficult as more stakeholders integrate digital communications platforms into their lives. Organizations with names that are also commonly used words, phrases, or abbreviations (for example, "CN," "Standard Life," and "GAP") face additional filtering challenges.

5. Digital communications are making some parts of the job easier for public relations practitioners than ever before. For example:

- Online surveys allow for fast, targeted distribution and near real-time analysis of results. This reduces costs and improves accuracy and efficiency.
- Lists of media and other stakeholders are more easily managed, updated, and shared using online databases, and these can be helpful for distributing news releases and other messages to specific target audiences.
- Online monitoring tools can help with the timely detection of emerging issues and help prevent and manage crises, as well as help identify new opportunities. Managing a crisis through digital channels is considerably easier if you already have an established presence on the platform where a crisis emerges. This is one more reason to encourage organizations to start using digital communication before there is an urgent need to do so.

In 2009, results from Wright and Hinson's three-year international survey of more than 300 public relations practitioners affirmed that social media are shaping the ways in which organizations communicate with their stakeholders. As they explain, the methods used in digital communications are complementary to more traditional methods:

Findings suggest social media complement traditional news media, and that blogs and social media influence coverage in traditional news media. The study reports blogs and social media have made communications more instantaneous by encouraging organizations to respond more quickly to criticism.[4]

The growth of digital communications has not fundamentally changed the job description of the public relations practitioner, although some of the required skills have changed. (See "Important Skills for Effective Digital Communications" later in this chapter.) Organizations continue to look to public relations practitioners for their expertise in areas such as media relations and crisis communications. The most significant changes caused by digital communications relate to the speed at which messages are communicated, the platforms on which they are communicated, and the potential reach of these messages. As Daniel Lamarre, former president of NATIONAL Public Relations, said back in 1995, "For the public relations industry...[new technologies mean] more immediate transmission of more customized information to more of the right people in more varied ways."[5]

It is not so long ago that corporate websites, a digital communications tool seen as very basic today, signalled a profound change in how organizations connected with stakeholders. The digital communications tools emerging today are changing the public relations industry in much the same way. Thanks to websites such as YouTube, businesses can easily create, share, and promote multimedia content at a reasonable cost, including time. As a 2009 article in *Advertising Age* noted, "If you wanted to reach [millions of] people using traditional media, you would have to pitch and place in dozens of outlets."[6] Today, hundreds of millions of people can be reached across multiple digital communications platforms.

Traditionally, public relations practitioners crafted messages and tried to distribute them to target audiences via the media. While this remains true today, in addition to these traditional methods, public relations practitioners can now reach target audiences directly by engaging existing communities of stakeholders or by encouraging the development of new ones.

Any claim that digital communications have replaced traditional communications is misplaced at best. Traditional communications cannot be meaningfully pitted against digital communications as neither is inherently better than the other: they complement each other. Unless an organization has *extraordinarily* specific needs, the public relations strategy and tactics used should be based on how well they meet the organization's needs. The decisions about whether and how to incorporate traditional and digital communications tools must be made in consideration of how well they respond to the organization's needs. They must also respond to other constraints such as time and budget.

Regardless of whether traditional or digital communications are used, organizations rely on public relations practitioners to craft and communicate their messages to target audiences effectively. However, some considerations must be made when deciding between traditional and digital communications. These include

- audience;
- control;
- cost;

- outcome;
- metrics; and
- speed.

Audience

Where do target audience members spend most of their time? Younger audience members typically spend more time online while older members spend more time offline, but the demographics of digital communications usage are changing.[7] Be sure to use current data about target audiences rather than assumptions. Remember that a combination of traditional and digital communications may make it more likely to reach all audience members.

Control

Control is much easier to achieve using traditional communications methods. If the organization absolutely needs control (of messages, platforms, etc.), then traditional communications may be preferable. Be sure to explain the benefits and risks of digital communications to otherwise apprehensive organizations. It may be worthwhile to note that people may be discussing the organization using digital communications regardless of whether the organization is participating or even aware of these conversations, so it may serve the organization well to have some kind of official digital presence and conduct monitoring.

Cost

Budget can affect an organization's choice to rely more on traditional or digital communications. The assumption is often that digital communications are less expensive than traditional communications, but if an organization has no existing presence in the digital world at the start of a campaign, the time involved in developing platforms and connecting with influencers may be more expensive and less effective than running a traditional communications campaign.

Outcome

The nature of the desired outcome will inform the choice of traditional and digital communications activities. For example, if an organization is looking to increase visits to a website, a digital communications campaign that targets audience members by age and interests may be preferable. If an organization is attempting to promote its position in the face of federal legislation, it may be more useful to publish an opinion piece in a national newspaper.

Metrics

If an organization needs various metrics related to the performance of a number of different elements in a campaign, digital communications may be preferable. Keep in mind that digital communications cannot always measure the elements an organization wants to measure.

Speed

If an organization needs to communicate information quickly, digital communications are generally preferable, particularly if the organization can use an existing digital platform; otherwise, the time needed to develop, configure, and promote the platform properly may make the initiative moot.

HOW PR PRACTITIONERS AND JOURNALISTS USE DIGITAL COMMUNICATIONS

Given the complementary nature of the roles of public relations practitioners and journalists, it should come as no surprise that many journalists are increasingly using digital communications in their work. Understanding how journalists use these tools can help public relations practitioners craft content that is more likely to be viewed and used by journalists.

Journalists are under tremendous and increasing pressure to produce content. To help in their work, they are increasingly using "non-public relations content from user-generated and social network sites" for a number of reasons,[8] including to

- monitor existing sources, situations, organizations, and so on;
- investigate, research, fact-check;
- engage with audience members;
- nurture relationships with contacts;
- distribute information; and
- for personal reasons unrelated to their roles as journalists.

Even as digital communications offer new ways for public relations practitioners to bypass journalists and connect directly with target audiences, they also offer new platforms on which public relations practitioners and journalists can establish and grow their relationships and exchange information. At any rate, as Avery, Lariscy, and Sweetser said in their 2010 study, "it is highly unlikely new media will enable practitioners to ever completely circumvent gatekeepers when seeking to place their stories in the news."[9]

At present, it appears that public relations practitioners use digital communications tools slightly more often than do journalists. This can be explained by the fact that public relations practitioners generally use digital communications tools to create content, monitor various platforms, and conduct outreach on behalf of their organizations, whereas journalists are more likely to use the tools available to them to consume content.[10] Public relations practitioners would be well advised to start using digital communication tools, including social media, now so that, as journalists increase their use of these tools, public relations practitioners will already be present and ready to work with them. Journalists may even be more likely to work with public relations practitioners who use digital communications tools as these can facilitate access to organizations and help make managing relationships easier so long as offline contact and real world relationships are maintained.[11]

WHO "OWNS" DIGITAL COMMUNICATIONS?

As digital communications grow increasingly attractive to organizations, and as sites like Facebook and Twitter continue to capture media attention through their roles in global events, a claim of ownership of digital communications is being made by various groups. Public relations agencies, advertising and marketing agencies, specialized digital agencies, and boutique agencies all claim digital communications as theirs. Similarly, numerous departments within organizations including public relations, marketing, sales and customer service, human resources, and legal have all staked their own claims. So, who really owns digital communications?

The short answer is, "It depends who you ask," because a number of very different but critical functions all take place within the sphere of digital communications. Some marketing professionals would say that digital communications is a subset of marketing communications, which is led by marketing departments. On the other hand, senior lecturer in management communication Margalit Toledano argues that the training and experience of public relations practitioners positions them as the natural leaders of digital communications functions:

> [Public relations practitioners are better suited to] prepare for crises
> (often more fast moving and intense in the online environment);
> they focus on two-way communication and on building relationships
> with different stakeholders; they are better trained to...communicate

with small groups rather than mass audiences; and they are experts in creating content for news stories.[12]

Compared to advertisers and marketers, public relations practitioners may have better training and more experience in creating and managing sustained multi-directional interactive communications. However, as digital communications occupy an ever-growing place in advertising, marketing, and public relations, this may not be true for much longer.

There is serious competition for ownership of digital communications, particularly social media. Myriad books have been written discussing how digital tools affect each field and why each is the rightful owner, but rather than an all-out war, it seems more likely that convergence will inevitably occur. Public relations could continue to integrate some of the functions of advertising, and marketing may find new ways to engage target audiences more thoroughly, perhaps by asking them to help develop the very advertisements they will ultimately see. However, to claim that any one field owns digital communications is to misunderstand these tools because each can be used in a variety of means to any number of ends. For example, a single digital service can be used to promote a brand, recruit new talent, manage discussions, distribute information, and more. Digital communications ultimately require the input, expertise, and skills found in several departments.

IMPORTANT SKILLS FOR EFFECTIVE DIGITAL COMMUNICATIONS

While there is considerable overlap in the skills required for effective traditional and digital communications, certain skills and the ways in which they are used are unique in the context of digital communications.

Skill: Create, Edit, and Publish Content

The ever-changing landscape of digital communications means that public relations practitioners need to do more than write effective copy: they need to be able to create compelling image, video, and audio content in addition to copy, and it must be received favourably by influential users and search engines alike. It is therefore imperative that content is created in such a way that is not only compelling to human audiences but that is optimized for the machines that make this content discoverable to target audiences, a skill known as search engine optimization (SEO).

Numerous free and paid services are available to help with SEO. Keep the following in mind when developing content destined for digital platforms:

1. Identify the keywords that target audiences associate with the organization and campaign and, wherever possible, use these in place of jargon. This technique will increase the likelihood of the content being found and shared by audience members.

2. Adapt the content to each platform on which it will be published. For example, blogs allow for essay-style content and often welcome multimedia; in contrast, many social networks have technical limits that may require shorter versions of the same message.

3. Include a "call to action" wherever possible. This is a short message that encourages readers to act in a way that is meaningful to the organization. Calls to action should be easy for readers to complete and should be measureable. They include leaving comments, sharing stories or indicating their approval of the content.

4. If the platform is social, try to maintain a conversational tone. Many organizations have difficulty shedding their formal images, but users of social platforms tend to respond better to human interaction than "business speak."

5. Refrain from making a hard sell to target audiences on social platforms. Instead, try to make content informative and entertaining. Make sure audience members can connect with the organization should they wish to make a purchase but do not make this the focus of the content.

6. Before publishing content, always review it to ensure it is of the highest quality, appropriate to the platform for which it is destined, and meets legal and ethical standards.

7. Refine messages so they are first distributed among the most passionate audience members and their influencers. Studies have shown that structure of a digital network, rather than its size, may be more important for achieving virality. It appears that in order for a message to "go viral" and reach a larger public, it must first resonate with many members of a smaller group.[13]

8. Publish content to the digital platforms that can have the greatest impact to the organization. For example, research indicates that coverage on personal blogs is more useful for reaching influencers in the entertainment industry while professional blogs are more useful for reaching political influencers.[14]

Skill: Monitor and Measure

Public relations practitioners working in digital communications need to have the ability to identify, track, and measure various types of digital content, including content created by stakeholders. They also need to be able to measure the impact of their digital activities and adjust for optimal results. Finally, they need to analyze and evaluate the information collected to determine whether and how to react. Measurement is useful for myriad other reasons, including guiding strategy, establishing return on investment, determining the success of a campaign's goals, and detecting, preventing, and managing crises.

The metrics required will vary based on the campaign's goal, how the organization and its industry measure success, and the features and limitations of the digital tools used in the campaign. A campaign that seeks to raise awareness may more accurately measure success by examining impressions rather than clicks, whereas a campaign that seeks to change perceptions may find more value in measuring sentiment among a limited group of stakeholders. (For more on impressions, see Chapters 8 and 12.) The parameters measured should be defined before the campaign begins, and an appropriate budget should be set aside for the work involved in collecting, analyzing, and communicating metrics.

Digital communications have changed how metrics are obtained and used. In offline campaigns, metrics are generally available only after the campaign's conclusion. With digital campaigns, it may be possible to obtain real-time or near real-time data that can inform the campaign's direction even while it is ongoing. These digital metrics are leading a "transition from impressions to engagement."[15]

Determining what to measure can be a challenge. Measureable attributes may not be the same across tools, and the tools themselves can and do change. Whatever tool or tools emerge to measure social media across platforms will therefore need to be flexible even while they should strive to provide some sort of industry benchmark.

Here is a list of some attributes that may provide valuable information about digital communications campaigns:[16]

- **Conversions:** The number of readers who complete a desired action, such as providing contact information or making a purchase as a result of viewing the content.
- **Demographics:** The reader's age, gender, location, and so on.

- **Engagement:** An activity the reader completes after consuming your content, such as clicking a link within the content, commenting on it, or sharing it with others.
- **Influence:** Relative reach and/or relevance of readers and commenters.
- **Sentiment:** The positive, neutral, or negative sentiment about the content that the reader expressed.
- **Time:** Duration of time spent with content; number of times the reader refers to the content.
- **Velocity:** The speed at which a particular piece of content is distributed through a network or to other networks.
- **Views:** Number of unique readers; percentage change in traffic over time.

One of the most important things that digital communications can help an organization do is listen to its stakeholders. Regardless of whether an organization is active in digital communications, chances are increasing that someone somewhere is discussing it or its people, products, brands, competitors, or industry.[17] The question should not be whether to monitor but what needs to be monitored, at what frequency, and how monitoring should be accomplished. Monitoring can alert an organization to a potentially damaging situation before it becomes a crisis. It can also help with customer service, stakeholder engagement, and competitive intelligence.

A number of free and paid tools are available to assist with monitoring. Some are better than others for monitoring specific digital communications platforms, but none can monitor absolutely everything all the time. There is simply too much content to monitor. Keep in mind that new content is being created by billions of people across the digital world every second of every day. Using multiple monitoring tools means that an organization will probably need to remove identical content detected by multiple tools (a process known as de-duplicating), but this technique will provide a better chance of identifying more relevant mentions than relying on a single monitoring tool.

Monitoring should begin *before* an organization begins a digital communications campaign as this will help with benchmarking (influencers, sentiment, volume, etc.) and provide an overview of the kinds of conversations that are taking place in various digital communities. Monitoring early in the digital communications campaign also allows more time to improve the quality of results detected by monitoring tools by revealing keywords that need to be refined or removed. This is particularly important for organizations that monitor very common words.

Monitoring can be passive, whereby mentions of keywords that the monitoring tool identifies are sent to the organization on a regular schedule or as detected. Monitoring can also be active, whereby someone monitors keyword mentions in real time. It is important for the monitoring system to incorporate an assessment component that evaluates identified mentions to determine whether and how they should be handled. For example, if a highly influential person says negative but accurate information about the organization, it would probably be relevant to report the mention to the organization immediately— along with some context about the person who wrote it, the platform on which they published it, and the audience who may have interacted with it. In contrast, if a blog with little traffic republishes a previously debunked urban legend involving the organization, it may be best to note this fact at a regularly scheduled meeting rather than sounding the alarm.

Skill: Assess and Engage

Since most digital communications are multi-directional, meaning audience members can openly send their own messages to an organization, a procedure must be in place to account for evaluating whether and how to respond to a mention of the organization. This skill is critical for successful customer service and stakeholder relations, and a flowchart or "decision tree" can help the organization evaluate messages in context and, when required, craft an appropriate response.[18]

A major part of the job for public relations practitioners is conducting outreach. Among other things, this is a very effective way to

- build relationships and use them to help achieve goals;
- engage with media, bloggers, the public, or other stakeholders;
- raise awareness;
- develop a brand; and
- raise funds.

The challenge is in establishing the right relationships and leveraging them at the right time. Before reaching out to a source, make sure you know as much as possible about that source. For example, if you plan to reach out to a blogger, spend some time reading the posts and comments on the blog to develop a sense of the tone and style of the blog as well as who contributes what content.

Keep in mind that the best way to have a campaign's message propagated is not always by targeting the sources that have the most followers. Recent research indicates that there may be considerably more value in targeting small but highly focused groups with specific messages because the passion these groups feel towards their preferred subjects can create a stronger force to propagate the message than can a vast group with many divergent interests.[19]

Skill: Crisis Management

A robust monitoring system can help identify potential crises before they explode, in some cases providing enough time to address the causes and prevent it from ever unfolding in public. Regardless of the measures taken to detect or avoid a crisis, one can happen at any time, and digital communications increasingly play a role in how crises unfold and how quickly they end.

Digital communications tools are ideally suited for crisis management because of their speed and accessibility. Information can be broadcast globally in a short period of time, but misinformation and negative comments can spread just as quickly. However, if digital communications are used effectively, their role can be critical to managing and resolving a crisis.

To use digital communications tools effectively in a crisis, they should already be up and running. A team that is familiar with their use should be established before a crisis occurs. The organization's protocol for crisis communications will be useful for managing information during a crisis, but this tool should be developed before a crisis and updated on a regular basis.

To manage a crisis using digital communications:

- Ensure a plan exists that outlines roles and responsibilities for the crisis management team.
- Since the regular flow of official information is critical during a crisis, ensure that monitoring and response flowcharts are updated for use in crises before they occur.
- Manage information and misinformation carefully: do not make the crisis worse.[20]
- If approval is normally required before content is published, ensure there are clearly defined exceptions for crises; for example, obtain permission at the outset of a campaign to re-post excerpts of and links to official material during a crisis.
- Make sure key people have access to all platforms (such as usernames, login information) and keep this information current throughout the crisis. For the sake of security, change sensitive information, such

as passwords, after the crisis has passed, and ensure the updated information remains accessible at a moment's notice by at least two trusted people.

- Wherever feasible, respond to a crisis on the same platforms to which it has spread. For example, if a video that is extremely critical of an organization appears on a video sharing website, consider posting an official video response on the same website.
- It is considerably easier for an organization to respond on a platform it actively uses than on one it has never used. Using a new platform to respond in a time of crisis can lead to unintentional misuse of that platform. It can also cost the organization credibility among frequent users of the platform. It is also important for the organization to consider what it will do with its presence on that platform once the crisis has passed.
- Organizations should use monitoring to identify the platforms most used by their stakeholders and consider creating an official presence on those platforms. This way, in a crisis the organization will be able to direct its communications to the platforms where their stakeholders are already most active.
- Run drills to test the crisis plan before a crisis occurs.

(See Chapter 16 for more about crisis communications.)

Skill: Learn and Adapt to Change

The skill of learning and adapting to change is perhaps the single most important skill for public relations practitioners working with digital communications. Technologies and platforms change rapidly, so it is critical to stay abreast of the opportunities and risks each affords. It is also important to have a good sense of which emerging trends may become the next big things and which may fizzle out so time is not wasted with trivial platforms.

It was not so long ago that fax machines and email revolutionized the public relations industry. The dominant platforms today include social networks, mobile apps, and tablet computers. The landscape for public relations practitioners tomorrow will inevitably be very different.

To keep informed of current trends, make a point of closely following industry leaders and issues. Keep in mind that many platforms are simple variations of each other, so learning about one may help you learn about many. For example, almost all modern social networking platforms feature "user profiles," so if you understand how these work on one platform, there is a good chance you will have an understanding of how they work on others.

SOME IMPORTANT TOOLS FOR EFFECTIVE DIGITAL COMMUNICATIONS

The nature of digital communications is such that the tools available to public relations practitioners change faster and more frequently than traditional tools, so only four are reviewed below. Important tools such as podcasts and wikis (digital encyclopedias containing articles written by their users) are not covered below but should be studied further for their relevance to the profession.

Tool: Editorial Calendar

An editorial calendar is an internal planning tool created by public relations practitioners to co-ordinate which messages will be distributed on specific channels at specific times. It is one of the most powerful yet easy-to-use tools available to ensure compelling content is regularly shared with target audiences across social media. An editorial calendar is useful for

- content curation and aggregation (finding, selecting, and maintaining a collection of the most appropriate content for a given audience);
- stakeholder identification and outreach initiatives (learning about the people and organizations that affect and/or are affected by the organization and planning how best to connect with them); and
- stakeholder engagement (connecting with specific stakeholders).

The calendar can and generally should include content from a number of departments other than public relations, such as

- corporate communications (such as news, events, awards);
- human resources (such as employee news, job openings, milestones); and
- marketing (such as new products and services, getting the most from existing tools, participation at industry conferences).

Additional content from other departments will ensure that relevant, timely material will be shared with stakeholders across digital communications platforms.

The editorial calendar should note important civic and religious holidays (such as Canada Day, Labour Day, Christmas), other events that are regularly celebrated (such as Valentine's Day, Administrative Assistant's Day, Earth Day), and dates that are important to the organization (such as anniversaries, accomplishments, roundtable discussions).

Tool: Corporate Blog

A blog can be a very useful tool for an organization but only if it is updated regularly with content that is compelling to its target audience. A blog should appeal to both external and internal stakeholders, so the content published on it should incorporate the human side of business. This means the blog should feature conversational language rather than jargon wherever possible. Posts should discuss topics related to the organization but should not always focus on the organization itself. A blog should be thought of as a place to nurture lasting relationships with target audiences rather than as another channel used solely to distribute marketing material or investor relations information, though a blog can legitimately serve those purposes as well.

In general, comments are allowed on blog posts, but to ensure they are appropriate, post a clear comment moderation policy and enforce it diligently. Keep in mind that negative feedback should be welcomed and addressed as long as it does not violate the established guidelines. This kind of transparency will demonstrate openness and accessibility while providing a platform through which the organization can correct misinformation, clarify its position, or address a crisis.

Content on the blog should be updated regularly. It is important to create timely posts that reference holidays, current events, and more, but it is also important to ensure evergreen content is available. This is content that can be published at any time, and it is important because it ensures new content is always available to readers. An editorial calendar (see "Tool: Editorial Calendar") can help with content development and ensure material is available for publication year-round, well in advance of dates important to the organization's target audiences.

To keep content fresh and interesting, use a variety of formats for posts. Consider the following types of blog posts:

1. Client services issues: Relate an anecdote about a recent client services issue that was resolved to a client's satisfaction.

2. Culture of the organization: Describe what makes the organization great or unique.
3. Current events: Present the organization's view on current events that are important to the blog's readers.
4. Guest author: Invite someone that interests readers to contribute a post.
5. List post: Briefly discuss several elements related to a single subject.
6. Milestones: Update readers with interesting blog or organizational milestones (such as current number of readers or number of employees).
7. Presentations: Make the organization's presentations available to a global audience by sharing them on the blog and solicit feedback.
8. Questions and answers: Solicit questions from stakeholders in one post and publish the responses in another.
9. Tips and tricks: Provide advice for using the organization's products or services.
10. Tour of the organization: Take readers on a virtual tour of the organization, its facilities and its employees using photos and videos.

It is very important to be patient with a blog. Unless the organization already has a strong following in the digital space, it can take a good deal of time to communicate the existence of the blog and to build a following. Despite potentially low initial readership, it is important to continue publishing fresh content on a regular basis to grow the audience. To help with this, consider promoting the blog on corporate websites, through newsletters and other platforms on which the organization and its stakeholders are active.

Tool: Social Networks

Loosely defined, a social network in the context of digital communications refers to any platform that allows its users to connect with each other to create and share content. Social networks can be efficient channels for directly connecting with stakeholders.

At the time of writing, the dominant social networks in most Western countries include Facebook, Twitter, YouTube, and LinkedIn. It is important to remember that only a few years ago this list was very different, and it is likely to change again in time. (Remember Friendster?)

The most important skill a public relations practitioner can have with regards to social networks is the ability to keep abreast of changing opportunities, trends, and features. The nature of social networks is such that they tend to evolve rapidly, so something that may not have been possible at one time may very well become the norm almost overnight. Staying informed of this changing landscape is a challenge, and one of the most effective ways of leveraging social networks for organizations is to follow those networks' blogs as well as blogs that cover the social media industry. Numerous books and academic writings are also available, but these often lag well behind the rapidly changing realities of social networks.

Tool: Social Media Release

A social media release is a tool that allows public relations practitioners to distribute an organization's news in a format that can contain digital content in addition to the text found in traditional news releases. This digital content generally includes hyperlinks as well as images, videos, and audio files. While social media releases are considered a somewhat specialized tool today, it would not be surprising to see the standard press release format increasingly incorporate social elements as social networks continue to gain in popularity.

Social media releases tend to be created in a way that makes their content easily reusable across digital platforms such as blogs and social networks. Bullet points, short quotations from multiple sources, downloadable multimedia content, and more all make the social media release ideally suited for the Digital Age. Their growing popularity means that today individuals outside the media view social media news releases too. As a result, in addition to creating them for the traditional audience of journalists, analysts, and other organizational stakeholders, they are increasingly being written with a broader target audience in mind. As with most other social tools, they may encourage conversation around their subject rather than just distribution of the news.

DEVELOPING A DIGITAL COMMUNICATIONS PLAN

Creating a digital communications plan is a very important step for public relations practitioners. While every plan will be different, the following steps can help inform and guide plan development and roll out. The plan will help ensure that

- the campaign goals are understood;
- the best tools are chosen to meet those goals;

- measurement and return on investment are accounted for; and
- crises can be managed or avoided altogether.

Without a plan, public relations practitioners unnecessarily risk degrading trust in digital communications as well as the organization itself. It is also a good bet that time, money, and other resources will be wasted.

Before the plan is created, ensure there is a common understanding of the reasons for choosing digital communications in addition to or instead of other tools to further the organization's goals. Public relations practitioners should be able to answer any questions regarding the decision to use digital communications, particularly if they are replacing rather than complementing traditional communications. Be prepared to manage others' expectations if asked to "tack on" a digital component to an existing plan because, in spite of the speed of digital communications, it takes time to plan a successful digital communications campaign properly, just as it does to plan a traditional communications plan. The steps below outline the general process for creating a digital communications plan.

1. Determine objectives and how success will be measured.

Understand the goal of the campaign, particularly in consideration of the organization's overall goals. Consider how this project will fit with current and future programs. Digital communications should be used to further business objectives, not to keep up appearances.

Ensure there is a commitment to the continued use of digital communications beyond the immediate campaign. Doing so is one of the most significant benefits public relations practitioners can bring to a campaign, particularly compared to their advertising and marketing counterparts. If a commitment to continue with community engagement is lacking, be prepared for a backlash from stakeholders because, at some point in the future, they may feel abandoned when a campaign they actively participated in ends. This is particularly true for short-lived campaigns (marketing contests, for example), more so than with long-term public relations strategies, but it is important to consider the post-campaign reality awaiting the stakeholders you seek to engage today.

2. Establish an inter-departmental team.

Assemble a team from all relevant departments. Define the roles and responsibilities for team members and establish workflow principles, and be prepared to adjust these based on team feedback as the campaign progresses.

3. **Research issues, audiences, influencers, and other stakeholders, and configure monitoring and reporting mechanisms.**
Develop a profile of target audiences based on demographics and psychographics. (See Chapter 11 for more about demographics and psychographics.) Conduct a digital audit to help identify and track key issues, influencers, and stakeholders to inform future outreach. Remember that it is important to develop relationships with people before you ask them for something.

Use this research to configure monitoring platforms. Make sure to measure the elements necessary to determine success, since different campaigns will need to measure very different things. Some campaigns may even interpret the same data very differently depending on their goals. In short, make sure the organization "listens" before it uses digital communications to "speak."

4. **Configure digital platforms, prepare advertising, and prepare to capture metrics.**
Research which platforms are best for connecting with the influencers and other stakeholders targeted by the campaign. Begin configuring these platforms by securing usernames related to the campaign and/or organization. Develop the visual styles unique to each platform and ensure visual elements are consistent across platforms. Use research from Step 3 to determine the keywords and interests most relevant to your stakeholders, and use these keywords to connect more effectively with target audiences in any complementary advertising campaigns. Consider the metrics available on each platform and whether any third-party tools are available to measure additional data that can help you evaluate the impact of your campaign.

5. **Prepare policies and start developing content.**
Create or adapt guidelines and policies including

- **Social media usage policy** for company employees. This policy should account for how different types of employees may use social media in a way that is acceptable to the company while respecting individual rights.

- **Editorial tone and style guide** for content published on social media. This policy should guide content development to ensure it is aligned with the company's persona. For example, a blue chip company may prefer a more formal style while an Internet startup may wish to keep digital content more casual in tone.
- **Comment response and moderation policy** for content about the organization posted by others on the digital communications platforms the organization controls or monitors. This policy will guide the process of deciding whether to allow the publication of content submitted to a platform the organization controls or delete it. It will also guide the process of deciding whether and/or how to respond to content about the organization posted on a platform it does not control. For example, the organization may choose to respond to any mention about itself detected online or instead ignore criticism if it is determined a detractor does not have a meaningful audience.
- **Crisis communication policy** for use in the event of a crisis. This policy should include the contact information of an inter-departmental team with the authority to respond to crises and outline how information will be developed, approved, and distributed within and outside the organization. It should also clarify how to identify the start and end points of a crisis.
- **Editorial calendar** to co-ordinate which messages will be distributed on specific channels at specific times. The calendar can and generally should include content from a number of departments other than public relations.

Begin developing content for each platform before the launch of the campaign to ensure visitors do not arrive at a wasteland. Use the editorial calendar to note dates and events important to the organization, key holidays, and other milestones, and begin creating content aligned with those dates and events. This preparation will ensure the content you publish is timely and advances your organization's goals. Deploy guidelines and policies to all content creators. Ensure all policies are clear to internal and external stakeholders.

6. Train staff.

Train team members, other involved parties, and the organization's executives in publishing, monitoring, and whether and how you will respond to relevant third-party content. Prepare the team for crises and run drills.

7. Publish, promote, monitor, and engage.

Begin publishing content on the organization's platforms and, where appropriate, other existing platforms. Showcase the content to relevant stakeholders and encourage their participation. Continue monitoring existing channels and add new channels as they emerge. Respond to stakeholder content according to the comment response and moderation policy.

8. Evaluate and optimize.

Evaluate the plan against the objectives defined in Step 1. Use findings to adapt strategy, content, and policies to the plan's objectives. Use key learnings from successes and failures to improve the program's quality, quantity, and speed in order to fulfill the plan's objectives. Repeat until the campaign is over.

RISKS ASSOCIATED WITH DIGITAL COMMUNICATIONS

Digital communications are not without risks. Obvious risks include the loss of control, particularly in terms of an organization's messages. Many organizations express fear with regards to how employees may use new technologies to the organization's detriment. This fear has led many organizations to forsake the use of digital communications tools or to limit them to small groups of hand-selected employees. Although these fears are reasonable, they are unlikely to persist in the long term. Consider this thought, recounted by communicator, author and speaker Shel Holtz to Scott Monty, head of social media for Ford Motor Company: "If you don't trust your employees enough to not damage your brand with their online actions...why did you hire them in the first place?"[21]

Embracing digital communications means accepting their inherent risks and training staff to use them properly just as they must use all other communications tools at their disposal, such as email and the telephone. Organizations can ignore digital communications for only so long until the pressure from their customers, competitors, and industry compels them to engage.

Risks of digital communications include

- account squatters and imposters (fake accounts purporting to represent an organization; these are more likely to occur when an organization does not have an official presence);
- technology-based attacks (directed at digital properties, service providers, or specific individuals);

- lack of discoverability (whether the organization's content can be found by target audiences);
- lack of audience participation or inappropriate participation by audience members; and
- hosting issues (reliability and other service provider issues).

To mitigate these and other risks, be sure to conduct research before selecting tools for the organization's use from the many available; have a thorough understanding of the features and benefits, risks, obligations, and scope of the tools selected; and research mistakes made by others before using similar tools, in order to avoid them.

Linguistic Challenges Facing Canadian Communicators

There is no definitive answer to the question of how to manage digital communications campaigns that take place in more than one language, but the following guidelines may help:

- Establish and post a clear language policy on the digital platforms on which the organization has a presence.
- Where possible, provide options that allow content to be displayed to users in the language of their choice. For example, a platform may allow an organization to automatically publish updates targeted to users based on their language or location. In other words, messages about a new product could be distributed on exactly the same platform in multiple languages but be visible only to users whose designated language corresponds to the language of the message.
- If the platform does not allow for selective distribution of targeted messages, consider whether to create and manage separate language-specific versions of the organization's presence on the platform. If the size of the audience for each language is relatively equal, this option may make sense. If the size of one audience is significantly larger than the size of others, consider whether you can use both languages on a single platform.
- It may be possible to accommodate all languages on a single platform even when that platform does not allow messages to be targeted to users according to their language and/or location. This accommodation can happen when all messages are visible to all users but each simply chooses to communicate in their preferred language.

CASE STUDY: CANADIAN CENTRE FOR ENERGY INFORMATION'S WEBSITE

Overview

The Canadian Centre for Energy Information's website was launched in 2003.[22] Over the years, the website had more than doubled in size, and its users were becoming frustrated because site performance had slowed. The organization was also encountering new competition online and needed to streamline access to its well-stocked content library, refresh the user experience, and continue to demonstrate value to funders.

Solution

The Centre for Energy engaged NATIONAL Public Relations to improve the website's performance. NATIONAL first completed a Web audit to confirm the site's usability and technical requirements. NATIONAL's strategic approach to the redesign was to make use of the Centre for Energy's existing content and offer users more interactive options for accessing information.

NATIONAL updated the site map, refreshed the site's design and format, and reorganized the content library. New drop down menus, quick links, and animations were added to offer visitors a more personalized Web experience. The resulting reorganization and reduction in the number of pages on the site helped improve the speed and performance for users.

Impact and Results

The new-look website was released in April 2009, and monthly visitor statistics initially decreased because of two main factors: a delay in visitors updating their bookmarks and the confusing error messages displayed to users when they tried to access previously bookmarked website pages that no longer existed. This visitor decrease was only temporary, and traffic resumed its upward trend. Notably, total visitors in 2009 were the second highest in the Centre for Energy's history. The website user experience is now friendly, performance is quick, and access to information is direct and easy. NATIONAL Public Relations continues to develop the website.

Project Details

- The Centre for Energy's content library includes information covering 10 different energy sources and is designed to be a hub for Canadian energy information.
- The website features an energy events calendar that is managed through a content management system (CMS), a tool used by website editors to publish text, images, audio, and video.
- Live stock market feeds (20-minute delay), commodity pricing, and a Google news feed are features on the site that prompt repeat visits. Feeds allow visitors to subscribe to notifications whenever the source information (e.g., stock price, new articles, etc.) changes.
- The Canada's Energy Map is interactive and showcases energy source locations and statistics across the country. Energy By the Numbers is an education resource that consolidates key provincial facts related to the map. Other education resources include Grade K-12 curriculum-linked materials available in both French and English, and Energy Drives Canada, an education program that explores Canada's energy system.
- The Centre for Energy's newsletter publications for subscribers and government are also managed through the website's CMS.

CONCLUSION

Major shifts in the way humans can interact with each other occur very rarely. The continuing rise of digital communications is, however, one of these shifts. Digital communications offer many exciting opportunities for public relations practitioners and other communicators to help the organizations they serve connect with stakeholders in new ways. Thanks to digital communications, many previously unimaginable opportunities, such as communicating in real time with hyper-targeted groups of stakeholders, now take place around the clock. Some organizations remain reticent about using digital communications in a truly multi-directional way, choosing instead to pretend these new platforms are just digital versions of traditional communications. This mindset is likely to hinder or hurt such organizations, but the ones willing to engage publicly in a true dialogue with the people they want to influence have the most to gain. Our role is to guide the organizations willing to take a chance on the future through this process as trusted advisors.

KEY TERMS

Digital communications: The various means by which people connect using technology. Digital communications include text, photos, audio, and video distributed through electronic devices including computers and mobile telephones whether to individual users (for example, through email or text message) or groups of users (for example, on social networks).

Multi-directional interactive communications model: The process by which messages move between multiple sources of information, such as public relations practitioners and the audiences they target.

One-way asymmetric communications model: The process by which a message travels from a public relations practitioner to targeted audiences through an intermediary such as a journalist.

Search engine optimization (SEO): An ever-changing collection of techniques used to increase the likelihood specific digital content appears as close as possible to the first result on the results pages of search engines such as Google and Bing.

Social media: The various means by which people electronically create and share content including text, images, audio, and video.

Social media release: A news release that incorporates content that can be easily shared on social networks.

Social network: A digital platform that connects users and enables them to share content.

Virality: The process whereby a message reaches a much larger audience than the one initially targeted.

FOR REVIEW AND DISCUSSION

1. What distinguishes digital communications from social media?
2. In which ways are digital communications similar to traditional communications? In which ways are they different?
3. How is the role of public relations practitioner changing in light of digital communications?
4. Do you agree that public relations practitioners are well placed to develop and manage digital communications campaigns? Defend your answer.
5. What has changed in the digital landscape since this book was published? Give your opinion on how these changes are affecting public relations.

ACTIVITIES

1. Create a Facebook page for a fictitious organization without making it public. Use a consistent visual style on all page elements including the cover and profile photos. Review every available configuration option. Describe the benefits to configuring a "Username" and "Admin Roles." Be sure to delete this Facebook page after your instructor has evaluated it.

2. Create (but do not complete a purchase for) a Facebook ad to promote the page. Explore available targeting options and the cost benefits of targeting a small, well-defined audience rather than a broader group. Be sure to set your budget to the smallest possible amount to avoid incurring a large cost should you inadvertently complete the purchase process. If you do complete the purchase process, you should be able to easily pause or delete your ad before incurring a charge for it.

3. Develop an editorial calendar that outlines the types of content that should be created (such as blog post and Facebook update), the audience it targets, and how you will track the performance of each piece of content.

4. Write two different kinds of blog posts. For example, write a new product announcement and a "Top 5" blog post. To which websites would you link? What kinds of content would you include in each post (such as text, audio, photo, and video)?

FURTHER READING

Bush, Michael. "How Social Media Is Helping the Public-Relations Sector Not Just Survive, but Thrive." *Advertising Age*, August 23, 2010, 21.

Cha, Meeyoung, Hamed Haddadi, Fabrício Benevenuto, and Krishna P. Gummadi. "Measuring User Influence in Twitter: The Million Follower Fallacy." *Proceedings of the 4th International AAAI Conference on Weblogs and Social Media (ICWSM)*, Washington, DC, May 2010. http://www.mpi-sws.org/ffigummadi/papers/icwsm2010_cha.pdf.

Crawford, Alan Pell. "When Those Nasty Rumors Start Breeding on the Web, You've Got to Move Fast." *Public Relations Quarterly* 44, no. 4 (Winter 1999): 43–45.

Croft, A.C. "Emergence of 'New' Media Moves PR Agencies in New Directions: Competitive Pressure Threatens Agencies' Livelihood." *Public Relations Quarterly* 52 (2008): 16–20.

Iyengar, Raghuram, Sangman Han, and Sunil Gupta. "Do Friends Influence Purchases in a Social Network?" Harvard Business School, Working Paper 09-123, May 2009. http://www.hbs.edu/research/pdf/09-123.pdf.

Jaffe, Joseph. "Who Owns Social Media?" *Brandweek*, March 16, 2009, 2.

Kent, Michael L. "Critical Analysis of Blogging in Public Relations." *Public Relations Review*, 2008: 32–40.

Morrissey, Brian. "Digital Dips Toes Into PR Waters." *Adweek*, May 24, 2010, 6.

———. "Marketers' Use of Twitter Goes Beyond Just Tweeting." *Brandweek*, January 25, 2010, 6.

Schiller, Marc. "Crisis and the Web." *Adweek*, March 5, 2007, 16.

Seo, Hyunjin, Ji Young Kim, and Sung-Un Yang. "Global Activism and New Media: A Study of Transnational NGOs' Online Public Relations." *Public Relations Review* 35 (2009): 123–26.

Simpson, Steve. "Hope, Change, Spam." *Mediaweek*, January 18, 2010, 22.

Singer, Natasha. "Why Some Twitter Posts Catch On, and Some Don't." *New York Times*, February 5, 2011.

Steyn, Peter, Esmail Salehi-Sangari, Leyland Pitt, Michael Parent, and Pierre Berthon. "The Social Media Release as a Public Relations Tool: Intentions to Use among B2B Bloggers." *Public Relations Review* 36, no. 1 (2010): 87–89.

NOTES

1. Eileen M. Searson and Melissa A. Johnson, "Transparency Laws and Interactive Public Relations: An Analysis of Latin American Government Web Sites," *Public Relations Review* 36, no. 2 (2010): 121.

2. Maureen Taylor and Michael L. Kent, "Anticipatory Socialization in the Use of Social Media in Public Relations: A Content Analysis of PRSA's Public Relations Tactics," *Public Relations Review* 36 (2010): 207.

3. Whenever an organization tells me they want to create a campaign that has viral content, I reply, "So do I..."

4. Donald K. Wright and Michelle D. Hinson, "How Blogs and Social Media are Changing Public Relations and the Way it is Practiced," *Public Relations Journal* 2, no. 2 (2008): 1.

5. Daniel Lamarre, "Messaging in Bits and Bytes: Technology Opens New Channels for communications Professionals," *Marketing Magazine*, October 23, 1995, 17.

6. Michael Bush, "As Media Market Shrinks, PR Passes up Reporters, Pitches Directly to Consumers," *Advertising Age*, September 26, 2009.

7. Steve Lohr, "Now Playing: Night of the Living Tech," *New York Times*, August 21, 2010.

8. Ruthann Weaver Lariscy, Elizabeth Johnson Avery, Kaye D. Sweetser, and Pauline Howes, "An Examination of the Role of Online Social Media in Journalists' Source Mix," *Public Relations Review* 35, no. 3 (2009): 314.

9. Elizabeth Avery, Ruthann Lariscy, and Kaye D. Sweetser, "Social Media and Shared— or Divergent—Uses? A Coorientation Analysis of Public Relations Practitioners and Journalists," *International Journal of Strategic Communication* 4, no. 3 (2010): 191.

10. Ibid., 200.

11. Ibid., 202–03, 194.

12. Margalit Toledano, "Professional Competition and Cooperation in the Digital Age: A Pilot Study of New Zealand Practitioners," *Public Relations Review* 36, no. 3 (2010): 233.

13. Jaewon Yang and Jure Leskovec, "Patterns of Temporal Variation in Online Media," paper presented at ACM International Conference on Web Search and Data Mining (WSDM), February 9–12, 2011, Hong Kong, China, http://ilpubs.stanford.edu:8090/984.

14. Jaewon Yang and Jure Leskovec, "Modeling Information Diffusion in Implicit Networks," paper presented at IEEE International Conference on Data Mining, December 2010, Sydney, Australia, http://ilpubs.stanford.edu:8090/989/.

15. Michael Bush, "PR Metrics Evolve to Show How Discipline Drives Sales," *Advertising Age* 80, no. 33 (2009), http://adage.com/article/news/pr-metrics-evolve-show-discipline-drives-sales/139430/.

16. For a good discussion of measureable attributes in digital communications, see Jeremiah Owyang and Matt Toll, *Tracking the Influence of Conversations: A Roundtable Discussion on Social Media Metrics and Measurement*, Dow Jones White Paper, August 2007, 5–7, http://www.web-strategist.com/blog/wp-content/uploads/2007/08/trackingtheinfluence.pdf.

17. Rogers Media Inc. Publishing, "Crisis Talks," *Marketing Magazine* 15, no. 8 (2010): 30–31.

18. The Emerging Technology Division of the United States Air Force's Public Affairs Agency developed and published a flowchart to help their staff effectively evaluate and responsibly respond to online mentions. It can be used "as-is" or modified to accommodate almost any organization's needs. See the flowchart at http://www.af.mil/shared/media/document/afd-091210-037.pdf.

19. Yang and Leskovec, "Modeling Information Diffusion."

20. Beware of the "Streisand effect," defined on *Wikipedia* as "the phenomenon whereby an attempt to hide, remove, or censor a piece of information has the unintended consequence of publicizing the information more widely, usually facilitated by the Internet" (last modified March 6, 2014, http://en.wikipedia.org/wiki/Streisand_effect).

21. Justin, "What Companies Fear Most about Social Media," *Creative Concepts, PR, Marketing and New Media Solutions!* (blog), September 11, 2009, http://creative-conceptsllc.com/what-companies-fear-most-about-social-media/.

22. See the Canadian Centre for Energy Information's website at http://www.centreforenergy.com.

Sheridan McVean

14

Government Relations

LEARNING OBJECTIVES

After reading this chapter, you will be able to

- explain differences in terminology used to describe government relations;
- describe how governments in Canada can have a significant impact on organizations and individuals;
- explain how to plan and execute government relations programs using the research, analysis, communication, and evaluation (RACE) formula; and
- describe basic government relations strategies and explain how they can be applied to a specific case.

INTRODUCTION

Government relations is a practice area in public relations that attempts to influence one or more governments to adopt your organization's point of view. As an example, consider a non-profit organization—such as a provincial automobile association—that seeks to reduce traffic accidents by improving traffic safety. Such an organization would communicate with government to attempt to have the government create laws requiring passengers in motor vehicles to wear seat belts and refrain from using cellphones while driving.

In this example, the organization's point of view is that if government adopted these laws, traffic accidents would be reduced. The organization would use government relations activities to attempt to influence government to adopt the measures. The activities would include communicating the organization's point of view to the government and perhaps providing the government with the organization's commissioned research demonstrating the connection between traffic accidents and the lack of seat belts as well as distracted drivers. The organization could also contact the members of their organization to ask them to write letters to their elected representatives recommending these measures be adopted as laws. Other government relations activities could seek to establish, maintain, or enhance the organization's relationships with government, including attempting to convince government of the organization's expertise and knowledge about traffic safety.

In defining government relations it is important to note that some academic literature on public relations focuses on "government public relations." This term is used to refer to conducting public relations on behalf of government as a government employee or a contractor to government. For the sake of clarity, this chapter is not about "government public relations" but rather about "government relations" as a practice area in public relations for organizations attempting to influence governments in Canada.

GOVERNMENT RELATIONS AS A PUBLIC RELATIONS PRACTICE AREA

There are several reasons government relations is considered a public relations practice area. First, consider a definition of public relations: "the management function that identifies, establishes and maintains mutually beneficial relationships between an organization and the various publics on whom its success or failure depends."[1] Governments are clearly an important "public" for business and non-profit organizations, and these organizations work hard to create and maintain mutually beneficial relationships with governments.

Consider also how the actions of governments can contribute to the success or failure of business and non-profit organizations. In Canada, consider how government regulations impact business and industry in areas such as taxation, telecommunications and broadcasting, energy and mining, banking and insurance, land use, zoning, and business licensing, to name a few. Regulations are rules determined by government as to how laws function.

All non-profit organizations in Canada are required to comply with government regulations. The regulations are even stricter for those non-profits who want to become or maintain their status as a registered charitable organizations authorized by the Government of Canada to issue income tax receipts. Business and non-profit organizations in Canada can be dependent upon government for their success or failure.

Second, consider other practice areas in public relations. Community relations focuses on communications and relationships with "the community" as a "public" or audience. In a similar way, media relations is concerned about the media. It is consistent, therefore, to have government relations as a practice area in public relations that focuses on communications and relationships with government.

OTHER TERMS USED TO DESCRIBE GOVERNMENT RELATIONS

When the phrase *government relations* is mentioned, the first response tends to be something like "oh, you mean lobbying." A less frequent response is "isn't that public affairs?" These responses point out the use of various terms to describe government relations activities.

Lobbying involves direct contact with elected representatives, such as government cabinet ministers, to attempt to influence their decision making. Lobbying activities can also extend to senior officials in government, such as deputy ministers, who provide advice to cabinet ministers. As lobbying involves direct contact, it can be referred to as a "contact" program to differentiate it from other government relations activities.

In Canada, the Government of Canada and numerous provincial governments require lobbyists to register their lobbying activities publicly and report on their direct contact with cabinet ministers and others. These regulations apply to certain types of individuals who are in direct, typically face-to-face, contact with government decision makers. Because significant penalties are associated with not complying with lobbying regulations, anyone planning to conduct government relations activities in Canada should check lobbying laws and regulations to ensure they are aware of them.

Regarding the term *public affairs*, some provincial governments, such as the governments of British Columbia and Alberta, have branches of government responsible for public relations activities that are called the "Public Affairs Bureau." *Public affairs* has also been used by large corporations to describe corporate departments that conduct government relations activities. Non-profit organizations in Canada, however, typically use *advocacy* to describe their government relations activities, not *public affairs*.

GOVERNMENTS IN CANADA

Canadians typically have three types of government: the federal government (Government of Canada); provincial and territorial governments;[2] and municipal governments. Each type of government has different responsibilities and these are referred to as their "jurisdiction" or areas of responsibility of that government.

Areas of responsibility for the federal and provincial governments were originally determined in 1867 when Canada was created. Two sections in the British North America Act of 1867, sections 91 and 92, described which government had the authority to enact laws and make decisions in specific areas. For example, the Government of Canada was given the authority to make decisions on foreign affairs and international trade. The provinces were given the authority to make decisions on education and health care.[3] Since 1867, some changes have been made to give jurisdiction to the provinces for non-renewable natural resources, forestry resources, and electrical energy.[4]

Many Canadians are surprised to learn that municipal governments, such as city and town governments, are creations of provincial governments. If a provincial government wants to change, abolish, or combine municipal governments, the province has the authority to make those changes. For example, the Government of Ontario amalgamated seven municipalities into the new City of Toronto in 1998. Provincial governments also create health boards and health regions, school boards, and post-secondary educational institutions.

If you are seeking to influence government to adopt your organization's point of view, it is critical to know which government has the authority (or jurisdiction) to make those types of decisions. Approaching a government that does not have the jurisdiction is typically a waste of time, although some organizations attempt to get one government to pressure the government that has the ability to make the decision.

WHY ARE GOVERNMENTS IMPORTANT FOR BUSINESS AND NON-PROFITS?

As you read earlier, governments in Canada make decisions that can have a significant impact on business and non-profit organizations. Some government decisions can mean the success or failure of an organization. For example, the Government of Canada in 2011 removed the ability of natural gas exploration and production companies to be income trusts by changing corporate tax laws so it was no longer financially advantageous to be an income trust. This decision was a disruptive surprise for many of the existing natural resource income trusts and forced many of them to reorganize their businesses.

More often government decisions either favour or hinder the activities of your organization. For example, the Canadian Revenue Agency has been very careful when considering the applications of non-profit organizations for charitable status. When non-profits are granted charitable status, they can issue tax receipts to their financial donors, and the Government of Canada will allow those donors to use the donation receipts to reduce their personal income tax. This due diligence by the Canadian Revenue Agency has delayed or denied the granting of charitable status to some non-profits.

The two examples provided above may be seen as small in scope, but consider the wide range of decisions governments can make. They create and amend laws; adopt and revise government policies; regulate or de-regulate organizations; and purchase and restrict the purchase of goods and services.

In the business world, Canadian companies including those in manufacturing, mining, energy, and forestry require multiple approvals from multiple governments to approve their

- use of public lands and water;
- handling of hazardous materials;
- construction of facilities;
- environmental care;
- land use and zoning requirements;
- business licences;
- transportation;
- labour standards for employees;
- import and export rules;
- customs duties;
- withholding of government portions of employee income tax;
- workers compensation; and
- payment of corporate, land, and sales taxes.

Non-profit organizations must abide by some of the same rules as business as well as rules unique to their sector, but must do many more things if they receive funding from governments for their work. They must also handle all financial donors in a prescribed way to maintain their charitable and non-profit status.

WHY ARE GOVERNMENTS IMPORTANT TO YOU?

If this does not convince you of the importance of governments, consider what you did this morning and how a Canadian government was involved in some way in your personal activities.

Did you get dressed? Then...

- your clothes were likely imported to Canada and subject to international trade rules, import tariffs, and the Goods and Services Tax (GST) or Harmonized Sales Tax (HST), which are all decisions made and imposed by federal and provincial governments.

Did you eat breakfast? Then...

- your food required approvals by the federal government (meat can also be approved by the provincial government), and hopefully you are eating according to the Canada Food Guide, and
- if your tomato was imported from Mexico, governments were involved with import taxes, customs inspection, highway transport rules, and Canadian rules on labelling.

Did you get in your car? Then...

- your car is required by the federal government to have daytime running lights unless it is an older model,
- some provincial governments require regular inspections for roadworthiness,
- an extra federal government tax was paid on air conditioning,
- the tires required payment of a provincial tire recycling fee,
- you are required by your province to wear a seat belt,
- texting or talking on your phone would violate law in many provinces,
- maybe you received a ticket from a red light camera (municipal and provincial),
- buying gasoline included federal and provincial taxes, and
- you drove on roads designed and paid for by municipal, provincial, and occasionally the federal government.

Did you catch the bus? Then...

- the bus stop was designed by your municipal government who selects the location and enforces laws around the stop,
- the bus was operated by a municipal or provincial government,
- the bus was purchased by a municipal, provincial, or the federal government, and
- the diesel that went into the bus was regulated, controlled, and taxed by the provincial and federal governments.

In short, governments are involved in many aspects of your life—whether you realize it or not.

GOVERNMENT RELATIONS PROGRAM PLANNING

As in public relations, planning for government relations programs follows the RACE formula: research, analysis, communication, and evaluation.

The advantage of planning government relations using the framework of public relations planning is that government relations activities can be easily integrated into other public relations activities. So, for example, ongoing media relations activities directed towards multiple publics could easily include media relations directed towards influencing government.

It is both important and helpful to use public relations planning and public relations strategies for government relations. Some individuals, such as some registered lobbyists and even some public relations practitioners who believe government relations involves only lobbying, may not realize the strengths that public relations planning and strategies can bring to improving the results of government relations. Government relations programs that fully use public relations do not rely solely upon "who you know" in government and have far more likelihood of success even when people or the political party in government changes.

The following sections highlight some unique aspects of planning government relations programs compared to the public relations programs.

Research

In addition to typical public relations research, government relations requires a fundamental understanding of current government policy and government perspectives on changes to policy. Government policy is the decision of government on a course of action as stated in documents such as speeches, news releases, announcements, backgrounders as well as regulations and legislation. For example, if one is seeking to ensure drivers of motor vehicles do not use cellular telephones while driving, it would be important to understand what the current government policy is towards use of cellphones in motor vehicles. Currently, many Canadian provinces have laws (legislation) that prevents use of cellular telephones by drivers in moving vehicles, while others do not, or the legislation is pending. In the research phase it is helpful to determine exactly what needs to be changed to achieve a modification of current government policies, regulations, or laws and the creation of new ones.

When laws are approved by provincial legislatures or the Parliament of Canada, the governments are permitted to create regulations describing how the laws will be implemented and applied. These regulations are written by government and typically require approval of the cabinet through what is known as an "Order in Council." Well known examples of federal regulations include the Food and Drug Regulations, the Consumer Packaging and Labelling Regulations, and the Meat Inspection Regulations.

It may be that your organization seeks a change in regulation rather than legislation. Changes in regulations are typically easier and faster for governments to make compared to legislation. Unlike legislation, changes to regulations do not require discussion, debate, and approval by a provincial legislature or the Parliament of Canada.

As noted previously in this chapter, one of the first research steps for government relations programs is to determine which government or governments have decision-making authority for the area in which you are seeking change.

Research for government relations programs also includes researching previous and current media coverage on the issue or subject you wish to change. In fact, public relations practitioners working in the field of issues management are already familiar with this type of research.

Knowledge of the processes governments use to change policy and legislation is also helpful. Discussion of the details on how governments make decisions goes beyond the scope of this chapter. Most provinces and the Parliament of Canada currently have information on their websites about how legislation is passed as well as information on how governments make decisions.[5]

A typical research plan would include the following steps:

1. Determine which government has decision-making authority for the change you seek.
2. Research current government policy and the government's attitude about change.
3. Determine if you are seeking a change in legislation or regulation, as you will want to be specific about the change you seek.
4. Research or determine how governments can change legislation and regulations.
5. Research previous and current media coverage on the issue or change you seek so that you know what has happened in the past and other organizations that would support the change you seek.

Public relations practitioners interested in government relations can check courses in Canadian politics and governments at post-secondary educational institutions or seek lobbyists or other consultants with knowledge of government decision-making processes.

Analysis and Communication

The following strategies are typically used in government relations programs:

- contact program (lobbying)
- grassroots contact program (lobbying)
- coalition building and maintenance
- election techniques
- media relations
- digital communications

Contact Program (also referred to as "Lobbying")

A contact program strategy involves a program of direct contact with decision makers in government. Federally in Canada, the Lobbyists Registration Act does not outlaw lobbying but rather requires the registration and reporting of any person (with some exceptions) who is paid to communicate on certain topics with a person who holds public office or to arrange meetings with that person.

Government relations practitioners should review the Lobbyists Registration Act before considering a contact program.[6] In addition, many provincial governments have lobbying registration and disclosure laws; these additional requirements should be reviewed as well.[7]

Many organizations contract (hire) registered lobbyists to conduct lobbying activities. Other organizations register specific employees, such as their chief executive officer or executive director, as lobbyists under federal and provincial laws. As a result, government relations practitioners generally work with lobbyist consultants or senior management within their organization rather than becoming experts in lobbying themselves. However, government relations practitioners typically prepare and provide written and visual materials for lobbyists to use.

Grassroots Lobbying

A grassroots lobbying strategy involves engaging employees and members of an organization to help persuade government decision makers to adopt changes proposed by the organization. For example, members of a local Chamber of Commerce or Board of Trade could send emails to its members asking them to contact local elected representatives to express the member's support for a reduction in property tax rates. This strategy clearly relies upon the strength of government relations practitioners who are skilled in communications and building mutually beneficial relationships with members of the organization as well as elected representatives.

Coalition Building and Maintenance

An important government relations strategy is to build a coalition of different organizations representing different perspectives that agree on and support a specific change in public policy. Public policy is a course of action or inaction chosen by government to address a problem or interrelated set of problems. Building and maintaining a coalition can be time-consuming and challenging, but a coalition can greatly influence the government to change a policy.

An important consideration prior to setting up a coalition is to anticipate the amount of ongoing effort required to maintain a functioning and effective coalition. Most government relations practitioners should also consider if there are existing coalitions that could be convinced to support the desired change in public policy. For example, most industry associations can be viewed as an existing coalition. The Canadian Manufacturers and Exporters and the Canadian Association of Petroleum Producers are two examples of industry associations.[8]

Election Techniques

This government relations strategy involves encouraging or mobilizing employees or other groups of stakeholders to vote during elections. Public relations plays a key role in election techniques because this strategy relies upon communicating with employees or stakeholder groups and motivating them to vote.

An example of an election technique would be communicating with employees to point out the impact of a future government policy decision on the organization and its employees. There would be additional communication regarding the importance of voting for candidates or parties who agree with the organization's stance on the policy decision.

In previous federal elections in Canada, restrictions were placed on organizations other than political parties or candidates ("third parties") to outlaw their purchase of advertising if the content involved political issues and appeared during an election period (the time from the announcement of the date of a general election to the day in which voting takes place). In 2004, however, the National Citizens Coalition challenged this law in the courts, and the law was changed. Now, the Canada Elections Act regulates "third parties" who engage in election advertising, requiring organizations spending more than a specified amount to register.[9] In other words, third parties can advertise during election periods if they register. Any organization contemplating advertising about political issues during an election period should double check with Elections Canada or similar provincial bodies to determine the current rules.

Government relations practitioners considering election techniques should consult the Canada Elections Act and Elections Canada to ensure they are well aware of current requirements on third-party advertising.[10] Provinces and municipalities have election laws that should be consulted as well.

Media Relations

Media relations can be used to build support for a specific policy change or demonstrate existing support by publics. Typical media relations tactics for government relations include op-ed pieces, news releases, general public opinion research, letters to the editor, public policy research papers, media interviews with organizational spokespeople and public policy experts, as well as attempting to attract media coverage on the organizations' policy preferences.

The timing of media relations as a government relations strategy can be critical. Some organizations use media relations to bring desired public policy changes to the attention of government before actually expressing their views to government themselves. This technique, however, can give the government a negative perception of the organization, especially if the government is surprised by media coverage on the issue.

Digital Communications

The power of digital communications, including websites and social media such as Facebook and Twitter, for government-related issues became very clear during the uprising against the president and government of Egypt in early 2011. The Canadian Broadcasting Corporation (CBC), the British Broadcasting Company (BBC), and other media networks reported the significant role social media played in mobilizing demonstrators against the Egyptian government.[11] The dramatic result of these actions—the resignation of long-time Egyptian President Hosni Mubarak and the return to military rule in Egypt—was spectacular in demonstrating the use of social media. Social media used for political purposes also occurred prior to 2011. In the United States, social media is credited with contributing significantly to President Barack Obama's election victory in 2008.[12]

Other uses of digital communications include large business organizations posting government relations information on their intranet sites for their employees to access. Some organizations will include their policy preferences on their external websites as well as links to websites of industry associations that support their policy views.

Non-profit organizations typically include policy preferences on their websites, often under a heading such as "advocacy." Some non-profits create online petitions that allow website visitors to add their signatures electronically. Some websites go beyond the petition by generating a personalized email for the individual to send to their elected representative via the organization's website.

A coalition can create its own website and use the tactics noted above. The organizations involved in the coalition can provide links on their own website to drive traffic to the coalition's website. This tactic can be combined with other strategies such as providing an online media kit for the coalition.

Evaluation

Evaluation for government relations programs uses the same evaluation measures as public relations programs. It is important to distinguish between interim measures and final measures. For example, current knowledge of a particular policy issue by specific "publics" can be used as an interim measure of awareness. Using public relations to increase awareness among elected officials of the need for a specific policy change can be measured. Increasing awareness of the need for change must occur before the actual policy can change. That is why the increase in awareness can be described as an interim measure.

The ultimate or final measure of a government relations program is whether government adopts or rejects the desired change in public policy. Government relations practitioners are well aware that it may take years to achieve a desired change. The delay can be caused by opposition from the political party that is currently in government; it may be necessary to wait for another party to be elected to form the government.

Since the success of ultimate measures may take years to achieve, government relations practitioners can detail measures of the campaign by breaking them into smaller pieces achievable in a shorter time frame (perhaps a month or a year at a time). Take the historic example of requiring seatbelts to be used in motor vehicles. While an organization may have sought to achieve laws that require everyone to use seatbelts when travelling in a motor vehicle, the starting point could have been to require children under a certain age to wear seatbelts. When this goal was achieved, the organization could have pressed for a change in the legislation to make it applicable to older persons.

In government relations, as in public relations, it is important to distinguish between the business goals of the organization and the government relations goals. Using the seatbelt example again, the business goal of a non-profit organization focused on vehicle safety would be to require all persons in motor vehicles to wear seatbelts. The goal of a government relations program would be to have a majority of government decision makers support legislation requiring use of seatbelts.

It may take several government relations campaigns to achieve the goal of government support for seatbelts. For example, an early government relations campaign may focus on getting a specific political party to adopt a new policy that seatbelts must be worn in vehicles. The next campaign would then press for legislation that would require mandatory use of seat belts.

CASE STUDY: CONSTRUCTION OF NEW HOCKEY ARENAS IN CANADA

This case on construction of new hockey arenas is presented to demonstrate how government relations strategies could be applied to a hypothetical but realistic situation in Canada. The case is hypothetical and is intended as a learning opportunity to point out the general application of government relations strategies. It is not intended to provide professional advice.

The case has been selected because several communities in Canada are currently considering the construction of new hockey arenas to serve professional and amateur sports teams as well as providing space for conventions, meetings, concerts, and other events. The case is intentionally written without a named location but adding your own specific location to the case could add greater depth to the learning experience. Another interesting variation on the case is to consider professional football stadiums instead of professional hockey arenas.

The Situation

Assume you are an employee of a professional hockey team in Canada and you have been assigned the responsibility to consider strategies for a government relations plan that would influence government to support the construction of a new arena in your city that would be suitable for the team to use.

There may be many reasons a new arena is required. For the purpose of this hypothetical case, assume a new arena is required because the current arena and others in your area do not have sufficient seating capacity for current demand and have older systems that are not efficient in terms of energy and design. In addition, constructing a new arena has the potential to decrease operating costs and generate additional revenue for the team.

The team has secured an option to purchase a suitable parcel of raw land on which the arena could be built. The raw land is surrounded on two sides by residential communities and light industrial areas on the other two sides. Re-zoning of the raw land would be required for the new arena. Although the light industrial areas are currently accessed by a large capacity highway, the existing standard intersection would have to be replaced with a new elevated overpass to accommodate the additional traffic to the arena. The parcel of raw land is large enough to accommodate the new arena as well as the required parking, with some extra land left over that could be sold or developed for related purposes.

Initial architectural designs and estimates of the total construction costs for the new arena have been completed. The team cannot afford to finance the entire cost of the new arena by themselves. Therefore, the team must seek additional funding from government and other sources. The team is prepared to work with other organizations that can use or rent the arena for events when the team is not using it.

Questions to Ask about the Case

Answers to several key questions must be determined prior to consideration of a government relations plan and determining strategies for the plan.

1. *What is our organization attempting to achieve that government(s) can help or support?*

   The case as presented would require government approval of

   - zoning or re-zoning of the raw land for use as a hockey arena;
   - infrastructure improvements such as the highway interchange and additional roadways, water, and sewer; and
   - some amount of government funding as a contribution to capital costs (the cost of building the arena).

2. *Which government(s) do we need to influence?*

   The municipal government would make decisions about zoning, local roads, and infrastructure such as water and sewer. Improvements to the interchange could be a municipal, provincial, or federal government decision depending upon which government owns or is responsible for the existing highway intersection. Requests for government funding would likely be made to all three governments.

3. *What specifically are we asking governments to do for our organization?*

   While re-zoning is required, which exact zoning category is being sought? Similarly, what type and capacity of interchange is required? For funding, how much is being requested from which governments and how much will be provided from non-governmental sources?

   Governments understandably want and need to have specific details when considering and making decisions. If the details are not available, governments delay making decisions and the momentum for decision making stalls.

Applying Government Relations Strategies to the Case

The following sections describe specific tactics that could be used for the scenario outlined in "Case Study: Construction of New Hockey Arenas in Canada." These strategies are intended as a learning opportunity rather than professional advice.

Case Summary

- Perspective: We represent the local professional hockey team.
- Government(s): Municipality, province, and federal government.
- Issue: Funding and approval for a new large indoor hockey arena to be used by a professional hockey team and others.
- Current government policy: Would need to research the current zoning of proposed land and servicing possibilities as well as the possibility and methods for governments to provide funding for the construction costs of the arena.
- Desired policy (what the organization wants adopted):
- Zoning and infrastructure approvals, and
- Funding for arena construction and ongoing maintenance.

Contact Program

As you read earlier in the chapter, a contact program involves direct contact with decision makers in government.

The contact program for this case would likely be divided by government. The municipal government is responsible for zoning or re-zoning, sewer and water, and for approvals and funding for roadways. If the provincial government is responsible for the current interchange, they would be a decision maker on the upgraded interchange. Funding contributions for the arena would be asked of the municipal, provincial, and federal governments.

Other key tactics for the contact program would include the following:

1. Research the process by which the municipal government makes decisions related to zoning, infrastructure, and arena funding.
2. Acquire information about previous requests and the current attitude of elected representatives towards approving zoning, infrastructure, and arena funding.
3. Contact municipal officials (unelected government employees) about the process, regulations, expectations of the process, and requirements for zoning, infrastructure, and arena funding.
4. Maintain ongoing contact with government through the entire process of requesting approvals and funding. Answer questions and provide information about the proposed arena.
5. Research arena funding policies of provincial and federal governments.

6. Appear at public hearings and meetings of the municipal government related to zoning, infrastructure, and arena funding.
7. Write briefing notes, backgrounders, the case for action (the explanation of why action needs to be taken), presentations, and other materials to provide to elected representatives and government officials.
8. Monitor progress and the media, addressing issues as they arise.
9. Work with in-house or contract lobbyists.

Coalition Building and Maintenance

This strategy involves creating a coalition of different organizations representing different perspectives that can agree on and support a specific public policy change.

Typical tactics would include the following:

1. Research and identify specific organizations willing to join a coalition to influence government to approve and help fund construction of a new arena, such as

   - amateur sports associations, other professional hockey teams;
   - businesses and business associations that would benefit from a new arena (restaurants, bars, other entertainment venues);
   - organizations dedicated to increasing tourism, including tourism bureaus, hotels, hotel associations, and local convention organizations;
   - current suppliers to the hockey team that are likely to see additional sales from a new arena;
   - hockey fans and season ticket holders; and
   - current and potential sponsors of the hockey team.

2. Approach and persuade these organizations to support zoning, infrastructure, and arena funding. Have them communicate their support to members of their organization as well as governments through initiatives such as joint or linked websites, joint coalition presentations to government, joint position papers, joint research to support the cause, and news releases.

3. Communicate regularly with coalition members to maintain their support throughout the process. Provide information about progress and answer questions as they arise.

Grassroots Lobbying

This strategy involves engaging employees and members of an organization to help persuade government decision makers. When combined with a coalition building strategy, the grassroots campaign is extended to all employees and members of all organizations involved in the coalition.

Tactics would include the following:

- Identify individuals and groups associated with the professional hockey team including employees, sponsors, and donors. Request their support and involvement in expressing their view to government.
- Create online petitions or an email that is sent directly to elected representatives.
- Use social media, such as Twitter, to alert employees to the immediate need to persuade government.
- Identify the elected representative for the area where an employee lives and encourage and facilitate the employee to contact the representative directly by telephone, letter, or email.
- Hold events, such as hockey games, to which elected representatives are invited and where they interact with individual supporters.
- Encourage employees to become politically involved.

Election Techniques

This government relations strategy involves encouraging or mobilizing employees or other groups of stakeholders to vote during elections.

Tactics would include the following:

- Communicate with employees and stakeholder groups and motivate them to vote in an election.
- Communicate with employees to point out the benefits of the government's financial support and its potential impact on the future of the organization and its staff.
- Provide information about voting, including voting qualifications and voting locations.

- Approve time off from work to vote, and encourage employees to run for election.

Media Relations

Media relations involves working with journalists and reporters to get information the organization wishes to communicate into the media and, therefore, communicated to specific desired audiences.

Government is a specific and desired audience that can easily be reached through media relations. The purpose of using media relations is to build support within specific publics or audiences for the position an organization is proposing in order to influence government to adopt that position or make a specific decision.

Typical tactics would include the following:

- Introduce new information about the benefits of a new arena to attempt to capture the attention of the general public (and government).
- Use the media to ask the government questions about the potential economic gain from building a new arena.
- Demonstrate to government that the "general public" supports a specific policy or action, such as the additional traffic safety benefits of upgrading the highway interchange that accesses the new arena.
- Release results of commissioned research that supports a specific policy advocated by an organization, such as the increased economic spinoffs of constructing the arena and the additional tourism it would generate.
- Highlight the abilities and knowledge of the spokesperson for the organization to help build credibility of the organization.
- Attempt to increase the importance of a specific issue or proposed policy so that government recognizes the need and urgency to make an immediate decision, such as the need to make a decision before arena construction costs escalate.

Digital Communications

Online communications refers to use of the Internet for government relations, including websites, intranets, email, and social media.

Tactics for using digital communications would include the following:

- Provide information regarding elections and public policy on the organization's intranet site for employees to access.

- Provide information about public policy, such as the organization's public policy preferences, on the organization's website.
- Create and maintain a website for a coalition supporting a specific policy.
- Provide links on the website to other organizations, such as think tanks, that support the organization's public policy preferences.
- Create and provide online petitions that allow website visitors to add their signatures electronically.
- Include the ability for website visitors to generate and send a personalized email to their elected representative.
- Set up and maintain a Facebook presence to create, build, and demonstrate support from the general public for a specific public policy.
- Use Twitter to provide news and progress updates on getting government agreement on roadways and financing as well as inviting supporters to "town hall" or similar meetings to express their views.

CONCLUSION

This chapter has taken a practical approach to explaining and illustrating how government relations strategies can be used to influence government.

Government relations is a growing and evolving practice area of public relations. In 2009, a global survey of senior business executives conducted by the management consulting firm McKinsey and Company identified three key conclusions relevant to government relations. First, more senior executives believe government has a greater effect on the economic value of the company than employees, investors, or suppliers. Second, senior executives believe company processes to manage relationships with government are less robust than processes to manage relationships with other stakeholders. From this, the survey concluded, "Most companies would benefit from making government more of a priority by building integrated capabilities to manage their government relationships."[13]

Government is unlikely to give up its authority in our lives, which means that the opportunities for government relations and government relations practitioners will grow. As the practice area grows, the field will continue to evolve. For those who are willing to get involved, there are likely to be significant rewards.

KEY TERMS

Advocacy: The term used by non-profit organizations to refer to government relations activities.

British North America Act: Legislation (laws) approved by the Parliament of the United Kingdom originally in 1867 that are the core of the constitution of Canada.

Coalition building and maintenance: A government relations strategy that involves building and maintaining a coalition of different organizations that represent different perspectives but agree on and support a specific change in public policy.

Contact program (also called *lobbying*): A government relations strategy that involves a program of direct (typically but not necessarily face-to-face) contact with government decision makers.

Digital communications: The various means by which people connect using technology. Digital communications include text, photos, audio, and video distributed through electronic devices, including computers and mobile telephones whether to individual users, (for example, through email or text message) or groups of users (for example, on social networks). In government relations, this technology is used to identify potential supporters and promote a specific point of view to influence government to adopt a desired public policy or policies.

Election period: The time from the announcement of the date of a general election to the day on which voting takes place.

Election techniques: A government relations strategy that involves encouraging or mobilizing employees or other groups of stakeholders to vote during elections.

Federal government: A reference to the Government of Canada.

Government policy: The decision of government on a course of action as stated in documents such as speeches, news releases, announcements, backgrounders as well as regulations and legislation.

Government relations: A practice area in public relations that attempts to influence one or more governments to adopt your organization's point of view.

Grassroots lobbying: A government relations strategy that engages employees and members of an organization to help persuade government decision makers to adopt changes proposed by the organization.

Legislation: Laws as determined by government through parliament and legislatures.

Media relations: A traditional public relations strategy to generate news media coverage used in government relations to push for a specific policy change or demonstrate existing public support.

Municipal government: The government of a Canadian municipality, such as the City of Calgary.

Provincial government: The government of a Canadian province, such as the Government of Ontario.

Public policy: A course of action or inaction chosen by government to address a problem or interrelated set of problems.

Public relations (PR): The management function that identifies, establishes, and maintains mutually beneficial relationships between an organization and its various publics on whom its success or failure depends.

Publics: Groups of people with similar characteristics who are important for some reason to the organization conducting public relations. Publics are also referred to as *audiences, target audiences,* or *stakeholders.*

RACE formula: An acronym that stands for research, analysis, communication, and evaluation. This describes the commonly used four-step planning process used by professional public relations practitioners in developing a public relations plan and is applicable to a government relations plan.

Regulations: Rules determined by government as to how laws function.

Territorial government: The government of a Canadian territory, such as the Government of Yukon.

FOR REVIEW AND DISCUSSION

1. What is the ultimate goal of government relations?
2. Examine your activities during a typical day and determine which ones have no government involvement. Be prepared to defend your answer. (You may be surprised at the extent of government involvement in our lives.)
3. In your opinion, what are the advantages of using the RACE formula for planning government relations programs?
4. Explain why it is important to know which government has jurisdiction in a particular area.
5. Why is it necessary to know how governments make decisions?
6. Compare and contrast the differences between a contact program and grass-roots lobbying.

7. Assess the value of setting up a coalition of organizations.
8. When would you advise an organization seeking changes in government policy to use media relations?
9. How can social media best be used in government relations?
10. What are the three questions that should be answered prior to developing a government relations plan?

ACTIVITIES

1. Identify something you would like to see government change. Propose arguments for and against making that change.
2. Select either a for-profit organization or a non-profit organization that you are familiar with. Create a list of policy changes that the organization would need or want from government. Brainstorm how the organization could use government relations to obtain what it needs or wants.
3. Analyze a topic currently in the Canadian news media that involves a government making a decision. Evaluate the arguments various organizations are making to attempt to influence government.

FURTHER READING

Broom, Glen A., and Bey-Ling Sha. *Cutlip and Centre's Effective Public Relations.* 11th ed. Upper Saddle River, NJ: Pearson, 2013.

Harris, Phil, and Craig Fleisher, eds. *Handbook of Public Affairs.* London: Sage Publications, 2005.

Mack, Charles S. *Business, Politics, and the Practice of Government Relations.* Westport, CT: Quorum Books, 1997.

Miljan, Lydia. *Public Policy in Canada: An Introduction.* 6th ed. Don Mills, ON: Oxford University Press, 2012.

Pal, Leslie A. *Beyond Policy Analysis: Public Issue Management in Turbulent Times.* 5th ed. Toronto: Nelson Education, 2014.

Stanbury, W.T. *Business–Government Relations in Canada.* Toronto: Methuen Publications, 1986.

Williams, Huw, and Lou Riccoboni. *A Guide to Government Relations for Directors of Not-for-Profit Organizations.* Toronto: Canadian Society of Association Executives, 2003.

NOTES

1. Scott M. Cutlip, Allen H. Center, and Glen M. Broom, *Effective Public Relations*, 6th ed. (Englewood Cliffs, NJ: Prentice Hall, 1985), 4.

2. For the sake of brevity, subsequent references to provincial governments in this chapter should be considered to include territorial governments, although differences in areas of jurisdiction exist between the two.

3. For a brief summary of the British North America Act, see Canadian Human Rights Commission, "A Three-Minute Guide to the BNA Act, 1867," accessed March 10, 2014, http://www.chrc-ccdp.ca/en/browseSubjects/bnaguide.asp.

4. For the full text of constitutional documents, see Department of Justice Canada, Justice Laws Website, "Constitutional Acts, 1867 to 1982," last modified February 17, 2014, http://laws-lois.justice.gc.ca/eng/Const/.

5. See Legislative Assembly of Alberta, *Citizen's Guide to the Alberta Legislature*, 7th ed., 2010, http://www.assembly.ab.ca/pub/gdbook/citizensguide.pdf; Parliament of Canada, "About Parliament," accessed April 27, 2014, http://www.parl.gc.ca/About.aspx?Language=E.

6. See Office of the Commissioner of Lobbying of Canada, http://www.ocl-cal.gc.ca/eic/site/lobbyist-lobbyiste1.nsf/eng/home.

7. See Office of the Ethics Commissioner of Alberta, Lobbyists Registration, http://www.lobbyistsact.ab.ca/LRS/GeneralSettings.nsf/vwEnHTML/Welcome.htm.

8. See the Canadian Manufacturers and Exporters at http://www.cme-mec.ca/ and the Canadian Association of Petroleum Producers at http://www.capp.ca/.

9. Elections Canada, "Spending Limits for Election Advertising," last modified August 24, 2010, http://www.elections.ca/content.aspx?section=pol&document=index&dir=thi/pla&lang=e.

10. The Elections Canada Act is available through Elections Canada, "Federal Electoral Legislation," last modified June 4, 2013, http://www.elections.ca/content.aspx?section=res&dir=loi/fel&document=index&lang=e. Also see Elections Canada website for more information: http://www.elections.ca/.

11. CBC News, "Egyptian Crisis: How Did It Happen?" January 29, 2011, http://www.cbc.ca/news/world/story/2011/01/29/f-faq-egypt-uprising.html; Anne Alexander, "Internet Role in Egypt's Protests," *BBC News*, February 9, 2011, http://www.bbc.co.uk/news/world-middle-east-12400319.

12. David Carr, "How Obama Tapped Into Social Networks' Power," *New York Times*, November 9, 2008, http://www.nytimes.com/2008/11/10/business/media/10carr.html.

13. Andrea Dua, Kerrin Heil, and Jon Wilkins, *How Business Interacts with Government: McKinsey Global Survey Results*, McKinsey and Company, January 2010, http://www.mckinseyquarterly.com/How_business_interacts_with_government_McKinsey_Global_Survey_results_2495.

Wendy Campbell

15

Internal Communications

LEARNING OBJECTIVES

After reading this chapter, you will be able to

- explain the role of internal communications under the broader communications umbrella;
- describe how internal communications can help an organization achieve its strategic goals;
- identify appropriate strategies to overcome issues and barriers to internal communications;
- describe how to develop a strategic internal communications plan;
- discuss the role of internal communications in crisis communications planning; and
- describe the basic issues in communicating organizational change.

INTRODUCTION

Imagine yourself in a communications supermarket where you are treated to tempting displays of communications practice areas such as media relations, government relations, digital communications, internal communications, and crisis communications. Which would you choose and why? If you chose internal communications, great! If you did not, ask yourself why. You may believe internal communications lacks the glamour and excitement of many of the other practice areas or does not command the same level of respect and resources. The good news is that you could not be further from the truth, if you are working for an organization that understands the value of the internal communications function.

Internal communications deals exclusively with groups of individuals (audiences) within an organization. Using the same strategic techniques and tools as most other communications practice areas, internal communications enhances communication among employees, management, unions, staff associations, boards of directors, and some stakeholder groups associated with the internal aspects of an organization. Strategic internal communications, in effect, throws down the gauntlet to an organization's managers and leaders to "walk the talk" of acknowledging, enhancing, and embracing the enterprise's most valuable asset—its employees.

Consider the following example. Both Organization A and Organization B have implemented formal employee recognition programs. Organization A's multi-layered employee recognition program was developed by an employee committee with representatives from each part of the organization. The committee asked each work unit for input while the program was in development and has built in an annual mechanism for evaluating employees. Recognition components include a selection of long-service awards, company funding of a baseball team, a shower room and small gym—specific "pat on the back" initiatives within work units and several opportunities each year for employees to talk directly with members of the senior management team.

Organization B is also composed of several different work units. The organization's senior management team agreed 10 years ago that morale throughout the company would be stronger if all employees, whether they are truck drivers, computer programmers, or senior managers, are recognized in the same manner. Organization B's employee recognition program consists of long-service awards, from a lapel pin for five-year employees to a mantle clock for 30-year employees, given out at the annual Christmas party and a list of recipients published in the employee newsletter. Managers of each work unit are free to recognize their own employees as they deem appropriate.

Which company "walks the talk" of supporting their most crucial asset?

On a broader front, consider the plethora of ads, annual reports, speeches, and recognition ceremonies that allude to the value of an organization's employees. It is interesting to note that many of these common vehicles are directed at audiences outside the organization itself, ensuring the message is spread to stakeholders, customers, communities, and others.

Are organizations investing comparable diligence in communicating the same messages of worth and importance to their internal audiences(employees)?

In many cases, the answer is a satisfying and resounding "Yes." Excellent organizations—those making the list of best employers or consistently reaching their business targets or building a name for innovation—invariably see internal communications as an essential element of their success. The CEOs of these organizations understand the entire mandate of the organization is dependent on the skill, dedication, and motivation of its internal audiences. Simply, internal communications helps organizations get the best results from their internal audiences, which is essential in helping the organization achieve its business goals.

Too many companies, however, yield to the temptation of focusing their resources outside the organization, believing customers and stakeholders to be the key to sustainable success. For private enterprise, this is particularly true during tough economic times when competition is fierce and profit margins become perilously thin. For institutions in the public sector, the never-ending mantra to serve the public often results in a lack of attention to the individuals who provide the service. Some leaders fall into the trap of believing those who walk the same hallways and attend meetings in the same buildings share the same knowledge base, objectives, and motivations as management and therefore do not need the same level of formal communication as external audiences.

Think of internal audiences as an organization's extended family. The family is composed of various branches, quite possibly situated at various locations. Each branch becomes defined by unique characteristics and synergies, and each member within a branch adds richness and depth to the whole. As in families, there are often challenges in communicating the right information, at the right time, to the right individuals so that everyone understands the big picture and why the other members are taking certain actions.

Consider the approach you and your nuclear family take when you are communicating with each other. You assume a certain level of knowledge of the subject being discussed and start your conversation at that point. To some degree, you also know before you begin a conversation how the individual members in your nuclear family may react and what information they need to respond appropriately to the topic. Now consider introducing the same topic to your grandparents, aunts, uncles, and cousins, some of whom you do not see more than monthly and some you do not see more often than every year or two. In fact, while you are proud to have them as part of your family, you really do not know some of these people very well. Your communications approach will be very different depending on the individuals you are talking to. Assumptions become very dangerous, and you have to take time to paint the larger picture—the context—so everyone has the same basis of facts and understanding with which they can contribute to the discussion and act in a meaningful way. Such are the challenges and rewards of being part of the internal communications team.

WHY COMMUNICATE WITH INTERNAL GROUPS?

Consider a common Canadian consulting environment: a two- or three-person consulting firm has set up its office space for maximum efficiency. The workstations are physically close to each other and, for operational ease, are set up so the consultants can hear each other's phone conversations and can interact with each other at the turn of their chairs. Clearly, the consultants share virtually identical business goals and are in constant contact with each other throughout the business day. Communication occurs naturally and routinely among them. Even then, however, there is the potential for miscommunication: assumptions may not be shared, successes not celebrated, or periodic reviews of business goals and successes not completed.

Now consider a larger organization of 75 employees, all located under one roof but with various job duties from production to sales to administration. Because egocentricity is human nature, every individual defines his or her world first by what it means on a personal level. Our 75 employees strive first to understand their own jobs, getting comfortable with the job duties, their colleagues and superiors. These things create the environment within which they manage their working lives. They may—or may not—expand their working environment as time goes by. If their small environment satisfies their working needs, they may have little incentive to extend their original context. Various reasons, however, may lead them to venture outside their original circle of acquaintances. These reasons could involve a personal habit such as smoking (smokers naturally congregate during their breaks and discuss an amazing amount of workplace topics), a desire for greater social contact during or after working hours, professional curiosity about the organization or other co-workers, or a desire to move up the corporate ladder. Most of these employees will not be managers and probably do not have direct contact to the organization's senior leadership.

A savvy organization will recognize these varying levels of interest and awareness and will address the wide range of employee communications needs. Multiply the complexity of this scenario when considering the internal communications needs of the three orders of government (federal, provincial, municipal) or large multinational organizations with international workforces and many work locations.

Effective internal communications helps an organization achieve its strategic goals, such as

- increasing market share;
- remaining competitive in an increasingly competitive global marketplace;
- recruiting more members;
- building a customer base; or,
- in the case of government organizations, serving the public more effectively.

Effective communications gives employees the information they need to understand not only the organization's vision, goals, and objectives, but how their function contributes to the whole organization. An organization employs individuals for one fundamental purpose: to do the work the organization needs to achieve its goals. An employee who does not understand how he or she fits into the organizational vision cannot contribute to the fullest extent of his or her capability toward the ultimate goal.

In short, effective communication helps ensure the organization can achieve its goals by building and maintaining loyalty throughout the organization. Effective internal communications offers multi-layered opportunities for two-way feedback, building employees' sense of belonging to the organization and contributing directly to its success.

More than any other practice area in communications, internal communications demands the highest degree of direct two-way communication. Two-way communication pays dividends by harnessing internal support for organizational plans, ensuring the individuals expected to implement the initiatives are enthusiastic, knowledgeable, and focused as they execute their duties.

The happy results of effective internal communications also become evident outside the organization. Clarity and focus of internal messages help the organization maintain consistency with external messages, a crucially important factor in creating a corporate image of transparency, sincerity, efficiency, and professionalism.

Informed and motivated internal audiences also become far more effective spokespeople for an organization than those kept outside the communications loop. Rarely is the employees' role as spokespeople formal; rather, employees chatting with friends, family, and neighbours or voicing their opinions in a plethora of public forums all leave an impression of their employer. The broader community will form a collective conclusion about the organization from formal and informal input. The opinions of those close to the source of the action—employees—carry considerable weight.

INTERNAL AUDIENCES

As you read in Chapter 9, identifying your audiences—and their demographics and psychographics—is a critical element for a successful communications plan. You must understand the target audiences of your intended messages, the environment within which they will receive the message, and how they are likely to react to the message.

The list of internal audiences, and whether they should be considered primary or secondary, depends on two basic factors:

· the issue or opportunity being communicated, and
· the size, scope, and geographic breadth of your organization's operation.

Primary audiences are crucial to your plan. Secondary audiences are not critical but would benefit from formal communications.

Whether you are identifying external or internal audiences, remember that large, homogenous groups do not exist. It is more accurate and more useful to identify target audiences as specifically as possible by their common characteristics.

Consider this example. The chief executive officer (CEO) of a large organization with 5,000 employees decides to reorganize the entire organization. The reorganization will result in as many as 20 per cent of employees moving to new departments. The job duties of many of these employees will change. Some layoffs are expected. To minimize disruption to the organization's business, minimize the adverse effects on employee performance and morale, and maximize the benefits of the reorganization, communication should focus on the following primary and secondary audiences.

Primary Audiences

- communications team
  - corporate communications team
  - communications staff working with the operational work units
  - external communications team
  - media relations team
- middle management (those with supervisory responsibilities)
- unions/staff associations
- unionized employees
  - those changing departments/work duties
  - those facing layoff
  - those in geographically diverse work locations
  - those without routine access to online communications tools
  - those on shift work
  - multicultural employees who consider English as their second language
- contract employees
  - those changing departments/work duties
  - those facing termination of contracts

Secondary Audiences

- unionized employees whose departments/work duties do not change
- contract employees whose duties do not change
- retirees
- internal "service centres"

When determining your list of primary and secondary internal audiences, remember your lists will vary depending on the issue being communicated. Avoid the trap of becoming complacent about your audiences; targeting your message to exactly the right audiences is crucial for the success of your communications strategy.

INTERNAL COMMUNICATIONS PARTNERS

As an internal communicator, you are responsible for

- identifying and developing an appropriate communications plan;
- communicating internal messages accurately and completely; and
- determining the effectiveness of your plan.

Regardless of whether you are the sole professional responsible for internal communications or part of a larger internal communications team, you will never be isolated from others who will support your endeavours. Your larger communications team is your first resource. Even if you are the only communicator dedicated solely to internal communications, you can parallel the strategic considerations and messages of your external teammates. Remember, an organization's external and internal messages must be consistent with each other to build and maintain trust and respect. The messages are presented differently, but their essence will be similar.

If your organization has a dedicated marketing team, they, too, become a valuable resource for reasons similar to the external team. Marketers have a product or service to sell and build their success on their understanding of that product or service, how it supports the organization's mandate, and how it will help their audiences.

Your organization's senior management team represents a huge resource. Team members are your senior leaders, with experience, vision, and the ability to view the organization from a strategic perspective. Together, they also represent very different operational perspectives. All of these characteristics help you to develop a well-rounded picture of the organization, offering an avenue for the wise communicator to step out of your comfort zone to gain some appreciation for the realities of the organization.

While senior management team members may not have time for face-to-face meetings with you, a director or manager reporting to the senior leader or an executive assistant (EA) may be able to help you directly or know where you can find the information you need. Whichever route you follow, you are achieving your short-term information-seeking goal and, as importantly, showing senior management your diligence in serving the communications needs of his or her area.

Your organization's human resources (HR) team can also be powerful allies. There have been discussions and debates roughly since the time of dinosaurs about the optimal relationship between an organization's communications and HR functions. The discussions are understandable. Both functions focus on people (albeit from different perspectives), both are corporate functions (serving the overall needs of the organization itself), and both involve a mix of science and sociology. Many organizations have communications and HR report to the same member of the senior management team, often under a title related to corporate services. For the purposes of this chapter, we will assume the two disciplines are very separate but collegial teams.

How, then, can HR serve as your ally? Very importantly, the HR team knows what is allowed—and what is not—when dealing with unions or staff associations. With their orientation toward legal matters and organizational process, HR professionals should be your first stop for matters related to collective agreements or other labour management topics. Union or staff association matters have complex labour relations and legal implications, so you are well advised to ask for, and take, the advice of those who understand the labour relations environment.

The HR team can also connect you to a wide circle of new contacts. Take advantage of their knowledge. As well, this team is responsible for a wealth of information you will want to communicate to your internal audiences. This information includes staff expectations in the workplace, employee benefits, orientation packages, employee honours, acknowledgements and long-service awards. HR may have its own avenues for distributing this information to employees, but making yourself known and supportive of their efforts will pay dividends over the long term. If they do not have their own distribution methods, your relationship with HR becomes symbiotic, with each team needing the expertise and information of the other.

Finally, the informal leaders of the organization can be significant communications partners. These are the individuals, at every level of the organization, who fall naturally into a leadership role within their own work environments. Colleagues listen to them, believe them, and seek them out for interpretation and corroboration of news coming from formal channels. When they are well-informed and have the organization's interests at heart, these leaders become informal champions and powerful allies.

Consider an initiative undertaken within one ministry of the Government of Alberta. The ministry's formal internal communications channels—the deputy minister's office and the communications team—were becoming increasingly ineffective as direct avenues of news dissemination. Research showed emails emanating from those sources were being opened less and less often, let alone embraced and acted upon.

Where were the effective internal communications conduits? The ministry undertook an interesting project to find the answer. Being careful not to breach employee privacy, it undertook a detailed analysis of workplace emails to determine the virtual connections of employees within the department. Who was communicating via email with whom? The results showed little regard for formal work units, with many individuals connecting far more with members of other work units than with their immediate colleagues. With this information in hand, the ministry conducted further analysis to determine the influencers (the "go-to" individuals, the natural leaders) and the "connector" individuals who were providing communication bridges among various groups.

With the influencers and connectors identified, the ministry had their answer of who was capable of disseminating ministry news and getting it read. They then developed a number of communications tools and tactics, including online discussion boards, blogs, and even YouTube clips, suited to this effective but informal network of "communicators." Readership of and participation in ministry communications soared. The project became a very effective means of illustrating the power of informal leaders, of virtual connections, and of the evolving role of communicators to harness all available resources to disseminate messages. It also gave the ministry some valuable data for future strategic communications development.

ISSUES AND BARRIERS TO COMMUNICATING INTERNALLY

The verdict is in: communications is a challenging and dynamic profession. Engineers, accountants, and lawyers often categorize communications skills as "soft," dealing within a murky world of human issues and relationships where there are few well-defined correct or incorrect solutions. They are partially correct. Communicators employ a mix of science (technologies and tactics, for example) and sociological principles to develop solutions that address a wide range of issues and barriers. Because the human factor plays such a critical role in defining each communications scenario, some major challenges facing internal communicators are outlined here.

Organizational Leadership and Culture

As surely as water flows downhill, an organization reflects the approach and character of its senior leadership. Many organizations benefit from the integrity, vision, and ability of their CEO and his senior team to "walk the talk" of a sound enterprise.

When leaders of an organization do not set a strong example for their employees, however, the ripple effect is felt at every level of the organization. When employees feel senior leaders are not being honest, are not giving the whole truth, are not communicating the same messages to everyone, or are not respectful or caring, employees lose their motivation to support the organization. Loss of motivation will affect employee morale, attendance, productivity, and, ultimately, the organization's bottom line.

Can an internal communicator have any effect? Yes. You are not alone in your quest to work within an organization that values its employees and strives to create a healthy internal culture. Talk to like-minded colleagues, supervisors, and senior managers. Ultimately, you need one or several senior management champions to work toward an improved workplace culture. Changing a culture takes perseverance and time, but you and your colleagues can make a difference if you approach the issues with professionalism, forethought, and tenacity.

Multicultural Communications

Ask Canadians coast to coast for some characteristics that help define us and many will point to our nation's great history of welcoming newcomers from around the world. Canada is justifiably proud of its multicultural makeup, with new Canadians continuing to fill vital roles within our society. Using Statistics Canada's medium growth population projection, immigration could account for more than 80 per cent of Canada's population growth starting in 2031, compared with about 67 per cent in 2011.[1] The implications for internal communicators are clear. We need to master effective multicultural communications within our organizations.

On one level, addressing cultural differences in the workplace starts with recognizing and addressing the issues created by language:[2]

- Avoid cultural humour. Humour can be dangerous even within the different regions of Canada. (Do residents of Newfoundland and Labrador really appreciate "Newfie" jokes? Do Saskatchewan residents really laugh heartily at flatland jokes?)
- Be aware of the use of language. Avoid idioms, colloquial expressions, metaphors, analogies, and other constructions that may be confusing.
- Choose communications tools that prove effective for individuals for whom English is an additional language.
- Be aware of Canadian political, historic, or geographic references.
- Speak distinctly and avoid rushing your speech.

On a deeper level, successful multicultural communications is far more challenging because it requires knowledge of systemic or inherent cultural differences. It is easy to assume our way of approaching communication is universal and accepted, but that is not the case. For example, North American business practices tend to favour the direct approach, keeping the time required to convey information to a minimum. We call that efficiency. Other cultures, such as those in Latin America, Africa, Asia, and the Middle East, base good communication on the quality of the relationship they share within the workplace. They appreciate face-to-face contact, like to feel they are part of a larger work "family," and respect hierarchy more than do most North Americans. A short email stating only the facts and work request may be interpreted as too abrupt, causing a Latin American or Asian employee to wonder why the business relationship is deteriorating.[3]

That is one example of many but it underlines the need for internal communicators to be aware of the potential of cultural differences and to plan for them. A first step is to ensure your communications team has access to representative cross-cultural resources. Form a communications advisory group or establish contact with key individuals from various areas of your organization who can help bridge the cultural divides. Then, ask the advice of your cultural panel when choosing the best tools and tactics to implement your internal communications plan.

Many organizations have developed effective tools. Multicultural orientation packages, English as a Second Language (ESL) or as an Additional Language (EAL) formal and informal sessions, mentoring clubs, print pieces meant to be taken home are great tools for making new Canadians feel welcome and more productive.

An organization's challenge goes far beyond the welcome mat, of course. All workers have a responsibility to contribute to the organization's mandate to the fullest extent of their abilities. To do that, they must understand the Canadian culture and participate effectively within it. The responsibility of Canadian workers is also clear: in a respectful and open manner, help newcomers function effectively in our society.

The Edmonton Region Immigrant Employment Council (ERIEC) offers a good example. ERIEC was established in 2008 to ensure that job-ready professional immigrants participate fully in the economy. The organization is achieving laudable results with the Career Mentorship Program, developed to help internationally trained professionals increase workplace skills, learn Canadian workplace culture, and access professional networks. Local, senior-level professionals are paired with the newcomers to offer hands-on advice. Mentors say they learn valuable aspects of other cultures, information they can use within their organizations to make their operations more effective locally and more competitive globally.

Multigenerational Communications

Just as Canada needs immigrants to address its labour needs, our country also needs the expertise and experience of older workers. More and more, Canadians older than 55, 60, or 65 are choosing to remain active in the workforce, and Canadian workplaces are developing strategies to either keep older workers at work or entice them back to work.

Consider the Government of Alberta's action plan, "Engaging the Mature Worker: An Action Plan for Alberta,"[4] launched with the hope of avoiding "a perfect storm for the labour market" as the economy again gears up to a fever pitch and experienced labour is desperately needed. In 2011, mature workers (age 45 and over) made up 38.8 per cent of the Alberta labour force; that percentage will continue to increase as the population ages.[5]

As the number of older workers increases, the need to address real and potential strife between the generations in a workplace becomes very important. Simply, every generation sees the world more clearly from its own perspective and naturally understands its own value more readily than it embraces the value of other generations. Human nature dictates that younger generations often see mature workers as slower, less innovative, less energetic, rigid, and less technologically savvy. What they miss is the value of experience, problem-solving abilities, attention to detail, patience, perhaps a nice sense of humour, and more.

On the other hand, mature workers often see younger workers as lacking discipline and commitment, disrespectful, ruled by a "me first" mentality, and consumed by technology. What they miss is the value of energy and fresh spirit, the mastery of the new technologies, the evolving rules of protocol in the twenty-first century, perhaps a nice sense of humour, and more.

Consider this example of different generational perspectives. An advice column in the *Edmonton Journal* featured a letter from a young woman whose father had recently died. She was hurt when her mother-in-law texted her condolences. The grieving young woman believed an email of condolence would have been more appropriate than a text. This scenario would have left most readers over a certain age shaking their heads in disbelief that sympathies were not expressed in person (the best option), by phone, or in a handwritten note.

The internal communicator's job is to bridge the generations so they can appreciate each other's strengths and share their expertise in a respectful way. Since assumptions tend to melt away when individuals get to know each other, think about strategies that involve face-to-face collaboration. These might include project-specific task teams, mentoring situations (with the younger worker assuming the role of mentor when appropriate), or even getting a multigenerational team working together on a special holiday promotion or employee recognition event.

Communicating in a Unionized Workplace

While each situation differs, the common advice when communicating within a unionized environment is to work closely with your organization's HR department or legal department to ensure communications plans do not contravene collective bargaining agreements. Most provinces restrict the employer from directly communicating collective bargaining issues with staff, requiring instead that these issues be communicated through the bargaining agent.

As well, if you are a non-supervisory communicator, you may be facing conflicting loyalties in the event of a strike, work slowdown, or other labour/management conflicts. On the one hand, your professional responsibility is to support your organization. On the other hand, if you are a member of a union involved in a labour dispute, you must abide by your union's directives. Labour disputes very often result in strong emotions on both sides of the issue. Your union steward and/or your direct supervisor will clarify your responsibilities; if this doesn't occur, ask questions until you understand what is required of you before, during, and after the labour dispute.

Choosing Between New or Traditional Communications Vehicles

Which statement best represents your thoughts?

- I believe traditional media are far more effective communications vehicles than the new technologies.
- I believe the new technologies are far more effective communications vehicles than traditional media.
- I believe choosing the best communications vehicle depends on the situation.

Texting, tweeting, and emailing have become so prevalent in our lives that many people assume new media offers the best communications options. If you chose the traditional media option, you are a member of a shrinking minority. If you chose the third option, determining the best solution depending on the situation, congratulations!

Research has shown, in fact, that new media is not making traditional communications tools obsolete.[6] Studies that examined the effect of email on workplace efficiency, for example, show a huge proportion of our work days are spent simply managing our email. One study concluded that knowledge workers invest 28 per cent of their work day in email.[7] A 2007 Ipsos Reid study concluded that Canadians divert 42 per cent of their email directly to the junk file, with only 43 per cent of respondents believing email increased their efficiency at work.[8] Interestingly, this percentage was down significantly from the year before when 52 per cent thought email increased their efficiency.[9]

At one time, the corporate communications department at the City of Edmonton required its employees to keep time logs, recording how they spent their days. Despite the inevitable grumblings about the need to account for their time, the time logs proved to be a valuable management tool. The time logs showed that employees would routinely capture time spent as "doing email." When urged to record that time under specific projects rather than just "doing email," employees often couldn't recall how email related to specific projects.

The volume and efficiency of email is one issue; its effect as an internal communications vehicle is another. Email has become so entrenched, so familiar, that we often treat it as an informal means of communicating. That's a mistake, and one that could have legal implications. Emails are considered to be as formal as memos and letters and are included under the broad umbrella of communications vehicles that are searchable under freedom of information legislation. Think about the implications of firing off that testy email to your colleague and how your CEO would react if it showed up in the news media or in a courtroom.

As well, email's very ease of use throws more challenges in its way. It takes seconds to compose an email. We do it countless times a day. Are we paying attention, however, to whether our grammar, word use, semantics, and context are sufficient for the receiver to understand what we want and to answer our query? Are we taking the time to edit an email before we hit "Send"? As with virtually every form of business writing, most emails improve when their writing is tight and business-like, which takes discipline.

Finally, email has become so much a part of our work lives that it has eclipsed many other effective communications tools. Lamentably, two tools that have lost the popularity contest to email are face-to-face communication and phone calls. Whether individuals find it easier, more convenient, safer, or more familiar, email cannot replace the value of face-to-face communication. The case can also be made that one phone call, where both parties can talk through the subtleties of an issue and come to a satisfactory compromise, is far more efficient than starting a string of emails that can last for days. Get into the habit of following up each business phone call with a brief email or other method of documentation so you have a paper trail of decisions.

While the above examples focus on email, the same basic observations can be made about texting and tweeting. Are these technologies making our work lives more efficient or are they detracting from our workplace productivity?

New and traditional tools all have their strengths—and limitations—and the dedicated internal communicator will create an effective program using a mix of both.

DEVELOPING THE INTERNAL COMMUNICATIONS PLAN

See Chapter 9 for the fundamentals of developing a communications plan for external audiences. The same strategic thinking and parallel steps are required to develop an internal communications plan.

The first critically important point about an internal communications plan is that every organization needs one. Think of the plan as your roadmap showing where you want to go, how to get there, and how to identify when you have achieved success. The complexity of the plan depends on factors such as the organization's size, complexity of its operation, business goals, employee composition, number of worksites, and any recent changes to its mandate, size, or strategic direction. A good internal communications plan focuses on key strategic elements, reflects the organization's character, and offers consistency with the organization's external communications strategy. The following are the steps for creating an internal communications plan.

Situational Analysis

Start with a SWOT identification of strengths, weaknesses, opportunities, and threats.[10] Use all available resources of research and documentation available to you. These will certainly include previous employee satisfaction or awareness surveys, internal focus group results, and any evaluation on hand of individual communications tools such as newsletters and intranet use. Gauging employee awareness and satisfaction is a crucial starting point for an internal communications plan because these individuals need to know where the organization is headed and what role they play in moving the organization forward before they can contribute to their fullest extent. It is also important to understand employee satisfaction; a satisfied employee is more efficient than his or her unhappy colleague and will contribute more productively toward the organization's bottom line.

Less obvious but still useful materials might include workplace surveys or demographic overviews conducted by HR, comparative efficiency reports of various departments or divisions of the organization over a number of years, absenteeism reports by department over a number of years, and even union grievance reports.

Many organizations understand the value of conducting formal employee research. Establishing benchmark results (a starting point of quantitative research from which future research can be assessed) takes the guesswork out of your communications efforts, allowing you to compare your results against your stated goals. While many organizations have already established a history of conducting formal internal research, others still need to be shown the value of investing time and budget to get this seminal work completed.

While your counterparts in external communications may give a cursory nod to the organization's internal environment, you would be wise to include a full examination of the organization's external factors in your situational analysis. Everything your organization undertakes has direct impact on your workforce. Whether your senior leaders want to enter new markets, develop new products or services, cut back on some facet of the operation, merge with another company, maintain a steady course through the shoals of economic uncertainty, or counter community attitudes or perceptions, your workforce has a right to complete, accurate, and timely information. Your organization will be stronger when its workforce is well-informed.

Audience Analysis

Earlier, this chapter outlined some considerations for identifying your internal audiences. Wearing your strategic communications hat, identify those groups—formal or informal—who are crucial to your plan (your primary audiences) and also those who, while not critical, would also benefit from formal communications (your secondary audiences).

Strategy and Tactics

When you are ready to set your communications goals and objectives, remember to keep operational or corporate goals and objectives distinct from communications goals and objectives. Consider the example of the Environmental

Figure 15.1 Strengths and Weaknesses of Communications Tools

Communications tool	Strengths	Weaknesses
Face-to-face		
Formal employee meetings (e.g., annual general meetings, town hall meetings, announcements of substantive news)	Employees hear directly from CEO and other senior managers	Requires time commitment from senior management team, perception of taking time away from "real work"
Department/work unit update sessions	Employees hear directly from direct supervisors	May present some logistical challenges to schedule
Project team meetings	Employees benefit from face-to-face communication	None, assuming meetings are well structured and well led; may be perception of taking time away from "real work"
Special events (e.g., recognition and award events, retirements, barbecues)	Opportunities for personal interaction with peers and management, different venues and perspectives from the norm	Require substantive resources, must understand employee motivations and perceptions to be successful
Focus groups	Direct contact with representative employees, cost-effective, easy to locate at various locations, proven effective	Requires experienced facilitator, participants may not buy in or participate, results are subjective
Electronic		
Intranet	Convenient, generally accessible, quick to update, familiar to most employees	Not accessible to employee groups without computers, requires command of English for comprehension, system establishment can be costly
Email	Convenient, generally accessible, an easy way to communicate to one individual or a small group	Potential for misunderstandings, informality may lead to legal issues, cumbersome when too many individuals are included
E-newsletter	Often a trusted, anticipated source of organizational news, timely, generally easy to scan, can offer interactive components, responsive, uses corporate messaging, easy to evaluate, offers good return on investment of staff time and resources, easy to analyze employee readership and interaction, can easily be evolved into different newsletters for different employee groups	Needs access to computer, keeps employees at their screens, requires command of English for comprehension, need for fresh, relevant, well-written content
Phone/cellphone	The next best thing to face-to-face communication, reduces potential for misunderstandings, efficient, cellphones are portable	Increasingly ignored as an effective communications tool, receiver must answer call or return call promptly, tempting to use cellphones while driving
Video conference/conference call	Offers a next-best solution to face-to-face communication for large groups or small meetings, generally easy to arrange, accommodates divergent worksites and times, cost-effective	Somewhat less effective than face-to-face meetings but a good alternative

Figure 15.1 (cont.)

Communications tool	Strengths	Weaknesses
Smartphone	Offers quick updates, easy to give cursory reply, portable	Easy to divert attention from task at hand, difficult to deal with attachments, potential of incomplete data transfer to main computer files, tempting to use while driving
Employee-specific site on public website	Ensures consistency and transparency of messages, no cost to establish network, easy to update, accessible to employees with computers	Employees may feel they deserve a discrete site (intranet), need access to a computer
Company blogs	Can be an effective way to start constructive conversations, share key messages and gauge employee awareness and perceptions	Messages cannot be controlled, need constant updates and fresh material
Social media	Responsive, familiar, and popular particularly with younger demographic, informal, effective way to gauge employee awareness and perceptions	Messages cannot be controlled, require constant updates and fresh material, not exclusive to internal audiences, use may be restricted or prohibited in some regulatory environments
Print		
Newsletter (hard copy)	Cuts through the clutter of electronic communication, provides permanent record, can be taken home for future study, helps with English comprehension, can be distributed to all employee groups and worksites, even those without access to computers such as construction site crews, manufacturing crews or mailroom employees, offers room for in-depth analysis	Younger employees may be more comfortable with electronic vehicles, not as cost-effective as e-newsletter, distribution takes time
Magazine	Offers space for in-depth features and analysis of articles and news that support the corporate vision, provides an archival record of the organization, appeals to employees who want more than "quick hit" news, can be mailed to homes, which offers a strong personal connection (and can be shared with family and friends), helps with English comprehension	More costly to produce and distribute than electronic tools, care must be given to ensure content appeals to all demographics
Letter or memo	Offers direct communication from a senior leader, short and to the point	May be lost in the in-basket, distribution takes time
Poster	Effective way to target specific campaigns or messages, graphics attract attention, readily accessible in high traffic areas	Effectiveness decreases over time
Employee annual report	Offers space to tell a year's story at a glance, provides historic record, can be mailed to homes, helps with English comprehension	More costly to produce and distribute than electronic tools, care must be given to ensure content appeals to all demographics
Special use products (e.g., calendars, one-time leaflets, laminated vision statements)	Command high attention initially, generally portable, can be kept for reference	Generally limited shelf life, generally more costly to produce and distribute than electronic tools

Services Department of the Regional Municipality of Wood Buffalo in north-eastern Alberta. In 2007, the department set an operational objective to divert 50 per cent of its waste stream from its landfill within five years. To achieve this objective, the municipality needed its residents to increase its recycling efforts significantly. To that end, external communications objectives focused on increased awareness of and participation in local recycling programs and initiatives. Internal communications focused on increasing municipal employees' recycling efforts, building their sense of environmental leadership, and sharing recycling successes. By the end of the third year, 2010, the municipality was confident its communication with both external and internal audiences would help achieve its ambitious operational goal. By the end of 2012, the municipality had achieved a waste diversion rate of more than 50 per cent.[11]

With all this plan development in place, you are now ready to consider which communications tools and tactics will help get the messages to your workforce most effectively and efficiently. Figure 15.1 outlines the strengths and drawbacks of some options. Here are some fundamental guidelines all internal communicators should be able to recite in their sleep:

1. Two-way face-to-face communication is the most effective form of communication. Use it whenever possible.
2. Employees want to hear news from their direct supervisors.[12]
3. Successful communication must be timely and consistent.
4. Traditional tools and new technologies all have advantages and disadvantages.

Determining the best tool to use depends on what you want to accomplish. Beware the communicator who jumps up and says, "I know! Let's start a blog!" before working to develop the strategy's goals and objectives.

Figure 15.1 offers an overview of many tools but should not be considered an exhaustive list. While the options may seem intimidating initially, the choices will become clearer as you work through the development of your plan.

Budget and Evaluation

With your tactics chosen, you can now work out your budget and evaluation measures. Evaluating your efforts is crucially important so you know which strategies were effective and which need to be improved. Measurement can be a mix of quantitative and qualitative measures, formal and informal. Begin by measuring the effectiveness of each communications tool.

Be clear about the objective of your chosen tool and design measures to answer the objective. For example, if your newsletters (hard copy or e-newsletters) are intended to reinforce corporate messages, ensure employees know how to access support resources, and increase participation in corporate events. Then, design a readership survey that probes those three areas.

You also need to measure how well your strategy is supporting overall corporate goals. An employee attitude and awareness survey is an excellent way to do this and an efficient way to measure the change in attitude and awareness over time. A well-written survey is an excellent tool; build the cost into your budget of having it written by a research professional. Contracting the services of a research specialist will pay big dividends and ensure statistically valid information.

INTERNAL RECOGNITION PROGRAMS

A 2011 survey by an American non-profit organization that focuses on global human resources issues concluded that 86 per cent of respondents indicate their organizations have employee recognition programs.[13] This statistic shows organizational leaders understand the inherent principle of recognition: employees work harder, more efficiently, and far more happily when they receive positive motivation.

To develop an effective recognition program, consider the exercise as a mini-strategic plan. Work out your goals and objectives, audiences, environmental assessment, tools, budget, and evaluation measures—remembering to link this program to your organization's business goals.

In developing your mini-strategy, keep a few points in mind:

1. **Develop a mix of formal and informal elements.**
   The following are some recognition vehicles that can be effective depending on your objectives, corporate culture and timing:

   - awards gala
   - long-service events
   - recognition component as part of significant employee gatherings, such as strategic planning workshops
   - CEO roll of honour
   - recognition feature in newsletter or on intranet
   - "time out" coffee party recognition (for specific work groups)
   - work group acknowledgement (silly or serious, depending on the worksite culture)

- personalized note or memo from supervisor or senior management
- invitation to serve on a committee or advisory group of interest to the individual

2. **Question traditional elements such as long-service award evenings—but do not assume they need to be replaced.**
Tradition and sentimentality cannot stand in the way of program effectiveness. The "We've always done it this way" philosophy cannot be defended, but be sure to measure the value of the program before deciding that it's destined for the history books. You may be pleasantly surprised to learn that a traditional favourite may only need some cosmetic changes to make it relevant to today's synergies.

3. **Get direct input from employee representatives of your organization (from various staff and supervisory levels, different work functions, and different work locations).**
The ivory tower syndrome, where corporate employees develop their programs and strategies in isolation of the rest of the organization, still exists in many organizations. Recognition programs are designed for your entire workforce. Who better to tell you what they want than the employees themselves? Organize online or hard copy suggestion plans, focus groups, special advisory committees, or other mechanisms to ensure you are getting input from all levels, all demographics, and all worksites.

4. **Ensure fairness and simplicity in nomination processes.**
In all likelihood, your recognition program will include some elements in which employees nominate their peers for recognition. Ensure your program in inclusive and simple enough to encourage strong participation.
If you want to test your draft program, call on your employee representatives and have them work through the logistics.

5. **Ensure timely recognition.**
Formal vehicles may recognize achievement from the past year—but rarely longer. Less formal vehicles, from letters and memos of thanks to newsletter recognition, should be completed within a month of the achievement and preferably sooner. Informal vehicles such as impromptu coffee parties are easy and quick to organize—and offer the recipient instant reward.

Many organizations are well meaning with their intent to recognize employees but fall short on implementation. What message does it leave, for example, when a long-service award is presented a couple of years after the anniversary? If you think this does not happen in the real world, think again. It does, often because those responsible for the recognition complicate the process. Set an objective of presenting long-service awards within a month of the anniversary.

6. Measure your results.

Your overall employee attitude and awareness survey gauge overall employee satisfaction levels and will pinpoint specific areas of the organization where worked is needed, but be sure to measure the individual vehicles you use as well. Focus groups, exit surveys, event evaluations and, again, employee advisory groups will all offer valuable feedback.

CRISIS COMMUNICATIONS FOR THE INTERNAL TEAM

Organizational crises come in all shapes and sizes. Many, including most natural disasters, accidents that knock out utilities, the unexpected death of a senior executive, or allegations of criminal wrongdoing within the organization, descend with no warning and often outside the regular work day. Others, including slowly developing natural disasters such as floods or labour disruptions, can be anticipated, at least to some extent.

The focus of this section is internal communications in a crisis, according to the three stages of an internal crisis communications plan:

1. **Before the crisis:** plan development and practice
2. **During the crisis:** implementation and documentation
3. **After the crisis:** debrief and amend the plan

Chapter 16 will look at crisis communications in more detail.

Before the Crisis

Determine who you need on your crisis communications team and compile their 24-hour contact information, remembering to allocate shifts around the clock should internal communications be required. You need the same information from your senior management team and other individuals who have specific roles to fulfill in the event of emergency.

You also need to detail your organization's command protocol for emergency situations. For example, what is the role of your CEO in communicating with employees? If your CEO's focus is on external issues, who is the senior leader (and an alternate) dedicated to informing internal audiences? Your primary spokesperson and alternate should be members of the senior management team. At all times, and particularly during times of high stress, employees want to get their news directly from a senior leader. The protocol should also include a checklist for communications approvals during and after the emergency so that everyone on the team clearly understands the approval requirements.

Communications vehicles are another important consideration. Cellphones have eased these challenges for crisis teams, but be sure to think through a range of scenarios to ensure cellphones would be effective in all instances. The need for instant and reliable emergency telecommunication service cannot be overstated. In many emergency scenarios, telecommunications becomes the one means of communication both with decision makers and with your employees.

Alberta Blue Cross, for example, has a 1-800 emergency phone system in place, and they have used it. A gas leak in downtown Edmonton in 2011 forced the evacuation of some downtown buildings, including the one used by Alberta Blue Cross. The crisis management team used the 1-800 number to update employees on whether they could return to work the next day.

Create an emergency kit for your lead internal communications person to use. The kit should include all the phone numbers, lists, and supplies that may be required throughout the emergency. Store the kit with other emergency supplies and label it clearly for the internal communications team.

Once you have your plan in place, your next step is to practise it. Practice is an absolutely essential step in preparing for effective communications management during a crisis. Establish a practice schedule—at least once a year—and stick to it. Involve your entire crisis team and take notes on what worked and where improvements should be made.

During the Crisis

With your plan in hand, you are ready to help your organization weather the emergency. You will have to co-ordinate initial requirements with the external crisis team, but be persistent in having employees hear the bad news first if possible. When your employees are included early, their sense of value to the organization rises and they become better, more accurate company ambassadors.

Remember, too, that nature abhors a vacuum. If employees are not given regular updates—or full updates—the rumour mill will fill in the blanks. You can count on it. Ensure your updates offer a complete story and address any rumours that already exist.

Finally, have your team take the time to document everything possible. This includes communications actions taken, any possible photos or videos of the occurrence, and a general timeline of events as they unfolded throughout the organization. During a crisis, you will be tempted to let this important step slip down your list of priorities, but your diligence will be appreciated and your record used after the event when your organization assesses events and responses.

After the Crisis

Your work does not end with the passing of the emergency. Your first duty is to close the information loop with employees. Next comes the decompression period. Depending on the emergency, those directly involved may need some help recovering from the trauma. While employee assistance falls outside the communications mandate, ensuring employees know what help is available and how to access it will be part of your communications responsibilities.

Debriefing comprises the final stage of crisis communications management. This generally occurs on two levels: corporate wide and specific to the communications function. Your activities logs, photos, videos, and other documentation recorded during the emergency will be needed for both exercises. After a critical review of which parts of the communications response worked well and which parts need improvement, amend your plan accordingly.

COMMUNICATING ORGANIZATIONAL CHANGE

From senior management's perspective, organizational change is undertaken to move the organization from its current state to where it needs to be to achieve its long-term goals. Goals include maintaining competitiveness in the marketplace; making more effective use of public dollars; and making better use of current technologies.

Change, however, affects the workforce quite differently. It is almost always unsettling for employees and, at worst, becomes a demoralizing, destructive, and fearful process that takes months or years to overcome. Communicating organizational change effectively is a key to making the process as smooth, painless, and productive as possible.

Human beings are egocentric. Almost always, individuals assess a situation from a me-first perspective. "How will it affect me?" or "What is in it for me?" Change communications should start from this perspective, with a clear articulation of why the organization is undertaking change and what its anticipated results will be. This corporate-wide vision sets the context for more specific communications directly applicable to the organization's various work functions and, therefore, how the changes will affect the individuals within each work group.

Change occurs on two fronts: technical and human. Integrating aspects of both helps ensure success. A good starting point for communicators of change is to search out the most likely allies for change in all levels and all functions of the corporation; then assess the technical/process changes needed to take place. With people you can rely on to support the start of change, focus on an "easy win" technical or process change with your allies close at hand. When a work unit can see some successes, even small ones, and someone within their work unit is championing the advantages of the change, you are on the road to success.

Continue building your successes and the momentum for change, and keep involving the affected work groups in their implementation. Individuals will feel far less threatened and become far more receptive to change if they develop a sense of ownership for the process and its positive results. When you communicate the results, focus your communications on the individuals involved and underline how the change helped the organization move toward its goals.

Communicators are naturally oriented toward the positive, but it is very important when communicating change to be optimistic, to keep looking forward toward the benefits of the change. The process of change focuses the energy of everyone involved, and, without a strong environment of optimism, it is easy for work units or individuals to focus instead on uncertainty, negativism, and the former, familiar way of operating—exactly what the organization has chosen to leave behind.

Timing is another crucial element of successful change communications. By all means, develop your plan and your intended timing but be prepared to be flexible if another event or operational imperative commands the attention of the work unit you were targeting. Imposing your own priorities over theirs may alienate the group, ultimately hurting your long-term objectives.

Finally, some organizational change will involve a reduction of staff. When that occurs, your HR team will take the lead to ensure the individuals involved receive all the information and support they require.

COMMUNICATIONS PROTOCOLS

Communications professionals hold a privileged position within their organizations. They generally have access to corporate-level decision makers, are in the "inner circle" of corporate headquarters, and yet get a taste of other areas as they execute their duties. With privilege, however, comes responsibility—the responsibility of setting good examples of business communications in our everyday working lives.

Here are some internal communications protocols that make corporate life more efficient and more satisfying for everyone involved.

Conducting Personal Business on Company Time

Make sure you know your organization's policies about checking out your Facebook page or phoning or texting your friends on company time, and be diligent about following the policies.

Email

With the exception of information sharing, your work colleagues send emails because they need information from you to do their own jobs. Check your email often and answer promptly. If you cannot give a complete answer immediately, tell the requester when he or she can expect the information and then honour your commitment. Your colleague will respect your professionalism rather than wondering if his or her request ended up in cyberspace.

Remember that emails are professional forms of communications and write them accordingly. Guard against becoming too informal and too wordy. Take a few seconds to proofread emails to help ensure their intent is clear and their grammar correct. It is also helpful to remember that emails can be forwarded without your knowledge or permission—another excellent reason for keeping them professional.

If you are on vacation, attending a training session, or otherwise not available to check your email for more than a day, use your out-of-office feature to advise others of your absence so they won't wonder why you are not responding.

Phones

Like email, colleagues phone you because they need your help. Your phone courtesies reflect your professionalism. When you answer your phone, always answer by stating your name even when your call display feature tells you it is a friendly, familiar person who is calling. Many work spaces use open area configurations; be conscious of the volume of your voice so you do not disturb your nearby neighbours.

When work duties pull you away from your phone, ensure your voicemail message is relevant and up to date. As with email, use your out-of-office feature to let callers know you are unavailable and when you will be returning. After you return, clear your voicemails and make time to respond to them promptly. Do not force your callers to make multiple calls to reach you; this annoying practice leaves the message that your time is more valuable than theirs. Keep your voicemail inbox clear of messages so there is room for callers to leave messages when you are not available.

Mobile devices give us a range of options for keeping in touch with our virtual worlds. The technology, however, is a double-edged sword. While keeping in touch has never been easier, being rude, discourteous, inattentive, and inefficient in meetings and other sessions has also never been easier. The best professional practice is simple: shut off all mobile devices when you are attending any professional gathering. Otherwise, you leave the clear message that the meeting or session is not worth your time and attention—and whoever is phoning or texting from outside the room is more important than the colleagues you are facing across the table.

There is an exception to most rules. With the knowledge and approval of the meeting chair, you can keep your mobile device active if you are expecting an urgent call that demands immediate attention.

CASE STUDY: ALBERTA BLUE CROSS

The following overview of the internal communications program at Alberta Blue Cross was provided in an interview with Brian Geislinger, vice-president, corporate relations for Alberta Blue Cross.[14]

Figure 15.2 describes the primary internal audiences within Alberta Blue Cross.

Alberta Blue Cross uses the following strategies to communicate with its employees:

- integrated print and electronic communications tools
- face-to-face formal and informal events
- employee satisfaction evaluation and evaluation of individual communications tools
- consistent recognition of employees in public communications vehicles (for example, employee features and photographs on the public website)

Figure 15.2 Primary Audiences within Alberta Blue Cross

Group	Considerations
Senior management team (executive operations committee)	This group of nine senior leaders is responsible for the vision, direction, and day-to-day operations of the organization. It is crucial that all members of this team are kept abreast of all substantive initiatives and their implications for each area of the organization.
Management staff • senior managers • team managers and supervisors	This internal audience is key to organization-wide understanding and acceptance of organizational initiatives.
Staff • employees • consultants	Frontline employees are the organization's face to the public and clients. These individuals illustrate the Alberta Blue Cross values and commitments at every contact point with the organization's 1.5 million customers as well as with the thousands of health service providers and other stakeholders with which it interacts on a daily basis. There are also a large number of on-site consultants working on specific projects.

Internal Communications Tools

Alberta Blue Cross uses a range of tools to ensure employees are well informed and have ample opportunities to offer feedback. "Any effective internal communications program that targets multiple audiences must include a variety of media including both low-tech and high-tech tools and approaches," says Geislinger.

Alberta Blue Cross considers its employee intranet site to be its most critical internal communications vehicle. Designed to reflect the culture of the organization and updated daily, the site has sections for each department as well as a myriad of employee resources ranging from a phone directory and floor maps to process manuals. To encourage regular visits, the site also includes photos and biographies of new hires and an events page that includes photos from recent staff events. The site receives over 52,000 visits per month.[15]

Another fundamental tool is a weekly internal newsletter, "News to Use," which evolved in 2011 from a traditional paper newsletter to electronic delivery. "Many employees consider the newsletter as a welcome break in their work day," says Geislinger. "When it arrives, many individuals take a quick break and read it right then and there."

A great deal of thought was put into the decision to move the newsletter from print to an electronic version. "There are clearly efficiency gains and cost savings with an electronic version, but the challenge is that this moved us from a principle of push where we brought the communications medium to each employee to a pull system where the employee now has to take the initiative to access the information we provide." The transition from print to electronic delivery has been a great success, with over 85 per cent of the organization's 1,000 employees still reading the newsletter on a weekly basis.

The intranet site and weekly newsletter are supplemented with a variety of other communications tools from bulletins to inform employees about marketing campaigns and new products, to elevator posters to promote upcoming events such as staff barbecues and fitness classes. "We use everything from email to elevator posters to keep our employees in the loop. There is no substitute for face-to-face communication, so we encourage a range of special events and more formal meetings where staff can meet executive members," says Geislinger.

Face-to-face communication includes quarterly review meetings hosted by the executive team for all managers, a presentation of the organization's strategic plan each January to the full management team, and regular staff meetings at a department level. Recognizing the value of face-to-face communication, the organization also added a CEO roundtable in 2011; employees have the opportunity to sign up to participate in an informal lunch-hour meeting directly with the CEO to discuss their ideas and suggestions for organizational improvements. The executive team even hosts a rooftop barbeque each summer to promote dialogue and interaction, with proceeds donated to charity.

Events include everything from department-specific informal events to an organization-wide staff assembly held every two years. Objectives of the assemblies are to motivate employees, celebrate successes, and offer updates. Senior executive members greet employees at the door and spend as much time as possible mingling. "This is a great opportunity for employees to talk directly to our senior leaders. It places all executive members front and centre and enables every one of our employees to hear the same messages at the same time," Geislinger explains.

Alberta Blue Cross does not use social media as a tool for internal communication; its use is limited to external communication only.

To measure the effectiveness of its internal communication program, Alberta Blue Cross conducts employee satisfaction surveys annually. The survey measures corporate values, employee attitudes, engagement, satisfaction levels, and other indicators of the health of the organization. As well, the organization conducts an annual readership survey of its newsletter and measures other internal communications tools individually. For example, attendees at each employee event are asked to complete a post-event survey.

CONCLUSION

Internal communications offers an exciting, challenging, ever-changing professional opportunity. The internal communications team fulfills a pivotal role in helping an organization achieve its goals because the internal communications team has responsibility for communicating with an organization's most important audience—the employees who do the work. Effective internal communications results in employees who understand the organization and its business, understand their own role and how it interacts with others in the organization, and are motivated to fulfill their role efficiently and effectively.

To be an effective internal communicator, you must first understand the business of your organization and how the various departments within your organization complement each other and contribute toward the organization's bottom line achievements.

You must also understand the various communication vehicles and tools at your disposal, and how to combine their use to offer effective, ongoing two-way communication to all your internal audiences. Some are formal tools but there are also many informal means of communication that can prove useful on their own or in combination with the formal communication vehicles.

It is important to define internal audiences according to their communication needs for each communication initiative. Key messages for these identifiable groups of employees will require different emphasis depending on the situation or opportunity being communicated.

As a professional communicator, you will deal with routine communication matters, positive subjects and also negative (or crisis) communication. For each instance, you will follow the same basics of communication planning and implementation, taking time to understand the situation and its effect on your internal audiences, then mapping out the most appropriate communication methods to reach your key internal audiences in a timely and effective manner.

Follow-up is also important. Effective evaluation of both individual initiatives and the overall internal communications function is needed to understand which initiatives are effective and which need to be changed or eliminated.

Finally, internal communicators have both the privilege and responsibility of being stewards of all forms of communication—from cellphone use to attendance and participation in meetings. You become a role model of professional communication practices—and can underline the corporate values of your organization when you are perceived to be a disciplined professional.

KEY TERMS

Employee recognition program: An integrated strategy (research, goals, objectives, budget, tools, and evaluation) to recognize the contributions of individual employees and groups of employees in helping the organization achieve its mandate.

Internal audiences: Groups of individuals within an organization, generally identified by characteristics such as union or management position, type of job (such as administrative support, operations, maintenance, corporate support), geographic location (assuming the organization operates out of more than one physical location), accessibility to specific communications tools (such as email or other types of online communication), and demographics (such as retirees, new employees, multicultural employees).

Internal communications: The communications practice area dealing with groups of individuals within an organization. Internal communications employs the same strategic analysis, development, and evaluation tools and techniques as other communications practice areas and adapts specific tools to suit an internal environment.

FOR REVIEW AND DISCUSSION

1. What organizational characteristics support excellent internal communications? Why is it important to communicate to internal audiences?
2. Multicultural and multigenerational workforces present specific challenges for an internal communicator. How can these challenges be successfully addressed? What opportunities do multicultural and multigenerational workforces offer?
3. Discuss the advantages and disadvantages of new communications tools compared with traditional communications tools. What mix of communication vehicles would you choose for your organization?
4. The health and effectiveness of an organization can be measured many ways. What formal or informal research may be available within an organization to help you establish internal communications goals and objectives?

5. What is the most effective form of communication, and what communications tools and initiatives could you develop to take advantage of it?
6. Discuss the elements of effective internal recognition programs.
7. Discuss the major challenges organizations face in successfully communicating organizational change. Explain how internal communicators can help ensure successful reorganizations.

ACTIVITIES

1. Working in groups, develop appropriate goals and objectives to address a large organization's internal communications challenges related to multicultural and multigenerational communications. How would you evaluate your initiatives?
2. Imagine you are part of the internal communications team of a large organization. Your organization has about 3,000 employees who work across Canada both in traditional office settings and also in production plants and warehouses. Working on your own, draft an appropriate employee recognition program. After you have completed your draft, work with a small group to develop one team approach from the individual plans. As a team, explain why you kept some program components and discarded others.
3. Working in groups, examine the organizational benefits of strong internal communications during and after a crisis. Sketch out two scenarios using the same crisis as a foundation for both. Develop the first scenario assuming weak or inconsistent internal communications. Develop the second scenario assuming strong, consistent internal communications. Compare the results and present them to the class.

FURTHER READING

Ansell, Jeff, and Jeffrey Leeson. "Manage Your Risk—And Your Response." *Communication World* (January–February 2011): 31–33.

Apud, Salvador, and Talis Apud-Martinez. "Effective Internal Communication in Global Organizations." *CW Bulletin*. April 2008. http://www.iabc.com/cwb/archive/2008/0408/Apud.htm.

Crincoli, Dom. "Is the Employee Newsletter Dead?" *Ragan Report*. April 2011. http://www.ragan.com/Main/Articles/Is_the_employee_newsletter_dead__42848.aspx#.

Dulye, Linda. "Managers Play a Key Role in Employee Recognition." *CW Bulletin*. July 2011. http://www.iabc.com/cwb/archive/2011/0711/Dulye.htm.

From, Jennifer. "The Difference Is in The Details." *Communication World* (March–April 2011): 22–25.

Gochman, Ilene. "Communication Impact Surveys That Work." *CW Bulletin*. August 2008. http://www.iabc.com/cwb/archive/2008/0808/Gochman.htm.

Henderson, Jeremy. "Supercharge Your Workplace with Meaningful, Strategic Recognition Programs." *CW Bulletin*. July 2011. http://www.iabc.com/cwb/archive/2011/0711/Henderson.htm.

Holland, Robert J., and Katrina Gill. "Ready for Disaster?" *Communication World* (March–April 2006): 20–24.

Krausova, Marika. "Are Employee Newsletters Obsolete?" *CEC Insider*. March 2011. http://www.executiveboard.com/blogs/are-employee-newsletters-obsolete/.

Langton, Nancy, Stephen P. Robbins, and Timothy A. Judge. *Organizational Behaviour: Concepts, Controversies, Applications*. Custom Edition for Grant MacEwan College. Toronto: Pearson Custom Publishing, 2010.

Larkin, Sandar, and TJ Larkin. *Communicating Change: Winning Employee Support for New Business Goals*. New York: McGraw-Hill, 1994.

McCasland, Robin. "Employee Focus Groups: A Reality Check For Your Communication Strategy." *CW Bulletin*. August 2008. http://discovery.iabc.com/view.php?cid=1018.

O'Neill, Ann-Maree, and Shaun McKeogh. "Low-Cost Recognition Ideas that Work." *CW Bulletin*. July 2011. http://www.iabc.com/cwb/archive/2011/0711/ONeill.htm.

Rewers, Angelique, and Melissa Erdman. "The Dos and Don'ts of Employee Recognition Programs in Today's Economy." *CW Bulletin*. July 2011. http://discovery.iabc.com/view.php?cid=2896.

Shaffer, Jim. "Changing Course. Taking the Wheel." *Communication World* (March–April 2011): 16–21.

Shockley-Zalabak, Pamela S. *Fundamentals of Organizational Communication: Knowledge, Sensitivity, Skills, Values*. 8th ed. Toronto: Pearson Education, 2011.

Smith, Larry, and Dan Millar. "Next Steps: The Aftermath of a Crisis." *CW Bulletin*. April 2011. http://www.iabc.com/cwb/archive/2011/0411/SmithMillar.htm.

Smythe, John. "Engaging Employees to Drive Performance." *Communication World* (May–June 2008): 20–22.

Spring, Natasha. "Interview with Russell Grossman, Head of Internal
Communication, BBC." *CW Bulletin*. July 2004.

Trompenaars, Alfons, and Charles Hampden-Turner. *Riding the Waves of
Culture: Understanding Cultural Diversity in Global Business*. New York: McGraw-
Hill, 1998.

Voss, Rebecca. "Communicating Internally—Achieving Your Balance."
CW Bulletin. July 2002.

Whitworth, Brad, and Betsy Riccomini. "Management Communication:
Unlocking Higher Employee Performance." *Communication World* (March–
April 2005): 18–20.

Wright, Marc. "Cultural Barriers to Internal Communication." *CW Bulletin*.
April 2008.

Xenitelis, Marcia. "Are Your Communication Strategies Really Engaging
Employees?" *CW Bulletin*. August 2008.

NOTES

1. Statistics Canada, "Population Growth in Canada: From 1851 to 2061," last modified
    December 18, 2013, http://www12.statcan.gc.ca/census-recensement/2011/as-sa/98-310-
    x/98-310-x2011003_1-eng.cfm.

2. Nancy Langton, Stephen P. Robbins, and Timothy A. Judge, *Cultural Barrier, Organizational
    Behaviour: Concepts, Controversies, Applications*, 5th Canadian ed., custom edition for Grant
    MacEwan College (Toronto: Pearson Education Canada, 2010), 284.

3. This and other examples are offered in the IABC April 2008 *CW Bulletin* on cross-cultural
    internal communications.

4. The plan is an initiative of Employment and Immigration Alberta.

5. Statistics Canada, *Labour Force Historical Review, 2011*, last modified December 19, 2012,
    http://www.statcan.gc.ca/pub/71-001-x/2011002/part-partie1-eng.htm.

6. George Sciadas, "Our Lives in Digital Times," Statistics Canada Research Paper,
    Connectedness Series, Catalogue no. 56F0004MIE, no. 14, November 2006, http://www.
    publications.gc.ca/Collection/Statcan/56F0004MIE/56F0004MIE2006014.pdf.

7. Christina Cavanagh, "Email in the Workplace: A Productivity Study" (research paper, June
    2002, used with author's permission, http://www.christinacavanagh.com/research.htm).

8. Cited in Langton, Robbins, and Judge, *Cultural Barrier, Organizational Behaviour*, 277.

9. Ibid.

10. SWOT is the acronym for a strategic management model developed by Kenneth Andrews
    and described in his book, *The Concept of Corporate Strategy* (Scarborough, ON: R.D. Irwin,
    1980).

11. Jarrod Peckford (supervisor, Environmental and Public Services, Regional Municipality
    of Wood Buffalo), personal communication, February 2013.

12. Many studies come to the same conclusion as outlined in Brad Whitworth and Betsy Riccomini's article, "Unlocking Higher Employee Performance" in IABC's March–April 2005 *Communication World* magazine.

13. WorldatWork, *Trends in Employee Recognition: A Report by WorldatWork*, May 2011, http://www.worldatwork.org/waw/adimLink?id=51194.

14. Brian Geislinger, interview with the author, June 2011.

15. Alberta Blue Cross website (https://www.ab.bluecross.ca/) visitor count taken December 2012.

John E.C. Cooper

Crisis Communications

16

LEARNING OBJECTIVES

After reading this chapter, you will be able to

- define *crisis*;
- explain the need for issues management;
- describe how to develop a crisis plan and other communications tools used in a crisis;
- list the stages of a crisis and describe strategies a communicator can take to manage it;
- explain the role of leaders in a crisis;
- describe the role of digital communications in a crisis; and
- explain what must be done after a crisis is over.

INTRODUCTION

When a crisis hits, organizations are too often unprepared to take action. People are killed or hurt. The power goes out. A natural disaster strikes. There can be any number of causes for a crisis. Everything spins out of control and no one seems to have an answer. Communications grind to a halt. A great gulf of unknowing widens, fuelled by fear, anger, suspicion, and anxiety.

A crisis is a situation where an organization's normal control measures have passed beyond a responsible point of stability because of a catalyst that puts it past the tipping point for effective management, altering the way an organization does business. Timothy Coombs, a professor in the Nicholson School of Communications at the University of Central Florida, defines a crisis as "a significant threat to operations that can have negative consequences if not handled properly."[1] Otto Lerbinger, a specialist in corporate affairs and communication theory, identifies eight types of crisis:

1. Natural (as in a disaster)
2. Technological (a computer glitch)
3. Confrontation (boycotts or sit-ins)
4. Malevolence (a violent act, such as a kidnapping or terrorist act)
5. Organizational misdeeds, which include

   - skewed management values (wrongdoing based on a misreading or misunderstanding of responsibilities within an organization);
   - deception (the misrepresentation of a company's intentions for its own gain);
   - management misconduct (such as misappropriation of funds)

6. Workplace violence
7. Rumours
8. Terrorist attacks or disasters caused by human error[2]

A crisis can also be categorized as externally driven (such as a natural disaster), or internally driven (such as crime taking place within a company).

An organization needs to shift resources to resolving the crisis, which may mean changing its day-to-day operations. Otherwise, it risks losing its level of public trust, the confidence of stakeholders, and its bottom line. As communications specialist Linda Smith, who worked with Maple Leaf Foods during the 2008 listeriosis crisis, says, "Companies are judged quickly by the way they respond to crises—and by the way they communicate that response. And judgment can be harsh."[3] A crisis is always an emotional event, supercharging feelings inside and outside the organization.

Crisis communications is a growing subset within the communications field—finding a niche in business and government in which digital communications have created the need for organizations to respond quickly, accurately, and decisively in crisis situations. Crisis communicators must focus on safeguarding an organization's reputation. They must promote an understanding of an organization's goals and build support for those goals among the organization's publics as they work through the crisis.

The stages of a crisis will be outlined further in this chapter. As a rule of thumb, communications practitioners Alfonso Gonzalez-Herrero and Cornelius B. Pratt offer a definition of four stages in the actual management of a crisis:

1. Identifying the crisis as it presents itself or develops.
2. Developing the strategy for managing it (sometimes called a turn-around strategy).
3. Implementing the change process and monitoring its progress.
4. Evaluating the success of the crisis plan, after the crisis is over.[4]

This chapter outlines an approach to crisis management that applies to whatever type of crisis your organization may face.

ANTICIPATING AND PREVENTING CRISIS

When is a situation an issue and not a crisis? When and how does it turn into a crisis?

Issues management is the practice of a communicator who examines all aspects of an organization, from gathering public responses to announcements and corporate practices, to the analysis of the opinions of stakeholders, clients, and consumers. Issues management takes the pulse of the organization's publics.

An issue is any question that may be asked about an organization that might provoke debate and polarize those publics. A trigger could be a potential event, procedure, practice, action, or statement by a member of the company or one or more of the company's internal or external publics. Issues managers ask, "Where are our practices taking us, and how will our future be affected?" Crucial to the approach of issues management is the notion that the issue is a factor that the company can *manage* or *control*.

Issues monitoring is about reputation management. Reputation management is about fixing a company's image in the public eye. According to communications guru Peter Sandman, reputation management is "two jobs: trying to be more loved and trying to be less hated."[5]

Reputation management is a major reason it is essential to think about the issue before the crisis hits. Steven Fink talks about the prodromal stage of a crisis (the "early warning" stages of a disease or an attack) when what appear to be insignificant events are in fact the distant signs of a potential crisis.[6] David Weiner identifies crises as arising from companies failing to identify and control contentious issues months before the crisis hits; most organizations, if they are attuned to what is happening in the business environment, can forestall a crisis.[7]

Communicators learn to recognize these signs by being sensitive to their organization's environment and by planning well in advance for what might happen. Organizations need professionals who can take a step back and ask, "What if something happens? What will we do?" and determine the steps necessary to address the event and to communicate those steps in a way that will salvage the company's reputation. By identifying issues, communicators are able to recommend actions that will benefit the company and its publics before a crisis occurs—in fact, their identification will often help communicators head off a crisis before it starts.

Two Kinds of Issues

Let's consider, for instance, two kinds of issues: *potential* and *concrete*. A potential issue is something that may or may not be a threat. Get enough customers angry about the quality of a product, then do nothing about it, and those customers begin to protest, which becomes something that is concrete. A concrete issue has the potential to become a crisis. Communicators need to deal with potential crises by flagging issues far in advance:

- The company must analyze its own potential issues and plan to resolve them before events turn them into concrete issues.
- A company must anticipate a crisis and plan to minimize its harmful effects.

A concrete issue is something that can still be controlled. It is any potential issue that has manifested itself as negative attention to the company. This negative feedback may be a forerunner of an imminent crisis, or it may be an indication of a controllable but deteriorating situation with a company's publics. Harm to the company's reputation is a given, and a crisis is likely if a crisis team does not act quickly and effectively. The point at which a concrete issue becomes a crisis cannot be precisely or quantitatively defined outside a specific case. In general, the tipping point from concrete issue to crisis is the point at which a company's publics' negative reactions are energetic or contagious enough that they cannot be diverted, absorbed, or otherwise controlled without an extremely expensive and time-consuming reorientation of a company's key personnel, focused specifically on repairing relationships.

Smart communicators will attack a concrete issue, once identified, with all the resources they can summon. The reason is that a focused, intense effort at this dangerous but relatively controllable stage along the issue-to-crisis continuum is likely to cost a fraction of the overall cost of a resulting crisis.

So, what separates a concrete issue from a crisis? First of all, not all concrete issues, not even those that go without remedy, will become crises. But even an issue that, left unaddressed, would not cause a crisis would likely be detrimental to the organization's reputation.

Methods of Issues Identification

Cervantes said "forewarned is forearmed." At the same time, communicators do not want to be fighting windmills, as Cervantes had Don Quixote do. What they do is put into practice a system of issues identification. This system includes assigning personnel to scan newspapers, websites, blogs, and news programming such as talk shows and newscasts. This review results in a clippings package (an archaic term in this era of electronic data collection). The clippings package can be done internally, or an external service may be employed to scan sources for all information dealing with the organization, its industry sector, or legislation relating to it. Such items will be compiled and additional transcripts (in the case of broadcast media) prepared and the information provided to senior communicators.

In addition to reviewing the media and publications from media, external stakeholders, and the industry, communicators must look at their organization and identify trigger points that could precipitate a crisis, such as

- the firing of top personnel;
- the death of a senior person, such as a CEO or president;
- a scandal involving top officials;
- plant closures or layoffs;
- the creation of a new company by former employees;
- a company product causing illness or death;

- natural disasters;
- terrorist attacks;
- a plant accident causing serious injury or death;
- disease outbreak;
- toxic spills;
- inquiries by government bodies or regulatory commissions;
- product malfunctions;
- class-action lawsuits; and
- industry disruptions, such as crises at other companies within the sector.

Communicators will want to look at the broadest range of issues possible to see what areas need to be addressed, plumbing their organization's depths for feedback on potential issues. A good communications department establishes and maintains a regular line of communication with all departments in its organization. A hospital communications department, for instance, keeps track of information dealing with everything from disease outbreaks in other hospitals to fundraising and government relations. It keeps track of investigations by government agencies into hospital practices. It also is linked to its community. For example, if there is a major manufacturing plant nearby, the hospital's communicators may ask, "What if there is a disaster at the plant? How would the hospital handle the extra load? To whom could we turn if we had to divert patients to other facilities?" This information is gathered from the media, external stakeholders, industry publications, and professionals. Communicators also garner information from meetings held with hospital boards and from discussion with practitioners at other hospitals.

Briefing Notes

Once communicators have identified potential issues, senior communicators may require more information, often in the form of a briefing note (the name may change from organization to organization, but the basic structure remains the same). A briefing note lays out the basic information on the issue, putting it into context and providing the company's planned response and next steps. It briefs senior communicators on an issue in three ways:

1. **Organizes information**. The communicator organizes into logical parts all the key information he or she can access on the issue. A briefing note suggests the basic structure for a crisis plan, should it be decided that

one is needed, and it also details further information that may be needed as the issue develops.

2. **Outlines the organization's position**. The communicator puts the issue into context and expresses the organization's official position on the issue succinctly, through key messages with some supporting basic information. Basic is the key here; while a briefing note may contain chronological history and messaging, it does not go into great detail. Whether the briefing note is used for a simple or complex issue, the focus is on saying, "This is where we stand on this issue."

3. **Outlines planned actions**. The document specifies exactly what actions the company will take to control the issue. It also predicts the outcomes of these actions.

A briefing note is a working document. The information it contains enables all members of the communications team to understand how the company is approaching the issue. Because it contains all the important information and key messages, the briefing note allows anyone in the organization who either leads the organization (and so is expected to speak on its behalf), or who must take on the role of official spokesperson (and provide updates on what is happening in the organization) to be ready to relay the most up-to-date information and the most current key messages. Generally speaking, leaders are always at the helm of the organization—they may be CEOs, presidents, or chairs-of-the-board. Spokespeople may be organizational leaders, or they may be personnel designated by leaders to speak on behalf of the company during the crisis. They can include vice-presidents, department heads, or subject matter experts (scientists, engineers, economists) within the organization.

A briefing note is typically no longer than two pages. It is used by internal staff only; it is not given to the news media or anyone else outside the organization. It is written in plain language. It provides the foundation for understanding how the organization will represent itself on an issue to the news media, general public, or external stakeholders.

Corporations and governments typically assemble all their briefing notes in one binder, called the briefing book. The communications department is usually the co-ordinator of the briefing notes and book, although some organizations may leave it to the responsibility of the risk management department.

See the provided template for a briefing note, along with Figure 16.1 for a sample timeline for preparing a briefing note.

TEMPLATE: BRIEFING NOTE

The issue: Provides a brief but clear overview of the issue in one to two sentences.

Sampling of quotations: Offers senior-level staff a chance to read what has been said in the news media and by stakeholders about the issue.

Suggested response: Provides key messages in a sound bite format. These messages concisely establish the organization's position on an issue. They express the actions the company will take, or at least communicate the company's direction (how they are dealing with the situation). These key messages may be used in media interviews or in discussion with the general public or external stakeholders.

Background: Positions the issue within the context of the organization's activities. It puts the issue into historical perspective and talks about future directions the organization is taking. It gives staff a chance to review quickly the major points that are not necessarily covered in the key messages.

Possible outcomes: Gives personnel a heads-up of what might happen if the issue is not addressed.

Contact information: Provides the name, title, department, phone number, and email address of the communications contact (the person who put the briefing note together).

THE CRISIS PLAN

Managing issues leads to the development of crisis plans. The process of communications planning is outlined in more detail in Chapter 9 and need not be reiterated here. Some elements of crisis planning, however, are unique, well-established, and worthy of note.

The first element is the preparation for a crisis:

1. Identify issues that may turn into a crisis.
2. Develop a plan for each potential crisis.

Figure 16.1 Timeline for Preparing a Briefing Note

6:00 a.m.	Communications staff review news and broadcast clippings. They prepare an issues report, which is a summary with basic notes on the information they have gathered.
7:30 a.m.	Senior communications staff review the issues report, identifying contentious issues.
8:30 a.m.	The communications head reviews the issues report with the CEO, president, or other senior staff.
9:00 a.m.	In the event that an emerging issue is identified, a communicator may be instructed to prepare a briefing note. In some cases, an existing briefing note may simply be updated with appropriate information in light of the new issue.
11:00 a.m.	The briefing note is prepared and sent to the communications department and shared with senior staff for review and approval.
11:30 a.m.	The briefing note is provided to key spokespeople, who are also advised of calls (or potential calls) from news media and external stakeholders.
Noon	Communications staff and spokespeople are prepared for interviews.

3. Create a crisis team with representatives from the organization's core businesses. Train them in their role of spokesperson to both internal and external publics.

4. Ensure that the public relations department is an essential part of the crisis team. The organization's PR professionals must have access to senior management, the legal department, and policy areas to share ideas and provide advice and direction every step of the way. They must not be relegated to secondary or stopgap roles.

5. Ensure that key personnel outside the crisis team know their role during a crisis. This point is not limited to the spokespeople, who may or may not be part of the crisis team (depending upon their role, spokespeople could include technical or administrative department heads, who may take their direction from the crisis team principals but not be involved in the day-to-day management of the crisis), and could also include other employees from across the organization.

6. Practise the crisis plan. Use outside personnel wherever possible to act as media representatives and run through the crisis plan from start to finish.
7. Review and update media and stakeholder lists. Ensure that the contact information is correct.

Details of key managers and spokespeople and where they or their backups can be reached at all times is essential; crises rarely arrive on schedule.

The following are well-established steps to take when a crisis hits.

1. Assemble the Crisis Team

The CEO or leader of the crisis team, as determined by the crisis plan, proclaims a crisis and authorizes the establishment of a room to be the emergency operations centre (EOC). Because the plan has been practised, all the right players or their backups assemble immediately. The EOC should have all the mechanisms to communicate internally and externally throughout the crisis.

The head of the EOC could be the CEO of the organization, or the organization's top communicator, often a vice-president of communications; that person will call for a situation report (often called a sitrep) to get a sense of where the crisis is; depending on the nature of the crisis, sitreps will come in as the crisis evolves, or on a time basis (e.g., a sitrep every two hours at first, then daily as the crisis is managed).

Senior staff in an organization may begin a process of planning on their own, away from the communications team. It is essential, however, to ensure that all members of the team are pulled together and working in concert. The first four hours are crucial for assessing the situation, disseminating information within the organization, establishing key messages, and creating the crisis timetable—a schedule that spells out the sequence of activities (like briefings) that will be rolled out over time as the organization addresses the crisis. These activities cannot be done alone.

During most crises, the team should meet face to face once or twice a day and stay connected by email and mobile phone the rest of the time. For the crisis team, there is no downtime until the crisis is over.

2. Establish the Timetable

Communicators need to establish a timetable to regularly release information and updates to employees, external stakeholders, and news media, usually twice a day (once in the morning and once in the afternoon). Updates usually take the form of briefings and Q&A sessions.

Communicators need to stick to the timetable. A timetable gives a sense of consistency and continuity for the company's publics, creating a level of comfort during the crisis.

It is important for communicators to outline and maintain a log of who has been notified during the crisis and details of the information provided. The contact name, title, organization, and phone and email information should be included, as well as entries for calls within the company.

It is up to the communicator to inform employees of what has happened and what they can expect and to ensure that they understand that all media calls are to be handled by the communications department. Communicators need to teach others how to handle media calls—no speculation, no discussion with media—and to route those calls to the communications team. "Blast" emails distributed internally to all staff during the crisis are useful for giving regular updates.

It is the communicator's responsibility to make sure that senior managers and directors provide an overview to staff within the organization. Employees often feel anxious during a crisis and will want the same comfort the company is providing to external publics.

While all of the organization's staff will not be privy to every element or aspect of a crisis, heightened employee confidence will reduce the likelihood of leaks from disgruntled or frightened people within the organization, particularly in cases where health is involved. The 2003 SARS crisis in Toronto is an example of where staff within an organization, such as nurses, hospital cafeteria workers, and caretakers, needed to be as well-informed as the doctors and senior executives. Keeping employees satisfied and in the loop is as much a goal of good crisis communications as is ensuring that the president and vice-president are well briefed on the issues. See "Case Study: The SARS Crisis in Toronto" later in this chapter.

Make sure employees are kept up to date by email, telephone trees, or meetings. A crisis communications telephone tree might look like this:

- The communications director calls the president and vice-presidents.
- The communications manager calls the company directors.
- Each company director calls his or her division's line managers.
- Each line manager calls his or her unit's supervisors.
- Each supervisor calls his or her staff.

In addition to managing their role in the telephone tree, middle managers will always be in touch with their own staff directly to provide information as the crisis moves toward its conclusion. Remember that it is not just one-way communications from the top down; supervisors should listen to their staff and elicit feedback. (See Chapter 15 for more on internal communications during a crisis.)

3. Update Materials

Communicators need to ensure that materials being distributed, whether externally or internally, are current, with all the proper approvals in place. These materials then must be distributed to the proper personnel: everyone who is part of the crisis team must be working from the same material, with no exceptions. The crisis plan must be updated to include all the specifics of the crisis that actually occurs.

Remember that revising materials and messages means approval through the chain of command, especially by the leader of the crisis team. The team leader may or may not be the spokesperson, but he or she will be expected to lead the organization in decision making. It is reasonable that in most cases, however, an effective leader will provide information to media, stakeholders, and the general public as the organization moves through the crisis. The communicator must ensure the messages are accurate and reasonably consistent within the nature of the evolving crisis.

4. Conduct Research

Communicators must keep on top of the crisis and gather as much information about the crisis as possible as it develops so that they can respond to it. This information includes who outside the organization is reacting to the crisis and what they are saying; what the organization is doing about the crisis; and other conditions that may be developing (especially in the case of a natural or man-made disaster).

Communicators may already have a template for research (basic questions that can be answered—what is the nature of the crisis, what are we doing about it, who is involved, are there casualties?)—but this template must be checked against new, incoming information. Research into the crisis—what the company is doing to deal with it (for example, product recalls, cleanup of spills, repair of computer software that created a customer service glitch)—is necessary because it helps communicators frame their evolving set of responses to the crisis against what has happened before and what is happening now. Communicators need to look into the company's past performance—as well as the performance of other organizations in the industry—to get a clear sense of how similar crises have been handled in the past. What worked? What did not? Being able to answer these questions allows them to anticipate upcoming questions and keeps the plan they develop as current as possible.

5. Maintain Vigilance

While you are dealing with a crisis, the day-to-day business of the organization must continue, even if it has to adapt business as usual to the needs of the crisis.

During a crisis, communicators need to beware of focusing on just the crisis. The business of communications is ongoing, and issues identification and management must continue. They need to be especially aware of arising issues that may have a further impact on the crisis.

MANAGING A CRISIS

An issue looms, cascading into a crisis. Or a crisis simply arises seemingly from nowhere, catching an organization unaware. During a crisis, communicators must understand the organization's ability to assemble a crisis team, plan a strategy, respond to the crisis, and ensure that there is a regular and controlled flow of information to the organization's publics.

The Strategies

Organizations may adopt different strategies in dealing with a crisis. According to Coombs, there are four major ones.[8]

1. **Forgiveness strategies** are implemented when an organization has made a mistake and is at fault. A forgiveness strategy gives an organization a chance to come clean and make wholesale changes in its organization, policies, and practices. See "Case Study: Maple Leaf Foods and the Listeriosis Crisis" later in this chapter.

2. **Sympathy strategies** allow organizations to portray themselves as equal victims in a crisis. Johnson & Johnson, during the 1982 Tylenol crisis, when cyanide-tainted Tylenol killed seven Chicago-area people, stressed to the general public that, not having any foreknowledge of the crisis, it was also a victim. A short-term strategy, sympathy often evolves into forgiveness, when companies move from a position of victim to activist.

In Johnson & Johnson's case, it meant compensating families of victims and creating new packaging standards for its products.

3. **Avoidance strategies** are employed by organizations that try to shift the blame. For instance, in 1993, the American hamburger chain Jack in the Box blamed the deaths of three children at a Seattle Jack in the Box on E. coli–tainted burger meat purchased from a supplier—one of the initial statements the company made was that the customers had eaten in other restaurants as well, so Jack in the Box might not be at fault. In this scenario, there was a denial of responsibility in the early stages until the company began the process of implementing more effective food-screening processes.

4. **Attachment strategies** are designed to get buy-in and public approval during a crisis. This is often done by promoting the organization's role in making change happen in a positive way. In 1979, following a train derailment in Mississauga, Ontario, in which more than 200,000 residents were evacuated after clouds of toxic chemicals spewed into the atmosphere, the City of Mississauga, Province of Ontario, and Canadian Pacific Railway took joint responsibility in resolving the crisis, ensuring the safety of citizens and planning for more effective control of the movement of dangerous goods by rail, as well as developing emergency evacuation plans in the future. All involved were lauded for their efforts by the news media, including (very importantly from a political perspective) the citizens who were evacuated, and who responded to the crisis in a very orderly fashion. There were no deaths and no looting during the evacuation.

THE STAGES OF A CRISIS

As you read earlier, Gonzalez-Herrero and Pratt outline four stages of managing a crisis. In terms of crisis development, it is important to establish a clear understanding of the crisis as it is likely to grow and change. Six main stages that characterize any crisis are as follows.

The Initial Stage

A crisis emerges that unbalances the organization. This stage is characterized by communicators working to get ready to manage the crisis. Plan or no plan, the crisis team is just forming. One or two senior communicators manage the teams, ensure that roles are assigned and understood, and mobilize company resources. The communicators prepare to move into action mode, reviewing their plans along with any mock scenarios they may have run in the past that bear resemblance to the current crisis.

Depending on the severity of the crisis, crisis team members and other staff may be anxious. If there have been incoming calls and pressure from publics, many communicators may be tempted to move into a reactive posture. To move easily to the next stage, they, especially senior communicators, need to resist this impulse.

The initial stage is best completed by activating everyone in their respective roles, letting everyone know what the internal information flow will be, taking questions, and then directing the relatively smaller number of people on the crisis team to prepare for the next stage and update all materials, including the crisis plan.

The Strategic Stage

Communicators and executives work to establish a game plan for the crisis. A communicator will make needed revisions to the plan and collaborate with senior communicators to anticipate as many contingencies as possible for the next phase. Communicators must always be thinking of how to maintain and, in some cases, rebuild a positive rapport with a general public that increasingly distrusts corporate organizations. Public opinion researcher and psychology professor Daniel Yankelovich has said that organizations must move away from "jealously managing corporate image or spinning the truth to influence public opinion and instead practice open and honest dialogue to build 'trust equity' with the public."[9]

The Information Stage

Communicators research and prepare press releases, website information, Q&As (a prepared series of questions and answers), backgrounders, and other communications products for use in news conferences and on the website. The organization's publics will form opinions about the organization as the crisis unfolds; providing proactive information will effectively answer questions about what the company is doing and will serve to underscore the positive steps it is taking to resolve the crisis.

The Tactical Stage

Communicators deliver information to their publics, and the organization takes action to contain the crisis (including conducting and drawing on opinion polls and surveys). This is very much a control mode stage of the operation, as the company works to get control of the situation, especially conditions that represent a danger to publics, such that initiatives such as product recall or suspension of operations may be the norm. This stage is the real test of the crisis plan's effectiveness and it represents the first delivery of information, context, and explanation to publics in an effort to close information gaps. The dangers inherent in this stage are failure to include all contacts into the information flow and a failure to follow up with contacts.

The Adjustment Stage

The crisis begins to draw to a close, but there may be changes in direction that demand changes to messaging or positioning of the organization. Either the information flow to the organization's publics has sufficiently addressed concerns and closed the gaps, or it has not. Sometimes publics are especially demanding or they are being carried on a tide of emotion. A company's messages may not have been perfectly targeted or drafted, and an information gap remains. Alternately, a new gap may form simply as a result of new information coming to light—for instance, a whistleblower turns up late in the crisis to criticize the organization and the crisis takes a new turn irrespective of the communicators' solid work.

After the tactical stage, when information has been presented along with key messages, communicators will receive feedback that will tell them whether the situation is coming under control. If the situation is not under control, they must go back to the crisis plan and add new strategy and tactics. New strategy may come in the form of new action, or new messages—but the adjustment stage represents responsiveness to the crisis as it moves toward completion.

The Evaluation Stage

Once the crisis is over, the company does a postmortem on its handling of the crisis, evaluating its successes and failures and learning from the experience.

Change inevitably happens. As a crisis unfolds and more elements are added to it, the crisis plan must be flexible enough to accommodate them. What changes within the plan are the minute-by-minute messages, which must acknowledge *every new element in the crisis*. The crisis plan must note these changes in subsequent versions of the original plan.

TRAINING THE LEADERS

A small number of people from the internal stakeholder group—the company's team leaders—will formally deliver the key messages to employees, other stakeholders, and the news media. From business experts to scientific spokespeople to the company's CEO or president, these leaders are the natural voices of an organization. The media and stakeholders will look to them for direction. And this makes sense: if they do not have the answers and the ability to stream this information through the organization and into the outside world, *who does?*

The communications team needs to get leaders trained and ready for a crisis before it happens because, once a crisis hits, an organization will have to work with precision to answer all the questions that are bound to arise from a wide range of sources. Leaders need the support of communicators to develop effective messages and to guide them through the process of handling the news media. They may even need public-speaking tips or media training. In many cases, communicators will not be able to develop a complete set of messages until after a crisis has unfolded, but they *can* train the leaders in public speaking and media relations beforehand. During a crisis, when the company's reputation—perhaps its very existence—could be on the line, time will be too scarce and pressure too high to be engaged in even basic media training. (See Chapter 12 for more about media training.)

Rehearsing the Crisis

The best way to prepare executives to perform the leadership role is to have them practise the role under pressure. Many organizations employ an outside company specializing in providing these practice services, or they hire former journalists to fire questions at a leader and see if they stay on topic. An outside company can

- help the organization's leaders understand how to handle the crisis and provide tips;
- work with experienced communicators to develop the format to deliver the messages and communications initiatives to handle the crisis; and
- work from a previously developed crisis plan that was created by internal communicators.

Here are recommended steps to rehearse a crisis.

1. Book Time to Run the Practice Scenario

Set aside time (two to three days) to run a crisis scenario. Create a scenario from the most likely issue your organization has that could turn into a crisis, from an industrial accident to a costly computer glitch. Use available briefing notes and a completed crisis plan. If you are able, hire an outside firm to provide staff who can act as news media and stakeholders during a mock crisis scenario.

2. **Begin the Exercise Using the Crisis Plan**

Pull out your crisis plan and review it thoroughly. How well does it match the current scenario? Turn the plan into a working document and update it daily. Make changes to the initial steps (appoint crisis team members, choose a war room [EOC], and so on). Have the next steps of the plan reviewed by senior communicators and returned quickly with any changes. Initiate the plan immediately, following the remaining steps, but ensure that communicators are empowered to revise and update the plans as often as necessary as the mock crisis plays out.

3. **Test Communications Products and Internal Communications**

Take products written in advance as part of the plan (fact sheets, speeches, news releases) and have leaders and communicators review them. How much customization do they need? Do they work well? Are they too detailed and in need of further distillation before they are ready for their audiences, or for the leader to use?

Have senior communicators and leaders test the internal communications links to other department heads to see how quickly information can be gathered from them in the event of an emergency. Do the internal communications lines function well to give you all the information you need as the crisis erupts? As it evolves? Is there too much information coming from departments or too little? Will new links to internal stakeholders be necessary to ensure a two-way flow of essential information from management, communicators, and staff?

4. **Prepare to Answer Questions from the News Media**

Prepare questions from news media as well as from stakeholder groups. Run through the questions with the spokespeople on your crisis team. Visually record the session—then critique it, using honest feedback to fine tune the responses.

5. **Follow Up**

At the end of the scenario, take your organization through the successes and failures of the crisis planning. Make necessary corrections to ensure maximum success the next time a crisis hits. Examine the lessons learned or the turning points that allowed your organization to move in a new direction.

THE COMMUNICATOR'S ROLE

During the crisis, communicators play several roles. On the strategic side, they plan the steps taken through the crisis. They advise senior management on what, how, and when to communicate, effectively putting the crisis plan into action and monitoring the organization's work during a time when anxiety and fear often cause organizations to close in on themselves, adopting a siege mentality rather than opening themselves up to the general public.

On the tactical side, communicators write the products (from news releases to speeches, question-and-answer documents, website updates, and briefing notes) needed for the proper flow of information to the news media, general public, and stakeholders. In the planning stages, crisis communications may take only part of the day or week. When a crisis hits, however, activity is a round-the-clock endeavour for as long as the crisis lasts. A crisis may demand short, intense bursts of activity for a few days, or sustained exercises that last months.

Handling Emotion

While structure and organization are key to managing a crisis, emotions must be handled as well. Public fear, outrage, and anger at the organization, harsh and critical news media coverage, stakeholder anxiety make a crisis an emotional experience for all to go through. The communications team approach is to allay this anxiety with an attitude of calm and professionalism akin to that of emergency responders who are trained to calm the fear and pain of the people they are trying to help. In a longer-term crisis of weeks or months, proper rest for all members of the crisis team is essential to help better manage the crisis.

CASE STUDY: THE SARS CRISIS IN TORONTO

In February 2003, an atypical pneumonia in China, Singapore, Vietnam, and Canada was earning international headlines. A month later, Severe Acute Respiratory Syndrome (SARS) would throw Toronto's Sunnybrook Health Sciences Centre into crisis mode.[10]

On February 21, 2003, a woman and her husband had stayed on the same floor of a Hong Kong hotel as a doctor who was seriously ill with SARS.[11] After travelling to her Toronto home a couple of days later, the woman fell ill with flu-like symptoms. In early March, Sunnybrook admitted her family members for observation. Soon after, the number of SARS cases increased rapidly. Within a month of the woman's return to Canada, the World Health Organization (WHO) issued a travel advisory recommending limited travel to Toronto.

SARS had been first detected in Toronto the previous November, and there were concerns at that time about it being spread. While it was highly unlikely the woman was the source of the outbreak in the city, the spread of SARS outside Asia raised concerns. On March 26, 2003, the government of Ontario declared a state of emergency. A state of emergency is a declaration made by a government that suspends normal, day-to-day operations of a jurisdiction; under Ontario's Emergency Act, it focuses on protecting safety, health, and welfare of citizens, and can involve travel restrictions and evacuation of people from danger zones until it is lifted. Sunnybrook went on to treat the largest number of SARS patients outside Asia.

SARS was a serious lung infection that began with flu-like symptoms caused by a form of coronavirus (an upper respiratory tract virus infecting mammals and birds) that likely mutated inside domesticated animals, such as chickens. The illness was severe and moved quickly when it spread to humans. The WHO, which also uses the term "outbreak" to describe an epidemic, considers such a situation to be underway when the number of cases observed exceeds the number expected under two conditions: in the same geographic area and in the same time period.[12]

SARS Timeline

- November 16, 2002: Guangdong province in China reports the first case of an atypical pneumonia.
- February 21, 2003: A doctor in Hong Kong becomes ill at a hotel and dies of SARS several days later. Other guests in the hotel also become ill. SARS is spread to other countries as a result, including Canada.
- February 28, 2003: WHO reports an unknown form of pneumonia in an American business office in Vietnam. Around the same time in Canada, visitors and Canadians returning from China report flu-like symptoms.[13]
- March 10–11, 2003: Dr. Carlo Urbani of WHO notes outbreaks in hospitals in Southeast Asia, China, and Canada and gives the illness a name: Severe Acute Respiratory Syndrome (SARS).
- March 15, 2003: WHO issues a global health alert, including a travel advisory, as more SARS cases are reported in China, Vietnam,

Singapore, and Canada.[14] A travel advisory recommends that travellers exercise caution and assess themselves for symptoms of the disease for 10 days after returning from travel.

- March 26, 2003: The Ontario government declares a state of emergency. It was lifted on July 2, 2003.
- March 29, 2003: Dr. Urbani dies as a result of SARS.
- April 23, 2003: WHO advises travellers to avoid Toronto, Beijing, China's Shanxi and Guangdong provinces, Hong Kong, Vietnam, and Singapore. Toronto is recognized as the epicentre of the Canadian outbreak of SARS. The travel advisory stays in place for three weeks.
- May 2003 to May 2004: Instances of SARS begin to decline.
- May 2005: SARS is declared eradicated by WHO, which reported that 8,098 people worldwide became sick with SARS; 774 died, including 44 in Ontario.[15]

Faced with the prospect of managing the news media, the general public, and hundreds of hospital employees, Sunnybrook's approach to crisis communications was to treat both external and internal groups as equally important.

In his thesis, "Effective Internal Crisis Communications," Craig DuHamel, then chief of public affairs and community relations (now vice-president, Communications and Stakeholder Relations, Sunnybrook Health Sciences Centre), explained that the focus of 70 per cent of communications in a Toronto hospital PR department is external, taking the form of media relations and lobbying the provincial government. The remaining 30 per cent goes to internal communications. During the SARS crisis, however, Sunnybrook turned this paradigm around, recognizing the anxiety of hospital staff as they raised questions about the safety of their work environment. Says DuHamel, "The main question hospital communications professionals in Toronto began trying to answer was how can they keep staff calm and informed so that they can continue to be productive and provide care for patients."[16]

Sunnybrook recognized that it was essential to be open and direct with medical staff, particularly nurses (who come into contact with patients more frequently than doctors) because they were putting themselves at risk by caring for patients. Hundreds of other staff also had information needs: administrators, maintenance staff, cleaners, cafeteria workers, technicians, and grounds workers. Over the course of five months, 180 hospital employees underwent the mandatory 10-day quarantine. Eleven employees were hospitalized with the disease.

Top to Bottom Communications

Although Sunnybrook had a complete emergency response plan to manage the needs of external stakeholders, it was not as well-prepared to handle internal crisis communications. As a result, DuHamel and his communications staff worked to put significant resources into communicating with employees. They created an electronic message system to deliver messages from the top down throughout the hospital (manager to staff, and staff to staff), all while "maintaining the original integrity or theme of the corporate message," DuHamel said in an interview.[17]

Messages were broadcast electronically to all staff through a telephone line with daily recorded messages, and email alerts. Frontline managers were able to complement this flow of information with face-to-face discussions with their own staff. This strategy allowed for consistent messages to be delivered, reducing confusion caused by media reports that were often at odds with what Sunnybrook's medical staff knew. As a result, hospital employees were able to rely on trustworthy lines of communications.

Communications originated from a single hospital meeting room that was the emergency operations centre. A gathering place for the crisis team, the EOC was the site of daily hour-long meetings to review and resolve issues. Team representatives then disseminated information to managers, who passed it on to staff. The information was reinforced through electronically broadcast communication from the CEO of Sunnybrook later in the day.

The hospital actively sought feedback from employees, offering an opportunity for input through a dedicated intranet site, telephone line a voicemail box, email alerts with response options, and all-staff Q&A meetings with the CEO and crisis team.

These efforts created an environment of trust, and the crisis team was able to gain the confidence of staff, according to DuHamel.[18] Questions and concerns from the staff ranged from the hospital's measures to control the outbreak, the steps taken to keep hospital workers healthy, to the treatment given to SARS-stricken employees.

Throughout the crisis, the hospital's communications were anchored in a cornerstone of corporate communications: an organization must have control of the messages it develops. This principle was necessary in the face of conflicting, hysteria-driven information that was being delivered by numerous parties. Internal messages competed with news media reports and information coming from the Ontario Ministry of Health, unions, and professional colleges (the schools that train nurses). According to DuHamel, the hospital's core of expertise resulted in the provision of better information than what staffers (from nurses and doctors to custodians, lab workers, administrators, and cafeteria employees) were seeing in the news.[19] The hospital's internal and external information was clear, concise, and free of media-fuelled speculation, thanks in part to the fact that the hospital had some of the world's foremost disease experts who in turn advised WHO on the crisis. The corporate commitment to staff made sure that clear messages came from the crisis team at all times.

LEADERSHIP IN A CRISIS

As you read earlier, the CEO or leader of the crisis team (as determined by the crisis plan) proclaims the crisis. The leader occupies a role that is essentially a performance task, prepared and supported by a communications team. The leader delivers messages as a means of healing relationships between an organization and its publics during a crisis.

The leadership role is usually performed by one person in a position of authority. As discussed earlier, that role can also be taken by someone who, while not at the top of the organization, possesses expert knowledge or leadership in a specific area within the organization. Leadership includes the ability to organize and focus the crisis team's efforts. The leader must understand the needs of stakeholders and be able to organize effective crisis responses as well as recognize the need to enlist occasionally the aid of outside experts and organizations.

With the speed of media today, however, leadership is often reduced to simply the ability to tackle a single crisis or issue head-on. The general public is not looking for a hero, just a competent professional who can answer their questions. A leader must have an ability to contextualize a crisis for people, with an ability to talk on a variety of subjects, and on a variety of levels, encompassing the company's work, as well as its relationship to the community at large, its immediate actions, and its plans for the future.

Sometimes the general public gets a hero anyway. Consider former New York mayor Rudolph Giuliani, whose profile was raised immeasurably by his actions during the crisis of September 11, 2001, when terrorists flew two airplanes into the World Trade Center. Giuliani demonstrated leadership and proved to be a good administrator who competently answered the public's questions while creating an emotional bond with New Yorkers. He explained not only what he was doing but *why*, linking each message he delivered to a demonstrable action being taken by the city.

A strong and effective leader will inspire trust from the general public, stakeholders, and news media and will do the following:

- **Come forward and deal with the bad news first.** It is not enough to do the right thing; you have to be *seen* to be doing the right thing. The effective leader tackles the tough issues first, never avoiding them.
- **Connect emotionally with their publics.** The effective leader recognizes and responds to the impact the crisis has on the organization's publics. The effective leader acknowledges and understands the pain, suffering, and inconvenience that their public deal with and will demonstrate that the organization is in tune with their public's feelings.
- **Be accessible.** The leader will be accessible as often as necessary—to internal and external stakeholders and news media.
- **Be confident in referring to expert advice or testimony.** A strong leader will be able to delegate with confidence and has the ability to say, "I am not an expert on the science of what happened during the crisis. However, I can tell you that we have an expert on hand who has done extensive work on this issue."

Giuliani was clearly ready for a crisis. Before September 11, he and his staff played out crisis management drills for 10 scenarios, from anthrax terrorism to poison gas attacks and truck bombs. It meant that the entire crisis team at city hall was ready when a crisis did occur. Giuliani was able to create a feeling of connectedness among many levels of government and the citizenry, from the person on the street through to police and fire departments and state and federal officials, that they were all in it together. He recognized what people needed to hear, what they wanted to know, and pulled those messages into compelling gestures that drew an emotional thread to anyone connected with the crisis. The mayor was also unafraid to be himself in the aftermath. Giuliani was the first to say that the impact of the crisis made everything else seem small; he was able to admit his weaknesses and his vulnerability in feeling the pain that all New Yorkers must have felt.[20]

When Leaders Mess Up

Unfortunately, leaders do mess up. In managing a crisis, leaders often do one of three things: they do the right thing by stepping up to the plate and delivering strong, clear messages that demonstrates leadership; they bumble their way through a series of platitudes that end up doing more harm than good; or they disappear until they feel the crisis is over.

In the spring of 2010, BP CEO Tony Hayward mismanaged his company's disastrous oil spill in the Gulf of Mexico by delivering a serious of messages that spoke more to safeguarding the company's reputation than tackling the crisis. In fact, he infamously said at a news conference, "I'd like my life back."[21] Not only did Hayward jeopardize his company's image, he added a road-block to dealing effectively with the crisis, negatively affecting the value of an entire industry.

Since the days of Johnson & Johnson and its adept handling of the poisoned Tylenol crisis in 1982, the methods for handling a crisis have changed. Organizations are almost painfully visible these days—all of their missteps counted and measured by both professional and amateur communicators, stakeholders and media. Organizations no longer have the option of "learning on the go" as they manage a crisis; they have to be prepared to step into the breach with strong leadership when a crisis happens.

On April 20, 2010, an explosion on BP's Deepwater Horizon drill rig 400 kilometres southeast of Houston, Texas in 1,259 metres of water created a massive fireball that killed 11 crew members and injured 17. Two days later, the rig sank, and oil from the well gushed out at the rate of almost 60,000 barrels a day—it would release a total of almost five million barrels before being capped on July 15. The accident has been called "a Project Failure of immense proportions...the inability of BP to stop the flow, communication blunders by BP management, negative media accounts and continuing coverage...resulted in serious negative consequences for BP, subcontractors on the project and the oil exploration industry as a whole."[22] By mid-December 2010, the US government would charge BP, along with the rig owner and drill company Transocean and several other companies, under the US Clean Water Act and Oil Pollution Act. The company established a US$20 billion compensation fund to manage cleanup and compensation.[23] On November 5, 2012, the company pled guilty to 14 criminal acts and pledged to pay US$4.5 billion. The company could end up paying US$21 billion in additional fines under the Clean Water Act.[24]

What went wrong with BP's handling of the crisis? In a May 5 interview with *Speigel Online*, Hayward focused on the challenges to BP's reputation and how it hinged on the company's ability to manage the situation quickly and forcefully: "If we do so, and are seen to do everything in our power to support the affected region and local communities, then I see no reason why we should not emerge with our reputation intact.[25] A couple of weeks later, Hayward said the disaster was a tiny spill in a very large ocean.[26]

As Jim Hoggan said in the *Huffington Post*, Hayward's attempts to deflect criticism were apparent, and the lack of compassion for those affected by the spill effectively dug the hole deeper: "The public doesn't trust BP, and for good reason. Where is the concern in BP's response? Does the company feel any real sense of responsibility behind their polished PR messaging?"[27]

BP spun out advertising about being responsible and was strategically involved in a joint website as a member of the "Deepwater Horizon Unified Command" (which included Transocean and eight US government departments) that offered regularly updated, consensus-driven information (information that represented the synthesis of fact and opinion from several sources) on the state of the situation in the Gulf of Mexico. While the website was well-received by commentators in the social media field, BP still was unable to create a sense of trust and confidence on the part of the public. A large part of that failure was in the less-than-contrite behaviour of Tony Hayward. Hayward was replaced as BP's CEO on July 27, 2010.

In another example of leadership missteps, US president George W. Bush failed to respond effectively to the crisis that followed Hurricane Katrina, which destroyed parts of New Orleans and other southern US cities on August 29, 2005. The hurricane killed more than 1,200 people and caused an estimated US$108 billion in damage.[28] Additionally, media reports from the aftermath of the storm said it displaced hundreds of thousands of people.[29]

Officially on vacation when the hurricane hit, Bush delivered a speech the next day that was focused more on the war in Iraq than on the devastation of Katrina. Later that day, in an interview on the nightly news, he told the people of New Orleans, "I'm confident that, with time, you can get your life back in order, new communities will flourish, the great city of New Orleans will be back on its feet, and America will be a stronger place for it."[30] Bush failed to get the message right, instead delivering a "buck up and take it" message rather than one of concern and empathy. A September 1 editorial in the *New York Times* said, "George W. Bush gave one of the worst speeches of his life yesterday, especially given the level of national distress and the need for words of consolation and wisdom. In what seems to be a ritual in this administration, the president appeared a day later than he was needed."[31]

Bush continued his vacation until it became clear that he had to return to work. Five days after the hurricane, he visited New Orleans. While his messages improved—he spoke of rebuilding, saving lives, and stabilizing the situation—he was still disengaged. Further problems and public outrage mounted in the following days: police resignations, major looting, the inability of the Federal Emergency Management Agency to manage the situation, and allegations of racism towards African Americans in New Orleans. Two weeks later, Bush took responsibility for his earlier lack of engagement by seeking to show a greater awareness of, and compassion for, the victims of the disaster.

DIGITAL COMMUNICATIONS IN A CRISIS

As you read in Chapter 13, the world of digital communications is changing every day, and so is the terminology used to describe a public relations world increasingly driven by the tools of the Web, from online newsrooms to social networking, blogs, podcasts, webcasts, email blasts, YouTube, RSS (really simple syndication), and viral marketing. More will develop in the future, and communicators need to be on top of new communications technology and how to use it.

Websites have a dual function as communications vehicles; they present an organization's messages to all publics, and they can create a channel of communication from the various publics to the organization—a channel that can be constrained in any way the communicators choose. The website, when fully exploited as a communications tool, is a powerful means of communicating during a crisis. It allows for rapid publication of key messages, news releases, Q&As, and backgrounders, and it provides an effective and customizable conduit for feedback from publics.

The key to effective use of digital media is recognizing that, while new, often exciting and certainly very flexible and organic, it serves to complement existing channels of communication. New and traditional media work in tandem—one does not replace the other. Traditional communications methods, such as the daily news conference, polling, surveys, focus groups, advertising, and marketing, will continue to be vital components of an effective crisis plan. Digital media will continue to evolve over time, and it is essential to keep track of new developments and determine ways to use emerging media in tackling a crisis.

The "next" Facebook, YouTube, or Twitter will be around the corner, and communicators will need to ask questions: Is this going to give me a platform I need to get the right messages out to media, stakeholders, and clients? How does this complement the methods I am already using? Such questions will be essential in determining what kind of new media you use—and how effectively you use those communications channels.

Dark Sites

The usual first stop for most news media, stakeholders, and the general public when a crisis hits is the organization's website. It is the place where people can expect to find comprehensive information and updates. Most organizations, however, do not have the time to create vast quantities of information about themselves from scratch during the crisis. To meet the anticipated need for fast, accurate information, many organizations will create a dark site.

A dark site is a website that is ready to launch as soon as a crisis hits. Anticipatory in nature, a dark site is built before the crisis happens, enabling communicators to prepare to release information to their publics quickly and accurately. The site is built at least two weeks before the anticipated crisis, generally when an issue looks like it may escalate, such as a product recall of tainted food or a potential natural disaster that could knock out operations.

The dark site becomes the place to go for information once the crisis erupts. It carries prepackaged and updated key messages targeting specific scenarios identified by the organization. The dark site can be used in several ways:

- It can replace the organization's regular day-to-day site.
- It can be linked from the organization's regular site.
- It can have its own URL that is based on search terms that reflect the organization and its business.[32]

The dark site offers a synopsis of the crisis, the organization's response, and a clear and concise description of the crisis's effect on the organization and how the organization is regaining control. Included on the site are

- a series of "what to do/what not to do" steps for media, the general public, and stakeholders;
- a description of the organization's work to bring the crisis under control;
- background on the organization; and
- contact information for both the general public and the news media.

The dark site is updated regularly as new information is added and as the organization works through the crisis.[33]

Dark sites are being lauded by media training companies as a tool to help organizations to shorten the time lag in gathering information and releasing a response to the general public in the face of negative media stories or perceptions that the organization is trying to hide the truth. The dark site provides members of the crisis team instant access to the facts that have been gathered ahead of time and provides the same set of key messages to everyone responsible for handling media inquiries. (The site also includes briefing notes and crisis plans for internal use only.) At the same time, news media, the general public, and stakeholders instantly have the organization's comments and position on the public record soon after a crisis erupts. The transparent nature of this information—available immediately—shows that the organization has control over the situation and can respond quickly and with authority.

Here are eight points communicators must keep in mind when creating a dark site:

1. Identify any and all issues that may turn into crises for the company.
2. Use briefing notes or a crisis plan to create a separate dark site for each crisis. Each dark site should be a separate site linked to the home page of the company website. Each dark site shares duplicate information; for example, background information and company history.
3. To eliminate the need for excessive revision when a crisis breaks, ensure that essential information pertaining to the particular crisis is as complete as possible.
4. Ensure that company information relating to its activities in managing and bringing closure to the crisis is as accurate and up-to-date as possible.
5. Include contact names and phone numbers for the key contacts within the organization, including spokespeople during the crisis.
6. Clearly identify the crisis (this may be modified accordingly before the dark site is launched).
7. Clearly outline the steps being taken to resolve the crisis.
8. Have information links in place, including a feedback link for handling inquiries and comments from the company's customer base. Make sure the dark site is equipped to handle high volumes of traffic without crashing.

RECOVERING FROM A CRISIS

The crisis is over, the dust has settled, and the organization has dutifully delivered on its key messages and wisely waited until the crisis ended of its own accord. So what's next?

Post-crisis, it's important for organizations to apply the lessons they have learned toward making improvements in how the organization does business. In "Seven Dimensions of Crisis Management," Lukaszewski says that a "lessons-learned approach" is necessary so that the organization "can learn to remember the mistakes, the miscues, the successes, and the victories in real time—meaning contemporaneously with problem resolution...Speaking publicly about lessons learned is a major corporate step toward obtaining public and employee forgiveness."[34]

In the wake of a crisis, organizations must be committed to rebuilding trust on the part of their publics. That means listening carefully to stakeholders, acknowledging mistakes, implementing honest recovery action, building coalitions with internal and external audiences, and being willing to monitor progress closely.[35] Most importantly, there must be positive, proactive steps taken to improve the organization. The measure of improvement can range from public trust or sales to measurement of positive coverage in traditional and new media. See 'Case Study: Maple Leaf Foods and the Listeriosis Crisis' for an example of how one company recovered from a crisis.

CASE STUDY: MAPLE LEAF FOODS AND THE LISTERIOSIS CRISIS

Maple Leaf Foods (MLF) is a well-established Canadian food processor with roots dating back to 1927. On August 17, 2008, a listeriosis crisis resulted in the recall of all products made at its Bartor Road facility in Toronto.

Three deli product lines manufactured at the Bartor Road facility had tested positive for the bacteria *Listeria* monocytogenes, which causes a potentially deadly infection called listeriosis. Twenty-three people died as a direct result of eating the tainted meat, out of a total of 57 confirmed cases of illness that were directly attributable to Listeria in MLF's products.

In response, MLF recalled all products made by the company going back to January 2008. It was the biggest recall in MLF's history, setting off months of intensive work. The recall affected a total of 15,000 business contacts (the people who purchased MLF's products for sale at the retail level) at 4,200 stores.

Media coverage of the listeriosis crisis was thorough. Within the first 10 days, there were 408 print, 1,959 broadcast, and 233 online stories. Within the first month, there were 1,011 print, 3,198 broadcast, and 443 online stories. Surveys showed that 100 per cent of Canadians surveyed were aware of the crisis.[36]

MLF, which at the time employed 22,500 at 90 plants in Canada, the United States, and the UK, took on the crisis as an issue of

- taking accountability;
- putting public health and consumer interests first, regardless of cost;
- leading in transparent, fact-based communication; and
- implementing a decisive action plan.

The reinforcement of company "core values" was essential, and customer service was placed above financial interest. The company focused on proactive communications and an acceptance of responsibility, deciding to acknowledge the issue, fix it, and implement new safety practices.

MLF launched an investigation in the middle of August when a panel of experts and the company began a "deep sanitization" of its Bartor Road plant. By September 5, the source of contamination was identified and food safety enhancements were implemented. By September 17, the plant reopened and production resumed under enhanced protocols. There was a hiccup in early October, when a positive finding of Listeria led to a temporary halt of distribution, but the company would go on to implement safety initiatives that included

- standardizing the food safety quality management systems in all of its manufacturing plants by working through the Global Food Safety Initiative and its benchmarked British Retail Consortium certification;
- in 2011, launching an internal audit program to monitor and enforce adherence to its standards;
- working with the University of Guelph and the Canadian Research Institute for Food Safety to deliver the Food Safety Foundations education program to more than 1,250 Maple Leaf employees; and
- launching an online training platform and establishing a 14-step food safety risk assessment process for all new products at MLF.

The crisis team was led by CEO Michael McCain and a small group of staff and advisors, which included representation from the company's communications department. The strategy and messages were simple and straightforward. The team reviewed its internal and external contacts, from employees and executives to customers, suppliers, media, and government. The senior management team at Maple Leaf Foods established a recall team (focused on ensuring that products were sent back to the company) and a project manager who was accountable for the team's activities.

Like all large organizations, MLF had a crisis plan in place and communication guidelines for recalls. The company focused on creating messages that were fact-based and simple—something especially important when telling the public that Listeria is pervasive, existing in any ordinary environment, and putting it into the context of the company's responsibility for the deaths of 23 Canadians.

A significant plus came from the leadership of CEO McCain, who was involved in all decision making as the company responded to media calls. The straightforward sharing of information directly with (and from) the CEO and the creation of a dialogue between the company and its publics—through the active engagement of the CEO—ensured that everyone received the same information at the same time.

MLF accepted responsibility for the crisis with an immediate public apology to victims and their families, which was digitally recorded and posted to YouTube. McCain personally appeared in this apology and as such established himself as the face and the voice of the company, creating a sense of accountability. He came across in all forms of media as caring and sensitive to the feelings of those affected and committed to improving the company's standards. He told reporters that "the buck stops here" and had the look of someone who felt personal pain but who clearly understood the steps being taken to rectify it.[37] In a television advertisement following the listeriosis outbreak, McCain used similar messaging, effectively expressing both sorrow and a commitment for the company to do better.

Immediate lessons learned by MLF during the crisis include the following:

- Lead with facts and be transparent in order to establish trust with media and the public.
- Build on two-way communications vehicles that are already in place. MLF used a CEO weekly note and employee conference calls.

- Use social media and broadcast media. MLF had 90,000 hits on You-Tube and found televised news to be the most effective means to get the message out.
- Use research. MLF used focus groups and corporate reputation surveys to determine the level of consumer confidence in the company following the crisis.
- Embrace the need for immediacy—be ready and willing to hold a press conference when it needs to be held.
- Make a commitment to bilingualism. The company's response in Quebec was negatively affected by a lack of qualified bilingual spokespeople.
- Use expert testimony. MLF used media-trained experts to manage technical questions.

Recovery

A significant challenge for MLF following the listeriosis crisis was moving from active crisis to maintenance mode. In the aftermath of the crisis, which was estimated to cost the company between C$25 million and $30 million (including money spent on making technical improvements to its operations), plus an additional C$15 million in sales,[38] the company

- established a best practices food safety program that it believes is the best in North America;
- appointed a chief food safety officer; and
- took a leadership role in global food safety by supporting public education on food safety and advocating for higher food safety standards industry-wide.

These initiatives won back consumer confidence in a big way.

In modeling Grunig and Hunt's two-way symmetry of communication, the company's website now offers updates and a "food safety pledge" from the CEO. There are links to "Food Safety 101" and an opportunity to ask questions of a resident food safety expert. The efforts address, rather than avoid, dismiss, or shy away from, the subject of food safety, clearly taking a stance of responsibility and commitment to both customer and product.

The successful management of the crisis resulted in McCain being named Canada's Business Newsmaker of the Year for 2008 by the Canadian Press. The company's efforts to rebuild consumer confidence resulted in it being named The Best of 2011 by *Marketing*: "The company has refocused

and revitalized its efforts around consumer-focused product innovation...Maple Leaf's strategy is paying off. Third-quarter results released
in October 2011 showed overall profitability of $43 million compared to a
$19.9 million loss for the same period" the previous year. "And in the 2011
Marketing/Leger Corporate Reputation survey, Maple Leaf Foods climbed
30 spots to 56th place on the top 100 list."[39]

CONCLUSION

We have seen in this chapter that preparation is vital to crisis management. The
best way to prepare for a crisis is to uncover all potential issues, create a crisis
plan, and rehearse mock scenarios with the crisis team. When a crisis hits,
come out strongly with a response that demonstrates understanding and a commitment to action and remediation.

Crisis management requires

- strong messages repeated through the course of the crisis but flexible
  enough to be modified as the situation changes;
- effective leadership from the top of the organization; and
- an ability to adapt so that the organization can achieve renewed stability.

After the crisis passes, communicators must thoroughly analysis how the
crisis was handled, revising their crisis plans and fully absorbing the lessons
learned.

KEY TERMS

Briefing notes: Working documents that contain information that allow all
crisis team members to understand the direction an organization is taking
in handling the crisis.

Concrete issue: An issue that is present within the sphere of influence within
which an organization operates. While not a full-blown crisis and not threatening to an organization's financial position or operations, a concrete issue
demands the preparation of a crisis plan, the assignation of spokespersons,
and the development of key messages.

Crisis: A situation where an organization's normal control measures have
passed beyond a responsible point of stability, usually due to a catalyst
that reduces effective management and alters the organization's normal

operations. If not handled properly, it can seriously threaten an organization's ability to return to normalcy.

Dark site: A website that is created by an organization in advance of a crisis and contains messaging and information that is useful to media, stakeholders, and the general public. During a crisis it can be quickly modified to provide continuous updates on the organization's actions to bring the crisis to an end.

Emergency operation centre (EOC): Sometimes called a *war room*, the EOC is a secure location that is used by communicators and leaders within an organization to monitor media and stakeholder response to a crisis, formulate key messages, and develop the crisis plan. It allows for complete control of information and messaging going into and out of the organization during a crisis.

Issues management: In issues management, a communications practitioner examines all aspects of an organization. The practitioner researches and examines public responses to everything an organization does, analyzes the opinions of media, stakeholders, clients, and consumers, and uses this data to plan for the future. Issues management helps organizations anticipate and respond to those trends that will affect them in the short and long term.

Reputation management: The process of establishing a clear understanding of an organization's reputation by recognizing and responding to the views of its stakeholders, the public, and the media. It works to ensure that the organization takes action to build and maintain a positive reputation among these key groups.

Potential issue: A situation or development that an organization is aware of but that has not yet become a concrete issue or full-blown crisis. A potential issue may exist with an organization's industry or on the periphery of an organization's operations. While non-threatening, it requires monitoring and awareness and action to prevent it from becoming a more serious (concrete) issue.

Situation report (sitrep): A report that provides a strategic overview of a crisis, including elements of the current status of crisis resolution and future potentials.

Spokesperson: The leader or leaders within an organization whose job it is during a crisis to respond to media, stakeholders, and the general public. The spokesperson is provided with key messaging by communicators within an organization, has a full understanding of the crisis on the organization's current and future position, and is part of the crisis team.

FOR REVIEW AND DISCUSSION

1. Why is issues monitoring so important? Think of real-life situations where effective issues monitoring could have averted a crisis.
2. Why is it important to update briefing notes continually?
3. Describe the five well-established steps for handling a crisis.
4. Describe the leader's role in managing a crisis. What about the communicator's role? What critical jobs are performed by the communicator behind the scenes? Compare and contrast the two roles.
5. What is a dark site? How have dark sites helped with reputation management during a crisis?
6. Take another look at the Maple Leaf Foods listeriosis crisis. What was the most important aspect of how the company approached the crisis? What can be learned about the steps the company took to recover from the crisis?

ACTIVITIES

1. Which of Coombs's four major strategies that an organization can adopt in a crisis do you think is most effective? Cite recent examples of such a strategy being implemented. Explain why you think this strategy worked in each example. Analyze the effect this strategy had on the organization's image.
2. The chapter describes a couple of situations where leaders failed to take a proactive approach to crises. Find an example of a recent crisis where a leader failed. Analyze the leader's actions, explaining how he or she failed to manage the crisis. Summarize your findings and contrast your example against a crisis that was successfully managed.
3. Find an example where the news media and stakeholders disagree on how well a company or leader managed a crisis. Provide your own evaluation of how the crisis was handled. Be prepared to defend your assessment.
4. Based on examples in this chapter and ones currently in the news, draw a conclusion about the way different types of organizations approach crisis management. What generalizations you can make based on the size of an organization, the type of industry, and other factors?

FURTHER READING

Alter, Jonathan. "Grit, Guts and Rudy Giuliani." *Newsweek*, September 24, 2001, 53.
CNN. "September 11, Chronology of Terror." *CNN.com./U.S.*, September 12, 2001. http://edition.cnn.com/2001/US/09/11/chronology.attack/.

The Corporation. Directed by Mark Achbar, Jennifer Abbott, and Joel Bakan. 2003. Vancouver, BC: Big Picture Media Corporation, 2004. DVD.

Cohn, Robin. *The PR Crisis Bible*. New York: Truman Talley Books, 2001.

Cooper, John. *Crisis Communications in Canada: A Practical Approach*. Toronto: Centennial College Press, 2007.

Covello, Vincent, and Frederick W. Allen. *Seven Cardinal Rules of Risk Communication*. New York: Center for Risk Communication, 2004. http://www.centerforriskcommunication.com/readings.htm.

Fyfe, Toby, and Paul Crookall. *Social Media and Public Sector Policy Dilemmas*. Toronto: Institute of Public Administration of Canada, 2010.

Gonzalez-Herrero, Alfonso, and Suzanne Smith. "Crisis Communications Management 2.0." *Organization Development Journal* 28, no. 1 (2010).

Howard, Carole, and Wilma Mathews. *On Deadline: Managing Media Relations*. Long Grove, IL: Waveland Press, 1994.

Lawrence, Dallas. "Three Crisis Survival Lessons for the Social Media Age." *Mashaable.com*. March 4, 2010. http://mashable.com/2010/03/04/crisis-survival-social-media/.

Sandman, Peter. "Risk Communications Lessons from the BP Oil Spill." *Peter Sandman Risk Communication Website*. September 13, 2010. http://www.psandman.com/col/deepwater4.htm.

Shiller, E. *The Canadian Guide to Managing the Media*. Toronto: Prentice Hall Canada, 2001.

Weil, Debbie. *The Corporate Blogging Book*. New York: Penguin Group, 2006.

NOTES

1. W. Timothy Coombs, "Choosing the Right Words: The Development of Guidelines for the Selection of the "Appropriate" Crisis Response Strategies," *Management Communication Quarterly* 8, no. 4 (1995): 447–76.

2. Otto Lerbinger, *The Crisis Manager: Facing Risk and Responsibility* (Mahwah, NJ: Erlbaum, 1997).

3. Linda Smith, "Trust and Transparency," *Food in Canada* 70, no. 4 (2010): 32–34.

4. A. Gonzalez-Herrero and C.B. Pratt, "An Integrated Symmetrical Model for Crisis-Communications Management," *Journal of Public Relations Research* 8, no. 2 (1996): 79–105.

5. Peter Sandman, "Two Kinds of Reputation Management," *Peter Sandman Risk Communication Website*, December 3, 2010, http://www.psandman.com/col/reputation.htm.

6. Steven Fink, *Crisis Management* (New York: Backinprint, 2000).

7. David Weiner, "Crisis Communications: Managing Corporate Reputation in the Court of Public Opinion," *Ivey Business Journal*, March/April 2006, http://iveybusinessjournal.com/

topics/the-workplace/crisis-communications-managing-corporate-reputation-in-the-court-of-public-opinion#.UyBfVl5aRHI.

8. Coombs, "Choosing the Right Words," 446–76.

9. Daniel Yankelovich and Steven Rosell, "Making Trust a Competitive Asset: Breaking out of Narrow Frameworks." *Strategy + Business* 35 (Summer 2004), http://www.strategy-business.com/article/04218?pg=all.

10. Sunnybrook Health Sciences Centre was called Sunnybrook and Women's College Health Sciences Centre in 2003.

11. World Health Organization, *Severe Acute Respiratory Syndrome (SARS): Status of the Outbreak and Lessons for the Immediate Future*, 2003, http://www.who.int/csr/media/sars_wha.pdf, cited in B.S. Kamp and C. Hoffman eds. SARS *Reference*, 3rd ed., *sarsreference.com*, 2010, http://sarsreference.com/sarsreference.pdf.

12. WHO, Global Alert and Response, *WHO Guidelines for Epidemic Preparedness and Response to Measles Outbreaks*, WHO/CDS/CSR/ISR/99.1, May 1999, http://www.who.int/csr/resources/publications/measles/WHO_CDS_CSR_ISR_99_1/en/.

13. Kamps and Hoffman, "Timeline," in SARS *Reference*, http://www.sarsreference.com/sarsref/timeline.htm.

14. Ibid.

15. "SARS," *WebMD*, accessed March 17, 2014, www.webmd.com/content/Article/62/71672.htm; WHO, "SARS."

16. Craig DuHamel, "Effective Internal Crisis Communications" (master's thesis, University of Stirling, 2004), 7.

17. Craig DuHamel (chief, public affairs and community relations, Sunnybrook Health Sciences Centre), interview with author, January 2005.

18. Ibid.

19. Ibid.

20. Rudolph W. Giuliani, *Leadership* (New York: Talk Miramax Books, 2002).

21. Benjamin Snyder, "Tony Hayward's Greatest Hits," *CNN Money*, June 10, 2010, http://money.cnn.com/2010/06/10/news/companies/tony_hayward_quotes.fortune/index.htm. Hayward was quoted widely by media on May 31, 2010.

22. David L. Pells, "Deepwater Horizon: Lessons from the Recent BP Project Failure and Environmental Disaster in the Gulf of Mexico—Part I," *PM World Today* 12, no 8 (July 2010), http://www.pmforum.org/library/editorials/2010/PDFs/aug/Editorial-Pells.pdf.

23. BP, "Deepwater Horizon Accident Response: Compensating the People and Communities Affected," accessed March 12, 2014, http://www.bp.com/sectiongenericarticle800.do?categoryId=9036584&contentId=7067605.

24. Clifford Krauss, and John Schwartz, " BP Will Plead Guilty and Pay over $4 Billion," *New York Times*, November 15, 2012, http://www.nytimes.com/2012/11/16/business/global/16iht-bp16.html?pagewanted=all&_r=0.

25. A. Jung, " BP CEO Tony Hayward on Deepwater Horizon: 'It Is Too Early to Talk about Liabilities.'" *Speigel Online*, May 5, 2010, http://www.spiegel.de/international/world/0,1518,693980,00.html.

26. T. Webb, "BP Boss Admits Job on the Line over Gulf Oil Spill," *The Guardian*, May 14, 2010.

27. James Hoggan, " BP's Crisis Communications Strategy is Fundamentally Flawed," *Huffington Post*, June 11, 2010, http://www.huffingtonpost.com/james-hoggan/bps-crisis-communications_b_609826.html.

28. Christopher S. Rugaber and Martin Crutsinger, "Hurricane Sandy to Cost Billions: Will the Economy Stand?" *Christian Science Monitor*, October 29, 2012, http://www.csmonitor.com/Business/Latest-News-Wires/2012/1029/Hurricane-Sandy-to-cost-billions.-Will-the-economy-stand.

29. Blaine Harden and Shankar Vedantam, "Many Displaced by Katrina Turn to Relatives for Shelter," *Washington Post*, September 8, 2005, http://www.washingtonpost.com/wp-dyn/content/article/2005/09/07/AR2005090702415.html.

30. "President Outlines Hurricane Katrina Relief Efforts," *National Business Association*, accessed March 12, 2014, http://www.nationalbusiness.org/?p=10730.

31. Editorial, "Waiting for a Leader," *New York Times*, September 1, 2005, http://www.nytimes.com/2005/09/01/opinion/01thu1.html?_r=0.

32. EMA Public Relations, "Reputation Management: Dark Websites for Crisis Response," accessed March 12, 2014, http://www.mower.com/micrositcs/reputation_management_services/dark-websites-for-crisis-response/.

33. Ibid.

34. J.E. Lukaszewski, "Seven Dimensions of Crisis Communications Management: A Strategic Analysis and Planning Model," *Ragan's Communications Journal* (January/February 1999), http://www.e911.com/monos/A001.html.

35. T. Martin, "Managing the Elements of Corporate Reputation During Crisis Recovery," *Perspectives: Ketchum's Online Quarterly* 2 (2004), http://www.ketchumperspectives.com/archives/2004_i2/.

36. Media, social media, and clipping searches completed by the author on September 11, 2012.

37. E. Reilly, "Maple Leaf President Michael McCain Proves Mettle in "Gut-Wrenching" Crisis," *Canadian Press*, September 1, 2008.

38. Kristine Owram, "Maple Leaf Foods Recovers from Listeria Crisis," *Toronto Star*, October 28, 2009, http://www.thestar.com/business/article/717348--maple-leaf-foods-recovers-from-listeria-crisis.

39. Kristin Laird, "All the Right Moves," *Marketing*, January 10, 2012, http://www.marketing-mag.ca/news/marketer-news/all-the-right-moves-43656.

Appendix A: Sample Communiations Plan

1. Template: Communications Plan for Government

2. Audience Analysis: Sidney Health Fair

3. Case Study: Arts Umbrella

1. TEMPLATE: COMMUNICATIONS PLAN FOR GOVERNMENT

Courtesy of John Barry, Director, Communications, BC Assessment Authority

This template contains potential categories that may be used in a communications plan for municipal, provincial, federal, or First Nations governments.

Front Pieces:

Title Page
    Prepared by
    Creation Date
    Last Updated
    Version
    Contact
Table of Contents
Executive Summary (where applicable)
Introduction
    Project Charter
    Project Plan
    Risk Management Plan (if required)
    Communications Plan (if required)
    How to Use This Document
    Communications Plan Acceptance
    Document Control

Communications Plan:

Background
Goal

SMART Objectives

Situation (SWOT) Analysis

Internal Communications Strengths and Weaknesses

External Communications Opportunities and Threats

Target Audience(s)

Internal and External Groups

Define Audiences

What do they say they need?

What do they already know about this ministry/Crown/organization?

How are they likely to react to message and why?

What are some factors that are influencing the audience that receives message?

How does the audience most frequently receive information (e.g., media, stakeholder newsletter, e-news)?

Key Messages

Message #1

Message #2

Message #3

Message #4

Strategy and Action Plan

Overarching Communications Methodology

Actions/Tools to Communicate Key Messages

Tactics

Internal Communications

Stakeholder Information and Education

Government Relations

Public Information and Education

Media Relations

Issues Management

Evaluation of Results

Qualitative Measurements

Quantitative Measurements

Budget

2. AUDIENCE ANALYSIS: SIDNEY HEALTH FAIR

Reprinted with permission from Britta Frombach, Sidney Health Fair/Sidney Integrated Wellness Community Society

Third Annual Sidney Health Fair: Target Audiences and Audience Reach

Audiences attending the fair are far-reaching. Primary audiences targeted are those interested in pursuing health options and living a more health-conscious lifestyle.

A profile of attendees demonstrates the width and depth of the fair's target market:

1. Seniors curious about blending current therapies with complementary choices
2. Families looking for affordable, effective and safe health options
3. Young adults and students searching for the best way to live healthy lives.

Seniors

Demographics:

Adults aged 65+, representing approximately 13% of the population; varying education; limited disposable income; and curious about blending current therapies with complementary choices.

Psychographics:

Moderately active individuals with increased time for rest and leisure following retirement. Activities include reading, watching television, and travelling to sun destinations. They have an increased understanding of their health and the effects of the external environment. They enjoy routine and consistency. They are willing to make small lifestyle changes for increased quality of life.

Baby Boomers

Demographics:

Men and women born between 1946–1966, with college or university education who earn between $50,000 and $120,000. Can include private-practice health care providers and professionals, nutritionists, naturopaths, and family physicians. Boomers account for approximately 33% of the Canadian population and have significant impact on the Canadian economy representing 75% of Canada's financial assets and about 55% of total disposable income (Source: Bureau of Broadcast Measurement RTS (Return-to-Sample) Survey, Fall 2006).

Psychographics:

If not retired, they enjoy stable, established careers in the higher level of corporate and business world, such as in upper management. Often have large disposable income. This generation has a longer average lifespan, due to major scientific developments and availability of health care. As boomers age, they are becoming increasing concerned with lifestyle and health planning. Planning for retirement becomes more important.

Boomers often lead hectic lives and are time-poor, leading them to seek conveniences to ease everyday life. They are conscious of their health and well-being. Baby boomers believe in extending their youth, staying healthy, active and focusing on enjoying their lives. They continually endorse and promote decisions and products (either formally or informally) that improve and maintain health. A large part of the boomer population is in their peak earning years and are savvy consumers of advertising and products. They are credited with being a heavily consumption-oriented bunch, even as they head toward retirement. Baby boomers are an important segment because of their market share and because people in this age group are typically larger spenders.

The private-practice professionals are passionate about helping people to attain and maintain healthy lifestyles. They are often also passionate about raising awareness of health-related issues and having the ability to suggest solutions, systems, and resources that may help improve the health of their clients and patients. Boomers are also interested in maintaining their health as they retire and age.

Families

Demographics:

Parents in their early thirties to late forties, with college or university education.

Psychographics:

They try to be good environmental citizens. Often active, health-oriented individuals who enjoy outdoor recreation. Product savvy, knowledge-driven consumers. Individuals who engage in health-oriented recreation, such as hiking, cycling, swimming, racquet sports, and other forms of fitness. Looking for affordable, effective, and safer health options that allow their families to live healthy lives.

Students

Demographics:

Teens and young adults aged 15 to 25 registered in secondary and post-secondary learning. Income is based on grants, familial assistance, part-time working, and summer employment.

Psychographics:

They like to meet new people and experience new cultures through socializing, networking, and travelling. They are highly social and experimental, always trying new fashions, music, sports and are curious about complementary health options. They are usually physically active, image-conscious, and technologically savvy. Although often opinionated, they are also open to new ideas and experiences. Many students are activists that lobby their universities, communities, and governments on a wide variety of topics, including tuition fees, some political decisions, the environment, health issues, and many other areas of concern. The typical student or future student is socially conscious and has a desire to "make a difference" in an age of heightened awareness.

It is recognized that health and learning are interdependent. Cognition, concentration, and co-operation are all enhanced when students are healthier. The same applies to teachers and their performance within a healthy workplace environment. The majority age of teachers is 50 to 54, followed by 45 to 49. As of 2003, 68% of teachers in BC were women. Average income is approximately $60,000 per annum.

Note

Schools play an important role in the development of good eating habits.Schools directly influence children's health and behaviours. Teachers lead by example when modeling healthy habits and a healthy lifestyle. To that end, the SIWC is establishing a relationship with the School District to assist with further awareness and educational platforms to broaden students' participation.

Fitness Buffs

Demographics:
Young urban professionals, heavily female-skewed, with post-secondary education. Income ranges between $40,000 and $85,000.

Psychographics:
They consume lots of liquids, including water and sports beverages. They are a large part of the vitamins/supplements and health bar consumer market. This group believes in staying active and maintaining a healthy diet. Lifestyles include healthy eating, where meals are balanced between the appropriate amounts of carbohydrates, protein, and unsaturated fats. Water and electrolyte consumption are also vital. Alcohol and caffeine consumption is average to minimal. Fitness regime often includes at least one type of cross-training activity, such as another cardiovascular activity, and/or weights, yoga or Pilates.

Sidney Residents General Segmentation
Population Breakdown:

0–19	16.3
20–29	6.4
30–44	14.4
45–64	27.6
65+	35.4 (23.4% of this population segment are 75+)

The 2006 census from Statistics Canada revealed that:

- The population was 11,315
- Total population 15 years and older was 9,995
- The median age of residents was 41 (males 39.7/females 42.2)
- There were 4,805 single people (single, separated, divorced or widowed)
- 5,200 were married or common law

Central Saanich Residents General Segmentation

Population Breakdown:

0–19	22.9
20–29	8.3
30–44	17.2
45–64	32.9
65+	18.7 (10.2% of this population segment are 75+)
TOTAL	100%

The 2006 census from Statistics Canada revealed that:

- The population was 15,745
- Total population 15 years and older was 13,275
- The median age of residents was 45.8 (males 45.5/females 46.1)
- There were 5,530 single people (single, separated, divorced or widowed)
- 8,605 were married or common law

North Saanich Residents General Segmentation

Population Breakdown:

0–19	19.6
20–29	6.9
30–44	12.8
45–64	38.9
65+	21.8 (9.7% of this population segment are 75+)
TOTAL	100%

The 2006 census from Statistics Canada revealed that:

- The population was 10,823
- Total population 15 years and older was 9,445

Greater Victoria Residents General Segmentation

The Greater Victoria region has a combined population of 330,088. The region comprises two of the fifteen most populous municipalities in British Columbia (Saanich, at number 7 and Victoria at number 13).

The 2001 census from Statistics Canada revealed that:

- The median household income was $46,387
- The median age of residents was 41 (males 39.7 / females 42.2)
- There were 83,680 single people (male 43,640 / female 40,040)
- 125,855 were married (male 62,895 / female 62,960)
- The majority were Canadian born—247,005 (male 119,110 / female 127,890)
- 57,590 were foreign born (males 26,455 / female 31,135)

The largest ethnic groups in Greater Victoria were:

1. English Canadian—222,450 (British/French/Old Canadian ancestry)
2. Scottish—79,275
3. Irish—56,655
4. German—34,345
5. French—29,440
6. Dutch—13,805
7. Ukrainian—12,770
8. Chinese—11,720
9. Aboriginal—10,230

Average home sale price in 2007—$624,450. The unemployment rate, which stayed below 4% in 2007, compared to the national average of 5.9%, did increase after the economic downturn in September 2008. Statistics Canada reported in February 2009 that it jumped to 6.1% in January 2009.

3. CASE STUDY: ARTS UMBRELLA

Arts Umbrella is a not-for-profit organization located in Vancouver, British Columbia. It provides high quality visual and performance arts to educate children and youth aged 2 to 19, including those who face geographical, cultural, or financial barriers to accessing arts education.[1]

Susan Smith is Arts Umbrella's director of programming. Her 23 years of communications expertise has helped shape the organization as a respected community player. With over 200 employees, artists, and educators, Arts Umbrella is a fast-paced environment that demands rigorous planning to support its broad-based programs.

When Smith and her team organized an event that brought together a diverse number of stakeholders, she outsourced a respected communications firm with extensive marketing communications expertise—NATIONAL Public Relations Inc.—to create a communications plan that combined all facets of the campaign. The plan, prepared by the agency and overseen by Smith, was built to match Arts Umbrella's objectives, expectations, deliverables, and anticipated audiences. It underwent several drafts because of the complexities of the event. Audience analysis was a critical component, as a large number of internal and external players were instrumental in the campaign's success. See the next section of this Appendix for the Sample Communications Plan for this campaign.

Ms. Smith was aware of the potential gaps and barriers to success for the campaign. She knew that stakeholder buy-in was critical. She also recognized that the Arts Umbrella brand was not synonymous for all stakeholders, as it meant different things to different groups (especially those in government positions), so messaging and media relations needed to be well managed. It was imperative that all stakeholders understood Arts Umbrella's history, mission, organizational objectives, and vision. She worked closely with the communications firm to address barriers that could surface during the pre-event, post-event, and day-of stages. As a result, the campaign was a resounding success that met all objectives and received critical acclaim.

This example highlights one of Arts Umbrella's many success stories. Each story contains a framework of planning, visioning, and implementation. Smith updates communications strategies annually, with various adjustments provided throughout the year. Where required, mini-plans are developed for larger initiatives to align deadlines and tactics to a more manageable level. Flexibility to change becomes an important characteristic for Smith's department because, when strategies are not producing expected results or when budgetary issues change, the plan's weaknesses will be changed to improve implementation.

About Susan Smith

Susan Smith's communications career began in 1986, where she studied radio broadcasting at British Columbia Institute of Technology (BCIT).

She spent almost a decade at a prominent Vancouver-based radio station that claimed top ratings in the marketplace shortly after its debut in 1991. In 1999, Smith was hired by a well-respected national agency—GENERATOR/IdeaWorks—to create sales promotions. Brands included high-stake firms such as Molson Canadian.

Cossette Communications Group in Vancouver hired Smith to manage its Blitz Promotion division. She also worked with Los Angeles-based Mobilico on an online NHL project. After a stint with Coca-Cola Limited as a marketing specialist, she transitioned to the not-for-profit sector in 2005 as director of marketing and communications with Arts Umbrella.

In 2007, Smith's position was expanded to include stakeholder development, where she spearheaded the organization's most successful fundraising campaign in its 30-year history. As director of programming, she continues to oversee marketing and communications.

NOTE

1. Smith Susan (director, programming, Arts Umbrella, Vancouver, BC), interview with Ange Frymire Fleming, May 31, 2011.

Sample Communications Plan: Arts Umbrella's Event and Media Relations Plan

Adapted with permission from Susan Smith, Arts Umbrella

Arts Umbrella
20XX Provincial Outreach Program

Event and Media Relations Plan

Prepared by:

NATIONAL Public Relations

December 9, 20XX

Table of Contents

1.0 Introduction

The following communications strategy sets out a step-by-step plan for the announcement of the 20XX Arts Umbrella (AU) Provincial Outreach Program. The plan includes an overview of objectives, the recommended strategic approach, as well as a tactical plan for the announcement in Kelowna, British Columbia.

1.1 Background

Arts Umbrella is Canada's preeminent visual and performing arts centre for young people ages 2 to 19. Its mission is to foster the creativity of young people by providing the highest quality visual and performing arts education that inspires their intellect, spirit, and passion. Each year, Arts Umbrella reaches 36,000 children (including students in Performance Outreach), with 86% of students accessing programs through bursaries and free outreach programs.

On February 9, Arts Umbrella will announce its 20XX mandate, which focuses on delivering visual arts and dance performance outreach programs in the Okanagan region. This initiative will include visual arts workshops and student art exhibition opportunities, a collaborative dance performance with the Kelowna Ballet and a number of school performances, and teacher training workshops.

Throughout the 20XX Provincial Outreach Program in Victoria and the Peace River Region, approximately 5,400 children had access to high quality workshops, and similar projections are forecasted for 20XX.

The Arts Umbrella Provincial Outreach Program is made possible by contributions from both the Province of British Columbia and Telus Corporation that were made to Arts Umbrella in 20XX.

Key details of the Arts Umbrella Provincial Outreach Program include:

- The donation amount from the Province of BC is $250,000 split over three years.
- The donation amount from Telus (matched funding) is $100,000/ year for three years.
- Costs to run programs will vary as per each program. For the first year, funding was used to implement two separate programs in Victoria (artsREACH) and in the Peace Region (Fort St. John and Dawson Creek).
- Regional sponsors are being identified and solicited to augment funding for the 20XX programs.
- All programs will be free to participating students. In some cases, there is free instruction/professional development for elementary/high school teachers and instructors in youth arts programming.
- Arts Umbrella will ensure the highest quality experience and may train instructors, program assistants locally as required.

2.0 Communications Objectives

The strategic objectives of this communications and event plan are as follows:

1) To officially announce the Arts Umbrella's Provincial Outreach Program at a high-profile event designed to generate province-wide media attention.
2) To profile the funding support for the Arts Umbrella Provincial Outreach Program provided by the Province of British Columbia and Telus.
   a. To profile the support of confirmed regional sponsors
3) To create awareness of the Provincial Outreach Program among educators, (teachers, principals, school district staff, etc.) parents, and students.

2.1 Strategic Approach

In February 20XX the visual and performing arts Provincial Outreach Program will be announced at a cocktail reception at the historic Laurel Packinghouse and will profile the new Okanagan program.

Local media will be invited to attend the announcement and cocktail reception; a news release will be distributed to major media in BC.

There will be a keynote speaker at the event, who will be a representative from Telus.

Media coverage will be pursued with the major media in Vancouver and Kelowna.

2.2 Strategic and Tactical Summary

Summary Table			
Key Strategic Communications Objectives	To generate news coverage of the Provincial Outreach Program	To create awareness among educators, parents, and students	To profile the funding support provided by the province of BC and Telus
Key Communications Tactics	· Media advisory · News release and backgrounders · Announcement in Kelowna with keynote speaker · Strategic media follow-up calls · Op-eds in targeted newspapers	· Website (AU, Province of BC, Telus) · Information for teachers and the school district	· Acknowledgement of funders in all communications materials and website · Pre-written article that can be provided to Telus for internal and external communications (employees and customers)

3.0 Key Messages

The following key messages are recommended for use in all communications to the identified target audiences.

1) The Arts Umbrella Provincial Outreach program will provide quality arts education in the visual and performing arts for children, regardless of their ability to physically access and/or afford classes, throughout British Columbia and specifically in the Okanagan in 20XX.

    Supporting points:
    - Arts Umbrella's programs enable young people to become well-rounded citizens who think critically, act creatively, and contribute to a healthy, thriving community.
    - Art educators/workshops provide the opportunity for mentoring and teacher training.

2) The Arts Umbrella Provincial Outreach Program is made possible by the generous support of the Province of British Columbia and Telus.

    Supporting points:
    - The Provincial Outreach Program is made possible by donations from the Province of British Columbia and Telus.
    - Arts Umbrella is very grateful to the Province of British Columbia and Telus for its commitment to children and communities across British Columbia.

3) The Arts Umbrella Provincial Outreach program brings arts and culture to youth, by enriching young people with arts education in the province of British Columbia.

    Supporting points:
    - Arts Umbrella shares arts education expertise with regional communities throughout British Columbia.
    - The Provincial Outreach Program provides the opportunity for youth to work with their peers, and for teachers to work alongside other teachers, which facilitates a learning exchange.
    - Arts Umbrella also seeks to learn from other communities.

4.0 Target Audiences

In considering the strategic objectives of this program, the following are the primary target audiences for pre-event communications:

Arts Umbrella Patrons
- Donors
- Teachers
- Parents
- Volunteers

Telus Employees

Telus Customers

Government
- Premier of British Columbia
- Provincial Ministers and MLAs, including:
  - Government bureaucrats
  - Director, Cultural Services Branch
  - Director, Cultural Services Branch
  - Deputy Minister of Education
  - Deputy Minister of Children and Family Development
- Foundations
  - BC Arts Council Chair
- Municipal (Okanagan region)
  - Mayor of Kelowna
  - Mayor of Vernon
  - Mayor of Penticton
- Other
  - President of the UBCM

Central Okanagan School District 23
- School District Office representatives
- Parents
- Students
- Teachers

Confirmed Regional Sponsors

General Public

5.0 Event Plan

The Provincial Outreach Program will be announced in Kelowna in February 20XX. It is recommended that a government MLA or Minister, a representative from Telus, and a member from Arts Umbrella announce this initiative through speeches at the cocktail reception in Kelowna on February 9, 20XX.

The event will be comprised of the announcement of the Provincial Outreach Program and possibly a performance by Arts Umbrella Dance Company.

5.1 Cocktail reception, Mission Hill Vineyard

Timing	Activity
4:00 pm	AV contacts arrive for AV set up
5:15 pm	Room set up and ready
6:00 pm	Guests arrive, light refreshments and hors d'oeuvres served
6:30 pm	Program begins
6:31 pm	Introductory remarks by Arts Umbrella M.C. • Introduce program and keynote speaker
6:34 pm	MLA or Minister remarks
6:37 pm	Arts Umbrella M.C. thanks MLA/Minister and introduces keynote speaker from Telus
6:38 pm	Telus representative remarks
6:43 pm	Arts Umbrella M.C. thanks Telus Rep and introduces Lucille Pacey, CEO of Arts Umbrella
6:44 pm	Lucille Pacey remarks and introduces AU performers/video
6:47 pm	AU performers or video
6:52 pm	Performance concludes and Lucille introduces Arts Umbrella M.C.
6:53 pm	Arts Umbrella M.C. concludes program

5.2 Action Items

Following is a list of action items that need to be completed prior to the announcement.

Date	Task	Responsibility
December 15	Finalize venue	AU
December 16	Develop invite list (include special guests, Ministers, MLAs, Municipal government representatives, etc.)	AU/National PR
December 31	Secure holding room for event speakers and VIPs	AU
December 31	Hire security company	AU
December 31	Book audio-visual company	AU
December 31	Design invitations	AU
January 6	Arrange travel and accommodation	AU
January 9	Distribute invitations	AU
January 9	Design and print backdrop–if necessary	AU
January 9	Co-ordinate AU student performance or video	AU
January 9	Develop media materials	AU/National PR
January 9	Develop media list	National PR
January 20	Conduct RSVP phone calls	AU
January 20	Develop Q&A document	AU/National PR
January 20	Develop key messages	AU/National PR
January 23	Co-ordinate catering	AU
January 23	Distribute draft copies of media materials	AU/National PR
January 30	Write speaking notes	AU/National PR
February 2	Finalize media materials	AU/National PR
February 6	Distribute media advisory	National PR
February 9	Distribute news release	National PR
Ongoing	Conduct media follow-up and co-ordinate interviews	National PR

6.0 Media Relations

Media will be an important tool to increase awareness of the Arts Umbrella Provincial Outreach Program. Major media and the appropriate local media will be invited to attend the official launch event.

Media relations efforts will be two-fold, focusing on the announcement of the Provincial Outreach Program as well as highlighting the generous donations made by the Province of British Columbia and Telus.

For maximum coverage and to achieve the strategic objectives, the following media relations activities are recommended:

1. Pre-event media advisory
2. Media press kit (including news release and backgrounders)
3. Brief media question-and-answer period (key spokespeople to be made available after announcement)
4. Ongoing follow-up media relations activities

6.1 Target Media

Following are suggested media to be contacted for all media relations activities.

Television
- CHBC TV Kelowna
- Global BCTV
- CTV
- CityTV
- CBC TV

Radio
- CKOV-AM 630 Kelowna
- CBC Radio Vancouver
- CKNW-AM 980 Vancouver
- CKWX News 1130 Vancouver

Ethnic Media
- Sing Tao
- Ming Pao
- Fairchild Radio
- Channel M

Print
- Kelowna Daily Courier
- Kelowna Capital News
- Vancouver Sun
- The Province
- Globe and Mail
- National Post
- Canadian Press
- 24 Hours
- Metro News
- Dose Magazine

6.2 Media Rollout

For media relations efforts, the following timeline is proposed:

Date	Activity	Assigned to	Status
January 9	Develop media materials (media advisory, news release, bios, backgrounders, etc.)	AU/National PR	
January 9	Develop media list	National PR	
January 23	Distribute draft copies of media materials for approval	AU/National PR	
February 2	Finalize media materials	AU/National PR	
February 6	Distribute media advisory	National PR	
February 9	Distribute news release	National PR	
Ongoing	Conduct media follow-up and co-ordinate interviews	National PR	

7.0 Other Communications Activities

The following communications activities are recommended following the launch event:

- Website updating (Arts Umbrella, Province of BC, Telus, Central Okanagan School District)
- Development and distribution of information newsletters to: Arts Umbrella stakeholders, Telus employees and customers, Central Okanagan School District and parents
- Letters to school districts announcing launch of the Provincial Outreach Program
- Copies of letters to regional sponsors

Appendix B: Tips for Media Interviews

1. Interviews on Television

2. Interviews on Radio

3. Interviews for Print

4. B-roll and Web Video Work

5. PR Photos

1. INTERVIEWS ON TELEVISION

- Focus on the interviewer, not the camera.
- Ignore camera operators and other technicians as they move about their business.
- You should consider yourself on the record from the moment you enter the TV station until you're in your car away from the studio. Asides can be heard and recorded in-studio, or even in the hallways or green room.
- Never talk over the interviewer.
- Avoid ums and ahs.
- Allow camera operators to get shots wherever they want, and don't necessarily demand the interview take place in your office behind your desk .
- Dress for the occasion. If you're in the plant, wear a hard hat and coveralls. If you're at an outdoor event, wearing a business suit may not be suitable.
- Don't be alarmed by re-asks, when the camera operator moves behind you and the reporter asks many of the same questions covered previously. This is for editing purposes.
- Stick to your original answers and stay serious. No bravado or silliness during these re-asks. You are still being recorded. Concentrate on the interviewer at all times. Look him or her in the eye. Use natural hand movements as emphasis to your answers. Listen carefully and actively.
- Avoid clasping hands tightly, gripping the sides of chairs or tables, playing with pencils, water glasses, and buttons, looking around, closing your eyes, blinking too much, swiveling in your chair (all these give the impression of nervousness, boredom, and even lying).

- Sit straight and avoid movement. Leaning slightly forward in your chair gives the impression that you're alert and in control.
- Wait until the lights are off, the red lights on the cameras are off, and the technician removes your lapel microphone. Then you may relax slightly, but only slightly. Manage your demeanour carefully because the cameras often stay on you and the host for several minutes while the show's credit roll. Nothing is worse than the audience seeing you and the host smiling after a serious interview. Never say, "I'm glad that's over," or "How did I do?"

2. INTERVIEWS ON RADIO

- Radio can be a deceptive medium. You may think your voice has energy and vitality, but by the time it makes its way through all the technology to a listener's speaker, your voice sounds flat.
- Remember to put about twice as much action into your voice as you would in normal conversation, and it will sound full of energy (but natural) on the receiving end.
- Vary your pitch, tone, rate, and volume.
- Overall, sound conversational and personal. Radio is a very personal medium.
- If doing a radio interview over the telephone, keep your mouth about six inches away to avoid the popping sounds caused by letters like p, because most telephone microphones are of poorer quality.
- Don't be disappointed if the interview took hours, but the resulting story is only about 45 seconds in length. Brevity rules radio news these days. Remember, your quotes, or sound bites (clips), should be short—less than 10 seconds.

3. INTERVIEWS FOR PRINT

- These interviews are generally longer than radio or television interviews.
- Print reporters generally require far more detail than radio or TV.
- It is common for a reporter to use a recording device. They should not mind if you do as well.
- Don't complain if some of the quotes aren't exact or some of the facts are slightly misinterpreted. Complaining will only antagonize the reporter. If there is a serious error or misquote, please see the following section on corrections.

- Be prepared for the reporter (or a researcher) to call back to check quotes and facts. If the reporter indicates the article will be published the next day, be reachable until after that newspaper's bedtime (anywhere from 6:00 p.m. to 10:00 p.m.). Ask the reporter about possible scheduling of publication, and ensure you are reachable. However, do not hand out your personal telephone (or cellular) numbers. Use a third party, such as public relations counsel, to co-ordinate such requests after hours. It is always better for you to call the reporter. This is one way to ensure authenticity.

4. B-ROLL AND WEB VIDEO WORK

B-roll is background video you provide to the television reporter to give supplementary video to the interview he/she may not have time to get. This may include shots at a factory, in the lab, in the retail environment to help the reporter provide some visual variety to his/her story.

Television news and Web video for online news outlets can be the most powerful and trusted news media these days, and to get a softer story placed must follow one paramount rule: have moving pictures.

In congested news markets such as Toronto, getting a videographer or camera assigned to your story is a challenge, to say the least. If you're lucky, you may get one or two cameras out to your news event. That leaves another three or four stations, not including the networks, that will not cover your story because they are not there with a camera.

PR practitioners can maximize their TV impact by investing in B-roll and hiring a news videography service.

Tips for B-roll and Web video:

1. Hire a videographer with news experience (and union credentials)— wedding video won't cut it!
2. Shoot it in high definition video formats.
3. It should be in edited, eye-catching footage and delivered in a timely manner.
4. Don't shoot shots—shoot sequences. Tell the story.
5. Produce a shot list to use as a rough guide.
6. Allow for time to light the shot properly.
7. Shoot as a news videographer would shoot it—don't make it too polished.
8. Keep the video visually entertaining.
9. Work with the camera operator/producer to capture the best shots and sequences.

10. Hire a staging company when it is a news event so lighting, backdrop signage, and audio feeds are all present and in working order.

Distribution of video is dependent on budget and timing. If it is a relatively hard news story with time sensitivities, courier delivery of the video makes sense, especially if it's a one-market focus or through satellite or Internet (FTP sites) and is of national interest.

Ensure concise hard copy news materials accompany the video and make sure the video is not too long—under 10 minutes is ideal. TV stations don't have the time or staff to go through long tapes!

These tips also hold steady for Web video, which is in high demand these days as print media market their online versions and use Web video on those online sites. The Internet is now a "broadcast medium," with moving pictures, as opposed to its tradition of being a print medium, with text and still images. Two service providers for Web video are Canadian Press Images and News Canada.

5. PR PHOTOS

One of the most effective tools for getting positive news coverage is the still photograph. Whether aimed at community newspapers or the larger dailies, public relations photos that get picked up by publications can powerfully convey your organization's message. But there is a real art and science to the news photo.

Ron Welch is general manager of the Canadian Press Images, Canada's only national news agency. Mr. Welch says, "editors know the value of good pictures—they draw readers' attention, they sell papers and they can make or break your chances of getting your point across."[1]

Welch, who has been in the photo business for decades, offers nine tips to help communicators get the best out of their news photo.

Tips for PR photos:

1. Hire a photographer with editorial experience. They understand what photo editors are looking for and will deliver them in the correct digital format, colour corrected and ready to go.
2. Good photos are new and in some way unusual.
3. A good photo shows action the instant it happens.
4. Strong photos portray people and appeal to the emotions.

5. They always relate to some important person, event, or place.
6. The photo should wrap up a story and provide an overall view of it.
7. Remember context—excellent news photos tie in with a current story, the season, the weather, a fad.
8. Large empty spaces should always be avoided in news photos— the entire frame should contain useful information.
9. Stand-up group shots, unless filled with VIPs, don't work.

PR photos can be distributed in a number of ways—through paid wire services such as Marketwired and directly to photo editors via email. The latter distribution tactic should not be overlooked because some community newspapers and smaller dailies do not subscribe to paid wire services, and they tend to be heavy users of photos generated by PR, especially of local events or people. Photo captions should be fewer than 50 words.

NOTE

1. Ron Welch, interview with author, June 2011.

Advertisers: Individuals, organizations, governments, associations, and others who sponsor (buy) advertising.

Advertising: A paid form of marketing communications from identified sponsors offered through the media that is designed to influence the thought patterns, attitudes, and behaviour of target audiences.

Advertising agencies: A service business composed of creative people and business people who plan, create, produce, and place advertising messages in advertising media for clients seeking to find customers for their products, services, and ideas.

Advertorial: A combination of an advertisement and editorial used primarily to promote ideas by an identified sponsor in paid media space.

Advocacy: The term used by non-profit organizations to refer to government relations activities.

Alternative media: A variety of media that reaches audiences when they are engaged in specialized activities. Alternative media can include movie theatre advertising, subway stations and tunnels, and other niche items designed to attract news media attention.

Association relations: Public relations and community outreach conducted on behalf of for-profit and not-for-profit associations concerned with promoting professional, industrial, or societal issues.

Audience profile: Economic, demographic, and social characteristics of the specific readership, viewership, and listenership of a particular advertising medium.

B-roll: Provided by organizations to media as part of media kits, B-roll is unnarrated video footage that is used by TV news producers to supplement news anchor narration.

Briefing notes: Working documents containing information that allow all crisis team members to understand the direction an organization is taking in handling the crisis.

British North America Act: Legislation (laws) approved originally in 1867 by the Parliament of the United Kingdom that are the core of the constitution of Canada.

Canadian Charter of Rights and Freedoms: A bill of rights forming part of Canada's Constitution Act, 1982 that guarantees political rights to Canadian citizens and protects the civil rights of everyone in Canada from the actions of all levels of government.

Canadian Constitution: The supreme law of Canada that establishes Canada's system of government, divides power between the federal government and provincial governments, and enshrines the civil rights of Canadians and residents of Canada.

Canadian Public Relations Society (CPRS): Established in 1948, the Canadian Public Relations Society is an organization of men and women who practise public relations in Canada and abroad. Members work to maintain the highest standards and to share a uniquely Canadian experience in public relations.

Canadian Radio-television and Telecommunications Commission (CRTC): Canada's regulatory agency that oversees broadcasting and communications.

Coalition building and maintenance: A government relations strategy that involves building and maintaining a coalition of different organizations representing different perspectives that agree on and support a specific change in public policy.

Code of ethics: A set of agreed upon principles for conduct within an organization or association used by members and employees to guide ethical decision making and behaviour.

Communication: The transfer of information from one person to another in an attempt to create a common understanding and generate a response.

Communications plan: A guide to an organization's internal and external communications needs that directs communications and marketing campaigns, initiatives, special projects, and annual planning.

Concrete issue: An issue that is present within the sphere of influence within which an organization operates. While not a full-blown crisis and not threatening to an organization's financial position or operations, a concrete issue demands the preparation of a crisis plan, the assignation of spokespersons, and the development of key messages.

Consumer protection legislation: Laws enacted usually by the provinces to protect the rights of consumers when they are purchasing goods and services in the marketplace and encourage fair competition among businesses.

Consumer-related PR: The public relations practice area in which public relations techniques are used to support consumer marketing and sales activities.

Contact program (also called *lobbying*): A government relations strategy that involves a program of direct (typically but not necessarily face-to-face) contact with government decision makers.

Copyright: A legal concept, enshrined in Canada's Copyright Act, that gives a creator of an original work exclusive rights to the use of that work, including the right to copy that work, to be credited for that work, and to benefit financially from that work.

Creative plan: A document prepared by an advertising agency that outlines the creative theme, message, tone, manner, and appeal method to guide the development of the writing and design of an advertising campaign.

Criminal Code of Canada: A Canadian law that codifies criminal offences, procedures, and punishments in Canada.

Crisis: A situation where an organization's normal control measures have passed beyond a responsible point of stability, usually due to a catalyst that reduces effective management and alters the organization's normal operations. If not handled properly, it can seriously threaten an organization's ability to return to normalcy.

Crisis communications: Consists of the planning and implementation of strategies and tactics, allowing organizations to identify real and potential crises that may disrupt the operations and materially detract from the organization's reputation.

Crisis news release: A crisis news release is a news release written in response to a company or organizational crisis. The public relations practitioner, on behalf of the organization, will write a news release on the latest happenings of the crisis to inform news media and the general public, continually keeping media updated.

Dark site: A website that is created by an organization in advance of a crisis and contains messaging and information that is useful to media, stakeholders, and the general public. During a crisis it can be quickly modified to provide continuous updates on the organization's actions to bring the crisis to an end.

Defamation: The communication of a false statement that may give an individual or business (or other organization or group) a negative or inferior image. Includes slander, libel, and criminal libel.

Defamatory libel: Also known as *criminal libel*, an umbrella term given to those forms of libel that are prohibited by law, including under the Criminal Code of Canada.

Defendant: In a lawsuit, a defendant is the party who is accused of some wrongdoing and must answer the plaintiff's complaint.

Demographics: Segmenting audiences by age, gender, race/ethnic origin, income, education, occupation, social class, marital status, and dependents.

Deontology: An ethical decision-making philosophy by which decisions are made based on what is right or what is wrong in a universal context, not on the consequences (which are not always easy to predict).

Diffusion of Innovations theory: A theory explaining how, why, and at what rate new ideas and technology spread through cultures. Developed by Everett Rogers (1995), diffusion is the process by which an innovation is communicated through certain channels over time among the members of a community.

Digital communications: The various means by which people connect using technology. Digital communications include text, photos, audio, and video distributed through electronic devices including computers and mobile telephones whether to individual users (for example, through email or text message) or groups of users (for example, on social networks). This definition is intentionally broad as it must account for not only today's products and services that enable these connections but those of tomorrow as well.

Digital media: Digitized words, pictures, audio, and video that can be delivered over the Internet or telecommunications networks. This type of media can be directed toward mobile phones, smartphones, and tablets. Digital media can also refer to new media.

Direct marketing: A strategy whereby marketers communicate directly to the home, office, or individual, rather than in the general marketplace. The consumer is invited to respond and interact directly. Direct marketing can involve direct mail, telemarketing, door-to-door interactions, home shopping networks, and social networking.

Direct response communications: The strategies and tactics used to target a single customer or prospect to generate an immediate and measureable response. Examples of direct response communications include flyers, promotional emails, and infomercials.

Economic determinism: A communications theory that proposes that the information we receive through the media is controlled by those who own the media.

Election period: The time from the announcement of the date of a general election to the day in which voting takes place.

Election techniques: A government relations strategy that involves encouraging or mobilizing employees or other groups of stakeholders to vote during elections.

Email pitch: A short, punchy email address to a journalist or blogger, suggesting he or she write about and publish a story on a certain topic. A news release with all the information appears below it.

Emergency operation centre (EOC): Sometimes called a *war room*, the EOC is a secure location that is used by communicators and leaders within an organization to monitor media and stakeholder response to a crisis, formulate key messages, and develop the crisis plan. It allows for complete control of information and messaging going into and out of the organization during a crisis.

Employee recognition program: An integrated strategy (research, goals, objectives, budget, tools, and evaluation) to recognize the contributions of individual employees and groups of employees in helping the organization achieve its mandate.

Ethical advocacy: As a tenet of professional practice, an ethical advocate is a public relations practitioner who communicates persuasively and truthfully on behalf of the client while recognizing his or her primary responsibility is to act in the public's interest.

Ethics: Ethics are the rules that help individuals, groups, and organizations to identify what is right or wrong, fair and unfair, honest or dishonest for themselves and for others in specific situations.

False representations: Statements that are held out to be fact but are found upon investigation to be untrue.

Federal government: A reference to the Government of Canada.

Frequency: The number of times that each person in an audience is exposed to an advertiser's message over a specified period of time.

Geographics: Audience analysis that identifies preferences and distinctions in sample or total populations. Differences include rural versus urban, one province versus another, or neighbourhoods within a city.

Government policy: The decision of government on a course of action as stated in documents such as speeches, news releases, announcements, backgrounders as well as regulations and legislation.

Government relations: A practice area in public relations that attempts to influence one or more governments to adopt your organization's point of view.

Grassroots lobbying: A government relations strategy that engages employees and members of an organization to help persuade government decision makers to adopt changes proposed by the organization.

Guerrilla marketing: A marketing strategy in which generally low-cost, unconventional means—such as flash mobs—are used to convey or promote a product, service, or idea to a specific group.

Impact: The effectiveness of the match between media and message to ensure the greatest potential audience will be exposed to the message, remember it, and be motivated to acquire the good or service or act on the idea.

Impressions: Generally, the number of eyeballs or ears reading, watching, or listening to a given media outlet. Some call this *reach*. Impressions are more than just circulation numbers, as is the case of print media, since a given newspaper or magazine is often read by more than one person in a household or office.

Industry relations: Public relations, intra-industry, or external relations used to support or promote a particular industrial sector's interests.

Internal audiences: Groups of individuals within an organization, generally identified by characteristics such as union or management position; type of job (such as administrative support, operations, maintenance, corporate support); geographic location (assuming the organization operates out of more than one physical location); accessibility to specific communications tools (such as email or other types of online communication); and demographics (such as retirees, new employees, multicultural employees).

Integrated marketing communications (IMC): IMC is the practice of coordinating various marketing communications disciplines in a single campaign to heighten the impact of a campaign on a particular target audience.

Intellectual property laws: Laws that grant certain exclusive rights to the creators of intangible assets such as original musical, literary, or artistic works, discoveries and inventions, or words, symbols, and designs.

Internal communications: The communications practice area dealing with groups of individuals within an organization. Internal communications employs the same strategic analysis, development and evaluation tools and techniques as other communications practice areas and adapts specific tools to suit an internal environment.

International Association of Business Communicators (IABC): An international professional association established in 1970 for communicators, including public relations practitioners. This association is a US-based international organization with over 15,000 members in 80 countries.

Inverted pyramid method of organizing information: A method of organizing information that requires the conclusion or main point to go at the beginning, not the end of the piece. Information appears in descending order of importance to the reader.

Investor relations: The public relations practice area in which activities are designed to support the reputation and the perceived value of companies whose common shares, bonds, or other financial instruments are listed on securities exchanges.

Issues management: In issues management, a communications practitioner examines all aspects of an organization. The practitioner researches and examines public responses to everything an organization does, analyzes the opinions of media, stakeholders, clients, and consumers, and uses this data to plan for the future. Issues management helps organizations anticipate and respond to those trends that will affect them in the short and long term.

Key messages: Primary, succinct statements about an organization, event, situation, or issue.

Legislation: Laws as determined by government through parliament and legislatures.

Letter to the editor: Sometimes referred to as LTEs; a letter sent to a publication by a reader, or a public relations person, on a topic or issue of concern. The intention is for that letter to be published in the publication so that other readers can read it.

Marketing: While often confused with public relations and sales, marketing is concerned with understanding target audiences through strategic research and interacting with them in a way that is beneficial to both them and your company. It is about identifying customer needs, aligning those with what you offer, and attracting and retaining the right customers to profit your organization.

Marketing communications: The various marketing and communications disciplines (e.g., direct response and advertising) organizations use to engage a particular target market and/or persuade them towards a particular action or purchase. Each discipline may be used on its own or in conjunction with others (integrated marketing communications).

Maslow's hierarchy of needs: A theory posed by Abraham Maslow in his 1943 paper "A Theory of Human Motivation." It outlines the stages of growth necessary to all humans from meeting physiological needs to self-actualization.

Mass communication: The distribution of a message to a large number of people through media such as television, newspapers, and radio.

Media alert (media advisory): A simple notice of the who, what, when, where, why (and sometimes how) of a news story, usually a simple or single event, such as a public appearance or a press conference.

Media buyer: The person who selects, negotiates, and monitors specific media space as necessary to place messages in media.

Media buying: The act of buying media space. Media buying is done by experts called media buyers.

Media content analysis: An analysis of media stories to help companies understand how they are portrayed by the media and, by extension, how they might be perceived by the public as a result of this coverage.

Media kit: A packet of information prepared for journalists, containing a news release and a selection of appropriate supporting material, such as a fact sheet, biography, or backgrounder article.

Media list: A detailed and time-consuming exercise to determine specifically which media will receive an organization's news. The media list comes from many sources, including media list brokers, and should include the contact name, media outlet, email and courier address, phone, cell, and fax numbers. The list can also include the media outlet's reach numbers, and the contact person's preference for receiving news by email, fax, or not at all.

Media planner: The person responsible for developing the overall strategy of a media plan by assessing the strengths, weaknesses, cost efficiencies, and communication potential of various media.

Media relations: The art and science of reaching your target audience with key messages through the news media. This public relations practice area focuses on interfacing with the news media, both proactively (through news releases and other tools) and reactively (providing information and facilitating interview requests).

Media relations plan: A formal plan that provides the detail for a media relations campaign, including details for researching target audiences, developing key messages, establishing which news media to target, creating a media list, and creating communications to send to the target audiences.

Media relations rating points (MRP): Created by an industry panel of PR experts and owned by the Canadian Public Relations Society, a rating system that provides both a qualitative and quantitative measurement paradigm for media relations.

Media room (press room): The designated section on an organization's website for journalists to access a media kit, an archive of current and past media releases, public relations contact information, photographs, and anything else an organization wishes to make accessible specifically to journalists.

Media space: A specified allotment of time or space in various categories of media, broadcast, print, Internet, digital, and direct mail available to sponsors who wish to purchase advertising.

Media training: The process in which spokespersons are trained in both theory and practice on how media relations works, with a specific focus on developing and delivering key messages. Ideally, everyone on the media relations team, including the support staff, should receive media training too.

Media vehicles: Specific print, broadcast, digital, or other media used in an advertising campaign.

Messaging: Statements that act as anchors for the organization's positioning on a given issue and are delivered with consistency by designated spokespersons.

Mind mapping: A visual brainstorming technique that identifies a central word or concept around which other related words or concepts are arranged. Once you have your main idea and have done a bit of research, start in the centre of the page with the main idea (thesis), and then work outward in all directions to produce a structure of related thoughts, words, or images. You can group like items together to produce a sort of visual outline.

Mobile advertising: A form of advertising delivered to target audiences via mobile devices such as smartphones and tablets.

Mobile marketing: Using mobile phones or devices to promote or market to customers through wireless networks.

Muckraking: A form of sensationalized journalism common in the early 1900s where stories were developed, largely for print newspapers, based on scandal and speculation.

Multi-directional interactive communications model: The process by which messages move between official sources of information, such as public relations practitioners and the audiences they target.

Municipal government: The government of a Canadian municipality, such as the City of Calgary.

National Policy: The policy of the Canadian government introduced under Prime Minister John A. MacDonald prioritizing the economic and political development of the country through policies of immigration and settlement of the West, tariffs and protectionist trade strategies, and the establishment of a national railway system.

New media: Media that are not yet fully established. Most new media has been developed since the advent of the Internet. This phrase is sometimes used interchangeably with *digital media*.

News fence: The barrier that exists between editorial and advertising in commercial news media outlets. The width of the news fence indicates to what degree advertising can influence editorial decisions.

News hole: The space in which proactive news can be placed. For example, business stories go into the business section of the news. Technology news can go into the technology section of the business area of the news but can also fit into other categories.

News release: An article that the public relations practitioner has written for the journalist in the hope that the story will make its way into the news either as written or used as an idea by the journalist for his/her own angle or story.

Newswire: Refers to a variety of services that will transmit a news release to a predetermined category of news media. Generally, newswires charge by the word.

Observational research: Collecting information through watching how people interact with each other and with products.

Official statement: Planned and prepared information supplied to reporters by an organization on a timely, significant, unusual, or controversial matter, or in a crisis.

One-way asymmetric communications model: The process by which a message travels from a public relations practitioner to targeted audiences through an intermediary such as a journalist.

Op-ed: An opinion piece that appears in the editorial pages of a newspaper (most often "opposite the editorial" article of the newspaper's editor), written by someone outside the newspaper staff and editorial board. Sometimes newspapers ask experts and relevant members of the public to write on a certain topic, and sometimes people will simply send an op-ed unsolicited in hopes it will be printed. It is also sometimes referred to as "opinion editorial." The topic or subject will likely be on a major news issue of the day that is timely, significant, unusual, or controversial.

Opinion research: The collection of stakeholders' opinions and attitudes using research techniques.

Paid media space: Specified allotment of time or space in various categories of media for which an identified sponsor has paid a fee, or exchanged a service of value, in order to place advertising.

Personal selling: The face-to-face process whereby a company's sales team encourages purchases by retailers and other buyers.

Pitch letter: A letter written by a public relations practitioner to an editor, asking him or her to write a story on a suggested topic.

Plain language: Writing in plain language is simply choosing appropriate vocabulary for the target public, using simple and direct words and sentence constructions arranged in easy-to-manage sentence lengths and paragraphs.

Plaintiff: A party who initiates a lawsuit and seeks a legal remedy from a defendant for the defendant's (alleged) wrongdoing.

Position paper: A publication prepared by an organization, most often the public relations person, that outlines the organizational perspective on a topic or issue related to the organization.

Potential issue: A situation or development that an organization is aware of but that has not yet become a concrete issue or full-blown crisis. A potential issue may exist with an organization's industry or on the periphery of an organization's operations. While non-threatening, it requires monitoring and awareness and action to prevent it from becoming a more serious (concrete) issue.

Press agent: This individual acted as a liaison with the press to share information on behalf of an individual or organization. This role typically reflected a one-way flow of communication from the organization to the media.

Proactive media relations: The part of media relations where PR actively seeks out media participation and coverage through a variety of tools, including news conferences, interviews, news releases, photos, audio, video, and articles.

Profession: Work that requires its practitioners to have specialized education, training, and skills developed over a long period of time, honed through practice and ongoing education and operating in alignment with public service.

Provincial government: The government of a Canadian province, such as the Government of Ontario.

Psychographics: Audience analysis that identifies lifestyle preferences (how audiences spend their time), activities, personality, interests, values, and opinions. In some cases, behavioural attitudes are also included.

Publicity: An uncontrolled (unpaid) method of placing messages in the media by creating interest among journalists for editorial content on the subject.

Public policy: A course of action or inaction chosen by government to address a problem or interrelated set of problems.

Public relations (PR): The management function that identifies, establishes, and maintains mutually beneficial relationships between an organization and its various publics on whom its success or failure depends.

Public service announcement (PSA): A proposed script for a broadcaster (television or radio broadcast) to read on-air that announces or discusses items of public concern and benefit (such as "stop smoking," "wear a helmet," a fundraiser, etc.). They are usually 10 seconds or 30 seconds in length, although they can be up to 60 seconds.

Publics: Groups of people with similar characteristics who are important for some reason to the organization conducting public relations. Publics are also referred to as *audiences, target audiences,* or *stakeholders.*

Qualitative research: A means of collecting information that uses conversations and interactions as the main data collection tool. This type of research generally asks questions that create a flow of dialogue rather than closed-ended questions. It is not representative of the whole population but is a great tool to understand how a group of people may feel about your product or company.

Quantitative research: Structured research that provides a statistically representative portrayal of a stakeholder audience.

Query letter: A letter written to ask an editor to publish a feature story or article that he or she has written. Freelance writers often query publications to accept their works, as do public relations practitioners. Public relations practitioners, however, are writing stories that will in some way enhance the reputation and image of their organizations.

RACE formula: John E. Marston's four-step process consisting of research, analysis, communication, and evaluation. RACE is a popular model for the PR process that is recognized by CPRS and IABC.

Reach: The number of different (unduplicated) people exposed to an advertiser's message over a specified period of time.

Reactive media relations: The part of media relations where the news media comes to PR seeking information, photos or video, or interview requests. The circumstances can be positive or negative.

Regulations: Rules determined by government as to how laws function.

Reputation management: The process of establishing a clear understanding of an organization's reputation by recognizing and responding to the views of its stakeholders, the public, and the media. It works to ensure that the organization takes action to build and maintain a positive reputation among these key groups.

Return on investment (ROI): The benefit a marketing or public relations professional receives based on the marketing or PR effort that he or she has created.

Sales promotion: A series of techniques used to increase immediate sales and consumer demand for a product, including in-store contests, coupons, and rebates.

Scrum: When a group of reporters surround a spokesperson to get news. Often scrums occur in a crisis situation but can also be a fast news gathering technique as opposed to a more formal news conference. Scrums are often visible in the political arena, when press gallery reporters gather news quickly from a number of individuals. These are also common for media covering the courts or police beats, where subjects are surrounded for news gathering.

Search engine optimization (SEO): An ever-changing collection of techniques used to increase the likelihood a particular website appears as close as possible to the first result on the results pages of search engines such as Google and Bing.

Secondary research: The use of previously published materials as a form of data collection.

Situation report (sitrep): A report that provides a strategic overview of a crisis, including elements of the current status of crisis resolution and future potentials.

Six-step communications process: A model that describes the process of communications: sender, encoder, message, receiver, decoder, and feedback.

SMART: A marketing communications term to describe creating objectives that are specific, measurable, achievable, realistic, and time-bound.

Social advertising: Social advertising is a practice area in which an organization purchases advertising to convey its message without interference or interpretation from news media.

Social marketing: Commonly used by non-profit or charity organizations, social marketing aims (through both traditional and modern marketing tactics) to influence the voluntary behaviour of target audiences to raise awareness of social issues with the aim of benefiting the user or audience and the larger community, rather than the organization.

Social media: The various means by which people electronically create and share content including text, images, audio, and video.

Social media release: A news release that incorporates content that can be easily shared on social networks.

Social network: A digital platform that connects users and enables them to share content.

Spokesperson: The leader or leaders within an organization whose job it is during a crisis to respond to media, stakeholders, and the general public. The spokesperson is provided with key messaging by communicators within an organization, has a full understanding of the crisis on the organization's current and future position, and is part of the crisis team.

Sponsorship: A financial or in-kind fee paid by a company in exchange for having their brand associated with a particular event or cause (typically sports, entertainment events, or a charitable cause).

Stakeholder: Any individual, corporation, or entity that you wish to impact with your marketing or public relations campaigns.

Strategy (as part of a communications plan): Broader, overarching methods that guide the organization on how to achieve the campaign's objectives and may include programming, public education, positioning, stakeholder or community outreach, and advocacy.

SWOT: An assessment tool that identifies internal strengths and weaknesses, as well as external opportunities and threats.

Tactics (as part of a communications plan): Day-by-day or week-by-week actions and duties that must be completed to achieve baseline milestones and meet objectives, which show how the strategies will be accomplished.

TARES: A self-test developed by Baker and Martinson (2002) that can be used by public relations people to guide them in ethical considerations about a piece of writing. It is an acronym that calls upon the writer to consider truthfulness, authenticity, respect, equity, and social responsibility in the preparation of communication pieces.

Technological determinism: A communications theory that proposes that changes in technology shape changes in society. Technology drives societal change through changes in how we create, distribute, and consume information.

Territorial government: The government of a Canadian territory, such as the Government of Yukon.

Trademark: A word, design, symbol, or phrase that identifies a product or service.

Traditional media: Established media, usually referred to as media introduced before the advent of the Internet, such as magazines, direct mail, newspapers, and broadcast television and radio.

Unpaid media space: A specified allotment of time or spaced in various categories of media in which a product, service, or idea is mentioned as a result of news media interest. Also called *earned media*.

Utilitarianism (situational ethics): An ethical decision-making philosophy by which decisions are made based on the greater good or perceived consequences of an action.

Virality: The process whereby a message reaches a much larger audience than the one initially targeted.

Viral marketing: Using social networks to promote a company, product, or service with the aim of increasing awareness and achieving other marketing goals. The word *viral* refers to the self-replicating nature of online promotion, similar to the way a virus spreads throughout the body. Messages are shared, forwarded, reproduced, and replicated to spread information quickly, cheaply, and easily.

Colin Babiuk (MA, APR, FCPRS) is the program chair and an instructor for the Public Relations Diploma Program at MacEwan University in Edmonton, Alberta. Colin has over 24 years of experience as a public relations practitioner in the private and public sectors. His experience includes issues management, stakeholder relations, strategic communication planning, media relations, and marketing. Colin is an accredited member of the Canadian Public Relations Society (CPRS) and a member of the CPRS College of Fellows. He earned his master of arts in professional communications at Royal Roads University in Victoria, British Columbia.

Sandra L. Braun holds a PhD from the University of Alabama, where she also taught English and business communication. She currently teaches public relations writing classes and crisis communication at Mount Royal University in Calgary, Alberta. She has worked in communications positions in the medical field, higher education, as a freelance writer, and as an account executive for a public relations and advertising agency in Florida.

Wendy Campbell (ABC) started her career in communications when typewriters produced words and film produced photos. An alumna of the University of Saskatchewan and SAIT Polytechnic, Wendy started her professional life in journalism then switched to communications. She has worked in both the public and private sectors in Alberta and Saskatchewan, offering her skills since 2004 as a principal with the Edmonton communications consulting firm of The DAGNY Partnership.

William Wray Carney (BA Hons.) has over 30 years of experience in education, journalism, and public relations. He is the author of In the News: The Practice *of Media Relations in Canada* (2nd ed., University of Alberta Press, 2008), the standard text on the subject in Canada. In 2009, he received the Award of Attainment from the Canadian Public Relations Society for "leadership that resulted in a pronounced contribution to the status and acceptance of the Public Relations functions as a whole." He maintains a communications practice in Regina, Saskatchewan.

John E.C. Cooper (MA) is a corporate communications specialist and writer. He worked for the Ontario government as a senior communications manager with the Ministry of Transportation. He has taught corporate communications at the college level since 2000 and is the author of *Crisis Communications in Canada: A Practical Approach*, published by Centennial College Press. He holds a master's degree in integrated studies specializing in adult education, a bachelor's degree in English, and a diploma in print journalism. At the time of publication, he was working toward his doctorate in education.

Marsha D'Angelo (MA) is a faculty member in the Applied Communications and Public Relations Departments of Kwantlen Polytechnic University in Surrey, British Columbia. Prior to joining Kwantlen, Marsha was a group account director with Cossette Communications in London, England where she led international media campaigns and provided senior counsel to corporate and education clients. Marsha holds an MA in history from the University of Toronto. She served on the Marketing Committee of the Vancouver East Cultural Centre and is a recipient of UNICEF's Dorothy McKinnon award for outstanding volunteer service.

Ange Frymire Fleming's (FCPRS, APR, MBA) expertise stretches over 30 years. A former broadcaster, freelance writer, and promotions director, she founded Vocal Point Communications in 1992, a boutique PR and marketing communications firm representing corporate, retail, not-for-profit, sports, and arts and entertainment organizations throughout western Canada. She is also a professor at Kwantlen Polytechnic University in Metro Vancouver, teaching in the Applied Communications and Entrepreneurial Leadership programs. A past president of CPRS-Vancouver Island and current board member with CPRS-Vancouver, she was awarded the 2011 CPRS Canadian Mentor of the Year.

Mark Hunter LaVigne, MA (journalism), APR, FCPRS (Fellow CPRS), has worked in media and communications since 1986. Mark sits on the Advisory Council to the Graduate School of Journalism at the University of Western Ontario and has taught part-time in the Corporate Communications Program at Seneca College, a graduate-level PR course, as well as at Ryerson

University. He has won a number of industry awards for his work with the private sector in media relations and has a practice based in Aurora, Ontario. He has written a book on media relations, *Making Ink and Airtime*, a compilation of newsletter articles he published since 2003.

Danielle Lemon is a lawyer in Vancouver with a practice focused on startups, technology, media, entertainment, and communications law. Danielle is a graduate of the University of Victoria and has a master's degree in media and communications regulation and policy (with merit) from the London School of Economics. Danielle has practiced law both in private practice and in-house in both Vancouver, BC and London, England.

Leah-Ann Lymer (BA) has worked as an editor in educational publishing for 20 years. She was a finalist for the 2008 Tom Fairley Award for Editorial Excellence (Editors' Association of Canada) and the 2009 Lois Hole Award for Editorial Excellence (Book Publishers Association of Alberta).

Allison G. MacKenzie (BA, MBA, ABC) teaches in the Faculty of Communication Studies at Mount Royal University in Calgary. Her extensive PR career spans more than two decades and includes leadership roles in the not-for-profit, for-profit, government, education, and legal sectors.

Sheridan McVean (APR, MBA, DMC) is a consultant in government relations, public relations, and marketing. In addition to consulting, he teaches at Mount Royal University, Royal Roads University, and the University of Calgary. He has worked with the Alberta Office of the Premier, Hill + Knowlton, Calgary Homeless Foundation, and his own consulting company. Mr. McVean has provided government and public relations consulting to a wide variety of organizations, including several Fortune Global 500 companies. He holds a BA in political science from the University of Calgary, an MBA from Royal Roads University, and a diploma in management consulting from the Grenoble Graduate School of Business (France).

Charles Pitts has spent much of his career in the telecommunications and pharmaceutical industries and the not-for-profit sector, achieving senior-level positions in Canada and abroad. He holds graduate and undergraduate degrees in psychology and heads Oromedia, a health communications firm. He is fluent in English and French and lectures in public relations, crisis and risk management at McGill University, Concordia University, and l'Université du Québec à Montréal (UQAM).

David Scholz is a partner and executive vice-president at Leger, Canada's largest independent research agency. He specializes in communication research and holds an MA in cognitive psychology from the University of Manitoba.

He developed a reputation measurement index for Leger and has published an annual report on corporate reputation in Canada every year since. He is an adjunct professor and teaches public relations research in McMaster University's Masters in Communication program and is a regular presenter at national communications conferences.

Jeff Scott works at Canadian National Railway, where he helps the company use digital communications, including social media, to engage with stakeholders. He also delivers training seminars to groups and individuals and is a regular guest lecturer at McGill University. Previously, Jeff worked as a consultant for NATIONAL Public Relations. While there he specialized in the development and implementation of digital strategies for businesses, governments, and individuals. Jeff holds a bachelor of arts degree in English literature with first-class honours from McGill University.

Charmane Sing is an associate at Borden Ladner Gervais LLP in Vancouver. In addition to being a lawyer, Charmane is also a registered trademark agent. Charmane graduated from the University of Alberta in 2005 and was awarded the George Bligh O'Connor Silver Medal in Law. Prior to attending law school, Charmane obtained a bachelor of commerce from the University of British Columbia. Charmane practises in the areas of intellectual property, technology, advertising and sponsorship, and corporate and commercial law.

Amy Thurlow (PhD, APR) is chair of the Department of Communications Studies at Mount Saint Vincent University in Halifax, Nova Scotia. Her research is in the area of organizational communication and change. Her experience in public relations includes work with government and community organizations in Canada and internationally.

Carolyne Van Der Meer has extensive experience in media relations, particularly media strategies for businesses and institutions. She has particular experience in media analysis, which she has undertaken for such Canadian blue chip companies as Bombardier Inc. and BCE Inc. Her experience as a corporate communications specialist and a journalist enhances her ability in the media relations field as she has an inherent understanding of both sides. In addition to holding undergraduate and graduate degrees in English studies from the University of Ottawa and Concordia University, Ms. Van Der Meer had done doctoral work in media theory. She currently teaches in the Public Relations and Communication Management Program at McGill University in Montreal and regularly does guest lectures on media analysis in client environments.

Ashleigh VanHouten holds an MA in professional communication from Royal Roads University in Victoria, British Columbia and a BA in public relations from Mount Saint Vincent University in Halifax, Nova Scotia. A marketing and communications professional from Halifax, Ashleigh has worked in corporate marketing and public relations agency roles in Canada, Bermuda, and New York City and is also a writer and editor, working for various consumer and trade publications in Manhattan.

Cynthia Wrate (ABC, CAAP, MBA) is an instructor in marketing communications management in the School of Business at Camosun College in Victoria, BC, where she teaches public relations and strategic communications. Prior to teaching, Cynthia's corporate and marketing communications experience includes leadership roles in broadcasting, telecommunications, retail, tourism, culture, manufacturing, and consulting. She holds an MBA from Royal Roads University, undergraduate studies in political science and English (the WRITE program) at the University of Alberta, and a diploma in creative communications from Red River College. She is an active accredited member and volunteer with the International Association of Business Communicators and frequent judge for the association's accreditation and international award programs. She is also a past member and volunteer with the Canadian Public Relations Society and is accredited by the Canadian Institute of Communications Agencies.

Anthony R. Yue (MBA, PhD) is an associate professor in the Department of Communication Studies at Mount Saint Vincent University in Halifax, Nova Scotia. He researches gossip in organizations and existentialism in organizational analysis. He co-authored *Business Research Methods* (Oxford University Press, 2011) and teaches courses in applied communication strategy, management, and international business.

Index

Page numbers with f refer to figures.

blogs
   activities on, 338
   comments sections, 327
   company blogs, 327–28, 383f
   impact of, 314
   public sphere participation, 102
   as resource on current trends, 329
   search engine optimization, 319–20
   writing content for, 239, 320
   See also digital communications; writing
      for public relations
Blue Cross (case study), 388, 392–95, 393f
Blumenstock, Dorothy, 93
bookmark sharing websites, 311
   See also social media
brainstorming and mind mapping,
      218–20f, 221, 252
brand consistency, 148
Braun, Sandra L., 211–57, 487
Brazil, public relations licensing, 73
briefing notes, 246, 406–09f, 434
   See also writing for public relations
Britain. See United Kingdom
British North America Act, 344, 361, 364n3
British Petroleum, oil spill, 137, 425–26
broadcast media
   advertising on, 267f–268, 275
   advertising revenues, 287
   code of ethics, 52–53
   crisis communications, 432–33
   current trends, 285–86
   hate speech, 41
   industry self-regulation, 52–53, 276
   interstitials (vignettes), 275
   media vehicles, 269
   obscene material, 41
   public broadcasters, 287
   tabloid journalism, 286
   See also Canadian Radio-television
      Telecommunications Commission;
   defamation; news media; radio;
   television; video
B-roll video, 77, 467–68

Broom, Glen M., 27
Buckley, Christopher, 248
Burnett, Tim, 227–28
Bush, George W., 248, 426–27
businesses
   about, 12, 15–16
   case study on government relations
      (arenas), 353–60
   crisis communications, 135–36, 387–89
   ethical issues, 47–48
   government relations, 342–45, 350,
      352, 360
   history of public relations, 27
   industry associations, 12, 17, 350
   industry relations, 17
   investor relations, 11–12, 15, 17
   personal selling in business-to-
      business, 138, 151
   power and media ownership, 99–100
   protection of personal information, 52
   regulations on, 342–43, 348
   sourcing news, 100
   See also crisis communications;
      internal communications; legal
      issues; sponsorships
businesses, writing for
   American/British/Canadian style,
      248–49
   briefing notes, 246, 406–09f, 434
   communication audits, 245
   company blogs, 327–28
   creative briefs, 245–46
   email, 246–47f
   letters and memos, 242–44, 383f
   marketing materials, 248
   reports and proposals, 244–46
   speeches, 216, 220, 248
   style and tone, 246–47f, 248–49
   See also writing for public relations
buyers. See consumers

calendars, editorial, 326–27, 332
calls to action, 121, 320

Spetner, Don, 240
sponsorships
about, 139–40, 151
advertising of, 267f–268
case study (Arts Umbrella), 451–62
communication plans, 176
Olympic Torch Relay Campaign, 146
See also marketing
sports and fitness
audience analysis, 448–50
case study on government relations
(arenas), 353–60
sponsorships, 139–40, 151
stakeholders
audience analysis, 184–85
audience analysis (Sidney Health Fair),
445–50
categories of, 184
editorial calendars, 326–27, 332
impact of digital communications on,
313
media monitoring, 322–23
research on, 162–64, 171
See also audiences; research
Streisand effect, 340n20
students in audiences. See
multigenerational communications
students in public relations. See education,
training, and competencies;
practitioners
stunts and guerrilla marketing, 121–23, 128
Supreme Court of Canada
on defamation, 44–47
on honesty in advertising, 48
surveys, 164–67, 181, 314, 381, 385, 394–95
See also research
Sutcliffe, Kathleen M., 31
Sweetser, Kaye D., 317
SWOT analysis
communications plans, 182–83, 201
internal communications plans, 380–81
resources for, 399n10

risks analysis, 183
terminology, 203, 399n10

tabloid journalism and muckraking, 26–27,
34, 286
Tannenbaum, Stanley I., 144
TARES test for ethical writing, 250f–251,
253
target audiences. See audiences
tear sheets, 298
technology
current trends, 285–86, 308–10
diffusion of innovations theory,
113–15f, 128
McLuhan's theories, 101–02
technological and economic
determinism, 98–103
See also digital communications
telecommunications
emergency systems, 388, 410, 422
industry self-regulation, 52–53, 276
language policies, 334
McLuhan's theories, 101–02
media interviews, 298–302, 465–69
mobile marketing, 123–27
statistics, 123
See also Canadian Radio-television
Telecommunications Commission;
mobile communications; radio;
television
telemarketing, 117–18
telephones, cellphones, and smartphones
advertising on, 276–77
crisis communications, 411–12, 422
current trends, 9
direct response communications,
140–41, 150
effectiveness of calls, 379–80
geolocation technologies, 124, 277
internal communications, 378,
382f–383f, 391–92
media interviews, 298–302, 465–69